ID0983976

WALTER CAMP

WALTER CAMP
Football and the Modern Man

JULIE DES JARDINS

OXFORD
UNIVERSITY PRESS

OXFORD
UNIVERSITY PRESS

Oxford University Press is a department of the University of
Oxford. It furthers the University's objective of excellence in research,
scholarship, and education by publishing worldwide.

Oxford   New York

Auckland   Cape Town   Dar es Salaam   Hong Kong   Karachi
Kuala Lumpur   Madrid   Melbourne   Mexico City   Nairobi
New Delhi   Shanghai   Taipei   Toronto

With offices in

Argentina   Austria   Brazil   Chile   Czech Republic   France   Greece
Guatemala   Hungary   Italy   Japan   Poland   Portugal   Singapore
South Korea   Switzerland   Thailand   Turkey   Ukraine   Vietnam

Oxford is a registered trademark of Oxford University Press
in the UK and certain other countries.

Published in the United States of America by
Oxford University Press
198 Madison Avenue, New York, NY 10016

© Julie Des Jardins 2015

Library of Congress Cataloging-in-Publication Data
Des Jardins, Julie.
Walter Camp : football and the modern man / Julie Des Jardins.
pages cm
ISBN 978–0–19–992562–9 (hardback)
1. Camp, Walter, 1859–1925.   2. Football players—United States—Biography.
3. Football—United States—History.   I. Title.
GV939.C34D47 2015
796.332092—dc23
[B]
2015008469

1 3 5 7 9 8 6 4 2
Printed in the United States of America
on acid-free paper

Frontispiece: Walter Camp at a football game, about 1920. Walter Chauncey Camp Papers,
Manuscripts and Archives, Yale University.

To Bastian—my man in the making

To Chris—my convert to American football

CONTENTS

———◦◦◦◦———

ACKNOWLEDGMENTS

IN GRATITUDE:

Thank you, Nancy Toff, for taking on a book about football.

And Ana Calero for thinking that it made all the sense in the world for a feminist to write about the "Father of Football."

And Ms. Jackie and the aftercare staff who took care of my kids so I could write. Thank you for giving me time to think.

And Carol Berkin, Thomas Heinrich, Vince DiGirolamo, and Clarence Taylor for being true friends as I grew disenchanted with CUNY. I'm lucky that our friendship continues.

And Catherine Allgor, my long-distance guardian angel.

And Linda Voris and Despina Kakoudaki, friends and scholars of the best kind. Something tells me that your enthusiastic viewing of an entire Thanksgiving football game was one of your many gifts to me.

And Susan Warner, Stacy Krieger, Kate Foss, and Marlene Glifort, perfect permutations of mothers, friends, and professional women.

And Bert Hansen, Randy Trumbach, and Jed Abrahamian for engaging my ideas, however partially baked.

And my workout pals Linda, Eric, Jeff, and Sid for being salts of the earth after a day of writing.

And my students, who convinced me that a story about masculinity was as important now as ever, especially one told through football.

And my twin, Jory, for empowering me to think differently.

And my sister, Jenna, who reads everything that I write, and my brother, Joe, who probably already knows much of what's in these pages.

And Chris for giving me space and support on my angriest days and always.

And thank you, Mom, for thinking that everything I do is worthy. I love you more than words can say.

PREGAME COMMENTARY

IN 1910, THIRTEEN-YEAR-OLD James Percy of East Cleveland, Ohio, sent a letter care of *Boys Magazine* to Walter Camp, the man known throughout the country as the "Father of American Football." Percy was like other boys on YMCA and high school teams who had written Camp to clarify the definition of a "scrummage," or a "snap," or "being held." One Chicago boy asked if a ball handed forward was considered a pass; in the early years of the game, it was unclear. In Percy's case, the inquiries were not merely technical; he wanted to know how to train for high school ball. He described himself as "physically weak . . . more or less what you would term a 'mollycoddle,' " and he wanted to change his image.[1]

"Mollycoddle" was a familiar term to any American boy coming of age at the turn of the twentieth century. Bullies used it to terrorize, and President Theodore Roosevelt invoked it to characterize men who had grown soft and "overcivilized" in the industrial age. Males who rejected Roosevelt's "big stick" diplomacy or his call to live a "strenuous life" were, in his estimation and rhetoric, milksops, sissies, pampered weaklings—effeminate and ineffectual men. Like Percy, they were mollycoddles, unprepared to lead in the modern age.

In his earnest attempt to become stronger and self-reliant, Percy decided to pick up football, a game he had never played a day in his life, but one that was popular all around him. College and high school competition was well established where he lived, so he could have turned to any number of men to teach him its technical aspects. And yet he turned to Camp in his quest not to be a mollycoddle. Roosevelt famously implored American boys to "hit the line hard," likening gridiron warfare to the rigors of modern life. Camp was most to thank for this conflation in the American mind. To this thirteen-year-old boy, it was apparent that football made the modern man, and that Camp was thus the arbiter of manhood as no other man could be.[2]

Percy was not alone. By 1915, members of the Business Men's League of St. Louis paid Camp to give the talk "What Shall We Make of Our Sons?" "Mr. Camp is one of the most distinguished and versatile men of our present time," touted the league. "He thinks, talks and writes about the training of youth with keen appreciation of the responsibilities and difficulties of the father."[3] It was true that Camp knew fatherhood firsthand: his son Walter Camp Jr. also achieved modest acclaim on the football field of Yale. But Camp's development of football made him, in the eyes of St. Louis businessmen, a father for all American boys. That scoutmasters and YMCA directors also sought him out as an expert on the making of boys into men tells us that they viewed the game he invented as inextricably linked to the transformation.

All of this supposes that Camp was in fact responsible for the origins of American football, and yet the annals of history reveal no single inventor. In the late nineteenth century, football grew in popularity across the country so quickly that multiple football conferences and rules committees emerged to shape it non-uniformly, making it harder for a single man to assert supreme influence over it. For a time, universities like Berkeley and Stanford resorted to English rugby rules to curb the mounting criticism that American football was too brutal, a development that Camp could not prevent and may have inadvertently accelerated. Can we call a staunch advocate of amateurism the father of one of the most profitable team sports played in the world today?

Football's place in the lives of American men is both due to and in spite of Walter Camp. His game took on meanings beyond what he intended, but that does not indicate that his influence was paralleled, or that it is not profound today. He, more than anyone, shaped the development of football and its popular image for fifty years. One of his former colleagues in the Intercollegiate Football Association likened him to an inventor with a patent on the game, making adjustments as he saw fit. A writer for the *St. Louis Republic* decided that he was to football what the Wright brothers were to the airplane: "He didn't invent it, but he made it work." Former pro player Michael Oriard sums it up when he describes Camp not as a "ruler" of football, "but the preeminent creator of its rules"; never an All-American, but a maker of them for thirty-seven years; never a paid coach, but a "coach of coaches" so successful that the sideline presence of a tactician—not just in football but also in baseball and basketball—has become a trademark of American sports.[4]

Although his place in national sports lore has been overshadowed by the memory of Knute Rockne, Babe Ruth, and legends who followed, Camp's significance to the American athletic tradition was not lost on Parke Davis, a football player and historian who eulogized him in 1925:

> Walter Camp pre-eminently was a philanthropist in American sport. His was the genius to play his country's games surpassingly well; to improve and to increase their technique; to surround them with customs and features that added immensely to their attraction; to accompany them with a code of chivalry and nobleness that coincidently trained player and spectator in American manhood at its best; and his was the talent so to popularize these games that from casual pastimes of schoolboys and collegians they became national institutions of entertainment, recreation and culture.[5]

Camp's role in football, as in sport generally, was often behind the scenes, but no one at the turn of the twentieth century or since can deny his impact on the game, or the brand of manhood he cultivated through it. His story is the tale of a particular New England, Anglo-Saxon set of college-educated men. And yet, viewed more broadly, it reveals just how much the developments of football and American manhood have cut across races and classes and been indelibly intertwined with each other.

Introduction

The Forgotten "Father of Football"

AMONG THE DOCUMENTS PRESERVED IN the Walter Chauncey Camp Collection at Yale University is a résumé Camp apparently typed near the end of his life.[1] It is hardly comprehensive, organized into categories and accomplishments that mattered most to a man looking back and taking stock. Although he published thirty books and more than 200 articles in some twenty magazines and countless newspapers in his lifetime, on the résumé, he listed only twenty titles, including a bridge-playing guide, a co-authored history of Yale, a book on golf, and a Young People's Library on sports and recreation. He listed six sports novels (apparently not thinking the others worth noting) and several books about fitness. Not surprisingly, he included a few volumes on American football.

Other parts of his résumé indicate that within northeastern social circles, he was a man who had clearly arrived. Belonging to all the right alumni societies and country clubs, he also served the state and local Chamber of Commerce and was trustee and treasurer of the Hopkins Grammar School. Incredibly, he also seemed to have an illustrious war record, despite never enlisting in the armed services. During World War I, he successfully lobbied for an appointment to the Commission on Naval Training Camps. Other titles—"Civilian Consultant on Fitness of Aviators," "Organizer of Senior Service Corps"—were not official, but he listed them, swept up in the martial spirit of his time. Men of his generation longed to feel effective through service that their fathers fell into by coming of age during a devastating civil war.

Something else is puzzling about Camp's résumé. The shortest list of entries falls under the heading "Business," where one might presume his itemization would be extensive. Certainly men who came of age in the nineteenth century were consumed with making a living; middle-class men's work was, it has long been believed, vital to their sense of who they were.[2] Camp could have listed an impressive sequence of positions he occupied on his forty-year climb up the ranks of the New Haven Clock Company, which employed several thousand people in its heyday. Instead, he summed up his professional ascent in a single line: "President for 20 yrs, now Chairman of Board." Why did work that took up hours of his days and years of his life not feature more prominently on a list of life achievements?

If modern men have been defined by their paying vocations, Walter Camp apparently was not—not to himself or nearly anyone else. "One of the most fatal things that can happen to any man no matter what his position in life is to become so tied up in his job that he does nothing else," he later mused. Years of selling clocks, keeping books, and dealing with factory fires, labor strikes, and economic downturns would have squeezed "the juice of life" out of him, as he put it, had he not defined himself outside the workplace as a man more profoundly fulfilled.

Because men of his generation did not always feel unconditional success in the professional realm, they started seeking solace in other pursuits. And thus, while Camp steadily worked his way up the corporate ladder, away from the office, he wrote for *Outing, Harper's Weekly,* and *Collier's,* in addition to newspapers across the country. If his pen helped him sustain feelings of self-worth better than corporate promotions did, it also betrayed his self-doubt. He wrote nostalgically in later years, "The halo of the college hero disappears like mist in the sun of the work-a-day world." Here, his use of the third person veiled his personal laments thinly.[3] His college years were epic in his mind, not because he was valedictorian of his class, but something better—a varsity letterman in the emerging realm of American sport.

"Athletics" featured first and foremost on Camp's résumé and in his self-assessment as a man. This would not have been the case decades earlier, when Americans still overwhelmingly worked on farms and sportsmen were more often bachelors of the South, the frontier, or the urban working class. But after the Civil War, as the country modernized and grew more industrial, middle- and upper-class men increasingly embraced the physical culture that their forebears would have thought beneath them.[4]

By the time Camp arrived at Yale as an undergraduate, athletics were not just respectable, but heroic, because they helped to soothe a crisis of identity in his generation. Although he did not have a war to fight or a thrilling climb up the corporate ladder, he belonged to the first cohort of American men who felt greatness in being athletic. In the words of Allen Guttmann, sport offered a chance for " 'man the breadwinner' to become, for a brief but glorious moment, 'man-the-hero,' " and Camp extended that moment out for as long as he could.[5]

Indeed, when athletics is the measure, Camp looks to be one of the most successful men of his generation. His résumé indicates that in this realm his accomplishments were many:

> captain of college baseball and football teams . . .
> college halfback for six years . . .
> varsity pitcher, shortstop, and left fielder for four years . . .
> leader of the Yale nine in fielding and batting average . . .
> class crew and the doubles intercollegiate tennis champion . . .
> high hurdles champion in the Fall Games . . .
> "coach" of Yale football for twenty years . . .[6]

More than his business, civic, or academic achievements, athletic accolades made him who he wanted to be—even if he achieved most of them before the age of twenty-three.

During the athletics revolution in America, Walter Camp was a household name. The nation's earliest football fans would have been familiar with pictures of him in his canvas togs, while younger Americans were better acquainted with his salt-and-pepper mustache and balding head—but acquainted with him they were. While his friends thought his intense, foxlike brown eyes and long features were

most distinctive, the man on the street likely knew him in caricature: fastidious and straight-backed, walking briskly in a trench coat
and signature bowler hat, his waistline trim and appearance neat.

Camp was popularly known for making football a rougher sport,
and yet his daughter remembered him as a gentle man who wrote
poetry. Football players are often presumed to be tough guys, and yet
the creator of the All-American was apparently the furthest thing from
a brute. When other men picked fights, he rarely lashed back, at least
not openly. He preferred reserve to flash, unlike most figures of tabloid
fame today, and he chose not to believe rumors or start them. Friends
remarked that he never spoke unkindly of someone, that he was diplo-
matic, congenial, wise, and never overbearing—the most "clear-headed"
and "clean-minded" man they knew. In the heat of competition, he was
said to maintain "poise so perfect that it annoyed."[7]

"One might conclude that he felt no emotion, and knew nothing
about the usual agonies of watching a hard-fought and doubtful
game," an admirer noted, but in fact Camp had passionate opinions
and summoned restraint to hold his tongue. There are glimmers of
anger, frustration, hurt, and yearning for revenge in the papers he left
behind, but he obscured his feelings from public view so that no one
thought him antagonistic or prejudicial—not for his sake, but for the
game he fathered and willed into permanence. Camp embodied the
self-possession of a gentleman to bring honor to a sport that might
otherwise have been viewed as ruthlessly gladiatorial, as evidence of
American civilization in decline. Although he sold clocks for decades,
his most ambitious project was marketing football as an antidote to
the degeneration of American men. And thus, while he ached for his
team to win, he wanted football to win in people's hearts and minds
even more.

Yale had been renowned for grooming the nation's religious, political, and military leaders and literary lights. Camp—an Episcopalian, a
Republican, and a "Navy man" (liberally construed)—was not remarkable in these realms of endeavor, but in new ones. He created a niche
as a football rule-maker, expert, and tactician, as well as an exemplar
of a chivalric sportsman's code. His writing was not the high art of a
Melville or a Thoreau, yet there was nary a red-blooded American male

who had not read something he had written by the turn of the twentieth century.

People who knew him attributed to him a properness characteristic of Boston Brahmins. And yet in his novels and on the gridiron, his tone was reportedly familiar and folksy. A sportswriter noted that his running commentary on a football sideline consisted of outbursts like "Shake 'em off!" "Jiminy!" "Cracky, they're 'hep' to that forward pass, all right."[8] He talked the vernacular of the sports page and had a hand in propagating it until it became the lingua franca of American boys.

Even those who did not read *Jack Hall at Yale* or Camp's annual All-America picks in *Collier's* felt his impact on their sense of self as boys and men, especially if they played football. He shaped the gridiron into a national text and used it to tell parables about being plucky, disciplined, and a good winner. Embedded in this text was yet another message: that American boys should be more athletic than anyone else in the civilized world. Camp maintained that what differentiated American boys from French or English boys—or American girls—was that they created tests of rigor for their bodies that were so intense that no one matched their ability to harness energy or dismiss pain. He told boys that superior physicality defined their manhood and that it could be achieved on a football field better than anywhere else.

Football hardened men to greatness, Camp swore, much like the Western frontier had until the 1890 census confirmed its closing. He liked to think that he was merely compensating for the loss, creating a new frontier that was equally rugged, delineated by chalk marks and nestled in less open spaces in urban centers, where American males needed outlets for their energy. The great artist Frederic Remington, his college teammate, agreed that the football field provided men in cities with the same man-making experience of physical danger that the frontier gave the cowboys in his paintings. When critics lambasted Camp for the roughness of his game, Remington implored him not to kowtow to their namby-pambyism. There was no longer anything in American life—not a mythical West or an Indian war—that counteracted the forces of feminization like football.[9]

To see how Walter Camp's propagation of football became the propagation of modern manhood, this story begins with his coming of age in New Haven in the 1870s, when he first started kicking around balls and building up his body. His life played out like a gridiron game—assessed thoroughly at halftime and fought vigorously in body and mind for four quarters. The clock ruled it too, rather stringently.

FIRST QUARTER:
ADOLESCENCE

———〜∘∘∘〜———

I

Survival of the Fittest in New Haven, 1860s–1880

IN THE 1980S, A RUSTED plaque barely hung on a dilapidated house on the corner of Gill and Chapel Streets in New Haven, Connecticut, announcing the spot as the birthplace of Walter Camp.[1] Today, the house is gone, and the plaque with it, yet the presumption that Camp was born in New Haven falsely remains. Camp is associated with New Haven like no one else, but the truth is that he was a boy of five when his family left New Britain and moved to this college town. The death of his maternal grandfather in 1863 brought the Camps to 170 Chapel Street the following year, then to 595 Chapel three years later, and 1303 Chapel in 1884, where the plaque still hung one hundred years later. Aside from a few years in young adulthood, New Haven was where Walter Camp resided for the rest of his life. Even as he built up a national reputation as the "Father of Football," he saw no reason to leave the place where he had gone to school, made a career, and raised a family of his own.

Camp belonged to a family that could be traced back to Essex County in England; Nicholas Camp, his earliest known ancestor, came to Massachusetts and settled in Connecticut in 1630. Nicholas married three times before fathering a son named Samuel in 1655; his son Nathan was born in 1688, his son Elah in 1729, his son Nathan Ozias in 1763, followed by a son who fought in the War of 1812, and his son Leverett in 1829. Leverett, like the Camp men before him, became father to a son. Walter Chauncey Camp, born on April 7, 1859, was a beloved and only child.[2] He came into the world the year that Charles Darwin's *Origin of Species* made it into print; decades later, he would borrow meanings from Darwin's biological theories and infuse them into a game he made useful for his generation.

Walter's mother, the tastefully hospitable Ellen Cornwell, left her modestly paid work as a schoolteacher to demonstrate the feminine art of moral instruction in the home, as proper Christian women did upon marriage. She was active in the church and volunteered tirelessly for the Home of the Friendless; no one was a more soothing bedside presence when neighbors were ill. Leverett shared her devotion to teaching. After graduating from the first class of the State Normal School in 1851, he became a public school teacher and principal, first of the Washington School and then the Dwight School, where he became one of the best paid educators in the New Haven school district. Leverett supplemented his salary with publishing and real estate ventures, affording a lifestyle that was comfortably middle class. The Camps enjoyed a sizable home in a respectable part of New Haven, a block from the Dwight School, as well as a summer home on Martha's Vineyard.[3]

Still, Leverett taught his son to esteem physical doing that seemed lost on the more moneyed families in town, starting a military drill squad among his students and encouraging Walter to run and play outdoors. He was moved by Protestant leaders who espoused "Muscular Christianity" back in England. Answering the call to make boys conspicuously virile, Muscular Christians tried to bring males back to the church by emphasizing the cultivation of the physical body and imbuing the work of perfecting it with spiritual import.

The novelist Charles Kingsley first coined Muscular Christianity in an effort to counteract what he and others viewed as the growing effeminacy of Protestant laities, but the concept had long appealed in England and soon would also in the United States, as anxieties grew over more women sitting in the pews and taking over the moral instruction of sons. Church leaders charged that sacrificing (read "feminine") images of Christ himself were having a softening effect on boys, made all the worse by mothers who raised sons while fathers worked long hours in the office.[4]

The Muscular Christians did not invigorate American youths en masse, however, until Thomas Hughes's novel *Tom Brown's Schooldays* became available in the United States after 1857. The exclusive Rugby School attended by the fictional Brown was a fount of Christian manliness and athletic heroism; on the playing fields, Brown's all-male peers experienced the restorative power of athletic competition and understood that their birthright afforded them executive assertiveness to excel there before moving on to Eton, Cambridge and Oxford, and eventually the halls of Parliament.[5]

Reading Hughes, young Camp drew his first connections between gentlemanliness and fair play, competitive sport and competitive life. That 225,000 copies of *Tom Brown* sold in America in its first year of publication suggests that he was hardly the only boy receptive to its message; his contemporary, the young Theodore Roosevelt, was also a reader of the *Tom Brown* novels and drawn to the Muscular Christians.

Men on both sides of Camp's family had tested their physical and moral mettle in the Civil War, as the Muscular Christians would have endorsed, but Walter came of age in decades when American males could never truly know the soldier's sacrifice. Sportsmen loomed larger in his childhood memories than did soldiers, because they were closer to his experience. Ironically, the Civil War may have contributed to this fact, since men of the comfortable classes of the Northeast had rarely cared to be athletic before being introduced to sport as Union soldiers. Before the war, boxing, wrestling, and baseball were decidedly lowbrow in their social worlds; but afterward, it was not unusual for a young boy to have middle- and upper-class role models who embraced rugged outdoor sport.[6]

For Camp, the athletic arena was the only amphitheater of physical combat he would ever truly know. It left an impression on him to see newspaper mogul James Gordon Bennett ride roughshod at the Newport polo grounds. But even more influential to his future endeavors were the Eton men who came to New Haven to introduce Yale undergraduates to the game of English rugby.[7]

The year was 1873. Camp, a lanky teen, studied the stately visitors in their white flannel pants and jackets trimmed in blue and noted that they were bigger than the Yale men he knew, averaging a good 170 pounds. He was particularly struck by the stature and status of one of them, a man who stood 6' 6" tall and went by the title of Lord. The evening following the match, he followed the Eton rugby players to the local theater, where a private box was reserved for them. "I looked at them a good deal more than I did the stage," he remembered. To an impressionable boy, these Englishmen were the walking embodiments of gentlemanly sport.[8]

The Eton players had arrived in a historically Calvinist town that had grown increasingly secular and commercial since colonial days. The New Haven of Camp's adolescence looked to have two distinct faces: While its industrial complexion showed in the factories and slums that proliferated along the town's avenues, the college section remained pastoral, residential, traditionally New England. Greek revival homes stood on elm-shaded streets, broken up by high brick mansions and white colonials with green shutters. "Like the columns of the houses," noted a proud resident, "the twin shrines in every heart were Reserve and Respectability." Most residents had already retired for the night when the chapel bell echoed through town at ten p.m. Yale undergraduates, meanwhile, carried on loudly on the campus greens. One professor likened the relationship between New Haven's "town and gown" to "a woman's club committee with a celebrity in tow, a credit to them but also an embarrassment and sometimes a nuisance."[9]

For a boy growing up in town, there was an implicit understanding that the college and its learned men made New Haven a privileged place. It was where the sons of the elite prepared for their leadership in national affairs, and where faculty and old families made a point of maintaining an aura of prestige. They tolerated campus hooliganism as the inevitable growing pains of God-graced boys becoming men.

And yet there was "ill feeling" between the undergraduates and, as one Yale man termed them, "the lower order of townies." Feuds led to Yale men organizing defense committees led by a physically imposing undergraduate—the "Campus Bully"—but young Camp observed that he did little to mollify aggressions. He recalled an incident on Chapel Street between local firemen and undergraduates that left a man stabbed and bleeding on the ground. Firemen secured the city cannon and had it turned on Old South College before the "peelers" (city police) intervened. Young men needed somewhere to vent their pent-up energies, Camp could see. He wondered if physical competition could effectively defuse their aggressions or channel them toward nobler ends. Would not both participants and spectators of sport benefit from taking pride in a common team, in supporting a common cause?[10]

Before the Civil War, Yale men had blown off steam through exercise of sorts—walking or gymnastics perhaps, if not hunting, riding, or fencing, which required little muscular development. Competitive team sport still seemed vulgar, until English collegians suggested the contrary. As Camp tells it, the first organized athletic outlet reared its head in New Haven in 1843, when a Yale junior purchased a nineteen-foot boat and started a collegiate crew club, the nation's first, to emulate those of Cambridge and Oxford. Harvard competed against Yale in 1852 in the first American interschool crew competition. Yale student James Whiton organized the regatta on Lake Winnipesaukee, and by 1858, the College Union Regatta Association brought Brown, Dartmouth, and Columbia into the fold. By the 1860s, Yale had a boathouse near Tomlinson's bridge, paid for by undergraduates. Young Camp traveled up to Springfield, Massachusetts, to witness Yale rowers take the intercollegiate title.[11]

Individual athletes now loomed large in Camp's eyes. Fayette Brown, a man in Yale's Sheffield School of Science, looked to him to be a perfect specimen, "handsome, courageous and . . . splendidly built" at 170 pounds. He noted that collegiate men were taking assiduous notice of their physiques and that he should as well before becoming a college man.[12]

Once, the only training equipment at Yale consisted of several rude frames and vaulting bars in the northwest corner of the yard. But the German Turners, who opened gymnastics facilities, or *Turnvereins*, after immigrating to the United States, inspired Yale men to build muscle at rudimentary gymnasiums near campus, until they raised $13,000 to build one on school grounds in 1859. The first Yale gymnasium was equipped with bowling alleys in the basement and weights and stroke machines on the main floor for the crew team. The largest crowds convened there in the half hour before dinner, turning exercise into a social affair.[13]

Gymnasiums also sprung up at Harvard and Amherst College, and the enthusiasm for strength training only intensified with the publication of William Blaikie's *How To Get Strong and How To Stay So* in 1879. When Camp was still a schoolboy, he obtained admission to the Yale gym and watched with wonder: "These men looked to me to be giants and I saw them wrestle, box and indulge in general horse play, and pull on the (then) very simple rowing weights."[14] He noticed too that, for these athletes, weightlifting was often a means, rather than an end in itself. They trained to box, ran to race, and practiced to play.

Competitive sport generated as much interest in Cambridge as in New Haven, perhaps because of the rivalry between their colleges since colonial times. Harvard had been founded in 1636 to prepare ministers for the Puritan theocracy, Yale in 1701 to train Congregational ministers. Ever since, Harvard and Yale men vied for primacy as the religious, political, and business leaders of the nation. Camp surmised that the athletic field was merely another arena of manly rivalry—not just for Harvard and Yale men, but soon for all American collegians. Spectators began wearing blue to show their allegiance to Yale, or crimson for Harvard. Camp remembered when Yale formed its first baseball nine and beat Wesleyan in its first recorded game, 39 to 13. Watching the players swing rudimentary bats and catch fly balls on a bounce, he dreamed of the day when he could compete for Yale himself.[15]

Yet again, his ambitions betray the influence of the Muscular Christians. Competition had hardly been perceived as a moral force in American life until Muscular Christians turned it into a mechanism of virtuous manhood, inspiring athletic contests at the interregional, intercity, national, and even international levels. American men started testing themselves against British and Canadian sportsmen, and college men chomped at the bit to compete against each other. Like Muscular Christians, young Camp internalized the passage in *Corinthians* that described the physical body not as the domain of Satan, as Victorian moralizers once insisted, but as a temple of the Holy Ghost.

In the industrializing world, man could neglect his body or keep it holy. Camp chose to cultivate it—to push its limits without sullying it with excessive food or drink—to prepare it for the reckoning of competition. The gawky teenager looked to harden his body out in the elements, where the deleterious effects of "civilization" had not reached. For a dozen summers, as the fashionable set hobnobbed in the resorts of Bar Harbor, he took advantage of his family's more rustic accommodations to swim away from the crowds, in the only wilderness this boy of the industrial age ever knew.[16]

Wealthy New Englanders were starting to send their dyspeptic sons overseas or to ranches out West to benefit physically from the rigors of the outdoors. The son of a schoolteacher, young Camp had no choice but to create rigor closer to home. He set out with a friend to the islands in Long Island Sound, and then camped out in New Bedford, Wood's Hole, and Nantucket. He caught a nine-foot shark and left for Martha's Vineyard, catching a boat to Portland to survive several weeks in the woods.[17]

Camp was living like a character in a Mark Twain novel and felt invigorated by the experience, deciding that this was the physically demanding existence that would make him successful in later years. Having read the biographies of self-made men like George Washington and Abraham Lincoln, he had come to conclude that their greatness stemmed from the arduous exercise of their youth. Great businessmen too, men like James J. Hill, Collis Huntington, and Marshall Field, had first put on muscle as construction workers and farmhands in their formative years. Camp was convinced that the strenuous exertions of their boyhoods had set the tone for the rest of their lives.[18]

The problem was that teenaged Camp was hard-pressed to find spaces near his tree-lined street where he could perform all this success-making labor. Baseball diamonds were just beginning to appear in urban areas; the first American tennis court was not built until 1876 in Boston; and the first championship tournament was not held until 1881 in Newport. So Camp became resourceful, running rigorously on the outskirts of town and doing calisthenics in his bedroom. He seemed to take pleasure in training and self-denial, even refusing his mother's famed cookies and cakes. He slept with his windows open and exercised daily, swearing even then that this allowed him to wake with the sun. He played golf before it was fashionable to build strength and coordination. As a result of abstaining from excess, one friend noted, he "had always a little more wind, a little less fat" than everyone else. Over time, he built a sinewy physique.[19]

These were years in which Camp also ran about the grounds of Hopkins Grammar School at the corner of High and Wall Streets, the eventual grounds of the Yale law school. Future Yale presidents Timothy Dwight and Arthur Hadley were both graduates of Hopkins, as were Josiah Willard Gibbs, the father of thermodynamics, and composer Charles Ives. When it came to placing students in elite colleges, Hopkins competed with the great preparatory schools of the Northeast. Three of every four graduates of Exeter went to Harvard, and the same ratio of Andover boys to Yale; after 1884, graduates of newly established Groton went to both, as well as to Princeton.[20]

With the proliferation of urban crime and immigrant populations, old-money elites began sending their sons to these boarding schools in the countryside to benefit from all-male staffs in wholesome settings. Like English Muscular Christians, they believed that fresh air away from urban decadence and mom's smothering influence would build character in their boys. Groton founder Endicott Peabody envisioned an American equivalent of Rugby, nestled in rural Massachusetts, where he could curb the overcivilizing effects of indoor life. His boys were not pampered with fine dining and hot baths; they attended chapel daily and trained rigorously for sport. The seclusion of the setting created an artificially competitive world in which boys developed pluck and self-reliance by necessity. Whereas Catholic schools placed emphasis on academics, Protestant prep school administrators stuck to the belief that athletic competition trained boys for college and the professional world beyond.[21]

For young Camp, Hopkins was as far away from home as he would ever get. Nevertheless, the headmaster William Cushing shared Peabody's views about sport, coaching the nascent crew team at Yale and encouraging his Hopkins boys to be sportsmen. "Digs" and "grinds" who kept their noses in books became less and less the objects of emulation than did classmates who exhibited greatness on the playing field. Competitions of running, throwing, and swimming established the pecking order in Camp's schoolboy universe. It was an asset to be taller and heavier and exhibit more prowess than one's peers. Camp was a good student, though not the best, performing consistently within the top fifth of a class of thirty-five. Although several classmates went on to perform more adeptly in the corporate world, Camp seemed to his peers to have struck the optimal balance between sports and studies. Because he was athletic, he was invariably popular.[22]

Soon he began to publicize the athletic events he participated in, writing them up as editor of the school paper and establishing an association to pay for equipment and travel costs to compete in baseball against nearby schools. Indeed, in the world of sport, he already seemed a pioneer, the first Hopkins boy to kick around a black rubber sphere at the vacant lot on Elm Street. When his classmates asked him what it was he was kicking, he told them it was a "foot-ball."[23]

To be clear, the future Father of Football did not "father" the game, so to speak. By the time Camp had entered the world, "football," "foot-ball," or "foot ball" had already found its way into American vernacular. Before the Civil War, journalists wrote of Negro slavery as a "political football," and once the fighting commenced, they reported that "foot ball" kept up morale in the army camps.[24] Some mark the genesis of football as a coherent game at the establishment of the first football club, the Oneida, in Boston in 1862, but in truth the game was never monolithic; variations had cropped up at Princeton, Brown, Harvard, and secondary schools before Camp imposed uniformity on it later in the 1870s, adding complication to the question of origins.

Back in the 1840s and '50s, Yale men had played a crude form of football as part of their freshman-sophomore rush. Administrators banned it, thinking it cruel and unusual for refined college men, and yet before the Civil War, a freshman class brought it back, posting a challenge on the door of the Yale Lyceum to play sophomores at a public square opposite the college grounds. Upperclassmen officiated as the freshmen rushed into a phalanx of sophomores, the end flanks engaging in one-on-one combat. The brutal spectacle caused town legislators to prohibit the game in public spaces.[25]

Four years after the Civil War, the first match of collegiate "rugby football" in America took place in front of a hundred spectators in New Brunswick, New Jersey, played with a makeshift ball that was supposed to be completely round when blown up properly, which it was not. Men of Princeton and Rutgers drew up makeshift guidelines for three matches, but the third was never played. Reportedly, a Rutgers professor came up to the field and, with his umbrella stabbing the air in front of him, warned the participants that they "will come to no Christian end" for having played. At the time, Camp was a boy of ten living in Connecticut, totally unaware that he would become central to debates about the moral and man-making functions of football.[26]

The game was thought to have gone defunct in New Haven until a rugby player revived play on Elm Street, and then in 1872 in Hamilton Park, two miles from the college on the horse railway line, in order to avoid detection. Juniors formed freshmen into twenty-five ranks four deep, the heaviest men in front, arms locked. The sophomores faced them on the other side of the field, ninety in number, relying on their superior strength once they reached their opponents and became entangled into a singular mob. Men at Columbia and Harvard had participated in similar rushes, which had been similarly banned, and soon undergraduate David Schaff, previously a student at Rugby, established the Yale Football Association to organize matches with these eager college rivals.

That October of 1872, Schaff's classmates came up with a rudimentary code of rules that set the dimensions of the playing field at 400 by 250 feet and the goalposts eight paces apart. Already, the code stipulated that a player not wear "projecting nails, iron plates, or gutta-percha on the soles of his shoes." Yale men were the first to call for game officials—two judges, who were partisan, and a referee. When they played Columbia that year, undergraduates littered the field at twenty per side. Rather than pick up the ball, men batted it to the ground and dribbled it with their feet as if playing modern soccer. It was just as well, since the ball was too large to be handled or thrown with much precision. The following year, Princeton men called a convention at the Fifth Avenue Hotel in New York to codify rules that the Yale men accepted—until Eton men introduced them to a more lively game with eleven players per side.[27]

From here, two forms of football rugby emerged: The "association game," which emphasized kicking and dribbling but not tackling, and the "Boston game," which permitted high tackling. Princeton, Columbia, Stevens, Rutgers, and Yale adopted the former, albeit disagreeing on the number of men per side; and Harvard the latter, having played it against the Canadians of McGill University and having seen that spectators loved it.

Camp also saw merit in a game of carrying as well as kicking the ball after watching the "concessionary game" between Harvard and Yale in 1875, so called because the teams agreed to play by a combination of rules. That afternoon, 1,200 spectators converged on Hamilton Park, paying fifty cents to watch their teams flail under the hybrid rules. Spectators did not seem to care, applauding both squads indiscriminately and appreciating the more physical game in front of them. The players had acquired standard uniforms—Yale men wearing blue shirts, dark trousers, and yellow caps with tassels, and Harvard men in crimson tops, stockings, and knee britches. The teams played intensely for three half-hour stints. There was no numerical scoring; four touchdowns were equivalent to a single kicked goal. Harvard's greater experience with more physical rugby was apparent in the final score of four goals and four touchdowns to none.[28]

Camp, a high school senior, stood on the sidelines taking mental notes. The Harvard men knocked down their opponents like ninepins, seeming "to score at will," he recalled. "After the first few moments of dazed and pained astonishment, the superiority of the Harvard team became so manifest that the Yale crowd were actually forced to laugh at the grotesque spectacle presented by their suffering team." But there were no hard feelings. Yale men were consummate hosts to the 150 Harvard men they housed at the New Haven House. Perhaps it was a token of gratitude for being introduced to the all-body contact they would adopt and hone better than any college men in the country.[29]

This was the moment when Yale men stopped playing soccer and started playing football. Camp was there to witness it and grew enamored with the more physical game. Soon to graduate from Hopkins, he showed up often on the Hamilton Park field to see the Yale men in action, volunteering to lay down boundary lines just to be around the game. He was entranced by the spectacle of it, as well as its tactical possibilities. When Eugene Baker, captain of the Yale squad, asked him if he would like to come to practice on the second scrub team against the varsity, it was an offer Camp would not refuse. He could not wait to become a Yale man, football, rather than academics, being foremost on his mind.[30]

In the year of the nation's centennial, not long after his seventeenth birthday, Camp sat for rigorous entrance exams in Greek, Latin, arithmetic, English grammar, and geography, and was admitted to Yale. Sixty percent of his incoming peers were eighteen or nineteen, though his class ranged in age from sixteen to twenty-five. For the majority of his classmates, financial success and political influence were birthrights. Ninety percent belonged to families that had been prominent since colonial days, and 15 percent had fathers who had gone to Yale.[31]

Upon entering the campus, these "youths" (as opposed to high school "boys")[32] were aware of the heroes who had entered the gates before them. There was the legendary Nathan Hale, a mere eighteen-year-old when he graduated with the Class of 1773, who Camp later described as a natural athlete. A soldier in the American Revolution, Hale had made the ultimate sacrifice during war, as had the more recent college graduate Henry Camp, who fought valiantly for the Union. Walter entered Yale as his own cousin Charles was making a name for himself on campus, graduating as valedictorian in 1877.[33]

As much as Camp felt awe for the men who had gone before him, he felt too that he had arrived at Yale at the perfect time to forge a different, modern path to success. A golden age was dawning; for the next forty years, the Yale man epitomized the best in American manhood in the popular mind, and his pioneering role in college athletics would have much to do with it. The college's prestige was predicated on a masculine image to which sport was key, as was the absence of campus coeds. Although female students were beginning to appear at the Seven Sister schools of the East and land grant colleges of the West, at Yale, the faculty unanimously supported limiting women's access. Camp went "snabbing" (picking up girls) in town from time to time, but his collegiate world was one in which females did not figure prominently. Though the first female graduate students enrolled as he entered Yale in 1876, their admittance as Ph.D. students was not official until 1892, and undergraduate women were not admitted until 1969.[34]

When women walked the campus greens, they were usually visitors or faculty wives. If they appeared to be of undergraduate age, typically they were students in the art department, the only academic enclave for women since the department was established in 1864. When Camp arrived on campus, only sixteen men were enrolled as art students, compared to 569 in the academic department and 206 in the Sheffield

School of Science. Artistry was apparently not an aptitude to which the virile aspired.[35]

Until the rise of second-wave feminism, Yale essentially remained a bastion of maleness—and in Camp's time, white, Protestant maleness; the undergraduates shared race and economic privilege that bonded them. Most slightly favored the Republican Party, though Yale men were notoriously apolitical. Any lingering resentments between North and South seemed to have eroded before Camp arrived, for Southerners now mixed with the rest of their classmates in tournaments of billiards and whist. Camp's contemporaries fondly recalled the "brown-skinned vagabonds" who played music for money along the campus fence and the affable Negro janitors in the dorms. The black men in physical proximity to campus were too servile to shake an undergraduate's sense of racial dominion.[36]

Camp the college man was not especially taken with the great intellectual questions or artistic works of his day. After a local performance of *Richard III*, he and his friends pelted vegetables at the stage. They left campus to drink and smoke pipes at Mory's, the alehouse at Center and Temple Streets, and occasionally skipped class to play cards or haze underclassmen; several times they were involved in drunken confrontations with the New Haven police. Vice was implicitly endorsed as evidence that one had "put away innocent things." Daring escapades were rites of passage that proved a man "plucky" and "mettled," hence there was no shame in getting caught hazing or chewing tobacco, or getting punished for either.[37]

Because there were few poor or immigrant students to contend with, the social hierarchies at Yale relied on distinctions of class in the collegiate sense: sophomores paid deference to juniors, juniors to seniors, and freshman to everyone. First-year students were not yet allowed to sit on the campus fence, smoke a pipe in the yard, carry a cane before Washington's birthday, or dance at the Junior Promenade. Bowing was proof of a man knowing his place: Walking the greens, a junior waited until he was regulation distance from a senior and then looked for the nod. "He, by right of superiority, gives the signal by moving his chin through an angel [sic] of three degrees," explained a junior, "to which I respond by an inclination five degrees lower."[38]

For all their bravado, Yale men had chips on their shoulders about Harvard coming to prominence first and remaining the nation's preeminent college in the collective mind outside New Haven. One of Camp's professors admitted feelings of inadequacy: "Our boys died as bravely for their country as theirs, but our knightly soldiers still await their poet. . . . At Cambridge no occasion lacks its poet."[39]

Standing watch over Harvard's reputation was President Charles Eliot, a Boston Brahmin who had been a Harvard undergraduate. His forty-year tenure as president was the longest ever, and he went on to live into his nineties when few men around him did. He contended that his longevity had much to do with his being an avid swimmer and outdoorsman in his youth. As an undergraduate, he had crewed in a boat alongside Alexander Agassiz, the son of the Harvard geologist Louis Agassiz. The experience made him believe that his undergraduate charges should also become disciplined through daily exercise, and he hired physical education pioneer Dudley Sargent to run athletic programs in the Hemenway Gymnasium. That said, he stopped short of supporting the rugged team sport of *Tom Brown's Schooldays*. Having experienced real life-and-death battle as a lieutenant colonel in the Civil War, he saw no reason to simulate war's intensity elsewhere. For now and always, his support of sport was as a recreational and individual pursuit.[40]

Thanks in part to Eliot's influence, Harvard men touted their scholarly credentials, whereas Yale men boasted of "well-roundedness." In New Haven, they liked to think that the campus spirit had been epitomized in Civil War-era undergraduate Clarence King, a visionary in the Sheffield School who founded the U.S. Geologic Survey. He exuded excellence as a Renaissance man: equal parts scientific thinker and patron of the arts, as he demonstrated aptitude in the classroom, rowed for the crew, captained the baseball nine, and spent summers conducting field research in rugged conditions.[41]

This all-around man was manly in a physical sense, a departure from the campus ideal a generation before, when youths came to Yale to become scholars or ministers. Most of the college presidents until then had been churchmen devoted to moral instruction. The ministry was their calling, not their occupation, and breadwinning was of little concern. But Camp's cohort increasingly valued the material, and consequently a different set of traits in men. Though their fathers emphasized faith and good works, they were often interested in works alone. Whereas nearly 40 percent of Yale graduates sought to join the ministry at the beginning of the nineteenth century, only 9 percent had similar ambitions in Camp's undergraduate years.[42]

Administrators responded by holding on to old traditions. Morning prayer remained obligatory, even as it fell by the wayside at Harvard, where the elective system took root. Still, the men in the pews were more interested in shoring up social connections than salvation, in looking the gentleman rather than embodying his moral sense. Henry Beers, a professor in Camp's undergraduate years, could see the change. His students stopped referring to "the campus"; now it was "the yard"—a playground rather than a place of quiet contemplation. Now men classified themselves as social types: "the sponger," "the croaker," "the bore," and "the chum." The "dig," whose bookishness was once an asset, was now too stuck in his head to be admired. The figure to be emulated was the "man about campus," not a scholar so much as a lounger in society.[43]

Before the Civil War, men filed into the halls and staircases of college buildings to hear the orators among them. Now, most debating and literary societies were defunct, replaced in students' minds by the secret societies and athletic teams. Yale men said their society system was more democratic than Harvard's, which they claimed had been ruled by old money, but the social game in New Haven was also rigged to a large degree. The men with whom one dined and boarded freshman year provided channels into the sophomore societies, and sometimes these had been predetermined at Andover and Exeter before a man even left an impression. "The faculty kept up a sort of routine which imposed upon the outside world, but their true function was to maintain a chessboard upon which youthful politicians could make their moves," recalled Beers. The distribution of class offices and honors was, as far as he could see, "for the sake of the society system."[44]

Camp soon boasted of being a man about campus in his own right, choosing paths to social success without appearing to try. His social collateral increased almost immediately after making the freshman crew and baseball nine, which he eventually captained. He ran track, played intercollegiate tennis, and fell into the right eating clubs and social cliques, paving the way for his invitations into the freshman society Delta Kappa, the sophomore society He Boulé, and eventually the junior society DKE. "Dekes" vied with Psi U men for top billing at Yale and appeared to have pulled ahead by the time Camp joined their ranks. The brotherhood included Charlton T. Lewis ('53), editor of the *New York Evening Post*, and highly decorated Civil War officers. But membership was never the end goal; it merely positioned Camp for the most coveted of prizes: a bid into the senior societies.[45]

Analogous organizations existed throughout the American college system. There was Axe and Coffin at Columbia, for instance, and Owl and Wand at Wesleyan. But the most prestigious societies were at Harvard and Yale, and in New Haven, there were really only two to which men aspired: Scroll and Key and the more highly coveted Skull and Bones. Though the latter had been in existence since 1832, its ominous hall had been built on High Street only twenty years before Camp arrived on campus. The structure intentionally resembled a tomb, and members had planted Virginia Creeper on it to add to its shrouded feel. Speculation abounded as to what one might find inside—the first college bell, the constitutions of defunct societies, perhaps evidence of crimes more serious than petty theft. Each year's initiates took a group photo around a table on which sat a skull, and behind them stood an antique clock whose hands always indicated the eighth hour ("Bones time," whatever that meant—no one was allowed to tell). Juniors knew nothing of their bid into Bones until the hour they were "tapped" or slapped on their backs and asked, "Do you accept?" If they did, they were whisked away and henceforward sworn to secrecy.[46]

As a networking organization, Bones offered a leg up after college that cannot be overstated, given the economic volatility of the times. A fraternity brother could put in a good word at an alumni convention and forge the connection securing a brother's future financial success. There was comfort in knowing that amid market fluctuations and the impersonal corporatism of the workplace, fraternal bonds were powerful and lifelong. In time, rosters of Bonesmen became rosters of magnates, executives, and college and American presidents. Yale faculty complained in the meantime, however, that the coveted status of Bonesmen caused undergraduate priorities to run askew. The arenas in which Bonesmen held primacy had changed by Camp's undergraduate years. Once, they were eloquent debaters or literary editors, much to faculty approval. Now, they were athletes above all else. Camp would usher in the era of Bonesmen becoming virtually synonymous with football players.[47]

Indeed, when Camp was one of the fifteen tapped for Bones in the fall of 1879, no one was surprised. His class included Standard Oil scion Walter Jennings and Henry Waters Taft, whose brother, the future president, had been tapped two years earlier. Few of Camp's activities in the organization are known because he rarely talked about them and never wrote about them, like a good Bonesman should. All members had secret names, and his appears to have followed him to his grave. The only hint of the organization in his correspondence is the occasional signoff "322," the importance of which is known only by other Bonesmen, though possibly linked to a legend about the society's founding by Demosthenes in 322 BC.[48]

A few disgruntled rejects of the society system turned into outspoken "neutrals" and established a mock society known as Bowl and Stones. But for the most part, the fraternal masculinity of Skull and Bones was the standard by which Yale men measured themselves. It was a masculinity defined through exclusion, even if not couched as such. Undergraduates bought into it for the same reason their sociology professor William Graham Sumner rationalized the existence of economic inequality in American life: because all was fair in the natural world of competition. "The societies are often denounced for exclusiveness, but we do not think the criticism a good one," opined a non-society man. "It simply amounts to saying that they are based on competition, like most of the good things to which men may attain. . . . For this reason it fosters that democratic spirit which is the boast and glory of Yale."[49]

Camp too believed that there was nothing more democratic—or American—than the drive to compete, and that he, a man who had built up his body and athleticism from scratch, had been the fairest competitor of all.

And yet there was more on his mind than athletics in his college years, Camp would later insist. He had won competitions for writing a class poem and "The Ivy Ode," and in the dorms, he played whist like a master. Still, he could not deny that he was better known as an athlete than as a scholar or literary man. He proved to be a talented pitcher, one of the first to acquire a curve ball; and he held individual records in fielding percentage at shortstop (.897) and in batting (.627). His grades were serviceable, by no means stellar, hovering around a 2.5 average when 2.0 was the required minimum. Friends noted that he studied, but "not too hard for companionship." To them, his placing in track meets, swim heats, class crew competitions, and tennis matches mattered more than attendance at chapel or a report card filled with A's. His hitting two home runs on two pitches in a Princeton game was legendary, to say nothing of his football exploits to come. Being an athlete meant that he had won the right to strut the greens with swagger. On campus, he was easily recognized and impeccably groomed. Enough facial hair had come in by his junior year that he wore a mustache that matched his easy posture and reputation as a gentleman athlete.[50]

One day he was on the baseball diamond when members of the newly formed track team caught his attention. He stepped over to the track to watch the runners, and before he knew it, the team manager had recruited him to run hurdles. He trained intensely for two weeks, making times in the hurdles and quarter-mile that qualified him for one of the first meets of the Intercollegiate Association of Amateur Athletes of America (IC4A). Lining up for his first race, his nerves had gotten the best of him; he felt queasy, regretting a big lunch. The gun went off, and almost immediately he tripped. But he was not discouraged. "A determination to win came over me," he recalled, and when all was over, he had won by a hair. The lesson he learned that day never left him: "Only those who have pluck, endurance, or some element within them which enables them to temporarily throw off the fatigue and depression will eventually win."[51]

After that he studied methods for clearing hurdles. He made the steps he took between each more efficient, and he mastered the technique of running through, rather than jumping over, the obstacles. The more literal and figurative hurdles he cleared, the more he learned about his strengths and saw the character-building value of what he was doing. Physical training was important, he acknowledged, but there was also a psychology to winning.

He remembered too in that first heat he ever ran that his competitors had been popular men with audible cheering sections, while he was too new to Yale to be recognized. But he heard a singular voice from an upperclassman who encouraged him on. He heard the voice again after the gun went off, and again as he neared the sixth hurdle, giving him the boost to make up the deficit and win the race. "I don't suppose it cost him much to yell for a poor freshman," he later reflected, "but I know that I always thought of him as one of the best fellows I ever knew."[52] That was when Camp realized how much athletes and their publics were mutually reinforcing.

Thereafter he preached that spectators should stay positive, regardless of which team or athlete they wanted to prevail. "In a boat-race or a foot-ball match the chances are that your own men will not hear you cheer," he later wrote, "but the men who may try for the team or crew the next season do, and they are encouraged to better efforts by it." Cheering an opponent's error was, he decided, "the worst kind of boorishness." Grace must always be on display, in victory or defeat. "Be each, pray God, a gentleman," he famously exhorted. A true gent wanted the best man to win; whether he was an athlete or spectator, he acted nobly, because he had been elevated by the experience of sport. Camp came to believe that moral lessons were not only gleaned in the heat of competition but in adhering to rules and regimens before and after the contest. It was the entire experience of sport that made the morally and physically superior man.[53]

In this and other ways, Camp exalted the same concept of athletic amateurism preached at Oxford and Cambridge, formalized in the Amateur Athletic Club of London, and popularized in *Tom Brown's Schooldays*. Like other Anglo-Saxons, he often presumed that what was English was right, because the English had purportedly seized on the time-honored wisdom of ancient Greece, whose ideals had been transferred to the next great civilization.

In truth, the Greeks had made no distinction between amateurism or professionalism, nor did they wax philosophical on fair play. But Camp embraced this myth as timeless truth. Sanctimoniously, he held that gentlemen played for glory, not compensation. Rich men likely had less reason to play for money than poor men, and more leisure time to embody the amateur ideal. But for now, the elitism of his formulation was beside the point. He articulated his gentleman's code in almost everything he went on to write, including the *Book of College Sports* in 1893. Yale Dean Henry Wright lauded its "manly tone" and predicted that "the boy who makes it his guide will not be satisfied with strength and skill and courage, but will also have an ambition to become an honorable man and master himself."[54]

Wright's enthusiasm for sport was not evenly dispersed among the Yale faculty, many of whom still tucked themselves away in libraries and believed that in so doing they demonstrated Victorian self-mastery better than did their students. One exception was a professor who Camp came to revere, a man who—while an appreciably better thinker than athlete—spoke of "doing" in the modern world, rather than of acquiring erudition for its own sake. He was political economy professor William Graham Sumner; with his hard-hitting lectures and adversarial style, his students viewed him as one of the few professors on campus who flexed proverbial muscles to demonstrate virility in the modern sense.

College President Theodore Dwight Woolsey had appointed Sumner in 1872, after he had graduated from Yale and trained for the ministry. Sumner became a tutor in math and Greek and an Episcopal minister before his intellectual interests led him to a pioneering path in social science. When the rest of his colleagues wore gray beards in emulation of Greek philosophers, Sumner remained clean-shaven; even in baldness, he looked relatively youthful, and his voice boomed at the lectern. "He broke upon us like a cold spring in the desert," recalled a grateful undergraduate. "No one was really entitled to say that he was a Yale B.A. unless he had taken 'Billy' Sumner." Indeed, Yale men hung on his every word: "This morning Billy Sumner gave us a very good talk on Sociology," a contemporary of Camp recorded in his dairy. "He claims that everything Government does is wrong, and I guess he is nearly right."[55]

When Camp arrived at Yale, Sumner had already been butting heads with department colleagues and conservative college President Noah Porter. Both objected to Sumner's assigning of Herbert Spencer's *Sociology*, whose chapter on "Theological Bias," they believed, contradicted the moral aims of the college. But to students, Sumner looked to privilege scientific truth over tradition, and it appealed. His laissez-faire philosophies also coincided with Social Darwinist logic that his students presumed would become useful after graduation in the world outside New Haven. In an age of expanding industry and corporatism, they agreed with Sumner's opposition to government intervention, protectionism, reform, and socialism. In life, it was "liberty, inequality, survival of the fittest," as he put it, or "non-liberty, equality, survival of the unfittest." Insisting that *Sociology* was the only scientific treatment of his subject matter, Sumner threatened to resign if Porter refused to let him assign it, and in the end, he got his way.[56]

"Professor, don't you believe in any government aid to industries?" an undergraduate asked him once.

"No! it's root, hog, or die."

"Yes, but hasn't the hog got a right to root?"

"There are no rights. The world owes nobody a living."

"You believe then, Professor, in only one system, the contract-competitive system?"

"That's the only sound economic system. All others are fallacies."

"Well suppose some professor of political economy came along and took your job away from you. Wouldn't you be sore?"

"Any other professor is welcome to try. If he gets my job, it is my fault. My business is to teach the subject so well that no one can take the job away from me."[57]

Sumner welcomed competition because he saw it as a law of nature. The fittest were those with the power to adapt. "What are we teachers of Greek going to do if Greek is no longer required?" a colleague once asked him. "Learn something else and teach it," he responded. Indeed, during the course of his career, he mastered French, Hebrew, Latin, German, Russian, and several other languages in preparation for the day when he might need them. He championed free trade, academic freedom, and the gold standard; his concepts of "ethnocentrism" and the "Forgotten Man" carried more resonance in later decades, but students were drawn by his convictions. They sensed that he preached the wave of the future and became his secular disciples.[58]

In these years of burgeoning collegiate sport, Sumner was emphatically unathletic, and yet his influence on young Camp's athletic philosophy was unmistakable. In due time, he became a father figure, or perhaps something more akin to the older brother that Camp never had. He was one of the first men to ask Camp to think for himself, rather than recite the ideas of others, and he influenced him to visualize football's application to competition beyond Yale. Football became, in Camp's mind, a rehearsal for the rigors of college "afterlife," about which Sumner always warned. Camp echoed his professor when he referred to afternoon football practice as "a general killing off and survival of the fittest." The practice field on Dixwell Avenue was ragged, and Camp thought it necessarily so. The piles of broken stone around its edges tore into him as other men pushed his face into the ground, but he believed the experience hardened him until he was impervious to pain. Every night after practice, his teammates met for a three-mile run that left him exhausted. Crawling into his room afterward, he would drop onto the bed and fall deeply asleep. He was preparing not just for the weekend game, but for the grittier life contests ahead.[59]

Even before Camp joined the freshman squad in 1876, football captain Eugene Baker could see that he was a powerful runner in spurts. He was instinctually a deceptive dodger, a skilled distance punter, and an able drop and place kicker who soon mastered a straight-arm technique to ward off tacklers. Baker recruited him and one other freshman for the varsity squad, and Camp showed "sand" in his first big game, hitting a Columbia opponent so hard that the man's head struck the frozen ground, leaving him lifeless on the field. "I was sure that the man's head had broken open like an egg-shell," Camp thought, as he stood over his bleeding scalp. He told Baker to take him out of the game, sickened by having inflicted his first concussion.[60]

As a freshman, Camp stood 5' 10"; he was skinny, not yet the 160 pounds he bulked up to by his senior year.[61] His fresh-faced visage belied his physical force. At the Harvard varsity match that year, the opposing captain pointed to him on the sideline and warned Baker not to let "the child" play. Baker laughed, assuring him that Camp was "all spirit and whipcord." Once the game commenced, a bigger, bearded man tried to exploit the seeming mismatch. He bore down on Camp when he did not have the ball, but the freshman responded by throwing his opponent to the ground and pinning his shoulders until the man flailed helplessly under his knees. Only later did Camp come clean about being clocked squarely under the chin in an earlier play. Although he wondered if his neck was broken, he held on to his man all the same.[62]

Camp was no bruiser by today's standards or even then, but his effectiveness was less about size than determination. He described his survivalist instinct as a heavy dose of pluck coupled with an internal sense of honorable play that told him never to start fights, but to end them with definitive force. He was willing to experiment and improve upon his attempts, and though it was a controversial play at the time, he made the first forward pass on record.

Teammate F. R. Vernon recalled that Camp had sharp, unreadable eyes, which seemed to see as well in every direction without much movement of his head. He was "quick on his legs and with his arms. His action was easy all over and seemed to be in thorough control." Sensing developments before they occurred, he was serene carrying the ball in his signature hand-satchel grip, zigzagging around men or warding them off with his free arm. Because he carried a ball with him to class, he had come to know every inch of its surface, juggling it in order to learn how not to fumble it. "The ball seemed to stick to his palm, like an iron to a magnet," Vernon marveled. And yet he transferred it easily from side to side while he ran, never losing it to opponents.[63]

One of the spectators who had come to see Camp in the Harvard-Yale match of 1876 was Harvard freshman Theodore Roosevelt. He had accompanied several dozen classmates to New Haven to weather a cold, wet November afternoon in the stands and stood witness to the field becoming a mud pit, men sliding into each other as they battled to win position. Following the Harvard loss, he whined that Yale boys did not respect the rules, loose as they were. More frustrating, however, was that he could only observe from afar, and not very well. His round-rimmed glasses betrayed the one physical limitation he never overcame: doctors insisted that he did not see well enough to play football. Gym director Dudley Sargent examined Roosevelt, as he did all incoming Harvard freshmen, and also decided that his heart was not strong enough for athletics.

Roosevelt paid him no mind. At 5' 8" and 124 pounds, he was slight, but like Camp, he had a work ethic that compensated for his deficiencies. In the *Harvard Advocate*, he extolled Camp's discipline to train, perhaps because he understood his motivation. As a sickly child, he had willed himself to health with regimented exercise to cultivate his body. As Camp ran miles in New Haven, the future president lifted weights at Wood's Gymnasium until his father built him an outdoor facility at home. He reversed the atrophy in his limbs and lungs and continued to seek tests of his physical prowess. At Harvard, he boxed—not just casually, but in timed rounds until men made pulp of his face. He wanted football to be another physical test to prepare him for life's others. But for now, he could only admire Camp from a distance and think him worth emulating.[64]

In an era before the advent of helmets or protective gear, Camp played football with abandon. He took jabs and gave them. No matter how badly he was trampled, he willed himself back up on his feet. It is remarkable that an eighteen-year-old saw enough character-building potential in football to stick with it, given how badly he suffered its early ambiguities. In his first two years of playing, four of his scores were nullified due to confusion about the rules. In the Princeton game of 1877, he had hashed his way through opponents for eighty- and fifty-yard touchdowns, only to see both field goal kicks missed and no scores result. The Intercollegiate Conference decided to alter the English rules and allow touchdowns to count as scores, but four were needed to equal one goal. The following year, in a game against Harvard, he kicked a goal thirty-five yards over the crossbar, only for the official to blow his whistle with the ball in mid-flight. The goal did not count, nor did it a year later, when he kicked the ball forty-five yards against Harvard and saw the goal nullified by a holding call. In a game against Columbia at the cricket grounds in Hoboken, he came up from a play so badly mauled that his pants were in tatters. The referee called time, as teammates circled him and he walked off the field in a state of undress. When he returned, men came to blows over the calls. Despite cheap shots to his stomach, he was responsible for the game's only goals.[65]

The free-for-alls did not deter him. Teammates remember Camp the next day with notebook in hand, dreaming up formations and game plans best suited to the rules as they ambiguously stood. In his quest for perfect play, he made defenders wear sealskin gloves so that in the cold their fingers had enough feeling to grab hold of ball carriers charging through the line. In his junior year, he bowed out of the Amherst game to scout out the strengths of the Harvard team, Yale's opponent the following week. He proved a natural at developing talent and finding uses for it. His most fortuitous surprise may have been the 5' 9", 200-plus-pound freshman Frederic Remington from upstate New York. Rumor had it that this budding artist of the American West was a crack boxer; Camp sized him up in the fall of 1878 and felt confident that he could do something with him.

Before meeting Camp, Remington had been reluctant about coming to Yale. He dreamed of emulating his father, a Civil War hero, and had gone to military academies to learn the ways of soldiers. Headmasters reported back, however, that he lacked focus and discipline, that he was better at sketching a soldier than embodying one. After being rejected from West Point, he came to Yale feeling defeated. Although his parents worried that his decision to be the only male art student in his class would emasculate him, football turned out to be a timely antidote. Though not fast or agile, he was good-natured. Camp built Remington's stamina with extra laps around the gym that gave him confidence. After playing only two seasons, Remington's father passed away, and his aimless son left Yale without finishing his degree. For the rest of his life, he searched for activities that made him feel as virile and accomplished as college football had.[66]

Camp was not a "trained leader," as one teammate explained. He was an "undisputed" one. As a natural mentor, he had the ability to moti-vate teammates, so they made him team captain in 1878. He took the job more seriously than anyone before him, banning tobacco during the season, as well as any fraternizing past eleven o'clock the week of the Princeton game. Looking back, his was also the first modern training regimen on record. Everyone complied with his rules but Johnny Moorhead, a talented runner, whose curfew breaking caused his captain to summon a meeting in the dorm. As a matter of principle, Camp threatened to resign as captain if Moorhead did not quit the team. The move seemed drastic, but it had the desired effect of galvanizing the men. Moorhead offered to quit if it meant that Camp would stay, though he eventually was reinstated.[67]

Camp's teammates never forgot the incident; it set the tone for the kind of discipline for which Yale men were famous for the next thirty years. In the nights before games, players assembled on Camp's dorm room floor, backs to the wall, nothing in the center of the room but a football and their captain mapping out strategy. He spoke, but he listened more; he had a knack for sifting through points of view and incorporating them into a singular plan of attack. Teammates thought him intense, but eminently democratic, as "class feeling" gave way to "Yale spirit." No one yet knew he was acting like a prototypical coach. In time, the drillers of men would come to be known as "advisors" and "coachers," but a coach as known today did not yet exist. As captain, Camp was a player, trainer, and advisor all in one.[68]

From the beginning, Eugene Baker had recognized Camp's leadership and involved his young protégé in the governing facets of football, bringing him to the annual convention of the Intercollegiate Football Association (IFA) in 1877. This body of Princeton, Harvard, Yale, and Columbia men met on neutral ground, the Massasoit House in Springfield, to hammer out a daunting number of technicalities. The playing fields at various locales, for one, had different dimensions; some even had clotheslines as field goal crossbars. As yet, there was no consensus on how to handle injuries or the substitution of players; it was not unusual for men to endure two and a half hours of continuous play before leaving the field. Players had no dressing rooms, trainers, or regulation uniforms. Instead of helmets, they wore knitted caps or nothing on their heads. Initially, in 1876, IFA regulators established the dimensions of the standard leather ball and playing field and agreed to sixty-one rules that largely conformed to English rugby's union code. They also agreed to hold a season-ending championship game, placing a premium on winning even in the early days.[69]

Arguments nearly caused the IFA to go defunct before it got off the ground, however. Yale and Columbia protested the meeting in 1877 over scoring procedures and how many men should be allowed on the field. As captain, Camp attended the following year, convinced that it was in Yale's best interest to have a hand in shaping the rules to its strengths. Yale men wanted touchdowns to be scored differently, and the number of men on each side to be reduced from fifteen to eleven. With fewer men on the field, Camp figured that speedier players like him would have fewer obstacles to run through, and as a strategist, he could more easily map out plays. Fewer players also made the transport of the team to and from games more affordable, but his proposals were rejected.[70]

Camp was not deterred. He proposed eleven-player teams the following year—and the year after that. Yale refused formal membership in the IFA until his terms were accepted, and they finally were in 1880. At this stage, Camp was the elder statesman of the group, and the contours of his larger plan were coming into view. He envisioned a game played by a more physically tuned variation of the gentleman athlete, one equally decorous to his British counterpart but more virile because he had more poundage and physical force. And thus he saw less need for the union rules handed down from across the Atlantic. Blocks and tackles below the waist, for instance, need not remain illegal in his physical game. He proposed counting "safeties," defensive scores that did not exist in rugby, and to make the field's dimensions 200 by 400 feet to heighten the competitive drama. Most radical of all, in October 1880, he proposed a total reorganization of men on the field, discarding the English formation of the scrum for an American line of scrimmage.

Camp thought the English scrum was ineffective for establishing clear possession: The rugby official restarted play merely by tossing the ball into a tangle of interlocking players, and more times than not, pushing the ball forward meant relinquishing it to opponents. Sometimes scrums pushed the ball back and forth for minutes at a time, leaving spectators confused about what was going on underneath the bodies. Camp thought the scene too chaotic to be an indication of skill, and he encouraged his teammates to seek order by pushing the ball backward, not forward, with their heels to ensure that they did not relinquish the ball.

Control was the key to his game, as it was to his sense of manhood. As players turned chancy scrum play into the skilled seizing of possession, they separated themselves from mere boys on the field. His scrimmage put a ball in play in order to reveal unambiguous possession, thus permitting teams a better vantage from which to strategize a full-fledged advance. In this formation, the opposing sides were more discernible, much as in the gentlemen's wars of an earlier age. Players lined up and created a clear delineation of offense and defense, suggesting that from early on, Camp wanted his game to be accessible to spectators.

By removing some of the seeming randomness of possession, Camp unwittingly created new facets of the game. There was now a need for a craftier tactician to premeditate plans of attack, for instance, and to gain the edge, teams needed to practice with specialized purpose to work through all the tactical possibilities. Although he emphasized a team concept for the American game, the scrimmage allowed for a field general to emerge: Camp called him the "quarterback" and decided he was more akin to a corporate manager than a coach, delegating the ball to his employees. The quarterback would have the ability to laterally move the ball and pass it off to others, but not advance the ball on his own, not yet. But with him in position, the standard T-formation offense started to emerge: seven men at the line—linemen (who stood up straight), the "snapback," eventually known as the "center" for his position in the line, and men who flanked him called "guards," for their function to protect. In addition to the quarterback, the "fullback" and "halfbacks" positioned themselves behind the line. Although the formations of these players would shift any number of ways, from this point on their names largely stuck, as did the term "tackle" on the defensive side.[71]

Now the general structure of the game was in place, and Camp made minor adjustments as needed. There was, for instance, the modification made after witnessing Princeton's "block game" in 1881. Until then, there was no consistent mechanism in place for the transfer of possession when a team failed to make forward progress with the ball. Camp had figured that proper sportsmen would punt the ball away in due time, but Princeton men, unable to gain yards on their own, simply held the ball for the entire first half of the game against Yale, reasoning that if they could not score, they would not give their opponents a chance to either. Yale men responded in the second half by prolonging their possession of the ball too, until Camp punted the ball away. The scenario was tantamount to a baseball player swinging through or ignoring pitches over and over, regardless of the strike count. Vowing not to allow "the football rules to become a refuge for weaklings," in 1882, Camp invented the concept of "downs."[72]

This was an innovation that kept pacing, as well as the spectator, in mind. The offense essentially would be given a limited number of tries or downs to make headway on the field. If it did not advance five yards or lose ten after three plays, it relinquished possession of the ball to the opposing side. To incentivize forward progress, Camp also proposed adding value to safeties, awarding points to defenders who

pushed offenses back past their own goal line. All this was fine, his
fellow rule-makers decided, but they warned that under the system of
downs, it would be hard for officials and spectators to discern whether
the ball holder made his five-yard gain to retain possession. Camp's
solution was to mark the field with cross lines spaced five yards apart,
from sideline to sideline, so that one could gauge a man's gained or lost
distance with accuracy. Fellow rule-makers begged him for clarification: "Like a gridiron?" they asked. "Precisely," he answered.[73]

But all was far from solved. At an 1883 rule meeting, it became
clear that scoring procedures also needed to be overhauled: if only
rule-makers could agree how. Initially, only goals counted as scores,
with touchdowns gaining value over time. IFA members differed on
how much value they should assign to them, depending ultimately on
whether their teams' kicking or running games were stronger. Safeties
were also a contentious matter, given their common occurrence in early
contests. Their value was ambiguous until Camp proposed a clearer
scoring scheme that distanced American football from English rugby
even further. By 1885, he convinced the committee to award six points
to goals from touchdowns, five points for touchdowns without goals,
three points for field goals, and two points for safeties—up from one
point the previous year. He believed the numerical system would maintain the competitive tension for players and eliminate ambiguity for
fans, creating sport and spectacle all at once.[74]

Still, ambiguity remained, partly because the official rules of college
football, decided upon by a mere handful of men, changed radically from one year to the next and were not uniformly understood
by the players. On December 5, 1883, the rules committee attempted
to minimize confusion by authorizing Camp to copyright and print
the changing rules in an annual guide to be made widely available to
college men. As editor, Camp would look to a wider public to be the
official official of collegiate football.

So began his forty-seven-year career as a college football rule-maker
and editor. For twenty-eight of those years, he served as secretary of the
rules committee rather than as chair, perhaps to underplay his influence. But make no mistake: His views prevailed, especially in the early
years. Although his presence on committees was never blustery, he
got what he wanted with stealth and finesse. He had a reputation for

solving problems and building consensus. When challenged, he diverted assaults and narrowed divides. He had a way of listening intently to all suggestions before someone invariably uttered, "Well, let us see what Walter thinks about it."[75]

If he looked surprised, the proceedings had likely already unfolded in his mind like moves on a chessboard—or plays on a football field. More times than not, in the end, men found Camp's suggestions most logical. He lulled them into acceptance of his power. What could possibly have been a better skill to refine for the professional afterlife that was to come?

2

The Disillusionment of Afterlife, 1881–1887

FORTY-SIX MEN DROPPED OUT OF Camp's Yale class by senior year, and another twenty joined it later, leaving 121 to graduate in the class of 1880. The transition out of college was daunting for some. One graduate described it as a "disillusionizing period," when he passed out of an "ideal world" to enter "life as it is." Yale professor Henry Beers noted that most of Camp's cohort tried to handle the transition from college stoically: While daughters the same age were encouraged to remain dependent and connected to intimates they had always known, sons were supposed to embark on college afterlife with a sense of detachment and sober responsibility. "Young men of our race have a wholesome shame of making a fuss about their deeper feelings," Beers reflected. They were encouraged to act assertively, rather than fall into deep, disabling reflection. The name of the game was "keep moving and mull over little." One hoped to will success by ignoring the prospect of failure.[1]

But failure was imminent as many men walked away from a social universe in which they had known the rules only to suffer a disorienting sense of anonymity and flux. They were entering a world in which their new associates were not always pals, but rather competition for limited resources. In the Darwinist realm of business, they could not necessarily fall back on class rank or fraternity brothers who vouched for them. If dad's connections had jumpstarted a social climb at Yale, they often had less pull in the workaday world. Some acquaintances were now hard to read, often because they did not share their cloistered collegiate experience.

That thousands of graduates funneled into alumni associations and fraternal orders like the Odd Fellows and Freemasons suggests that Camp's classmates were hardly alone in their search for backslapping camaraderie and rootedness after college. In a nation in which the rules about social order and mobility had grown ambiguous, at least they could summon up a great game or a legendary athlete and create a connection. On a train, in a meeting, or a hotel lobby, sport was already providing the common language and meaning that brought men closer. It was a bond when no other nostalgia connected them, creating a male community of sorts.[2]

In time, Camp became a self-professed workaholic; better to keep busy he figured and not have emotions or self-doubt catch up to him. And yet some of his classmates went on to sublimate their anxieties so fully that they suffered physically, and doctors diagnosed them with "neurasthenia." This was not the same neurological deficit thought to come from masturbation, though experts still advised exercising Victorian restraint. Rather it was a case of one's competitive environment taking its toll, hence causing one to suffer nervous strain and grow decadent. Identified by physician George Beard, the malady was the result of cerebral, rather than physical, overstimulation in the desk-relegated work of modern times.[3]

The white man's paradox was that he, as agent of civilization, had become its overthinking victim. His pallor and sunken-in cheeks and chest were evidence that he had lost vitality—and hence virility in the modern world. An estimated 68 percent of male neurasthenics of Camp's day were between the ages of twenty-five and forty-five, when expectations for professional success were greatest. More than a fifth of Camp's graduating class succumbed to physical breakdown by age thirty, some requiring years of rehabilitation away from the stresses of the workplace.[4]

If someone had asked these men what was making them anxious, few could have articulated an answer, their stresses often stemming from conditions too far beyond their control to identify. This generation of

Yale men likely never appreciated the extent to which they yearned for the simpler successes of their fathers, because they did not fully understand the extent to which those successes required economic conditions and dominance over men of other races and ethnicities that they would rarely have. The cessation of Indian wars and soaring immigration were contributing to their collective emasculation, whether they knew it or not. Despite rampant racism and ethnic chauvinism, black, Jewish, and immigrant men were beginning to enter college and the professions and to vie for political positions and resources that once seemed specially set aside for the Anglo-Saxon few.

Whereas nine of every ten American men had worked the land or were self-employed before the Civil War, fewer than one-third could say the same by 1910. The "marketplace manhood" embodied by their fathers was eroding now that men felt less autonomous and more anonymous in the market economy. Industrialization and urbanization were going to make them sedentary and interchangeable. They were likely going to suffer volatile shifts in the market and find it harder to achieve manly independence in periods of economic decline. Their primacy as breadwinners was no longer a given. The pressures of these new realities invariably took their toll.[5]

But Camp's contemporaries did not walk around feeling victimized, partly because their sensibilities were changing with the times. They were embracing a new ideal of manhood, one wholly unlike the Victorian ideal of old. Before the Civil War, a white, educated man only felt compelled to distinguish himself from men of his same breeding, which he did by flaunting his refinement, or stoicism, or erudition. He proved his right to hold power by defining his *manliness* over his former *boyishness*; it was maturity—internal self-mastery—that made him a man. But his preoccupations with manliness necessarily shifted as immigrants, blacks, and women began to have access to higher education and to compete for resources and power. Needing another way to distinguish himself from others, the white elite now unwittingly deemphasized manliness to place a greater premium on *masculinity*—not in opposition to boyishness but rather to *femininity*—defining it in physical, racial, and ethnic terms.[6]

In time, football facilitated this new mindset; as for Camp's own needs for football, these were more complex. Although he fell prey to the same emasculating forces as his classmates, he was not like them in all ways. True, he dressed and talked with the polish of the most genteel of his graduating class, but his identification with them had its limits. Born with neither business connections nor a silver spoon, he was able to create enough distance to study his patrician peers carefully and avoid many of their pitfalls. When he looked at them, he saw men who had been raised almost exclusively indoors by female parents and nannies; who anticipated post-college lives as organization men, pushing paper behind desks in urban settings; and who, bound by four walls and corporate rules they could not control, would grow disenchanted with the purgatorial ranks of middle management.

Over the years, he observed his peers' lower muscle tone, bulging middles, and anxiety-induced maladies and wondered if they had endured the physically rigorous rites of passage through which a more effective manhood is made. For all their privilege, they never experienced character-building war like their fathers, just the emasculation of the burgeoning industrial age. It became Camp's personal mission not to suffer physical and psychic deterioration to the same enfeebling degree.[7]

Professor Beers was also mindful of the lack of grit in the Yale Class of '80. He wondered if they could endure the Spartan existence of the New York boarding houses that assuredly awaited them now that they were graduates. Indeed those of Camp's classmates who did not train to be New York lawyers, trained to be New York executives or in rarer cases to go up to Boston. One-third of the Class of '80 became lawyers, another third businessmen. Only one classmate pursued a Ph.D., suggesting that life tucked away in an ivory tower had less appeal than it used to have. While a third of the class entered lifelong careers directly after graduation, others followed drift patterns, in no hurry to nail down professions just yet. Five of Camp's classmates followed Frederic Remington's lead and postponed office work to live out West as cowboys.[8]

Camp was neither so adventurous nor raring to become a professional. After devoting himself to collegiate sport heart and soul, it was hard to turn the page, but no one had paved a path of post-collegiate athletics that he could respectably follow. Professional baseball came into existence in 1871, but accepting money to play was still considered déclassé for a man from Yale. In the 1880s, the majority of the 240 players in the big leagues had never even gone to college. Camp had had the best batting average of the Intercollegiate Association, and rumors abounded that he was offered good money to join a professional team. Instead, he contemplated a more honorable appointment in baseball's league of umpires. For an enviable salary of $1,000 plus expenses, he would officiate on diamonds throughout the Northeast.[9]

This was where Camp needed to be, after all, to continue playing competitive football. The best squads were still Harvard, Princeton, and Yale, with Pennsylvania (Penn) and Columbia narrowly behind them. Given his loyalty to alma mater, staying put in New Haven was the only option he considered, but how could he legitimately do it?

In 1882, he decided to join twenty-four others and enroll in Yale's medical school, continuing his college athletic career as if graduation had never happened. Not yet were there restrictions on the athletic eligibility of graduates on college teams; ironically, Camp pushed for them later in the 1880s. Medicine looked to be a choice of convenience for now, but it also made some sense, given his limited options. Had there been a course of study in sports medicine or athletic training, Camp likely would have seized it, but ironically, these fields arose later as adjuncts of sport itself, rather than in medical schools. Camp had already studied the joints of pitching arms and the knees on tackles. After running enough races, he determined that football backs could shoot off a line better in a crouched position. He was drawn to the study of bodies, less to stave off disease than to prevent injury and maximize athletic performance. Attending medical school seemed the best way to follow in that line.

Several years earlier, Dudley Sargent had graduated from Yale Medical School and embarked on a career that combined his knowledge of physiology with the goal of making college men as hardy as their battle-tested fathers. As a pioneer of anthropometry, the study of body measurements, Sargent developed "corrective gymnastics" to achieve optimal body symmetry and determine the perfect physique for specialized athletic tasks.[10] But becoming a credentialed physician was harder now than in Sargent's time. When Camp entered, Yale Medical School had been revamped and its requirements made more rigorous. In advance of all medical schools other than Harvard, Yale instituted a longer, nine-month annual course of study for three years. After passing a written entrance exam, Camp was subjected to lectures, recitations, laboratory sessions, and grueling final exams. Administrators boasted that Yale men would have knowledge of the latest medical procedures, but this meant that the medical student took more time studying than he ever had in his undergraduate years. As this reality hit Camp's classmates, they started dropping out of medical school in droves. The average Yale medical class graduated only seven in the 1880s. Sixty percent of Camp's cohort left before finishing the degree.[11]

Camp relinquished his captaincy of the Yale eleven to pass the torch to undergraduate Robert Watson, and then to Frank Eaton. But when Eaton broke his collarbone in practice, Camp agreed to lead the team for a third time. He performed as doggedly on the field as he had in his undergraduate years. In a game in 1882, he kicked all nine of the team's goals against Rutgers. Every facet of play—offensive and defensive, physical and mental—were his to manage, though he began to delegate conditioning to another expert of sorts, a trainer, whose preparation of bodies started to loom as large as the mapping of strategy. Camp's knee, damaged in practice, was proof that injury management was becoming a factor in games. For the first time in his playing career, he started taking himself off the field to be replaced by substitutes. Only three games into his seventh season, a final blow to his knee put him out of commission. With cartilage damaged, he sat on the sidelines in a silicate cast from his hip to his ankle. Walking with a cane for the rest of the season, it struck him that his playing days were over.[12]

The realization was made easier by the fact that he remained integrally involved with the team, creating for himself an advisory role that he took to the sidelines. He was not paid for his leadership or expertise, which, he insisted, was how it should be: There was no place in amateur sport for salaried players or consultants. His teammates were so relieved to have his input that they did not much care if he gave it from the peripheries. In fact he soon started strategizing off the field completely, holding meetings in his parents' house on Chapel Street. On evenings after practice, teammates moved his mother's living room furniture to clear the way for demonstrations of his new formations.[13]

It was not long before Camp broadened his role in Yale sports even more by drafting terms of engagement with rival teams as an unofficial ambassador of athletics. His trips up to Cambridge made the Boston papers, one headline declaring that he went north bearing "Yale's Final Proposition for Harmony" between the nines, elevens, track teams, and crews. In December 1882, Harvard zoologist Alexander Agassiz, now a faculty supporter of the crew, called for a truce among the respective squads, and administrators again turned to Camp to mend fences. He had a hand in preparing Yale for the first intercollegiate tennis tournament in 1883, and then in forming its golf team. To give undergraduates competitive options in the winter months, he announced in the campus paper a meeting to start a wrestling squad, and he joined physical director William Anderson in forming a Gymnasium Advisory Committee to oversee the acquisition of training equipment.[14]

Camp would not have organized so zealously in the name of sport had he not seen its potential to fill cultural voids, as if sport were a modern religion. He envisioned it providing moral guidance and virile values in a nation detached from its traditional moorings, and thus while his editorials on sport initially only filled Yale publications, he soon sought a wider audience for them in *Outing*, a magazine first devoted to cycling that expanded its coverage to the larger, booming sports craze. He prepared a history of intercollegiate baseball that got the attention of Henry Chadwick, the first New York sports reporter, who floated the idea of *Camp's College Base Ball Guide* in 1885. Interest in his writing snowballed from there. He secured contracts with *St. Nicholas Magazine* and *The Youth's Companion* to write for boys and reviewed intercollegiate football for newspaper and magazine editors intrigued by the gridiron game.[15]

The timing of his literary rise was no coincidence. Football and the daily press relied on each other for their growing popularity in the 1880s and '90s. Joseph Pulitzer was first to prove the profitability of an entirely separate sports department for the *World*, and William Randolph Hearst expanded on his ideas by printing the nation's first sports page. Publications like the *New York Times, Herald,* and *Journal* followed suit and in time expanded coverage of college football to multiple columns, then multiple pages, and eventually front-page features and spreads with eye-catching illustrations and photographs. Thanks to the dailies, an intramural activity of elite college men grew into a national fixation. The passing of the five-yard rule in 1882 had given structure to football, and soon it lent structure to Camp's journalistic accounts of games, which unfolded play by discernable play in print across the nation.[16]

New York newspapers and magazines had covered sports intermittently before Camp came along, but the submissions were largely anonymous and intended solely to inform, rather than interpret sports' deeper meanings. Camp's pieces were different. While some of his first ones did explain the technicalities of football to confused novices, his others sold football as more than a game, but also as an antidote to male degeneration in modern life. In a piece for the *Yale Review*, he called young men to arms—or to sport: "How many parents urge their sons on coming to college to study hard and stand high! How few exhort them to play hard and be athletic! . . . At least half need the latter advice." Claiming that sports provided strenuousness in lives that lacked physicality, Camp created connotations for sports that empowered.[17]

The message would probably have been lost, particularly on young readers, had he not conveyed it through stories of modern sportsmen—especially footballers—set in heroic molds. Take his write-up of former teammate Ray Tompkins, whom he described as "one of the most ideal captains and linemen" he had ever seen. In Camp's hands, Tompkins was a historical legend in the making, his greatness emerging from his tenacity and ability to shirk off pain for the good of the team. As Camp told it, Tompkins mangled his ankle in the penultimate game of the season but refused to sit out the final match. Doctors insisted that his foot was too injured to walk on, let alone play on, and yet Tompkins knew that as the leader of the team he had to be out on the field. He bandaged his ankle to "absolute stiffness" to play, as a warrior would, and, as Camp intimated, a legend must. Doctors often cautioned players in Camp's writings not to take physical risks, but they had too much courage to heed the warnings. The moral: Football made real men, and real men played through pain.[18]

Camp's literary career was blooming while he was still a medical student being trained to use pain to gauge injury and diagnose ailments. It did not bode well for his future as a healer to idolize mythical men who never winced at pain, but other factors also caused him to reconsider his career options, not the least of which was having fallen behind in his coursework after being stricken with typhoid. He had already struggled to keep up with the rigorous pace of school and football at once, and things got worse once he enrolled in the anatomy course and struggled. Two courses shy of fulfilling his requirements, he decided to forgo his final year of medical school, telling friends that he was despondent over the death of a professor whom he had regarded as his mentor.

Fellow Bonesman Walter Jennings thought it very strange when he met up with Camp in New York and was told the news. "You are joking," Jennings said. "Why, you are practically a doctor now." Camp allegedly shrugged him off: "The fact is, I hate the sight of blood." What he purportedly said was hard to believe, given the blood he had seen spilled on the gridiron. More likely, Camp convinced himself of what he wanted to believe to justify giving up and taking another path.[19]

In total, Camp played on the Yale eleven for six years: four as an undergraduate and two as a medical student. For three years, he captained the team, and for five, he represented Yale in the IFA. His teams won twenty-five games, tied four, and lost only one. In some respects, he spent the rest of his life trying to return to the unambiguously glorious days of college life, even if he would not admit it. "Burn up your college sweater and replace your college cap with a derby," he stoically advised in later years. "No man should flaunt his gaudy past."[20] And yet the emotions he described in a piece for *Harper's* were ones he likely knew firsthand:

> To be a member of a varsity team is to be among the leaders of the college, and the captain is perhaps the most conspicuous character in university life. His fame is almost national; for college men, wherever they may be, are watching him. . . .
>
> Yet no matter how successful he is, he will probably be obliged to settle down at the close of his course to hard work at the bottom of the ladder, and the change is a pretty difficult one for youth and pride to accept. When it comes, it finds him handicapped, because he has become accustomed to fill an important position. . . .
>
> He has to learn the routine, the beginnings of the work before him; and no one who has not tried it himself can realize what a jump downwards that means. The new clerk, who knows nothing of business principles, finds himself far below men who seemed to look up to him but a short time before.[21]

Having abandoned medicine, Camp now confronted the hardships of starting over, of developing a reputation from scratch. Nevertheless, his success in the athletic arena assuredly had a hand in his landing a sales job with the Manhattan Watch Company in 1883. He made the trek to New York City, but left Manhattan Watch within a year to work for the concern he would stay at for the rest of his professional life, the New Haven Clock Company, which, as the name suggests, was head-quartered closer to home.

Clock-making had long been an industry bringing Connecticut capitalists into the international economy, Seth Thomas, Ansonia, Waterbury, and other local manufacturers also competing for market share. The New Haven Clock Company had been established by Hiram Camp in 1853 and produced brass clock movements for the Jerome Company. But by the Civil War, the New Haven Clock Company had taken over Jerome's industrial facilities, and Edward Stevens, the new husband of Jerome's daughter, expanded the operation in England. In time, New Haven's highly efficient assembly-line facility would span two city blocks and make 6,000 timepieces a day.[22]

Camp's first two years with this firm were in the New York salesroom at 16 Park Place, and the third year was largely spent on the road as he moved up into the selling and export departments. But when he became manager of the sales force, he was able to relocate to the head office in New Haven, returning to New York regularly for meetings. Because of football and clock company business, Manhattan would always be his home away from home.

Sales was a far cry from medicine, but hardly a step down in a society that defined prestige in masculine terms. The field appealed to a former collegiate athlete looking to channel his competitive spirit into activities that paid and integrated him into the virile realm of capitalist enterprise. Clerkships and other office positions had become feminized of late, but not sales jobs. These white-collar positions allowed for upward mobility and reinforced independence and individuality when industrialization threatened to strip both from American males. Men brokered deals by forging relationships in all-male contexts—on the road, in hotel lobbies, on the golf course, or in a gentleman's club over drinks. Selling was men's work, and Camp gravitated toward it naturally.[23]

Peddling timepieces was a stable living that had its perks. High-end clocks brought prestige to their owners, and Camp was quick to give them as gifts. In the decade after graduation, as friends married off one by one, he discovered that standing clocks made ideal wedding presents. He had Chippendales customized with special pendulums, glass doors, and mahogany panels, as requested, and engraved with cryptic markings that, unbeknown to a woman in the household, paid homage to the groom's fraternity—a small reminder of the intimate male world he left behind.[24]

Although Camp had a hand in modernizing the New Haven Clock Company, the business was never his passion. He plodded up the corporate ladder expectedly, becoming assistant treasurer in 1893, then treasurer, and eventually president in 1902. He never complained about the modest annual raises he received, but in truth, his place within the bureaucratic ranks never provided the same sense of daring or enterprise that invigorated other famed magnates of the Gilded Age. Looking back, it appears that his celebrity in the burgeoning field of sports brought more value to his business than the other way around. Any time he negotiated with suppliers or vendors or magazine men to buy space for his ads, his football prominence pulled more weight than anything else. One of his greatest professional victories was popularizing a pocket watch called "The Yale"; what better way to capitalize on the winning record of an alma mater?[25]

Camp recognized that it was probably more exhilarating to sell clocks than to punch them or make them on an assembly line, as most New Haven Clock workers did. His company, like many expanding businesses of its day, turned profits by mechanizing the labor of once autonomous artisans, turning them into unskilled, interchangeable cogs of an industrial machine. Protective legislation had not yet prevented the exploitation of women and children, and Camp's company took advantage to some degree. During his first year on the sales force, one of the manufacturing buildings caught fire, causing $20,000 in damage and injuring an employee trying to escape the flames. It was not the last fire to wreak havoc, or the last employee to suffer, or the last time Camp would find himself torn between people and profits. Threats of machinist strikes would prevent him from attending football games and rules committee meetings; disgruntled workers weighed on his conscience.[26]

Perhaps Camp was more ideally suited to the position his childhood friend Julian Curtiss took with Spalding, the burgeoning sporting goods company founded in 1876. Still, the business of clocks lent inspiration to his efforts to give order to football. As he watched workers punch in and out at the factory, making hands on pieces that methodically moved, he internalized a sense of regulation that was dictated by time. In the 1880s, engineer Frederick Winslow Taylor used a stopwatch to optimize the work of laborers in factories and he called it "scientific management." Camp soon also managed the pace of football by starting and stopping a clock, punching in and out, so to speak. While the stop-start nature of football was unrecognizable to Englishmen, he saw value in controlling the rhythm of play. For spectators, watching men compete against the clock added narrative tension to the drama before them. For players, being on the clock forced efficiency and effectiveness that Camp thought useful in the modern world.[27]

Occasionally, Camp traveled to company offices in Chicago, San Francisco, and London. Between appointments, he met with sports promoters, editors, and alumni for lunch and rounds of golf, selling timepieces and football at once. His affiliation with Skull and Bones won him invitations to alumni events at some of the most exclusive clubs in major cities, though New York remained the center of his professional, literary, and athletic operations.

Boston Brahmins established the nation's first country club in Brookline in 1882, yet even earlier, *New York Herald* owner James Gordon Bennett had built the Westchester Polo Club and the Newport Casino to allow New Yorkers to mix socializing with competitive sports. Seen as the "saving muscular grace" of desk-confined executives, athletic clubs sprouted up in the best parts of Manhattan and its environs. The New York Yacht Club was joined in the 1880s by the University, Crescent, American, and Manhattan Clubs. The flagship New York Athletic Club (NYAC) had 1,500 members and a five-story clubhouse replete with gym, pool, dining hall, bowling alley, and shooting range by 1885. Its facilities at Travers Island allowed for boating and tennis, and to add a competitive spark, it hosted amateur track-and-field meets and championships in swimming, wrestling, and boxing.[28]

Camp could see that elements of New York society were unlike the staid elites of Philadelphia or Boston. This fashionable set embraced a culture of play and made sports part of their conspicuous consumption, perhaps because so many of them were nouveau riche born elsewhere. The city's old families steadily mingled with men who recently converged on New York to make their fortunes. This new set had less reverence for Victorian restraint and helped to make New York society more permeable, with its respect for tradition and self-making alike. Although Camp did not have the money or pedigree of a Livingston, his Yale degree, combined with his newly appreciated athletic assets, turned his into social currency as good as any. Few were better positioned to find their name in the little black book, the *Social Register*, or on the rosters of the prestigious metropolitan clubs, many of which were now centered around athletics.[29]

Standard Oil executive and former teammate Walter Jennings wrote letters of introduction to the University Club at Camp's behest, but the list of candidates for membership was long. Men were admitted by regular elections, usually after a wait of a year or more, so Camp waited patiently until his athletic record made him a shoo-in at the University and Graduates Clubs. He repaid the privilege of being selected for membership by officiating at the clubs' amateur tournaments; more so than other members, he had participated on the committees that had authored the rules.[30]

Harper's now referred to New York as "the amateur athletic capital of the world," and on the surface it was true. In 1879, the most exclusive clubs of the city had formed the National Association of Amateur Athletes of America (N4A), and within a decade, the NYAC formed the Amateur Athletic Union (AAU), which took control of the amateur movement. By relegating club competitions to men who claimed never to play for compensation, members believed they kept true amateurs in and riff-raff out. Gentleman athletes were self-policing, the concept went, and their skill in sports purportedly came naturally, rather than being worked at. Perpetuating the English notion that lower-class men could never internalize their ethos of fair play, they were exclusionary in the name of purism.[31]

Camp managed to be a rare, self-made exception to the rule. Over lavish meals and cocktails, New York elites indoctrinated him further with their amateurist philosophy, even as their stronger impulse was to win sports contests by any means, much as they had in business. Camp could see that rather than truly promoting play for play's sake, they implicitly encouraged rule-breaking, a win-or-die mentality, break-neck training, under-the-table payoffs, and run-amok commercialism—in all sports, but soon in college football especially. IFA rules committee meetings migrated from Springfield to New York, another sign that alumni money was beginning to hold sway in the college game.

Although Camp was reticent to acknowledge it openly, he could see from his insider perspective that amateurism was an elitist fiction; "gentlemen" were often the very perversion from which amateur sport needed saving. The athletes for whom Camp officiated were often bought and sold; when convenient, working-class men with athletic gifts were made to appear as elites so that their sponsors could avoid the look of hypocrisy as they exploited them for personal gain.[32]

This was the paradox at which English amateurism turned undeniably American, and Camp sat uncomfortably in its crux. "A gentleman never competes for money, directly or indirectly," he professed—long after he knew differently. In truth, nothing was more antithetical to the materialistic individualism of the Gilded Age or any American age since. But for now, Camp did little to draw attention to the contradictions. His reputation in New York athletics was affirmed when he was elected president of the Crescent Athletic Association in Brooklyn in 1886.[33]

For this bachelor who roomed sparsely downtown on West 34th Street, dining at the Crescent and his uptown clubs meant rubbing elbows with important people and enjoying meals and pampered domesticity now that he no longer lived at home. More crucially, it provided the all-male intimacy lost since his college days. Mixing with sports editors and football regulators as he sold clocks and smoked cigars in the finest sitting rooms in New York, he had managed to build an afterlife that was discernibly virile and not so disillusioning after all.

The Walter Camp of New York society was, in a word, self-reliant. Looking back on these years, he would insist that his earlier experience of Yale athletics had set the tone for his life. Though faculty control of athletics was the preference at Harvard, at Yale, athletes controlled their own destinies, thanks to Camp's pushing to make it so. The scheduling of contests was put in the hands of student managers and team practices in the hands of captains; faculty gave input only upon undergraduates' request. With his student days not far behind him, Camp wrote on the merits of Yale's student-run system: "Athletic Sport teaches a race more self-government than politics," he professed. The self-regulated athlete "is safe from athletic degeneracy and professionalism but also reminded capable of carrying on organizations in a business-like manner. . . . The undergraduate is obliged to take care of his own financial, traveling and other troubles. *He is a man* and as such expected to look out for himself; and that is the way, the best way, to enable him to become a truly manly fellow . . . without the namby-pamby effeminacy of a child in leading string."[34]

Self-possession was critical, he told Yale athletes; less disciplined men succumbed to bookies and promoters when given the chance. The faculty did not question that he knew about whence he spoke. Their only intervention in athletics was to stipulate that contests take place on Wednesday or Saturday afternoons and that students miss no more than twenty credit hours traveling and playing in games. Yale's athletic management was almost no management at all—a handful of graduate advisors, whom Camp described as "elder brothers" giving counsel when asked. Apparently they were asked rarely, since they did not meet for years at a time.[35]

Sport was the Yale undergraduates' preserve. Their boathouse was built, as were the football stands, through undergraduate subscriptions rather than university funds. Gone were the glory days of the student literary papers; now, campus publications served as boosters for the major sports teams. Pudge Heffelfinger, a football guard at Yale in the late 1880s, recalled hundreds of schoolmates showing up to watch him practice every afternoon. "The students felt that they were part of the team," he explained; they made it their business to stay abreast of its progress.[36]

The most important mass meeting, in students' eyes, was the one at which they elected their managers and captains for the upcoming athletic season. Managers of the four major varsity squads—crew, base-ball, track, and football—kept separate books, but as gate receipts grew, in football most substantially, Camp created a clearinghouse for these monies called the Financial Union. Undergraduates officially managed the Union, as they did the teams, but Camp was appointed its treasurer and given a salary of $600 to keep the books. As an "advisor," not a coach or manager, he broke no amateur codes by getting paid. Once directors of other athletic departments recognized that Yale's Financial Union was the first body in college athletics to generate surplus, they asked Camp to explain its workings. His response was always to underplay his influence and describe Yale athletics as democratic in structure—run for undergraduates, by undergraduates, for better or worse.[37]

And yet in truth, little happened athletically at Yale in which Camp did not play a part. The undergraduates relied on him to make most financial decisions, and graduates turned to him to broker agreements with other schools. Without acknowledging the incongruity of it, alumni started referring to Yale's system of "self-government" as Walter Camp's "czarist regime," because from their perspective, that's what it was. He was instrumental, for instance, in sorting out the seating shortage at the Harvard-Yale annual game that left most graduates clamoring for tickets. Ironically, it had become easier to secure seats for contests in New York than for home games at Hamilton Field, since space was so limited. After the Class of '81 raised revenues to purchase land for a bigger venue, Camp drafted Articles of Association for the Yale Field Corporation and agreed to serve as its treasurer, a role he assumed for the next fifteen years.[38]

Camp collected enough money in subscriptions and mortgages to build a bigger venue in time for the Harvard-Yale game of 1884, as well as to give himself a hefty $1,200 salary as director of the field. The bigger facility stood on Derby Turnpike, a mile south of the old field, on New Haven's West River; for convenience, trolleys ran practically to its front gate. In 1884, the grandstand accommodated 600 patrons and the overflow funneled into the standing-room sections, causing clamor for more expansion until the stands accommodated 30,000 by 1905. Camp was involved every step of the way.[39]

Yale administrators did not object because they bought into his philosophy that college sport was good for the town, the college, and undergraduate men. Harvard officials were less convinced, much of the skepticism emanating from the president's office. A few years earlier, Charles Eliot and President James McCosh of Princeton had asked Yale's President Porter to join them in curbing the traveling of athletic teams during term weeks, but the dean of students assured Porter that this was not a problem at Yale. "From then the divergence of opinions began," Camp recalled. "With the growth of athletics the methods of various universities became more marked, Harvard's finally developing through a process of faculty control into an athletic committee with its powers from the Corporation."[40]

From its inception, Harvard's Athletic Committee was an obstacle to Camp's vision of student control. Its members insisted on being the negotiating party with Yale managers, stipulating when, where, and how often students could play in matches. It did not please Camp when the Harvard committee almost banned the big game of 1883. Its charge: Football "had begun to degenerate into a brutal and dangerous contest." There were too many cases of intentional offsides and blatant cheating, to say nothing, members claimed, of the men who punched opponents in premeditated fashion. The committee refused to allow Harvard to play more games until the IFA pushed through changes that allowed for stricter officiating.

According to John Heisman, who played at Brown before moving to Penn, the committee's allegations were not off the mark. He likened the college gridiron of the 1880s to the lawless West: There was not yet a clearly delineated neutral zone separating teams at the line of scrimmage, and men duked it out with "hammer and tongs, tooth and nail, fist and feet" to win position. There were no linesmen and no line sticks. The referee kept track of distance by dropping a handkerchief wherever he surmised the ball was last in play, and players moved it when they thought they could do it undetected. Arguments invariably ensued, ones in which "the whole team took part," Heisman joked. "A good linguist was a priceless asset." The ritual of partisan judges arguing calls like trial lawyers got out of hand on the sidelines, but what concerned the Harvard committee more was the uncouth behavior of the players. Members complained that a man could "hack, throttle, butt, trip, tackle below the hips, or strike an opponent with closed fists three times before he was sent from the field."[41]

Harvard administrators reluctantly allowed the big game of 1884 after the IFA gave the referee more power to disqualify unruly men, but their players were under probation. To monitor conditions, members of the Athletic Committee showed up at games that season, only to have their worst fears realized. "In every one, there were fist fights and men had to be separated by other players, or by the judges and referee, or by the by-standers and the police," they reported. "Gentlemanly spirit" had gone astray—on the field and in the stands. "We often heard cries of 'kill him,' 'break his neck,' 'slug him,' 'hit him,' and 'knock him down.'" "After deliberate investigation we have become convinced that the game of football, as at present played by college teams, is brutal, demoralizing to teams and spectators, and extremely dangerous."[42]

The Harvard Athletic Committee banned intercollegiate play for 1885, and Princeton reacted by relegating its team's play to college venues only. Camp's call to let college men regulate themselves had fallen on deaf ears; faculty members were desperate to take back some control. As the most veteran member of the IFA, Camp tried once again to appease Harvard administrators with substantive changes to the football rules. He proposed a five-yard neutral zone to curb sparring on the line, but the measure did not pass. Rule-makers did agree in 1886, however, to make it illegal to interfere with the center as he snapped the ball, which created some order on the line of scrimmage, and even more power was granted to game officials. The referee could declare a ball down and mete out penalties for intentional delays of game, offside play, and slugging. Partisan judges officially went by the wayside as the referee's authority increased.

Harvard officials seemed well-enough appeased to allow play in 1886, but it was hard to find game officials with whom all parties were satisfied. For the Harvard-Yale game, managers of both teams thought Camp the best choice. Princeton had also requested him that year and three years prior, as did Wesleyan in 1891, proving that even among rivals, his fairness and technical expertise were unquestioned. In the Yale-Princeton contest of 1885, he proved he could be impartial when he called back a sixty-five-yard run by Yale's Harry Beecher because his foot slipped out of bounds; Princeton went on to win by a single point. When Princeton and Harvard men accused each other of corrupt recruitment practices, they asked Camp to settle their disputes. No IFA member objected when he proposed in 1887 to institute a Graduate Advisory Committee, an arbitrating body consisting of a graduate from each of the five IFA member schools. Sitting on that, as well as the rules committee, allowed him, and only him, to advise on *and* consent to his own legislation. Under the guise of a committee system, Camp had found a way to impose his singular will.[43]

But he could not officiate in all games. With all of the referee's added responsibilities, he wondered if the time had come for more systemized training and screening for the position. Controversially, he proposed that referees be paid for the expertise required of them. Though the suggestion obviously deviated from the English tradition of self-regulation and seemed antithetical to the spirit of amateurism, he rationalized it for American officials, who, he pointed out, oversaw a far more technical game than rugby. Whereas captains settled disputes in the English game, he declared it "manifestly out of the question" in an American game that kept captains busy enough with specialized duties of generalship.[44]

Doing away with partisan judges, Camp divvied up the work of the referee among more sets of expert eyes on the field. In 1888, the umpire became the specialist responsible for identifying personal fouls so that the referee could focus on the course of the ball. Eventually, the linesman and field judge helped the referee perform his job with greater precision as they also took on specialized workloads. A player would, in theory, think twice about playing dirty, since he knew he could be seen and penalized. IFA men approved because they were confident that anything Camp conceived was in the best interest of the game.[45]

Camp's unvarnished reputation in the football world made it all the more shocking when his name appeared in the headlines of the New York papers on March 7, 1887: The man responsible for cleaning up dirty play on the gridiron was being implicated in a far dirtier crime perpetrated on the gridded streets of Manhattan. A man named George Condit Smith was clinging to life in a New York hospital after being shot in Madison Square at 1:00 a.m. by an unknown assailant. Smith survived, and when he came to, he told police that the shooter was a rival suitor of his fiancée Sallie Barnes of Paterson, New Jersey. Reportedly, she and Camp had once been engaged, though both emphatically denied it. Camp's possible involvement in Smith's shooting became the talk of the New York clubs.[46]

To this point, Camp's only appearance on a police blotter had been as victim of a stolen overcoat the year before, but now detectives shadowed him to and from the New Haven Clock Company offices and the 34th Street brownstone where he lodged with a traveling businessman. His landlord insisted that Camp was a model tenant and out of town the night of the shooting, but reporters continued to name him as the only suspect in the crime. Camp proceeded with plans to catch a train back to New Haven that weekend, but authorities apprehended him on his way to Grand Central Station. His father confirmed that he had officiated at a Yale sporting event the Wednesday night of the shooting and slept in New Haven. Still, Camp was subjected to more questioning at the precinct house. He claimed that he had not seen Sallie Barnes in years, but police confirmed that he was present at the reception where Smith proposed to her only weeks before. Now it looked as if he had something to hide.

Camp asked friends to come to the precinct, and the clock company arranged for a lawyer. Policemen escorted Camp to the hospital where Smith was recuperating, and made him walk back and forth in front of Smith for identification. But Smith did not recognize him. The police made Camp rewrite a letter that Smith had allegedly received from one of Barnes's former suitors, and the handwriting was not a match. Evidently, Camp was not their man. The police apologized for the mistake, and Camp was released. He went back to New Haven, where colleagues met him at the train station and issued exonerating statements to the press.[47]

Manhattan papers had reported that Camp was linked to the gun that shot Smith, and yet after his release, no link was mentioned again. The incident was over, and Camp saw no need to speak of it publicly. His mother never recovered from the notoriety of it, but he saw no point in suing for defamation; the indignation in New Haven seemed enough vindication to write off the incident and move on. Editorialists now expressed outrage that such an upstanding man could be arrested on mere hearsay and gossip. How could authorities question his ability to control his aggressions off the gridiron, they begged to know, when his football exploits exonerated him? Camp had shown that he was a master of his energies, choosing the most appropriate ways to channel them. "Every college man in the country knows of Walter's prowess," wrote a reporter for the *Boston Globe*; he would be "the last man to injure another."[48]

Ten weeks later, Smith confessed to staging the shooting. He had meant to put the bullet through his overcoat but clipped his shoulder instead. Apparently, it was his attempt to keep the affections of a woman whose eyes wandered toward more athletic men. Camp bore no ill will for the inconvenience of being accused of attempted murder, sending Smith a bouquet of flowers, as a gentleman would.[49]

SECOND QUARTER: MANHOOD EPITOMIZED

3

Alice and All-American-ness, 1888–1891

ACCORDING TO A JOURNALIST COVERING the Smith shooting for the *Times*, Camp was "popular with the ladies, and his word was law at Martha's Vineyard." This impression that he was something of a flirt or a jetsetter might have titillated readers, but it was far from the truth. Although this charming conversationalist had connections to important people in the Northeast, his corporate job, coupled with his writing and athletic advising, left little time for fraternizing with the fashionable set in the Vineyard. The accusations against him in Manhattan had belied the fact that he was traveling back and forth to New Haven to work, referee matches, advise varsity athletes, and spend time with his betrothed—a schoolteacher named Alice Sumner.[1]

The *Times* also reported in 1887 that Alice was the only daughter of Professor William Graham Sumner, but that was not true either: She was the Yale sociologist's much younger half-sister. Born in Hartford in 1861, she was Camp's junior by two years and Sumner's by twenty-one. It was common for men in her time and place to choose wives who were considerably younger, but Camp's choosing of a mate close to his age suggests that he was looking for a companion in the modern sense, a woman who was not a glorified breeder so much as his intellectual equal and emotional intimate.

Alice shared his penchant for discipline and industriousness. Her working-class father came to her brother's mind when he spoke of the "Forgotten Man," for he had been an independent artisan devoted to his family who left England with the rise of the factory system. According to his son, he instilled in his children the belief in hard work for a day's pay. Consequently, while Alice had a nationally recognized scholar for a brother, she was a practical, frugal, useful—rather than ornamental—woman. At twelve, she told people that she wanted to be a teacher—not the doting kind, but the kind that disciplined. "I don't think I [would] like a place where I could not give a child a good shaking, if he needed it," she told her brother. Even in girlhood, she felt boys had become too pampered to be effective adults.[2]

Alice passed competitive entrance exams for high school and was near the top of her class. She graduated at seventeen, when Camp was a junior at Yale. Her parents could not afford to keep her at home, so her brother took her in while she attended a New Haven normal school and trained to be a teacher. While studying, she practically reared William's sons Graham and Eliot. Jeannie, Sumner's wife, a classic Victorian sufferer of nervous illness, was sweet and affectionate, but too frail for hands-on mothering. Alice became her caretaker too, falling into the role of domestic helpmeet out of necessity and moral imperative.

Sumner approved; though he was a libertarian who thought all beings had the right to seek their potential, he was also a traditionalist who presumed that men's and women's separate spheres of influence were rooted in biological difference. He saw women's domesticity as natural law, and refused to discuss theories as seemingly innocuous as Malthusian reproduction near female ears, worried that the topic might denature tender souls. He did all he could to protect Alice from debasing influences; her mind had to remain pure for the day she would carry out the childrearing for which he thought her predisposed.[3]

He would have been less protective had his efforts to steer his other sister on a path of respectability not ended in failure. Alice was only a young girl during the earliest of her older sister's indiscretions, for at nineteen, Esther allowed men to accompany her to the local establishments most nights of the week, to her brother's dismay. He reminded her that it was imprudent to allow suitors to take liberties before being properly vetted at home, but she carried on as a public woman anyway.

By the time Alice was a teenager, her sister appeared to be damaged goods to any man who thought himself a gentleman. Esther lived alone making dresses and working as a shop girl in New York City until an older man married her to rear his motherless children, an arrangement that ended in divorce.[4]

Alice was too preoccupied by books for Sumner to worry about her similarly falling from grace. She might have become a scholar had she had the opportunity, but in the 1880s, this was still a nearly impossible path for American women. By the time she met Walter, Alice was highly respected in New Haven society, having graduated from the normal school and advanced to the highest position a woman could hope to achieve, as principal at the Welch School. The British writer Arnold Bennett thought her "one of the most brilliant women in America." Sumner's colleague, the literary scholar William Lyon Phelps, was taken with her ability to speak on modern movements and topics he assumed beyond the reaches of the female mind.[5]

And yet Alice walked a fine line. Tragically, there were women her age and circumstance who came to be known less than endearingly as "college widows," whose frequent interactions with college men seemed to have caused them to lose interest in marriage until it was too late—they turned "too old" to be courted. Other New Haven women were infamous as sophisticated girls who lost admirers as they aged and new classes of undergraduates passed through the college gates. Alice was growing older than the typical marrying age, but she had the timely good fortune of meeting Walter at her brother's home and falling in love; Camp's reciprocated affections had the effect of ceasing all speculation of her becoming an overly bookish bluestocking.[6]

Alice's father was no longer alive, so Camp had the awkward task that summer in 1886 of writing his former professor to ask for his sister's hand. "I do not imagine you need the assurance that I love her," he wrote Sumner; Alice assured her brother of their mutual affection. Jeannie sent Camp a belabored note of approval. "I shall always follow her life with great interest," she said of Alice. "I believe that with the right influences & opportunities she will become an unusually grand & fine woman." Sumner approved of the union since Camp seemed to share his same reverence for frugality and honest living—what Sumner referred to as the "golden mean." Despite the growing decadence of his peers, Alice's suitor, at twenty-seven, showed the restraint of an older, presumably wiser man.[7]

Alice and Walter's two-year engagement was not unusual; couples often waited to marry until the groom could support his household without help, and in this instance, Walter definitely needed the time. Like any proper lady, Alice planned to forgo her modest paycheck after she married, and thus the betrothed couple saved in the meantime, finally marrying in a traditional ceremony at Trinity Church in New Haven on June 30, 1888. The bride wore a gown of white silk, her bridesmaids in white, pink, and yellow dresses with flowers to match. Two of Camp's groomsmen, friends from the Class of '80, traveled from Cleveland and Syracuse for the occasion. The service was followed by a tasteful reception at Sumner's home on Edwards Street.[8]

Thereafter, Alice fell in with the married women of New Haven, becoming a member of the country clubs at Giant Valley and Pine Orchard. She belonged to the New Haven Lawn Club, the Saturday Morning Club, and an organization known among the most affluent in town as "Our Society." From her sister-in-law, she learned the ways of ornamental women, and soon her name appeared in the local society pages when she hosted teas and receptions. "Mrs. Camp is a tall, stately woman, with a graceful well-moulded figure, and is endowed with the quality of knowing how exactly to wear her gowns," noted a local columnist. Still, the pampered lifestyle of clubwomen was never fully hers. Though neat and tasteful, she had no fondness for lavish clothes or furnishings, at least not yet. Walter still earned only modestly, and her father-in-law had lost too much money on real estate investments to offer financial assistance. Nevertheless the couple lived at his house on Chapel Street until they could rent a home nearby. Notwithstanding their expenditures on Irish maids, Walter and Alice lived frugally, convinced of the propriety of that choice.[9]

In his newlywed years, Walter did not have the luxury of leaving the clock company at midday to run Yale football practices. It pained him, so Alice spent weekday afternoons at the Yale field in Walter's stead, notebook in hand, writing down her observations to show him at the end of the day. If her presence on the sidelines was awkward initially, the players got used to it and even came to appreciate it. She jotted notes with enough technical precision for Walter to draft game plans and then impart them to team captains in the evenings. Players fondly remembered coming to Camp's parents' home and later his modest abode at 12 Gill Street to discuss "Mrs. Walter's" reports. As Alice played hostess, the men circled around a checkerboard, plotting and planning for the day they could try out Camp's ideas with living pawns.[10]

It would have been impossible for Walter to advise the Yale eleven without the intrusion of football into Alice's domestic world. Conversely, her presence on the gridiron would have mired her reputation had she been single; marriage provided a social cover, allowing her to engage in the athletic and social life of Yale in unprecedented ways for a woman. Even when Walter could leave the clock company to direct practice himself, he pulled up to the field with his yellow cart and horse, Alice in the seat beside him. Such was the Camps' modern kind of partnership. Although Alice was not much older than the players on the field, hers was a maternal presence.

Alice seemed to know her place, even as a woman's place was becoming harder to define. Her part in her husband's world was more permissible than it would have been twenty years earlier, because middle-class women were seeking paid work, education, and service outside the home with greater frequency in the 1890s, engaging in public life in ways their mothers had not. Although American women could not vote until 1920, some were rejecting traditional domesticity for higher education, divorce, and paid work, or proving them not mutually exclusive. In the last quarter of the nineteenth century, the number of female professionals tripled throughout the country, but women's encroachment on traditionally male terrain was not uncontested. Medical experts cautioned that higher education and paid work sabotaged female reproduction and diminished the race. In the alarmist words of Basil Ransom in *The Bostonians*, "The whole generation is womanized . . . it's a feminine, nervous, hysterical, chattering, canting age." He echoed the fears of Camp's generation of American men.[11]

Alice was no suffragist or the embodiment of the sexually expressive "New Woman" coming to the fore, and yet many medical men would have thought her too familiar with the public space of the gridiron. When asked if the exhibitions of brute force were too much for the fragile constitution and temperament of a proper lady, Camp said he was unconcerned about Alice's peripheral presence at football games.

Female spectators boosted morale, after all, as they cheered players' heroic exploits, much as ladies had for the knights of eras past. "Some critics would urge us to believe that we are cultivating a taste in these girls for cruelty and hardness, because [they] can bear to look on and view the sharp crash of man to man in football," Camp conceded. "But you will find that every one of these girls is just as tender to helplessness as was her grandmother before her. Wise Old Mother Nature . . . has put somewhere deep down in her blood an admiration for courage, strength, pluck and all the manly qualities. It would be indeed retrogression to educate or refine that out of her."[12]

Camp had no anxiety because he assumed that football had built-in physical boundaries over which women could never pass. He felt assured that as Alice stood on the sidelines watching the crashing of male bodies, her fantasies would be only about gentlemen saviors, never of emulation; women understood that they could never be football players, only raisers and admirers of them. When Walter Jr. was born in February 1891, Walter could also rest assured that Alice would not coddle his boy to effeminacy. After reading *Tom Sawyer* and *Tom Brown*, she afforded her son opportunities for fresh air and physical tussles, the birthrights of effective males.[13] In poetry he wrote, Camp likened his wife to a woman of Sparta, who understood the man-making effects of physical pain. She was a true lady, and also, without contradiction, a "Gridiron Mother":

> A health to the Gridiron, bless her!
> She's a mother that's making men;
> She turns out none that are weaklings,
> She trains them in her den.
> And her pups they grow up sturdy,
> Their jaws they are undershot,
> And when she gets them ready
> They're a rugged fighting lot.
>
> They never whine or whimper;
> You may beat them 'til they blink,
> But their jaws you can't pry open,
> When once their teeth they sink.
> So here's to the Gridiron Mother,

And her downs and yards of ten;
For her lads are worth the raising,
This mother that's making men![14]

Camp sounded as if he wanted to sire a football squad, but his only other child was a girl, Janet, born in July 1897. He had had it so fixed in his mind that he would have only sons that he looked upon his little girl as a miracle, spoiling her in ways he never would a boy. Walter Jr. grew up exceedingly close to his mother, while Janet was an unmistakable daddy's girl, even accompanying him to football practices from time to time. When she was older, she would seek out her father at the clock company whenever she wanted something. Dad would listen to her intently; Janet could not recall him ever refusing a request.[15]

Camp's less affectionate relationship with Walter Jr. had likely to do with a father's high expectations for a son, as well as his acceptance of the prevailing thought that he must proceed with stoicism if he was going to raise a virile boy. Going into the new century, as educators discussed the perils of coeducation, middle-class children like the Camps' found themselves segregated from their siblings in order to cultivate traits that were gender distinct. Parents dressed their wee ones in appropriate colors and styles and gave them appropriate toys in appropriate spaces, where they played girl- or boy-appropriate games. Boys moved into trousers as toddlers, a symbol of the freer movement they were encouraged to have compared to their sisters. Lamenting the indoor existence soon expected of her, young Janet confessed that she wished she had been born a boy.[16]

Still, for a time, when Janet was small, Walter and Alice allowed her free rein in the natural elements. Unlike many medical experts at the time, the Camps were convinced that fresh air and exercise were prophylactics against nervous disease, regardless of gender. They supported municipal parks and any progressive movement that encouraged children to play outdoors. As reformers rehabilitated urban youth on playgrounds and during weekend trips to the country, the Camps took their children to nearby coastal Pine Orchard or the shores of Maine. At four, Janet had already proved fearless in water, Alice reporting that she "ha[d] to be caught to be got out." She was not concerned that her young daughter looked "rugged, fat, brown & red," not yet "delicate & peaked," as was the Victorian preference for girls. While Walter golfed and Walter Jr. swam and played baseball, Janet carried on wildly like a tomboy, once even falling out of a tree. After summoning a doctor, her parents discovered that their five-year-old's stomach pains and fever were not due to injury, but malaria caught during her outdoor escapades.[17]

Only later in her teens was Janet shuttered indoors to be taught the art of playing hostess. And for that, she had the best mentor in New Haven. Alice was famously affable to hundreds of guests on the weekends of the big games. Men were entranced by her hospitality, and Camp was relieved to have a wife so adored and easily acculturated to the worlds in which he hoped to make her an asset. Behind the scenes, she won her husband's confidence as his intellectual partner. She charmed executives and football men and wrote quips to newspaper editors when she thought her husband was unfairly judged. For this, Camp was not embarrassed but grateful and forever affectionate. In his household, football and femininity seemed compatible after all.[18]

In time, Alice covered football, as well as women in college athletics, for the *Woman's Home Companion*, and Walter helped her with the research. Editors complained about the poor quality of the photographs she obtained of Wellesley athletes, and Walter defended her, explaining that administrators at women's colleges did not want the faces of their athletes identifiable in print. And yet the fact was that more and more women were golfing, playing basketball, and swimming at the Seven Sister schools in the 1890s. The gymnasium director at Radcliffe reported that women even played lawn tennis and field hockey outdoors, where crowds could actually watch.[19] It only turned scandalous, apparently, when female athletes exposed limbs and toned muscles that looked too mannish on future mothers. Medical experts still echoed Edward Clarke's warnings of the 1870s that athletic activity was a threat to women's reproductive health. Dudley Sargent was progressive in his view of athletics for college men and had overseen the physical education program at Wellesley, and yet even he thought it ill-advised for women to participate in sports too intensely, fearing they would denature them.[20]

Camp kept up on the latest studies in England and the Seven Sisters and concluded that women should indeed get exercise—even pregnant women and even through organized sports. Still, while he endorsed Alice's outdoor excursions in sailing and archery, he stopped short of supporting competitive and team sports for his wife. These were manly outlets, and letting any woman participate here was the same slippery slope of allowing her sway in schools and churches, until she emasculated both. It worried him that Walter Jr.'s first teacher, a woman no older than twenty, seemed to have more influence over his son for now. The kindergarten movement, the rank-and-file of which was female, looked from many a male perspective to be mired in sentimentality; Camp waited for the day his son was old enough to learn the counter-balancing lessons of football.[21]

His philosophies about female physical activity suggest that he was less worried about women turning mannish through sport than about men looking effeminate in comparison. Muscle-building competition was a rare male realm left in his middle-class world, and he supported efforts to preserve its purity. The Young Men's Christian Association (YMCA), which had come to America from England in 1851, became a propagator of the Muscular Christianity Camp implicitly endorsed. By the 1890s, its network of associations conducted welfare work for poor men and organized physical training and sports leagues for middle-class youths around the nation. Luther Gulick, director of the YMCA Training School in Springfield, put his triangular concept of improving a boy's body, mind, and spirit to practice by supporting competitive sport to cultivate strenuosity in American males.[22]

Canadian missionary James Naismith invented basketball at the YMCA school in 1891, and YMCA director William Morgan invented volleyball four years later, also to promote physicality in boys. And yet football came to feature more centrally in the program of the YMCA, thanks to Camp and one of his charges, a Yale divinity student named Amos Alonzo Stagg, who Camp affectionately called "Lonnie." Already a star pitcher on the Yale nine when he tried his hand at football, Stagg was only three years younger than Camp, who had been out of school for nearly a decade. At twenty-seven, Stagg looked to be a "ringer," a man bought for his athletic prowess to win games. But he was honest and clean living, refraining from smoking, gambling, drinking, even cussing to devote his life to God. He attended public school until the age of twenty-one and took additional high school courses at Exeter, hence his delayed entrance to Yale. The son of a cobbler, not a banker, he needed to work odd jobs to afford school; even at Yale, he waited tables to defray his costs.[23]

It was not long before Stagg's classmates considered him another "man about campus." He sang in the glee club, managed the *Yale News*, and served as secretary for the Yale YMCA chapter in Dwight Hall. Because he was an athlete, he was better respected than his divinity school peers. Administrators believed that Stagg was the reason membership in the campus Y and signups for missionary work were up; his example seemed to prove to classmates, they liked to think, that there were "no antagonisms between spirituality and muscularity." Rumors abounded that Stagg had offers to pitch for professional baseball that he declined; his work for God and his amateur standing took precedence, proving, according to the Y's *Young Man's Journal*, "that strength in body, strength in mind, and strength of soul, may healthfully exist in one human form."[24]

Gulick thought no one better suited to preach the gospel of physical education, and he recruited Stagg to lecture throughout the Northeast on "The Modern Athlete." When Stagg addressed boys at the YMCA hall in Brooklyn, he sported a black eye and a bruised nose from a football game the day before, and yet a reporter decided that his "broad shoulders" and "marked muscular development" spoke to flat-chested, middle-class misfits, as well as immigrant boys of the streets. In years when Camp was hired to speak to youths groomed for Yale and Harvard, Stagg appealed to audiences of newsboys and bootblacks inspired by his humble beginnings. Projecting stereopticon images of classical athletes, he conveyed the idea that spiritual and physical manhood were indelibly linked. Be an aggressive sort of Christian, he told them, by wearing religiosity on your pre-industrial bodies. If reporters were to be believed, the novice speaker generated as much awe as the baseball player-turned-evangelist Billy Sunday, who was also working his crowds.[25]

Stagg went from divinity school to Gulick's training school, where his Christian service was starting a football squad. Administrators tried to lure him away through offers to coach football and baseball at Penn and Yale, but the most intriguing proposition came from his former divinity professor William Rainey Harper, now president of the University of Chicago. Stagg agreed to be director of physical culture at Harper's institution, where he would be paid to coach *and* play on an emerging baseball nine and football eleven.[26]

In *Outing*, Camp had only started using the term "coach" as a noun—an experienced trainer, strategist, and paternal influence rolled into one—and Stagg looked to be the nation's first prototype, with a pay package exceeding that of most deans and senior professors. Where athletic directors at other universities felt hamstrung by faculty boards, Stagg enjoyed unprecedented autonomy in building the athletic program. Retailer Marshall Field gave generously to build Chicago's playing field in 1894, and Stagg secured fellowships and other inducements under the table to bring talent to his teams. Familiar with Camp's system at Yale, in which "proselytizing" to high school athletes was officially forbidden, Stagg played by new rules out West, mailing recruitment letters to boys at feeder schools before anyone else could meet them. If his practices did not seem Christian, Harper did not stop him; Stagg brought money and prestige to a nascent university in need.[27]

Stagg had Camp to thank for elevating his celebrity to the point where a college president would choose him to organize his athletics department. Not only had Camp groomed him for greatness on the Yale eleven, he had also anointed Stagg to his newly invented "All-America team."

. . . as Camp tells it, at least. In truth, debate over the originator of the mythical squad has been contentious. Camp thought his word on the matter would be the last when he wrote in *Collier's* that he had invented the team, but it was not. The publication in which he claimed to publish his first selections was called *The Week's Sport*, and this list of men appeared in a column called "Amateur Sport," under the signature of editor Caspar Whitney. Although it is plausible that Whitney asked Camp to make the first selections, if they did not make them together, Camp insists that he made them alone, without prompting from Whitney. His claims are hard to prove, because in 1889, the inaugural year of the team, he wrote mostly incognito and under Whitney's signature—his way to report on games that he occasionally refereed.[28]

In the end, it might not matter who invented the All-America team, since it was Camp who invariably popularized it. At one point, early knowledge of his picks was so coveted that he had to submit names in installments to prevent stolen lists from being sold to other publications and prematurely disclosed. His daughter remembered weeks each winter when the family lived as if surrounded by spies. Everyone wanted to know who Camp was considering, other opinions not yet mattering for much.[29]

Like Camp, Whitney had been a college athlete, having played football, baseball, and lacrosse at St. Matthew's College in California before making a name for himself in sports journalism. Eventually appointed to the International Olympic Committee, he was second only to regulator James Sullivan in championing athletic amateurism in America, which made him both Camp's greatest admirer and harshest critic—often in print. When he suspected commercialism in Camp's arbitrating of football rules or in Yale's recruitment practices, he scolded Camp to make his actions live up to his words.

Whitney's mission was retaining sport as the activity of gentlemen, namely those with the pedigree to prove it. And yet, ironically, he tried to snuff out profit in sports as he made the field of sports journalism a commercial enterprise—first at *The Week's Sport*, and then at *Harper's*, *Outing*, and *Collier's*. The timing of his journalistic exploits could not have been better: The popularity of athletics coverage boomed as weeklies and monthlies were getting cheaper to make and circulate to mass audiences. And thus while Camp turned the Monday-morning reading of football results into an American ritual with his submissions to the *Herald*, the *Boston Globe*, the *Philadelphia Press*, and the syndicates, he had Whitney to thank for some of his earliest breaks. When Whitney moved his column to *Harper's* in 1891 and was given a collegiate sports department to run, he asked Camp to write about crew, track, and baseball throughout the Northeast. Needless to say, Camp and Whitney were also responsible for a disproportionate number of pieces on football.[30]

Camp initially appeased his editor with weekly scores and assessments of the teams, but soon Whitney wanted more. Knowing *Century* and other national publications pursued Camp for pieces, he was desperate for details that would make his publications look to be "leading the procession," not "following the bandwagon." "More vinegar!" Whitney demanded. Make each submission "bristle with comment and caustic criticism!" He resented that Camp made more definitive statements in the *Yale Alumni Weekly*, which Camp edited after 1891. Even in the new century, Whitney pressured Camp for the inside scoop, knowing it would violate Camp's contract with *Collier's*, the publisher of the All-America list after 1898.[31]

All of this made the relationship between editor and sportswriter more complicated than most. Camp and Whitney fought—sometimes for obvious reasons—as when Whitney did not pay Camp for his submissions, or when Camp wrote bad copy, or pulled his invest-ment out of *Outing* and resigned from its board.[32] But underneath the blow-ups was a more fundamental difference causing angst: While they both idealized gentlemanly sport, Camp and Whitney had conflicting ideas about just what it entailed.

Whitney, a privileged Anglophile at his core, promoted a brand of amateur athletics that closely approximated aristocratic sport overseas. In his eyes, the self-cultured standout (as opposed to unsung workers, plural) embodied heroism on the gridiron, and he presumed that any athletes who came from old money (and presumably Anglo-Saxon stock) would be inherently superior to the motley masses (or ethnic mongrels) beneath them. Over time, Camp proved to be less of a snob; given his self-made career, he had to be. Although he had his class biases, he thought football could further greatness that one was born into, but also assiduously worked at. Exalting the team, the corporate entity, as an enterpriser of the industrial age was more predisposed to do, he rejected Whitney's model of amateur sport for a homegrown one he called scientific, corporate, highly competitive, and eminently modern.

Both men viewed football as a test of leadership for the nation. But Whitney's presumption that this leadership would be white and elite was culturally British. In a contrast not to be overstated, Camp was open to leadership made anew, if fought for and deserved, which made his sensibilities more characteristically American. As early and influen-tial promoters of football, Whitney and Camp unwittingly built contra-dictory meanings within it, the game coming to represent elitism and democracy all at once. Camp believed that non-Anglo-Saxons could play up to his culturally Anglo-Saxon standards in time. Black center William Henry Lewis of Harvard and Native American players of the Carlisle Industrial School soon proved his point.[33]

As Camp conceived it, the All-America team was comprised of eleven college men who, taken together, created an effective whole more valuable than its constituent parts. He was not interested in highlighting All-Americans, in other words, as much as the All-America unit; in fact, he insisted that the relative anonymity of the football team built manliness like no "individual or selfish sport" ever could. In a piece called "Team Play in Football" (1891), he wrote, "If ever a sport offered inducements to the man of executive ability, to the man who can plan, foresee and manage, it is certainly the modern American foot ball." These leaders, as he initially envisioned, were not renegades and standouts, however; they were men with persistence, who worked thanklessly behind the scenes (or on the sidelines and under bodies), rather than showing fleeting flashes of brilliance. Instead of making the big play, they were reliable stalwarts, trudging on consistently throughout the season and showing the meaning of sacrifice.[34]

Camp's inaugural All-America eleven remains the most legendary, its members the first to be memorialized in the Collegiate Football Hall of Fame: ends Lonnie Stagg (Yale) and Arthur Cumnock (Harvard), tackles "Hec" Cowan (Princeton) and Charles Gill (Yale), guards Pudge Heffelfinger (Yale) and John Cranston (Harvard), center William George (Princeton), quarterback Edgar Allan Poe (Princeton), halfbacks James Lee (Harvard) and Roscoe Channing (Princeton), and fullback "Snake" Ames (Princeton). The honorable mentions, later to be grouped into second and third teams, were also exclusively from the Big Three. In 1891, the only wrinkle in this scheme was the addition of a Penn center to the first team, players from Lehigh and Wesleyan on the second, and a man from Williams on the third. Camp declared that the best talent came from Harvard, Princeton, and Yale, and for now, no one disagreed.

With Whitney's blessing, Camp published a guide to all things gridiron for Harper & Brothers, *American Football*, in October 1891. The title was boring, but Whitney thought it important to deemphasize the English origins of football and describe a game played by elite collegians as quintessentially American, as opposed to current versions played by immigrant workers in the textile mills of Fall River and Paterson, New Jersey. Ironically, for all Whitney's efforts to emphasize college amateurism in *American Football*, Camp's insertion of business metaphors left the more lasting impression. Football was a uniquely American phenomenon, he implied, in both mindset and purpose, because it brought out the penchant for planning in the nation's men. In the light he cast, football could not be as chaotic as rugby because it was not recreation but work—industrial *and* corporate work and hence *modern* work; highly organized, disciplined, productive, and specialized work, and hence work with moral and pecuniary value.[35]

Camp's definition of football as work contradicted Whitney's conception of it as amateur pursuit and, by extension, leisurely play. *American Football* described a trajectory of casual (English) chaos to reasoned (American) order to argue that scientific rationalization, driven by an American will to win, made football a developer of effective men. Camp reconciled the sight of disorderly piles of body parts on fields by describing the scientific principles ordering them into well-oiled machines or hierarchically structured bodies like the New Haven Clock Company. In both cases, the workings of the whole exceeded the value of constituent parts. Camp's team concept coincided perfectly with the philosophies of Frederick Winslow Taylor's industrial efficiency movement, as he described his gridiron as a classroom, testing ground, and incubator for the most effective industrialists of the modern age.[36]

"Division of labor has been so thoroughly and successfully carried out on the football field that a player nowadays must train for a particular position as much as he would on a ball nine," Camp explained.[37] Indeed in *American Football*, specialization was a key to his game and a distinctively American phenomenon. Where the English rugby he described had only "rushers" and "backs," football had tackles, end-rushers, snapbacks, quarterbacks, halfbacks, fullbacks, and guards; each needing a tailored set of skills. The balance struck between brain and brawn differed ever so slightly among specialists, but was required to some degree. There were optimal sizes, temperaments, and talents for each specialist. Halfbacks, for instance, were workhorses who translated tacticians' ideas into physical action—the "ground-gainers," who concentrated all bodily energy into single intensive thrusts through defenders. To operate optimally, these men had to maintain a precise ratio of muscle to weight or experience the wear and tear that Camp likened to the grinding and stripping of gears.

Camp referred to players collectively as football "material" rather than as individualized personnel, and offered recommendations for the raw stuff from which to make the machine's parts, as well as strict eating and training regimens for upkeep. It was best if the quarterback had natural "executive" ability, like a magnate of business, for instance, though a quarterback would need it even more with the coming implementation of the forward pass. Camp's reticence to create a passing game just yet had much to do with his vision of the quarterback as an undifferentiated part of the whole. For now, he held up higher than the quarterback the selfless center, a utility man whose job was often unseen but essential to the work of the whole. He believed that the most important parts of systems—the engine underneath the hood of a vehicle, or the decision-maker behind the closed doors of an office, or the coach on the sidelines—were often obscured from view. In the center, Camp saw the ultimate team player of the corporate world.[38]

What also appealed about *American Football*, to a broader audience of readers than Whitney anticipated, was its assertion that any man, not merely one who looked the genteel part, could be made an asset specially fitted to the football machine. The bulk on a husky boy, for instance, could be hardened and channeled into productive service, while the scrawny boy could compensate for his lack of heft with "that peculiar type of courage called 'pluck.'" Camp's ideal man was disciplined, but not to mind-numbing complicity, as a less "fit" immigrant worker might have been. What differentiated the corporate footballer from the dutiful assembly-line grunt was that he had a mind to match his laboring body. Football required a sense for managing men and operations; the leaders on the field were team players suited to become the nation's managerial elite. The balance between heft and skill, tactic and execution, strength and speed, brains and muscle was crucial to his marketing of football to men who aspired to be virile and cerebral in the boardroom and other contexts.

Industrial metaphors were effective for Progressives sold on the soundness of science, and Camp found also that military metaphors resonated in this time of relative peace, when football gridirons promised the vicarious experience of war and its man-making lessons.

"There is no sport known that in its very nature so mimics that art [of war] as the game of football," he asserted. "The tactics, the formations, the strategies, the attack and defense, all belong equally to the military commander and the football captain." He described kicking as "artillery work," and the scrimmage as a battle line across which two sides of warriors "assailed" each other in a quest for territory. Like any good general, the quarterback conducted a forward assault while preventing any breach in his line, and he included elements of deception in his arsenal of weapons: "Any amount of disguise may be practiced in the way of taking a last glance at the wrong man, or calling out to some one who does not enter into the play," Camp wrote. As in war, football required a system of codes, or signals, to convey plays in ways opponents could not make out. He recommended a set of simple sentences for teams just starting out, omitting words or adding phrases over time.[39]

Camp received an advance of $300 for *American Football*, confident that the book would sell quickly and that he would earn healthy royalties in the future. Whitney marketed the book aggressively and made sure that follow-up articles in *Harper's* were generously illustrated with action photographs of gridiron men at work. He wanted Camp to obtain images of the best individuals in "characteristic positions," proposing, for instance, that he capture All-American Frank Hinkey blocking off, and his quarterback, All-American Vance McCormick, in the middle of a lateral pass. "The camera must be near enough to these men to make portraits," he told Camp, unaware that his own reporter was responsible for instituting a ban on the press at Yale practices.[40]

Whitney settled for men posed after the fact, leaving the more action-packed images to be rendered in oil by none other than Frederic Remington, the former Yale lineman. In addition to illustrating *Ranch Life and the Hunting Trail* (1887) for fellow Eastern transplant Theodore Roosevelt, he painted scenes of cowboys and gridiron men for the national weeklies. Like Camp, Remington was becoming an iconographer of American manhood.[41]

With the publication of *American Football*, Camp seemed to be an inventor, much like Thomas Edison. He saw gridirons, like laboratories, as sites of innovation and ingenuity, so he took his scientific game to athletic directors as Frederick Winslow Taylor took scientific management to industrial magnates. The parallel between the efficiency of industrial workers and football players was soon made explicit at Brown University, where industrial engineer Frank Gilbreth, a Taylor disciple, fine-tuned the center's snap to economize on his movements. The snap was in fact invented when time trials proved it more efficient than the 2.5-second relay of the ball between the quarterback and punter.[42]

Such was the beauty of football. It never stayed stagnant, evolving as men thought up ways to improve upon the old. In this vein of change, Camp steadily advised less and less on the Yale practice field, delegating more from above. His lessons were conveyed down the chain of command—from coach, to field coach, to captain and players. Football was becoming yet another corporate structure to manage and improve on in his American drive for perfection.

4

Manifest Destiny, 1892–1893

ACCORDING TO UNIVERSITY OF WISCONSIN history professor Frederick Jackson Turner, the 1890s marked the closing of the American frontier—both a momentous and foreboding occasion, depending on how one looked at it. White American men had essentially conquered a continent, and yet in the wake of the conquering, they would experience fewer opportunities to fight Indians and live ruggedly in uncharted lands, which meant fewer man-making rites of passage to experience. Camp thought long and hard about the shifting tides, but he was not worried. With his invention of downs, he had created a new way to teach Eastern boys the virile lessons of Manifest Destiny: Capture territory, hold possession, or surrender it to stronger opponents. As boys fought hard to eke out yards and progress from one chalk line to the next, he believed that they were morphing into men.[1]

And this transformation was spreading westward. Fifteen years earlier, Camp noted that football was "indulged in only by one or two of the colleges"; by 1890, he was able to boastfully declare, "The terms punt, drop kick and touchdown, which were Greek to many ears, are now intelligible to every boy."[2] Now more than fifty Eastern colleges fielded teams, with Williams, Amherst, Dartmouth, and Bowdoin forming the New England Intercollegiate Athletic Association. By 1892, football was in mid-Atlantic schools like Lehigh, Franklin and Marshall, and Gallaudet University, a college for the deaf. Forty schools in the Midwest now competed, and the Intercollegiate Athletic Association of the Northwest, a precursor to the Big Ten, was formed. Even further west, teams sprouted up at Colorado College, Washington State, Idaho, and Oregon State, where Camp's annual guides were bibles for first-time players.[3]

Football's spread was also southward, as Trinity (Duke), North Carolina, Wake Forest, and Virginia authorized intercollegiate games and Washington and Lee, Randolph-Macon, Maryland, North Carolina State, and the University of the South followed suit. Soon Tennessee State, Auburn, Georgia, Mercer, Alabama, and Mississippi established squads, and the first official match was played in Texas. Georgia Tech captain Leonard Wood refereed games throughout the South and reported to Camp, "Foot ball is all the rage down here." Indeed Southern Progressives saw potential in a game that allowed Southerners to take pride in their preindustrial bodies as they embraced the values of a rationalized, industrial society. It was a modernizing agent made palatable, because it did not turn men soft. Although the region's cultural conservatives complained of football's Yankee roots, they could not deny that the game paid reverence to the martial values of the South like nothing else since the Civil War.[4]

A representative from the Denver Athletic Club meanwhile reported to Camp that his team suited up for five games against college squads in 1892 and ten in 1893, their opponents including the Universities of Kansas, Missouri, Nebraska, Northwestern, Baker (Kansas), and the Colorado State School of Mines. In 1892 alone, his team drew more than $6,000 in gross receipts. Another informant from the Oklahoma territory confirmed for Camp that "football is played more and more every year here; in fact nearly every large high school in the territory has a team. Of course it[']s crude, but the spirit is there and we are learning." Caspar Whitney declared the game so widespread at the collegiate and high school levels that he thought it easier to list locales where it *was not* played. Camp likened the spread of football to a cultural revolution, as backward and effete men embraced the commercial spirit of the Northeast, as well as the ways of gentlemen.[5]

Football teams from different regions officially played each other as early as 1881, when the University of Michigan challenged Cornell.

In the early 1890s, Stagg suggested a Penn-Chicago matchup to bring East and West together in a truly *national* championship game, but the Northeastern establishment proved to be less than enthusiastic about playing non-elite teams. Instead, Stagg settled for playing California squads and the Salt Lake City YMCA, spreading football fervor further west. Camp was quietly ambivalent about the trend, wanting his game to expand, but in a way that allowed *him* to control football's meaning for American men.

For now, his Yale squad remained the undisputed gold standard for teams across the nation. From its final game of 1890 to its ninth game of 1893, the Elis scored 1,265 points to 0; in the decade that followed, Camp's teams lost only four times. Fans plowed Whitney's sports department with letters requesting details about the ages, weights, and regimes of Camp's players; they were becoming individual stars, despite Camp's veneration for the team.[6] Nearly every man on his rosters between 1888 and 1892 was nationally known and went on to the Collegiate Football Hall of Fame; for many, their football celebrity became currency that turned them into captains of industry and civil servants after graduation. Bonesman George Woodruff, for instance, became the attorney general of Pennsylvania after graduating from the Class of '88; Lee "Bum" McClung, captain of '91, became treasurer of the United States; Vance McCormick, a leader in the Democratic Party; George Carter, the territorial governor of Hawaii . . . and on it went. Football made their academic standing almost irrelevant; their future success seemed predetermined by their effectiveness on the gridiron.

Athletic directors across the country were desperate to know what Camp did to tune the play of these men to such perfect pitch. To appease inquiring minds, Whitney asked Camp to give readers of *Harper's* an inside glimpse at a week of Yale practice, and Camp obliged with a portrait of men at routinized, disciplined work: At two o'clock every afternoon, two four-horse barges stood outside the Yale fence to take the players to Yale Field. Upon arrival, men sloughed off coats, divided into squads, and drilled in front of hundreds of spectators. "The cries of the captain and the coach drive the men on, and neither rest nor respite is allowed," Camp divulged. "It is this relentless drive that has given Yale her remarkable record on the foot-ball field." Whitney noted that Camp commanded remarkable authority using few words.

The players viewed him as an oracle—never to be second-guessed. "There is no wild gesticulation or Fourth-of-July oratory in Mr. Camp's coaching," he explained. Camp was modeling the behavior of a modern coach, observing mostly from a distance as he organized human labor, primarily in his head.[7]

Whitney heard that Camp's quiet way of leading held true at IFA meetings too. Once, rule-makers planned a scheme to pass an amendment that would put mighty Yale at a disadvantage. They decided to start business at 10:30 in the morning, and if Camp was not there to the minute, they would elect another chairman to run the proceedings and propose their new rule. The conspirators had scripted their declaration of overthrow, but when Camp walked in the room at 11:05, no one said a word. He opened the meeting and asked for motions. According to Whitney, "not even a murmur of discontent was heard." His word remained unquestioned in football, because no one had the moxie to challenge him. Even as it was becoming increasingly obvious that he catered to the strengths of Yale's style of play, his reputation for serving the best interests of football did not suffer in a public way.[8]

Whitney perpetuated the fiction; if he thought Camp partisan, he told him privately, knowing that Camp's reputation as "the Father of Football" above the fray was good for selling subscriptions. In *Harper's*, he opined that there was nothing better for the future generals of West Point and Annapolis than to be trained in the Yale way, and he was sufficiently convincing to administrators at both military academies, who asked Camp to find them a coach. Camp helped Army secure Yale graduate Henry Williams in 1891 and teammate Lawrence Bliss in 1893. Determined to make the Army-Navy rivalry competitive, Annapolis men requested none other than Camp himself to mentor them, but Camp assured them that a fellow Bonesman, twenty-five-year-old Ben Crosby, was their man. Indeed Crosby's charges were more than satisfied with his direction until he contracted typhoid and died the following year. Navy applied to "headquarters" once again, and Camp found them Yale graduate Josh Hartwell. Harmon Graves (1894–95), William Wurtenberg (1894), Burr Chamberlin (1903), and Charles Gould (1903) perpetuated the Yale-military connection into the twentieth century.[9]

Whitney continued to seize on the aura around Yale men, as well as his connections with Camp, accepting requests from athletic directors around the country to be matched with Yale men to coach them. In 1893, a year in which even the most well-equipped college graduates felt the effects of the depressed economy, second-stringers on the Yale eleven could easily get coaching jobs, all expenses paid, for respectable compensation. At least thirty former Yale players served as head coaches at colleges across the country that season, to say nothing of prep and high schools. A headline out of New Haven declared that virtually all paid coaches of competitive teams were disciples of Camp, except at Princeton and Harvard, where pride was a factor. Making matches for North Carolina, Hamilton, Wake Forest, Exeter, Virginia, Bowdoin, Vanderbilt, Nashville, Vermont, Western Reserve, Union, Rutgers, Indiana, Minnesota, Nebraska, Tennessee, and the University of the South, among others, Camp helped to inaugurate programs that continue to thrive today.[10]

Often the only football instruction to be had at small institutions was through accounts of Yale games in the newspapers. As an unpaid ambassador of football, Camp doled out pointers for free in these instances. An Iowa youth from Coe College asked for any advice he could offer his men: "We are surrounded by wealthier schools[,] the State University, Grinnell and Cornell, whose means enable them to employ a coach. Our school is small and the foot-ball team is unable to stand such an expense. . . . I have written to you as the highest authority in the land for a few suggestions as to playing and training." Camp also received a letter in the fall of 1892 from James Kivlan, an administrator at a little Indiana school called Notre Dame: "I am an Instructor connected with this University and have been asked to coach the team. I know something of the Rugby game, but would like to find out the best manner to handle the men. I have seen a good many Yale games (as I came from New Haven). . . . And knowing you are an authority on the game, I would welcome any points you might give me."[11]

Men turned to Camp because they were convinced of the correctness of his football system—precisely because it was a "system"—a scientific way to manage men and tasks. Former Harvard captain J. H. Sears venerated this new scientific figure Camp called "the coach," declaring his "theoretical" or "head" work more progressive than in any other sport. Trying to explain Yale's winning ways, a New Haven journalist wrote, "It is not because the biggest and the strongest men come to

Yale, for Harvard has more men to choose football stuff from. But the material is handled in a way that makes the best use of it, and infused through it all is the 'Yale spirit.' "[12]

This spirit was so deeply inculcated that even as Camp doled out former players to nascent teams, Yale men voluntarily returned to New Haven to train new elevens. They made salaries at other colleges, but accepted that coaching for no compensation in New Haven was a matter of institutional pride. Camp justified his players receiving money elsewhere as a concession to a greater good; his men were missionaries, spreading Yale spirit to a nation needing tough guidance. In lieu of military conscription, they gathered willing warriors into armies organized across university gridirons and transformed them into men.

Little did proponents of amateurism realize that the growing importance of the paid coach meant that the days of a captain's field generalship were numbered. True to English form, the rules committee banned sideline coaching in 1892, but the ban did not prevent non-playing coaches from giving instructions to substitutes entering the game. In 1900, a rule prevented substitutes or any non-players from conveying advice to men on the field, and future rules prevented advisors from walking up and down the sidelines. Harvard's Athletic Committee referred to sideline coaching as a "shady practice" that violated the tenets of sportsmanship. But there was no stemming the tide once men saw how effective Yale coaching could be.[13]

In disseminating his protégées across the land, Camp had generated a reverence for the coach. Men saw that he was more than just a preferable presence, but a necessary one, soon to be a hallmark of American sport. Lonnie Stagg built his dynasty in Chicago, as Henry Williams brought football to Minnesota. A talented player under Camp, Williams had honed the art of coaching at Army before heading west. As a medical student in Philadelphia, he officiated at games and watched former teammate George Woodruff, the coach at Penn, stymie opponents with his "guards back" formation. Williams also became famous for his "Minnesota shift" and eventually cashed in on a summer institute for aspiring coaches.[14]

Indeed, Yale men innovated, just as Camp had encouraged them to. Stagg patented the tackling dummy, and George Foster Sanford laid claim to the "huddle," the "triple kick," and movable towers on the practice field. The same year Camp published the *Book of College Sports*, Williams collaborated with Stagg on a "Scientific and Practical Treatise on American Football for Schools and Colleges," which rivaled *American Football* in its comprehensive advice. The authors claimed expertise Camp had once exclusively claimed for himself. If their success was bittersweet to their mentor, he could only blame himself for instilling their enterprising spirit. All he asked was that some of his secrets not be shared. When Williams wanted to publish a few Yale formations, Camp reminded him of his promise "not to divulge certain points of the Yale play." Knowledge was power. Camp thought it more blasphemous "to pick the brains than the pocket."[15]

There lay his mixed message: Go forth and preach the gospel, but keep your cards to yourself. Minnesota sportswriters grew weary of Williams's closed practices, but Camp had taught him that success in football, like bridge or war, relied on an element of surprise. The mental game had value, and former players repaid the lesson by finding out things about Yale opponents and reporting back. Charles Gill, a Yale All-American-turned-coach at Dartmouth, told Camp what he gleaned about Harvard strategy in time to prepare for the Princeton game. Some informants were so secretive that they reported back under assumed names, such as the Bonesman who pretended to be a reporter to get a seat at the Princeton training table. "My conscience or whatever serves me as one almost revolted at taking a complimentary ticket to go in and spot their eleven," he admitted. And yet he gathered intelligence on the starting players so Camp could make his plans.[16]

"Scouting" was not yet an acceptable practice. For now, Yale men were conducting veiled acts of deception that Camp claimed no part in, even as they were becoming integral to his preparation. Harvard also used informants to beat Yale in 1890; one Harvard coach got caught and apologized for informants taking notes at the Yale field before the big contest in 1900. In time, the practice of gathering information on other teams became more transparent, albeit regulated. Camp eventually declared scouting aboveboard, as long as informants announced themselves in time to give a coach a chance to hide his best people and plays.[17]

No doubt, information about players was becoming as valuable as the divulgence of game plans, and though Camp still publicly condemned "proselytizing"—talking up the college game to prep boys (knowing that the next step was to recruit the talent for a price), his hands were less than clean. Yale alumni became concerned that other coaches might grab up raw material at the high school level before Yale could. In 1911, the *New York Herald* announced that "Loyalty to Alma Mater Impels Thousands of Graduates to Scout Country for Prospective Stars." This was not news, just a public declaration of what Camp had already been privy to for decades.[18]

In the 1890s, college teams often referred to the "coacher" and "trainer" interchangeably; but at Yale, Camp's players came up the ranks understanding each as a specialized expert to be respected in his own right. The distinction had already been made in the 1880s, when Camp hired trainer Mike Murphy for $1,200, an enviable salary at the time. A former sprinter and minor league baseball player, Murphy had been cultivating athletes in Massachusetts when Camp sought him out. He had handled men like no one else and fine-tuned boxing legend John Sullivan for his championship matches. He had a knack for rehabilitating bodies and spotting physical ability that did not announce itself; Camp thought it remarkable that he could watch some poor freshman flailing at the guard position and recognize immediately that he was better suited as a back or an end. He knew what to say to motivate men to become better at whatever position they played.

Murphy did not learn his expertise in college, nor did he have a medical degree. He knew men's bodies from being around them in constant motion. Growing up on the rough-and-tumble streets of an Irish Boston neighborhood, he suffered his share of black eyes and bruised ribs. The knowledge he accrued on the streets now had value in Camp's elite college world. Making men's bodies athletic became his way of making a living and a name in the modern age. Camp was one of the first to acknowledge what he brought to the table.[19]

Eventually, Camp followed his players and spread the lessons of football westward, accepting an invitation in 1892 to introduce his game to eager recruits at Stanford University in California. Alice was tending to her ailing sister-in-law, so Walter made the trek out West alone, Yale undergraduates deferring their election of next year's captain until he returned.[20] Unable to help himself, the Stanford team manager divulged news of Camp's expected arrival, and Berkeley men reacted by securing a Yale coach of their own, the All-American "Bum" McClung. In a San Francisco paper, a garment manufacturer placed a full-page ad in which Camp and McClung's heads were attached to bodies wearing his overcoats. Indeed the Yale men were celebrities before they even made it to California. By the time their train arrived in San Francisco, there were only seventeen days left in the football season, and yet the local Yale Alumni Association and University Club feted them with toasts and fight songs. The Berkeley chapter of DKE offered Camp its headquarters, and Harvard men also threw receptions in support of his mission: to convey to men in the West what was still virile about the East.[21]

But Californians were confused about what Camp officially did as a "coacher." He clarified in the *Daily Palo Alto* that he had come to teach men a respectable game: "In the East football is growing in importance every year. It is supported by the very best class of people and does not share with baseball that professional tinge." He piqued much interest, packing a Stanford auditorium as he preached the moral efficacy of football. "None can help admiring Mr. Camp for that faithful adhesion to the lightest moral and ethical principles which characterize his every thought in the game," reported one attendee. "With such ideas of gentlemanliness, football becomes a game which instills into players and audiences those higher qualities which mean success in every station in life."[22]

For all the reportage of Camp's mission in California, little in the local papers matched accounts of big games in the press back East. More and more, the New York dailies were painting images of players on football Saturday that were half hero–half hoodlum, and of spectators who were no longer minding their manners. After one recent Harvard-Yale contest, they described Yale men catching trains back to New Haven and carrying on like madmen. A pack of sixty undergraduates allegedly assembled at a local pub and purchased a bear that the proprietor had caged in his front window, only to let the animal loose on the old campus green. They plied the creature with booze and induced it to go up a flagpole until police officers arrived on the scene. A local man wondered how college men could stoop to the depravity of the "East Street gang," and another man representing proprietors in town wrote Camp to implicate him personally in the debauchery: "You ought to be ashamed of yourselves, skylarking & frolicking & trying to show off your monkey shines & make a big splurge through the newspapers & trying to get all the girls in town to look at you, so you can feel big. . . . Small boys like you should keep quiet & follow the example of your instructors & stick to your studies & not be filling up our newspapers & making the respectable citizens pay out their money for papers filled with a description of your monkey shines."[23]

These were fighting words that Camp ignored. In California, he saw no need to divulge details of any criticism football men received back East. Football was a virile, disciplining influence, he insisted. If he was not entirely convinced, he still believed that his game was too positive an influence to bother with a disgruntled few. "There will doubtless always exist a class of the community wholly inappreciative of the value of athletic sports and contests to our institutions of higher learning," he conceded, but "this is a small class, and not nearly so important and influential as it was a generation ago."[24]

Stanford administrators did not need to be convinced; they funded their new football team generously while Camp was there. Recruits enjoyed the amenities of a health resort in a hamlet of the San Francisco foothills, where local farmers showed up each afternoon to watch Camp work the men. He politely tolerated their curiosity at first, but then started instituting secret practices so as not to give away plays to Berkeley spies. The raw material at his disposal was encouraging, but still smaller than material back home, averaging 164 ½ pounds stripped. Camp decided to ease the running regimen and work the men harder in scrimmages. He made them eat a substantial breakfast at his scientifically inspired training table,[25] and he added beef and mutton to their diets. A strict schedule told the men when to eat and study; lights went out at 10:30. He described the signals work and rotations of the first and second teams, and reporters hung on his every word.[26]

Fifteen thousand packed into the Haight Street Grounds that December to watch Camp and McClung's recruits battle to a draw. San Francisco's most fashionable were in attendance, a reporter boasting that there were enough pretty girls in the stands "to fill every seminary west of the Rockies." For the following 1893 season, Camp dispatched Yale halfback Cliff Bliss to coach in his stead, and at Berkeley, McClung was replaced by All-American Pudge Heffelfinger. Like a good disciple, Heff checked in with Camp beforehand, making sure he knew which Yale plays he was forbidden to teach to Western men. Stanford secured Camp again the following fall, and another Yale man, Charles Gill, replaced Heffelfinger. Again, Camp refused all payment except for reimbursement for travel, though the Stanford manager arranged for a horse team and surrey and board at the former residence of university president David Starr Jordan, located a quarter mile from the practice field.[27]

Camp returned to Stanford for a final time in 1895, but stayed only until mid-October. The rival coach was slated to be yet another of his former players, All-American Frank Butterworth, and again, Camp asked for no payment other than travel reimbursement and passes to the games for Alice and their maid.[28] This time, his wife and toddler son captured the attention of an area socialite, who wrote a front-page "woman's perspective" on the "royal" football family. She was enamored with Alice but more so with Walter, who she described as both a heartthrob and a hero:

> The Father of Football and the idol of college hearts is big and brown and quiet and deliberate. He impresses even the passing stranger as a man who is not afraid of anything on earth, or in the waters under it. But my restricted feminine fancy cannot picture him in the active rush of the field of battle. He suggests, rather, the past master in the art of planning the campaign.[29]

Dining with Camp and the Stanford players at the team training table, she observed impeccable manners and concluded that this Father of Football was the best of paternal influences, a cultivator of Western gentlemen.

Camp's California experiment appeared to be a public relations win. "The empire of football has taken its way westward faster than people suppose," declared the *Morning Call*.[30] In San Francisco, Yale alumni sang his praises:

> In 1492
> Came old Christopher, the continental saint;
> And in 1892
> The whole continent is blue,
> And this Walter Camp's the man who mixed the paint.[31]

Manifest Destiny had been achieved. If more undeniable proof was needed, Camp found it almost anywhere in the country on Thanksgiving Day, as Americans gave their afternoons to football. Witness to 20,000 streamer-waving fans at the Haight Street Grounds, he could see that Thanksgiving football had come a long way since the IFA first hatched the idea of the two best Eastern college football squads facing off on Thanksgiving back in 1876. When his team played Princeton in Hoboken in 1879, it was the first Thanksgiving contest played off school grounds, and each team netted a modest $238.76 in gate receipts. The stakes grew exponentially bigger once the annual game moved to Manhattan, where it drew 5,000 spectators the following year, and 15,000 by the mid-1880s. In 1889, each team netted over $5,400 from the game; two years later, over $14,000. By 1893, the Thanksgiving game was the marquis athletic event for socialites in San Francisco, while 40,000 fans watched Yale face off against Princeton at Manhattan Field, thousands more standing around the field on barrels and boxes, hoping to get a glimpse. Some 120,000 athletes played in 5,000 Thanksgiving contests across the country that year, generating athletic heroism beyond the Ivy League.[32]

The Puritans who had sat down to the first Thanksgiving meal shunned sport as idle recreation, but now their secularized descendants admired the strenuosity of athletic competition. Camp occasionally heard complaints from traditionalists that he was to blame for making Thanksgiving something other than a day of quiet contemplation, but Americans apparently saw nothing wrong with football being part of their civic celebration. Journalist Richard Harding Davis remarked that Thanksgiving was "no longer a solemn festival to God for mercies given . . . [but] a holiday granted by the State and the nation to see a game of football."[33]

Thanksgiving game coverage in the papers included sightings of Yale's mascot "Handsome Dan," a bulldog who, as legend now had it, barked wildly at the sight of opponents and became as prominent a Thanksgiving symbol as the turkey itself. Following Yale's lead, the University of Georgia and other schools even acquired bulldogs of their own.[34] Camp was as responsible as anyone for creating tradition and spectacle with his journalistic coverage. His accounts of the annual Yale-Princeton matchups of the late 1880s and early '90s perpetuated a sense of awe with their panoramic and insider views of the action. College men took over Manhattan, as he told it, "eagerly discussing the prospects of the rival teams . . . as if upon the outcome of the match hung the fate of nations." As for the players, they spent Thanksgiving morning in deep contemplation, eating lunch behind closed doors and returning to their hotel rooms to lace up uniforms stained from earlier battles. In ritualized tales of male bonding, players collected in the captain's room before making their way out the side exit, where a driver took them to the arena. According to Camp, in these moments of initiation, the courage to win was forged:

> Hardly a word is spoken after the first few moments, and one fairly feels the atmosphere of determination settling down upon them as they bowl along through the Park. Every man has his own thoughts, and keeps them to himself; for they have long ago discussed their rivals, and each man has mentally made a comparison between himself and the man he is to face, until there is little left to say. . . .
>
> They are soon in, and, jumping out at the dressing rooms, run in and throw off outside coats, still keeping on the heavy sweaters. Now comes a slight uneasy delay, as it is not yet quite time to go out on the field lest their rivals keep them waiting there too long in the chill air. This is in truth the *mauvais quart d'heure* of the foot-ball player, for the men's nerves are strung to a high pitch.
>
> . . . A short silence follows, and then they receive the word to come out. As they approach the great black mass of people and carriages surrounding the ground, they feel the pleasant stimulus of the crisp fresh air, and their hearts begin to swell within them as they really scent the battle. Just as they break through the crowd into the open field, a tremendous cheer goes up from the throats of their friends, and the eager desire seizes them to dash in and perform some unusual deed of skill and strength.[35]

Camp had a flair for narrative. While filmmakers and commentators have since tried to capture this sense of rush and failed, he made the pregame warm-up so compelling that boys wanted to experience it for themselves.

Now, local and regional papers profited from syndication and wire services that allowed them to print Camp's reports of the big games of the East. He wrote prolifically in the dailies, and soon the *Illustrated Sporting News* and general publications like the *New York American, Chicago Examiner*, and *Independent*. "I shall be frank with you," he told one editor. "The work which I am doing in this line for various magazines and Weekly's [sic] is so extremely well paid on account of its being perhaps something in the nature of expert opinion, that I feel that my prices would seem to you out of proportion to the value of the article. . . . There has been such a growth in appreciation of the athletic side of life that satisfactory articles on the subject seem much less than the demand." Indeed, a Harvard man on a train from Kansas City to Philadelphia confirmed that he saw ten copies of *Collier's* being read in the seats, eight of them turned to the section where Camp's writings featured prominently.[36]

Back in the early 1880s, Camp had pounded the pavement to find editors who wanted his material, and he was one of the few self-proclaimed experts peddling it. Now, football commentators were springing up everywhere, hired by the dailies to appease reader demand for football coverage. Sports writing had become a lucrative profession that catered to a range of consuming publics. Business professionals could read extensively about football in upmarket publications like the *Times* and *Sun*, while readers of the working and amorphous middle classes seemed to prefer Sunday and evening editions of the *Herald, World*, and *Journal*, or perhaps even the seedier *Police Gazette*.[37]

Camp was still considered *the* authority on football, but he was hardly the sole interpreter of its cultural meanings anymore. Readers consumed stories now that made football as much about material conspicuousness and physical prowess as strategy and manly honor. Covering the Thanksgiving game between Yale and Princeton in 1893 for the cultured readers of *Harper's* (and receiving a staggering $500 for it), Richard Harding Davis called the event as much "social spectacle" as "athletic contest." Reportedly, Manhattan elites hired coaches a year in advance for the convenience of being driven through the crowded streets on game day, forming lines three deep for five blocks on the streets leading up to the grounds. They paid up to $15 for regular seats and ten times more for boxes. The Whitneys, Alexanders, Sloanes, and

Vanderbilts were at the game, as were the New York mayor, Tammany boss Richard Croker, soon-to-be police commissioner Theodore Roosevelt, and aspiring tribes of nouveau riche desperate to be seen.

The forefathers of these spectators might have shunned concerns about what one was wearing and who one was with at the game; and yet these wealthy socialites had come to measure success by how they were perceived by others, as many Americans did going into the new century. Nearly two million people not in the stands read about them in the dailies, now that reporters made a point of making the flashiest spectators part of the football story. The Thanksgiving spectacle provided an opportunity for elites to display pedigree through Ivy League colors, so they paid three times the listed price for the most conspicuous seats—all for the privilege of wearing their social prominence on their sleeves.[38]

The sociologist Thorstein Veblen lamented this conspicuous consumption in America's leisure class. During one of the most severe banking crises and fiscal depressions of the century, tickets to the Yale-Princeton Thanksgiving game of '93 were so eagerly sought that the University Athletic Club arranged deals with speculators to minimize the price gouging of scalpers. At the Hoffman House Hotel, headquarters of the Yale team, a bartender collected $50,000 in bets, while alumni gambled on the game on the floor of the New York Stock Exchange. It was hard for Camp to tout football as amateur sport when it took on a life beyond moral or fiscal responsibility. Either despite or because of economic depression, Americans paid handsomely for football. Fiscal uncertainty may have frayed their nerves so badly that they became desperate to witness physical manhood on the gridiron and to experience it vicariously. The spectacle curbed their own emasculation, if only for a time.[39]

Camp preached football's moral lessons, turning a blind eye to the rampant materialism on display, as well as the less savory lessons learned by college men in the stands. Within days, undergraduates had snatched up the 16,000 tickets made available for the Yale-Princeton Thanksgiving game of '93. Many ditched classes to camp overnight and partake in the surrounding hoopla before entering the grounds on game day. The football mentality apparently stayed with them once the match ended, for they meandered onto the streets and occasionally grew violent: "Many people bearing the appearance of gentlemen acted as brutally as could be expected of the lowest ruffian," the *World* reported. Men in college sweaters were seen shoving bystanders as they scaled elevated train car windows, and college boys made their way to the red light district along 25th Street, lingering in cabarets to heckle chorus girls. Anticipating the unfortunate scene, college administrators had instituted curfews that were summarily ignored. The policemen summoned to man the streets spent most of the night walking belligerents to the West 30th Street station to sober up and post their $5 fines. College presidents saw the tailgating as hooliganism, while law enforcers, as a disturbance of the peace.[40]

For the Yale and Princeton men in the stands, the game was clearly an opportunity to blow off steam, which might have been fine had their behavior not been on display for 150 newsmen at the match. For the first time, a press box had been arranged to accommodate them, and those hired by the penny press found college fans as titillating to write about as the game itself. Although there were reporters who wrote of the day's events in Camp's heroic terms, others could not help but share with their less-privileged readers the unflattering image of elite boys in drunken stupors. Reporters transformed decorous Ivy League men into stiffs who gambled and came to blows, appealing to fans who Camp, up to this point, had not fully acknowledged—men who had no access to high-brow athletic matches and did not belong to the college ranks. These budding football fans could not afford tickets, but they read dailies in which football coverage appeared alongside synopses of dog races and prizefights. To them, football was mass spectacle, not elite experience.

Men of the Big Three, who might have been referred to in the society pages as gentlemen of erudition and restraint, on many a sports page were transformed into lewd spectators and vicious tacklers. "Beef and brawn" distinguished them, as did their less-than-savory tactics. One reporter claimed that the only thing Princeton and Yale players feared in 1893 was the roving eye of the umpire: "The favorite methods of damaging an opponent were to stamp on his feet, to kick his shins, to give him a dainty upper cut, and to gouge his face in tackling," he added.[41]

Camp dismissed such "highly-colored tales of brutality" as "unscrupulous sensationalism . . . pandering to the tastes of the low and vulgar," not fully acknowledging how his dreams of Manifest Destiny were coming true East to West, as well as across socioeconomic stratums of American men. Football had been turned into entertainment for lower-class males whose physical prowess had once been stigmatized and used against them. Now it looked as though collegians emulated their physicality and redefined their sense of manhood acceptably on the gridiron. In hands beyond Camp's, football was becoming a language with wider meanings, creating a diverse but common male culture.[42]

5

Necessary Roughness? 1894

WALLY WINTER HAD JUST ARRIVED at Yale when he decided to show up on the practice field on West Chapel Street and try to secure a place on the freshman eleven. He wanted a spot so badly that he spent nearly all his money on a canvas jacket, moleskin pants, stockings, and shoes for his day of reckoning on the practice field. Once he arrived, he was summoned to crouch opposite a larger, more seasoned upperclassman to show what he could do on the line. The older man made Winter's lowly place in the pecking order known to him—very quickly—extinguishing his dreams of grandeur with a swift, unsolicited punch in the face. Such was the welcome given a freshman on his first day of practice.

Most recruits understood that, as unknowns, they demurred to senior men, but Winter did not. Rather than walk away, he gave his adversary an uppercut that nearly laid him out. Chappie Howland, the man in charge of the freshman candidates, reacted with fury and kicked Winter out of practice, shouting at the freshman to never show his face again. Winter lumbered off the field, dejected and stunned. Rather than take the streetcar, he walked back to campus alone to wallow in his failed attempt at athletic stardom. But that night, a janitor from Durfee Hall came to his door with a mysterious note. Winter was being summoned to the old New Haven House, to a room ominously known by upperclassmen as "117." There, in the dark, men of the varsity eleven sat Winter down for interrogation. Billy Rhodes spoke for the jury of upperclassmen:

"Know anything about football?"
"No, sir," Winter replied.
"Know how to box?"
"Yes sir—some."
"What do you weigh?"
"One seventy-eight, sir."
"Did you slug a man on the field this afternoon?"
"Yes, sir."
"Who was he?"
"I don't know, sir."
"Why did you slug him?"
"Because he slugged me—twice, sir."
"Where did you hit him?"
"On the chin, sir."
"How often?"
"Once, sir."
"Don't you know any better than to slug a man on the football field?"
"I do now, sir."
"Are you sorry?"
"No, sir."
"Well, you ought to be sorry. Let me tell you one thing—don't you ever let me hear of you slugging on the field—never. And tomorrow you come out with the varsity. Good night."[1]

Thus began the collegiate career of Wally Winter, one that culminated in his winning of the ultimate distinction—All-America status—in 1893. In 1891, his Yale squad scored 488 points against its opponents; in 1892, 435 points; no team earned a single point back until Penn and Princeton each scored touchdowns the following year.[2]

On that night in room 117, Winter was initiated into a culture that Camp had cultivated for nearly a decade among Yale men. He admitted as much in front of the 400 alumni who feted him and the team of '91 the following February in the concert hall of Madison Square Garden. From the looks of it, the banquet was a civilized affair. The *Daily Tribune* described the assemblage as "a splendid array of men, college-bred, appreciative of the best taste in all that goes to contribute to that which is manly and useful in life's pursuits." An orchestra played as the graduates gathered in order of class at bountiful tables. Sorbet was served in crystal footballs that mirrored the outlines of the leather-bound menus and wax centerpieces on the tables. Members of the recent championship team received engraved silver matchboxes, and Camp, who sat in the chair of honor, was presented with a silver loving-cup in the shape of a football, held up by three miniature players on a silver base. Caspar Whitney supposed the figures represented Camp's famed players Winter, Heffelfinger, and McClung in their characteristic poses.[3]

The toastmaster spoke:

> In this fair temple, devoted to prize exhibitions, another Canto will be added, another demi-god created, another niche in Yale's temple of fame filled. . . .
>
> In foot ball as in war, it isn't to the general who executes but to the chief who plans the campaign that the greatest credit is due for its ultimate success. And such is the case here. . . . For twelve years there has resided at New Haven a quiet gentleman, who has created there the game that has more interest and excites greater enthusiasm than any yet brought before the American people. His tactics and methods are original[;] all others are copies or variations. He is the master and the Yale teams have been his pupils.[4]

When Camp quieted the applause and took the podium, he was self-effacing, but then his tone oddly changed. He confessed how much the physical thrashing of Harvard men had ruled his thoughts since he first competed against them as a teenager. He hungered for victories and took no greater pleasure in seeing the more winning men in front of him looking "fat, sleek, well-fed" by comparison. This thirst for victory, nearly primal in intensity, was what he considered the key distinction between English and American players. In the English tradition, *how* one played mattered more than the outcome and said more about the man than the win itself. In America, there was no tradition to speak of, so the outcome mattered more. The championships listed on the leather-bound menus revealed how well Yale men understood this to be true.[5]

Camp went on to tell stories about his players. It amused him to think that when he first set eyes on Captain Bum McClung, he thought him too soft to be effective on the gridiron:

> Certain croakers in college had an idea when he was elected that he'd turn out to be too pleasant and easy. Why, I remember standing next to him at one of the smaller games in which he did not play. There was a man on the field whom McClung had been trying for some little time . . . for Mac never had much confidence in him. . . . The signal was given for this man to run. Off he started and came crashing through the line when he met some one's knee fairly in the face and went over with a limp drop and never moved. McClung's face fairly glowed with delight. 'He's dead, thank God, he's dead!' I heard him exclaim, and I made up my mind that Mac's tenderness would never injure the chances of the team.[6]

It was rare that newspapermen were within earshot of Camp divulging such things; their biggest complaint was that he did not reveal enough now that practices were closed to the press. Camp's editor at *Leslie's Illustrated* had wanted photographs of the men practicing before the big Princeton match, but Camp refused to give them. Newsmen figured that he wanted no leaks of his tactics, but perhaps he also had a team's gentlemanly image to protect. In interviews, he reiterated that the men in his charge never slugged, shoved, or kneed an opposing player when he was down. But privately, a whole other set of maneuvers was implicitly accepted, if not vigorously embraced. Yale men had quietly expected and caused their share of bruises and broken bones as far back as Camp's own playing days, when Frederic Remington allegedly dunked his uniform in animal blood "to look more businesslike" on the field. One Yale man admitted that he thought football without slugging was like a production of *Hamlet* without Hamlet.[7]

As a player, Camp had also taken pride in his reputation as harder-hitting than the rest. When he made the transition into coaching, he imparted to Yale men the idea that physicality was noble, even if opponents thought it crossed a line. It was becoming evident to anyone paying attention that Camp spoke out of both sides of his mouth, and encouraged the same in his players, since it proved their physical courage. His sense of honorable brutality spread to college campuses throughout the Northeast, as coaches filled their rosters with "gentlemen" who both shirked off pain and inflicted it when the need arose. As much as Camp had imparted the significance of honor, he also unwittingly encouraged men to ask whether a foul was a foul if an official did not see it. The implicit answer was no.

The IFA rules committee had retained ways to score through kicking, a nod to football's English origins. But Camp believed it was necessary to minimize its importance, since it deemphasized physicality in the American game. In an article for *Harper's*, he had justified his deviations from British rugby, emphasizing the importance of developing competitive intensity "more suited to American needs." In his mind, Americanizing the game meant prioritizing physical force, manipulating weighty bodies over the goal line, rather than the demure flicking of the foot. He had lobbied to situate action lower and convinced rule-makers to approve tackles from the waist to the knees, making it harder for ball carriers to evade men in the open field. In the English game, this was tantamount to dirty play, but the American conception of fairness diverged as Camp perceived the low tackle as the shot of virility that football needed. In his estimation, this maneuver was "far more effective than that of the ordinary English player." The American version of a tackle was swift and definitive, as a defensive strike should be.[8]

Although a seemingly minor adjustment, it changed the complexion of the game as thoroughly as did the line of scrimmage. The low tackle ushered in a peculiarly American form of physical play—bodies amassed together to form human battering rams. Camp justified the change as an attempt to avoid injury-making tackles around the neck, but in fact, the lower tackle opened up whole new ways to damage bodies. In the days of high tackling, linemen had stood erect with arms extended, and backs spread themselves out the width of the field to accept lateral passes or run wide. Now, the low tackle made ends sitting ducks when lined up near the sidelines, their midsections exposed to opposing tacklers. To protect themselves, they invariably moved in on the line of scrimmage and scrunched together shoulder to shoulder behind the linemen. The innovation made it harder for the ball carrier to run in the open field, shifting the advantage to the defender.

In the interest of maintaining competitive balance and narrative tension in matches, Camp belatedly also convinced the rules committee to allow for offside forms of "interference" under strict conditions: Men on the side of the ball carrier could, in other words, create barriers to tacklers with their bodies, not their hands and arms, while defenders could use hands and arms in breaking through. As Camp explained it, in the emerging block game, "the defense was given the right of way."

For every advantage given a defense, however, Camp proposed adjustments to the offense, a tactical tit for a clever tat. Through adjustments and counter-adjustments, his game evolved, just as men evolved by playing. That teams started developing more sophisticated padded armor was an indication that men were being toughened as never before.[9] By the early 1890s, the most physically devastating counters to defensive advantages were "mass" plays. Princeton had innovated first with a simple v-wedge that the bulkiest players formed behind the line of scrimmage to obscure the ball carrier and plow through first defenders. A defense unprepared for the wall of bodies might allow the ball carrier to gain twenty to thirty yards before being able to break the formation and bring the man down.

The wedge play became standard quickly, only to be improved upon by lending momentum to mass. In 1892, a businessman named Lorin Deland created the "flying wedge" for the Harvard eleven, named for the running start men generated behind the line of scrimmage before blasting through a defense. The play was highly effective, perfectly legal, and thought up by a man who never played football a day in his life. Deland claimed his expertise was derived from his knowledge of military strategy. A self-proclaimed authority on Napoleonic battle tactics, he could think of no better application of his knowledge than for gridiron use. "All I have done," he told a Boston reporter, "is to apply the art of war to football."[10]

Indeed, the momentum play gave football a new dimension and Camp a new challenge to counter. He stood on the Yale practice field trying to come up with defensive answers to Deland's maneuver, shifting men around like pawns. Less often now would he crouch down on the line and demonstrate the defensive moves himself. "I felt that I was too old, and that my duty to my family forbade anything of that kind," he later wrote. Admittedly, the element of risk had been amplified since his own playing days. He chose younger, unmarried graduates to be his substitutes, one of them privately confessing that he thought the flying wedge should be outlawed. While logical on paper, the amped-up tactic was terrifying to confront on the field.[11]

Still, Camp thought something ingenious about specially targeted applications of brute force; Deland managed to work around the written rules to intensify the competitiveness of the game. From the beginning, there had been a freedom of experimentation and interpretation of the rules that allowed, as Camp saw it, for the most perfected state of play to reveal itself. He thought there was something especially American about innovating before rules became too entrenched. English rugby never evolved into a game with the same intensity, he believed, because Englishmen were slaves to unchanging traditions. Momentum and mass plays had become the smartest adaptations in the evolution of his game; it was, as he saw it, survival of the fittest in the context of the gridiron. Ruthless though they were, these plays were eminently practical, and hence Camp's "Plea for the Wedge" in *Harper's* in 1893. All was fair in simulated war, he insisted, until rule-makers officially decided that it was not.[12]

Following the same logic, the Trinity eleven greased their canvas jackets so that defenders could not grab them as they ran with the ball. Yale players responded by clenching hunks of dry dirt in their hands until they got close enough to men to grab them with force and throw them down. Others used a sticky substance on their hands, Venetian turpentine, for a better grip, until the ball got too tacky and a rule forbade it. Men hid balls in their jerseys to confuse opponents—again, until a rule banned the practice. Players wore metal cleats that cut up opponents, and when those were outlawed, they turned to leather cleats sharpened into tips so small that they might as well have been metal—until an even more specific rule outlawed those. Camp had written deathly force into college football, and he encouraged players to be the strictest of constitutionalists.[13]

Though he believed he had charted a course toward perfection, others thought that the escalation of intensity and competitiveness encouraged troubling violence and dirty play. Cornell President Andrew White echoed the sentiments of other college presidents when he announced that the brutality in football was getting worse. "The sight of a confused mass of educated young men making batter-rams of their bodies, plunging their heads into each other's stomachs, piling upon each other's ribs, or maiming each other for life . . . is to me a brutal monstrosity." Critics had to wonder if a game that had to legislate against "hacking" or "throbbing" (shutting off a man's wind) was one in which brutality was incidental or implicitly endorsed.[14]

But Camp saw no contradiction in a sport that simultaneously generated violence and honor, nor did many men of his generation, since they viewed physical and moral courage as one and the same. A contributor to *Outing* called the violence of football acceptable, if not highly functional, since it trained men to be warriors: "The events of the Civil War showed that the men of best morals were the best fighters," he reminded readers.[15] Camp also waxed poetic on the man-making function of risk-filled sport in the *Sunday Globe*. "There are worse things in college life than a sprained ankle, a twisted knee, or even a broken nose," he preached:

> No game was ever worth a rap
> For a rational man to play
> Into which no accident, no mishap
> Could possibly find its way.
> There's danger even where fish are caught,
> To those who a wetting fear;
> And what's worth having must aye be bought,
> And sport's like life, and life's like sport,
> It ain't all skittles and beer.[16]

He believed that the youth of the comfortable classes needed exposure to physical struggle to become successful men. Performing a dangerous stunt for its own sake, or "doing a stump," was not without purpose; physically dangerous activities built character.[17] That other middle- and upper-class parents agreed was clear when they permitted their sons to participate in football and other activities once considered unseemly for their violence.

Take boxing, for instance. Decades before, no proper gentleman would be seen near a ring to watch a fight, let alone train for one, since it was associated with lowbrow vice. And yet by 1880, Theodore Roosevelt boxed until he was bloody in a college gymnasium; his Social Darwinist sensibilities told him that the physical prowess once associated with working-class men was now an asset for Anglo-Saxon elites. By the early '90s the sport appeared even more dignified with the adoption of the Queensberry rules, which required padded gloves. The YMCA offered boxing lessons to middle-class boys as a means of instilling discipline, courage, and self-control. Even Camp refereed rounds at the Lincoln Rink. John Sullivan, a working-class immigrant turned boxing champion, was a hero to working-class boys and college men alike because he represented a dying breed—the autonomous worker, the skilled artisan—a man with power over his domain.[18]

Although boxing celebrated the individual, not the team, Camp drew parallels to football and saw both sports as man-making. Like boxing, football was tinged with just enough danger to build physical courage, and yet football was even more cerebral, he argued, since it required the planning of multiple moving parts. Ultimately, the team facet of football required brain to complement brawn. In fact, Camp thought that the effectiveness of a football brain could be determined by the amount of brawn it effectively controlled. By emphasizing this relationship between brawn and brain, Camp was able to incorporate a more physical, working-class notion of manhood—an elemental brand of masculinity, really—into an elite image of gentlemanliness, without the appearance of contradiction.[19]

And yet, remarkably, when Sullivan the boxing great was asked if he had ever seen a Harvard-Yale football game, he could not see the parallels drawn by Camp: "There's murder in that game!" he exclaimed. "Sparring! It doesn't compare in roughness, or danger, with football. In sparring you know what you are doing. You know what your opponent is trying to do, and he's right there in front of you, and, there's only one! But in football! Say, there's twenty-two people trying to do you!"[20] These were revelatory comments, coming from a man who doled out black eyes for a living.

Camp had tried to mitigate the chaos of rugby with tackling regulations and a line of scrimmage, and yet Sullivan saw gridiron play as a free-for-all, the science apparently lost on him. He was hardly alone. Another prizefighter, Jim Jeffries, concurred in *World Magazine* that football was "far more brutal" than boxing. This working-class icon ironically added, "I don't see how any gentleman can feel at home in the game. I wouldn't go into it for a thousand dollars a minute."

Tallies of annual casualties in both sports also suggested that football, if more cerebral, was more debilitating. A North Carolina newspaper claimed that broken necks were far more prevalent in football than boxing: "Excepting the bullfights of Mexico and Cuba, there has been no sport quite so brutal."[21]

Camp boasted that he had created a game that encouraged strenuousness, not brutality; cunning, not deception; which was man-making, not man-breaking. But in 1893 and '94, traditionalists, medical ethicists, and religious moralists fought him on these points. Even if people believed that balance had been struck on the field, it often seemed lost among fans applauding the bloodletting from the stands. The big Thanksgiving games were hardly the only occasions inciting violence around the country. Low-profile matches also required the intervention of local law enforcement because spectators grew belligerent. An interclass game at Cornell got so out of hand that sophomores continued punching their freshman rivals well after whistles had been blown; police resorted to swinging clubs to disperse the crowds. Several journalists surmised that the aggression of spectators had everything to do with the fact that they were watching dirty play that made boys' primal instincts come to the fore.[22]

Camp was politely dismissive. Football was not the problem, he insisted. It disciplined and motivated college men, in fact, and campus hooliganism had been far worse when students did not have the outlet of competitive sport. "Scientific" studies added fuel to his claims, including one by Eugene Richards, a professor of mathematics whose son once played on the Yale eleven. Looking at disciplinary records of Yale students in recent decades, Richards noted that "trespasses on the discipline of the college, [had] grown steadily less." In the *Yale Review*, he lauded football for bringing "the death of that effeminacy which is so rapidly undermining the American nation."[23]

Richards's view of football as a safety valve for rowdy-ism and an antidote to emasculation was echoed by Civil War veteran William Conant Church, who called football "an outlet for superabundant animal-spirits which otherwise might find expression in the usual college pranks." One physician praised football for "ending a career of debauchery for more than one youth"; put more bluntly, the game was a remedy for delinquency, as well as masturbation, in his medical opinion. Such was the contemporary understanding of the "spermatic economy": A youth's libidinal energies needed appropriate channels before his procreative years, so experts believed, and football seemed to provide the physicality and sense of thrill necessary to keep them from being squandered in the meantime.[24]

None of this medical talk lessened the sanctimony of Harvard's Charles Eliot, who nagged about football's perilous effect on men's morals and bodies and decided that Camp was to blame. In his estimation, Camp had created an environment in which coaches and players felt tremendous pressure to succeed, as colleges fell into the business of entertaining the general public with their high-stakes contests. Unlike in rugby, a gentleman's tie in football was tantamount to failure, since American spectators bet money and reputations on empirical victories. He believed that the drive to win at all costs grew more soul-destroying as alumni offered inducements and started spy rings to gain an edge. The profit motive encouraged brutality and deception; "trick plays" persisted because rule-makers were influenced by Camp's tacit approval of them. Eliot's most thorough condemnation came in a presidential report in 1894. With the growing number and gravity of injuries, he concluded that "the game as now played is unfit for college use."[25]

Eliot likened football fans to the sensation-seeking lowlifes who had filled the Roman Coliseum in the years of that empire's decline. Theodore Roosevelt was "utterly disgusted" with his point of view; although he also drew classical analogies to gladiatorial sport, his lament was that too many modern men, like the declining Romans, preferred to be voyeurs in the stands, rather than hardened warriors themselves. More American men should play football, he exclaimed, to achieve the discipline and strenuousness missing in modern life.[26]

If football instilled discipline, as Roosevelt insisted, Eliot did not think that it mattered for much. He thought a man should develop his own internal compass and regulate himself without umpires or police officers, and yet both had become fixtures at football venues. Indeed, as the man responsible for establishing the elective system at Harvard, he did not favor discipline that was externally imposed, and yet Camp's books of changing rules seemed all the more proof that football could not regulate itself. At a minimum, Eliot recommended limiting play to college campuses, relegating spectatorship to collegians only, and shortening the season, perhaps even in alternate years, so that students could focus on studying. The injuries, the betting, the truancy, and the hooliganism would diminish, he predicted, if players spent less time on the field.[27]

On Eliot's points, medical and academic men were torn. Physician H. H. Almond called football a "moral agent" and the scrimmage "a great educator": "Football, when taken by the hand and guided, may be made the training-ground of a virtue which is so far modern that it has not yet acquired a distinctive name." Physicians William White and Horatio Wood also exonerated the game, concluding that nothing topped football for developing the "military virtues . . . of enormous value to their possessor in all the struggles of life." But there was also the editorialist in *Medical News* who called football "a worn-out, brutal old game," much to the agreement of college presidents Jacob Schurman of Cornell, Ethelbert Warfield of Lafayette, and James Angell of Michigan. A vocal contingent even made "A Plea for Association Football," or rugby, alleging that "in the family of British sports, always cherished by the rough-and-tumble Anglo-Saxons," Camp's football was a "wayward child."[28]

Most damning of the editorials were those in the *Evening Post* by E. L. Godkin, who described the connection between the "football craze" and campus violence as causal and direct. Godkin had not come of age playing sports, let alone football. In his college years in Belfast, he was president of the Literary and Science Society and came to America only in his thirties. As a man now in his sixties, he was offended by the homemade battles of the gridiron as much as he was by the corruption of Tammany Hall, and he wrote about both in scathing terms. He agreed with Eliot that the sensibilities of both players and spectators were blunted by the violence before them. In Eliot's words, "To become brutal and brutalizing *is the natural tendency of all sports which involves violent personal collision between players.*"[29]

By insisting that brutality was inherent, not incidental, to football, Godkin and Eliot had touched a nerve. Camp thought "brutality" an ugly word; it was the unwarranted violence incited in beer brawls of less civilized men, not the controlled, deliberate movement of gentlemen on the gridiron. "I have noted the *Evening Post's* attitude toward football," he responded. "There is a distinction to be drawn between illegal and brutal play because of incompetent umpiring, and 'hard play.'" Acting out of mad rage was futile in football, he explained, since it did not achieve the precision required to win. "There is an element in human nature which finds a powerful attraction in personal contest between man and man," he added. "We cannot suppress this element, but we may wisely direct it. While in some sports it leads to cheating, it has quite an opposite effect in football. . . . The man who loses his temper will be outplayed." Essential to Camp's defense was that Yale players appeared to be the moral specimens he idealized. He identified four of the last six captains as prominent members of the YMCA, and hence models of Christian manhood. He also pointed out that the aggregate grade point average for Yale football players was higher than for non-athletes on campus.[30]

Camp would not have had to be so zealous in his defense had the most victorious team in the nation not already acquired a reputation for cheap shots. Harvard men had long accused Yale players of being the dirtiest on the collegiate scene. Even divinity student Amos Stagg was said to have delivered a "ministerial uppercut" from time to time. A contributor to the *Harvard Daily Herald* maintained that the Yale game plan was to "maim opponents," and other collegiate men concurred. Tufts players claimed that Yale men "maul[ed] their antagonists with double fists"; another opponent alleged that a Yale player tried to drown his teammate in a puddle that had accumulated on a rain-soaked field. The accusations added to the perception that dirty play was required to be the most winning team in football.[31]

The most effective and brutal Yale player at this time was Frank Hinkey, a man who, off the field, seemed too mild mannered for the gridiron. By most accounts, his demeanor changed once the whistle blew; then, his controlled rage was revealed in calculated spurts. He was unusually slight, even for the time, at 155 pounds, and yet a teammate described him as "180 pounds of . . . flame and dynamite." His refusal to wear headgear or padding only accentuated his smallness, and yet he was said to have an inhuman ability to apply homicidal force that the media both shunned and glorified. "He solved the crushing power of the flying wedge. He broke up guards-back. He wrecked the old tandem within a few minutes after the opening whistle," teammate George Adee marveled. Camp called him "the Disembodied Spirit" and the name stuck, since he seemed able to penetrate any mass formation put before him. Harvard men called him needlessly violent, but Camp dismissed criticism of "Silent Frank" as the frustrated ramblings of men who did not know how to beat him.[32]

In the national press, however, Camp knew to sound less dismissive. In a highly publicized move, he asked captains from IFA colleges to sign gentlemen's pledges respecting the sportsman's code. Apparently this was an empty gesture, since allegations of dirty play continued and nearly tore the IFA asunder in 1893. Wesleyan and Penn withdrew their memberships, following the lead of Harvard, and for a time, only Yale and Princeton remained. Former Yale player Laurie Bliss confessed to Camp that he could not rein in all the dirty play in the games he officiated at and that substantive adjustments to the rules were in order. It might help, he suggested, if line judges and referees also had the umpire's power to disqualify players and fans for slugging.[33]

University of Wisconsin president Charles Kendall Adams also wrote Camp with proposals: "It seems to me no opponent should be allowed within five yards of the man making the catch." He also endorsed penalties against the "creeping" player who piled on men already down. Hundreds of others wrote Camp with ideas for reducing pile-ons, punches, and bunched up play. How about having teams line up six feet apart? Or allowing longer passes? Or more kicking? Or doing away with wedge plays? Or downing the ball where the runner touched the ground with any part of his body other than his feet? But Camp's colleagues could not come to consensus about which adjustments to make.[34]

Finally, public pressure for reform caused the University Athletic Club of New York to intervene. Given the disintegration of the IFA, it appointed a "neutral" body of experts renamed the Intercollegiate Rules Committee (IRC), which included the usual suspects from Harvard, Penn, and Princeton; Camp was appointed secretary and Princeton's Alex Moffat chair. There was one meaningful addition, Paul Dashiell, who played at Johns Hopkins before teaching chemistry at Lehigh and Navy. Like Moffat, he could speak to the officiating side of the problem, having worked so many Harvard-Yale games. The IRC's job was to eliminate brutality while keeping football's most compelling facets intact. Camp was unable to attend the first meeting in New York, but he outlined some focal points for reform during a speech at the University Club in Boston and later handed a list of proposed changes to a reporter. The list included calling for a fair catch, encouraging dropkicks, adding a line judge to the field, and reducing playing time. Flying and momentum plays were on the table, but there was no telling whether they would be abolished.[35]

The proposed solutions were relatively minor because Camp, unlike Eliot or Godkin, thought corrupting forces in football were ultimately external to the game. The "win at all costs" attitude Eliot bemoaned was not the problem, as Camp saw it, for any honorable gentleman played to win, by definition. The problem was that football had grown profitable to people *not* on the field; *they* were the ones who incentivized winning by dubious means. For every parent unnerved by the exaggerated violence of football, Camp swore that more parents were relieved to see their sons eating right, keeping curfew, and applying the discipline learned in training to their studies. All the evils in football were detachable from the game, he insisted. It just took a little will.[36]

He would have been more convincing had parents not grown horrified by the running tally of football fatalities in the national press. The *Times* reported twenty-three nationwide in 1890, twenty-two in 1891, and twenty-six in 1892. Calls to ban collegiate football grew to fever pitch in 1893 and '94 with deaths at several high-profile games: A Thanksgiving match in Washington, D.C., resulted in the paralysis of Georgetown quarterback George Bahen, who died of his injuries. Georgetown faculty banned football, as did administrators three years later, when Georgia player Richard Von Gammon was killed in a line-bucking play that got the attention of the state legislature; the governor vetoed a football ban in Georgia state schools, but not without criticism. In the early 1890s, Trinity, Columbia, Wake Forest, and Alabama instituted temporary bans on football. President Grover Cleveland fanned flames too when, reacting to reports of increasing injuries and tensions at West Point and Annapolis, he canceled the Army-Navy game. Methodist ministers, meanwhile, called for schools in the Kansas conference to ban play indefinitely. At Cornell, football had already been relegated to the campus, in hopes that the "hippodrome" effect could be minimized.[37]

A cover of a Sunday edition of the *World* featured a skeleton decked in the cloak of death—"the twelfth player on every football team." The image was typical of the coverage of the 1890s, evoking the haunting specter of brutality, yet glorifying the violence to sell papers. The press's mixed messages perpetuated the lack of consensus on where to draw the line between "necessary" and "unnecessary" roughness; hospital reports were both horrifying and titillating to readers. Camp emphasized the view that violence, in context, was a necessary good. He conceded that certain unsavory behaviors (punching, cheap shots, and the like) constituted unnecessary roughness, but he also argued that there was a level of physicality that was necessary for turning boys into men. In his worldview, punishment to male bodies was hardening as long as it did not corrupt or debilitate.[38]

Camp's position became harder to defend after the notorious Harvard-Yale game of 1894. He was at Stanford at the time and thus not present to witness the melee that occurred. The Yale football manager wired him prior to the game to assure him that all arrangements had been made for a public relations success. The stands had been inspected to avoid the fires and structural collapse that had plagued well-attended games in the past, and graduate coaches Billy Rhodes and Ray Tompkins thought the team well prepared, giving no indication that the contest would be an exhibition of brutality beyond the pale.[39]

And yet it was—in front of 25,000 witnesses. According to accounts Camp read later, it was a "bloodbath" on the gridiron. Reportedly, not a minute of the two-hour, twenty-minute game went by without demonstrations of gratuitous violence. Linemen shoved and punched, and injured players staggered about like the walking dead, clearly concussed, officials unheeding of their condition. Frank Hinkey delivered a late hit on Edgar Wrightington, the Harvard punt receiver, breaking his collarbone. Hinkey was penalized, but the umpire allowed him to stay in the game, to jeers in the Harvard crowd. The theme of the second half was more violence and injury. After suffering a disorienting blow to the head, a Yale tackle gouged the eye of a Harvard player. The Yale man suffered several more concussions before being removed on a stretcher, in a coma. Only at the end of the game did the umpire try to restore order by ejecting players for slugging. When all was said and done, nine substitutes replaced injured or ejected men.[40]

John Kieran, a messenger boy running newspaper bulletins at Hampden Park that afternoon, could not believe the sheer indifference to the carnage. "Practically all the players were bleeding from cuts or from kicks or smashes in the general mauling," he remembered. Yale's Fred Murphy was carried out of the game and unceremoniously dumped into a pile of blankets on the sideline. "Just out of curiosity, I went over and lifted the blankets apart and looked in," recalled Kieran. "There he was, still unconscious—and nobody was paying any attention to him." Murphy did not come to until he found himself in a hospital five hours later.[41]

Fans around the nation read about the bloodbath at Hampden Park. The *Times* called rebellion in South America "child's play" in comparison, and a Wisconsin journalist described a scene "more bloody than some battles history makes much of." In the *World's* "College-Bred Brutality," a spectator did not hide his disgust: "Prize-fighting is a human[e] recreation compared with such football as we have just witnessed under the auspices of Yale and Harvard." A Yale graduate in St. Louis confirmed for Camp that, locally, coverage of the game was damaging and "resulted in a great many people here in the city forbidding their sons to play football." The international press did not paint a rosier picture. A German paper alleged that backs were broken, eyes lost, and that seven players were carried off in dying condition. Crowds of surgeons and ambulances reportedly emptied onto the field as women fainted at the sights before them. True or not, it hardly seemed a tale of glorious manhood in the making.[42]

Yale player Brinck Thorne assured Camp that the scene was not as bad as he was hearing. Wrightington had allegedly been complaining of a bum shoulder before Hinkey ever laid into him, and yet teammates convinced him to deny it. Camp returned east to sift through all the hearsay on an investigatory committee. Not surprisingly, the testimonials he heard in New Haven exonerated Hinkey and underplayed the carnage. He offered to go to Cambridge to smooth things over with the Harvard Athletic Committee, but the damage was done. Harvard men believed that a new threshold had been crossed.[43]

By now, a larger movement to ban college football was afoot, and the pressure on Camp was palpable. Before 1894, his rhetoric seemed to be defense enough of the game, but now it became clear that he could not quiet critics or sway public opinion without more empirical proof of football's beneficial effects. And so he welcomed the request of the Harvard Board of Overseers to chair an investigative committee to determine the extent of brutality, as well as character-building, on college and prep school gridirons. His committee included Robert Bacon of the Harvard Board of Overseers, Reverend Joseph Twitchell and Judge Henry Howland of the Yale Corporation, James Alexander of Princeton, and Groton founder Endicott Peabody. Because Camp performed the legwork, these men were all largely figureheads. But they were powerful allies, especially Peabody, who extolled football, fairly played.[44]

One of the ways that Camp added credence to his study was to include the research of surgeon John Loveland, who culled medical data from men who played at the Big Three and Wesleyan between 1881 and 1890. Of 187 respondents, a little over 20 percent reported permanent injuries, though Loveland emphasized that many of these were minor and disproportionately suffered at Wesleyan, where he presumed football material to be "inferior in muscular physique" to that of the Big Three. In Loveland's estimation, injury occurred to men of smaller size and less maturity than their opponents. Ninety-six percent of his respondents said football had "good effect" on their general health, and he found no evidence that it was more dangerous than other sports.

Like Yale's Eugene Richards, Loveland believed that football prevented "dissipation" and was an "outlet for overflow animal life." "The hot blood of youth cannot develop muscle and bone without destroying some muscle and bone," he reasoned. "Most anything in life that is worth doing has its risks. . . . If our nation survives, the man of the future must be able to elbow his way among rough men in the foul air of primary elections; he may need courage enough to take his part in vigilant and safety committees and the like; he may need to 'tackle' an anarchist now and then and perhaps oftener. Where shall he develop his courage? Can he do it where there is no physical danger?" Apparently Loveland had no qualms about inserting charged political commentary into his empirical study of anatomical parts.[45]

Medical opinions proved helpful, but Camp knew that the public also wanted assurances from football men themselves. He sent out a circular to every man who ever played on Big Three or Penn varsities since 1876, as well as to every man on a college football roster in 1893 and to headmasters of schools where football was played. Modeled after a questionnaire of men who rowed on English crews in the 1870s, his survey asked if players had ever suffered injuries in their sport. If yes, were they permanent? Did administrators recommend the sport for boys? How did football affect schoolwork and discipline? Did respondents feel that football led to success in life after college?[46]

More than 1,000 respondents, nearly 90 percent of the men solicited, returned their surveys within a few weeks of receiving them. The most critical among them were school administrators rather than players. The headmaster of the Cambridge Latin School, for instance, reported that the discipline football allegedly imposed was not evident in his classrooms. "Now and then a boy stays from school (plays truant) because he loses interest in school on account of his greater interest in [football]." In terms of the physical risks of playing, he wrote, "more are injured than helped—I have many who have suffered from injury to their knees." A significant percentage of headmasters, professors, and administrators seconded Charles Eliot's sentiments, but thought the banning of football impractical, given its popularity. Instead, they called for substantial reform, most urgently in the rules permitting mass play. The principal of Colgate Academy thought that football, "rightly controlled," had the potential to benefit students physically and contribute to the discipline of the school. Not coincidentally, he was a former player himself. Nevertheless, he urged that football be made safer so that boys did not become invalids before their lives had properly begun.[47]

While administrators' responses were mixed, former players who responded to Camp's questionnaire almost unanimously exalted the game. Among the enthusiasts Camp surveyed were All-American Pudge Heffelfinger and Camp's former teammate Frederic Remington, who simultaneously aided Camp's cause with illustrations glorifying gridiron warriors for *Harper's*. Now rounder around the middle than when he played, Remington remained an unflagging supporter, voicing irritation with all the "namby-pamby talk" of football's evils. When he saw his old friend in New York City, he urged Camp to do all he could to prevent football from being "emasculated and robbed of its heroic qualities": "Camp, you are not going to civilize the only real thing we have left are you? It is the only game left for a man to play."[48]

Nearly all of the former players who responded to Camp's survey felt the same way. Of Big Three men, 328 (of 337) thought they personally benefited from football; and of the 364 who responded from other colleges, only ten reported injury during their collegiate careers. Some respondents described themselves as being of average health before training for football, but now of hardy constitution. Harry Brown reported that he entered college with debilitating headaches that were eliminated by the rigorous regime of football. Another respondent reported that he entered college weighing 150 pounds; by the end of his senior year, he weighed "183 stripped" and gained an inch on his chest. In his estimation, his physical improvements were a reflection of other, less-visible gains to his character. He called the benefits of football "physical," "mental," and "moral" at once.[49]

Most respondents agreed that the grinding contact of football did not hurt their bodies but hardened them, and made them less susceptible to sickness in the work world after college. The proof was that they took fewer sick days and put in longer hours than their peers. A New York physician explained that hospital work, with its long hours of confinement, had ill effects on many of his peers, but not on him. Football made him hardy, he believed, and also made him a leader. "In teaching us, as no other game does, the value of regular habits, good food, and avoidance of all excesses, it does a most excellent service. . . . I value the coolness of mind, reactiveness in emergency, and self control, which I am sure football playing gives." One man claimed that the game helped him to master the three "essential points" of his profession: self-reliance, quick judgment, and keeping his temper. Heffelfinger claimed that football readied him for professional life by training him to read the faces of men he would later face in business: "A good player will constantly study the men playing opposite to him as many men give away much by movement of muscles of face[,] eyes[,] etc."[50]

George Carpenter, a lawyer who played for Harvard, was typical when he told Camp that he could think of no greater experience than football for American boys. In its purest form, the game promoted health, endurance, and self-control, he asserted. Because he had not played recently, he could distance himself from the mass play currently plaguing the game. Today's players depend solely on "brute strength," he explained, "leaving very little opportunity for skillful maneuvering and brilliant playing," as he believed Camp had originally intended. Like most of his contemporaries, Carpenter did not dismiss the evils that had crept into football, but he did not see them as inherent to the game. The balance of power and skill, brains and brawn was the game's essence.[51]

Respondents also countered Eliot's concerns by insisting that football in no way detracted from their studies while in college. A former Yale man was typical, reporting that he had better grades during the football season than in the spring because the sport disciplined him and stimulated him to think. Another respondent, a valedictorian, insisted that football was a healthy distraction from over-studying, and he was therefore able to thwart the emasculation he saw in unathletic boys. In his estimation, football had provided the fresh air and activity that made him a well-rounded, flush-cheeked, modern man.[52]

Nearly all the respondents underplayed their injuries and turned a blind eye to football's physical dangers. W. P. Graves, Yale Class of '91, admitted that he suffered internal injuries to the stomach, yet concluded that the effect of football was "good in every respect." Similarly, W. S. Harvey, who played for Penn, claimed that his only serious injury occurred in 1883: "In a scrimmage behind the goal, I was knocked insensible, but recovered in about fifteen minutes," he recalled. "During the summer following I was sick with blood-gathering in the head that threatened with congestion of the brain, my illness being attributed by the Doctors to the above accident. I recovered fully from this injury, so that in the Fall I was again on the Team, although at that time I played under another name on account of family objections."[53]

Camp's mentor Eugene Baker reported having played football for ten years—five at prep school, four as an undergraduate, and one as a law student—and yet the only injury he remembered was a sprained toe that put him out of a single game. H. W. Cowan swore that he knew of no injuries, with the exception of a player leaving a game for exhaustion. "I was injured more by playing tennis," he joked. Heffelfinger surmised that men were "less liable to get hurt when playing against a scientific team" like Yale or Harvard. One Harvard respondent admitted that, in tallying injuries, he disregarded broken noses, viewing them as "necessary adjuncts of almost any sport."[54]

In one testimonial after the next, the only injuries deemed significant were the result of poor conditioning or lack of fortitude. The captain of Penn's eleven of '91 could remember no injuries, save one caused by Princeton's Edgar Allan Poe running into his own player. Remarking on a broken leg he witnessed on the Yale practice field, another respondent assured Camp that it was "an accident that could have occurred in any Drawing room." The resounding consensus in the responses was that injury happened to the weak and unfocused, not the disciplined men of the Big Three.[55]

Corporate executives thought that football cultivated traits they needed in their competitive worlds, but men of the cloth also extolled its virtues. The Reverend B. W. Bacon of Yale Theological School echoed other Muscular Christians when he admitted that he valued "what some would be pleased to call the 'inhumanities' dinged into me on the football field. There is a 'humanizing' in the true sense of the word which comes by tackling your college adversary in a good football game."[56] Camp's cousin Charles, now head of a divinity school, also absolved football of the evils Eliot attributed to it:

> It is sometimes said, and apparently often thought, that players are guilty of intentionally injuring their opponent. This, I believe from my own experience and observation, is scarcely ever the case. It is true that in the excitement of the game, contestants have been known to lose their tempers and strike out with their fists; but every captain of a team knows how the loss of self-control in such cases of temper injures the efficiency of his men and therefore does his utmost, independently of the rules, to prevent such outbursts. The general influence of the game is doubtless to teach men courage, endurance and self-control.

* * *

> While deprecating the betting which is often connected with college athletics, it ought to be always remembered that the tendency of the age and country, and of the legitimate part of the young men in our university, are responsible for this, and if baseball, boating, and foot-ball were entirely suppressed, the betting in some form, probably worse, would still go on.

* * *

College athletes have done much to promote the moral welfare of
our great universities—Forms of hazing and dissipation, formerly far
too prevalent, have been greatly diminished, or actively abolished,
since the revival of athletic interest[,] which dates from about the
time our colleges adopted the Rugby game of foot-ball.[57]

Camp could not have hired better publicity men to aid his cause.
Former players effectively countered Eliot's contentions; even Harvard
men like Perry Trafford waxed eloquent on the game's behalf: "If every
man who has the responsibility of directing the education of American
boys and young men could be made to understand the real character
of the game, there would be teams in every school in the country," he
wrote. "And if the game were played in all our schools the American
people might become the hardiest and bravest race the world has ever
known." It was hard to disagree when so many of Camp's respondents
occupied seats of power in politics, medicine, and industry. A survey
of 514 former Yale players revealed 50 percent of those in business to
be chief executive officers; 75 percent with law degrees went on to be
partners or judges.[58]

In his final report, Camp did not mention that many of these men
had also come from families that shored up their professional connections well before they picked up a football. Former Yale captain Henry
Ward Beecher was the grandson of the famous minister, a football
proponent no less; and Princeton's Edgar Allan Poe was a blood relative of the famous poet. Surely men like Bum McClung, who made
a fortune in the railroads before being appointed U.S. treasurer,
was helped by his All-America status, as well as the endorsement of
President William Howard Taft, a fellow Bonesman. J. H. Sears of
Harvard reported that all of his living teammates had remained pillars
of their communities after their football days were behind them. But
how much of their success was the result of self-perpetuating connections or the character-building of football?

Rather than speculate, Camp packaged his reports and testimonials into a book that Harpers published as *Football Facts and Figures*
near the end of 1894. In it, he concluded that elite college men had an
"almost unanimous opinion" that football benefited them both physically and mentally. Because of the statistical and firsthand nature of his

evidence, he declared his report the ultimate arbiter in the debate to ban football.[59]

Temporarily, his book served the public relations objectives he intended. And yet, his claims were hard to reconcile. How could the players of '93, for instance, report little to no knowledge of injuries that were so obviously evident? Spending a day with the Yale eleven that fall, Richard Harding Davis noted how "everybody limped—even those who were practicing; and the majority of them . . . were held together by yards of rubber bandages, which they wore concealed about their persons." He also noticed the miraculous recovery of Yale men from injuries that would have left average men in bed for a month. Implicitly, he acknowledged the culture that Camp continued to cultivate, one that compelled men to grin and bear what ailed them to prove that they were men.[60] George Woodruff's response to Camp's survey summed up the mentality of his former players, many of whom seemed indifferent to the rants of reformers:

> Changing the rules of the game will not, I am convinced, materially lessen injuries. . . . Discourage, as far as possible, this recently born but abnormally developed habit of playing baby on the field. There should be less delay of the game—less sponging during a game—less fuss about injuries already received and, consequently, inevitable. If the hurt is great, the player should leave the field and if small he should smile and play harder.
>
> There should be cultivated that determination and Spartan-like fortitude, which, in the days before water-buckets and sponges and regiments of Doctors, inspired some Williams College Poet to write:
>
> > The Yale men are no dudes
> > When they line up in the game.
> > Their shirts are all dirt,
> > But they never get hurt
> > And they get there just the same.[61]

An injured Yale man understood that he bucked up and put on his game face in front of the press. Forty-eight hours after thousands witnessed Fred Murphy lying lifeless at Hampden Park, he presented himself to reporters as if nothing had happened, vowing to be ready for the season closer that weekend. Like Murphy, teammate Frank Butterworth laughed off his injury to reporters, even as one observed that "flesh hung over his optic." No one would have guessed that permanent injuries had occurred at Hampden Park, but in fact they had: A Yale man named Jerrems had suffered a rupture to his side that ended his playing career, and yet there was almost no mention of him in the press. Camp was well aware of men like Jerrems; in fact his research suggested that up to 20 percent of former football players had suffered permanent injuries of varying degrees. But this fact did not get in the way of him concluding in *Football Facts and Figures* that football built muscle and character in American men.[62]

Perhaps his obfuscations allowed him to speak truths that more people wanted to hear. For all the injuries that may or may not have maimed, there was clearly something titillating about the violence of football. For all the dubious play, its brand of ruggedness had popular resonance. If older men were critical of its brutality, younger men believed it would shape them into corporate leaders for the modern age. An English acquaintance of Camp saw its functionality: "Football meets the demands of a commercial and hard-working people, as the tourneys and jousting of old met the demands of chivalry, for in both cases the spirit of struggle between man and man is first and foremost."[63]

Former teammate Ray Tompkins understood this truth. During the most precarious moments of the crisis of '94, he assured Camp that football was "too American to be stopped by any one faculty, or all the faculties combined." While Mark Twain called baseball "the outward and visible expression of the drive and push and rush and struggle of the raging, tearing, booming nineteenth century," Camp had convinced American men that football was the game for the century to come.[64]

6

Martial, Marketable, and Masculine, 1895–1899

FOOTBALL FACTS AND FIGURES DID not quiet all critics or consolidate minds in the IRC. To give the look of consensus, Camp published a tentatively agreed-upon set of rules in Spalding's *Official Intercollegiate Football Guide* that gave officials more power to penalize dirty play and holding, provided for line judges, and required kickoffs to travel at least ten yards, hence creating the kick return. But these changes were not uniformly endorsed. Regulations that shortened games to a less grueling seventy minutes and eliminated the flying wedge were supposed to minimize casualties, yet mass play persisted, and so did the injuries.

Soon, disagreements grew so intense that the IRC was rendered inactive, leaving Princeton and Yale yet again in charge of codifying rules as the barely resuscitated IFA. Harvard, Cornell, and Penn continued to embrace momentum plays that had been struck down by the IRC by setting no restrictions on activity behind the line of scrimmage. Yale and Princeton meanwhile limited motion to one man and prohibited more than three players from grouping behind the line. In 1895, college teams had a range of choices: They could emulate the game played by Princeton and Yale, or Harvard and Penn, or ignore both and revert to the 1894 code. Camp thought the whole thing an abomination.[1]

In 1896, the fragmented state of collegiate football was apparent in the Chicago-Penn series, which took place under alternate sets of rules. The seeming incompetence of the IFA and IRC in the East had led faculty in the Midwest to consolidate further into the Intercollegiate Conference of Faculty Representatives, later known as the Western Conference and the Big Ten. Critics grew louder west of the Alleghenies, as Eliot continued to rail against Camp in Cambridge. A letter Camp received from Theodore Roosevelt gave him some much needed solace:

> I am very glad to have a chance of expressing to you the obligation which I feel all Americans are under to you for your championship of athletics. The man on the farm and in the workshop here, as in other countries, is apt to get enough physical work; but we were tending steadily in America to produce in our leisure and sedentary classes a type of man not much above the Bengali baboon, and from this the athletic spirit has saved us. Of all games I personally like foot ball best, and I would rather see my boys play it than see them play any other. I have no patience with the people who declaim against it because it necessitates rough play and occasional injuries. The rough play, if confined within manly and honorable limits, is an advantage. It is a good thing to have the personal contact about which the New York Evening Post snarls so much, and no fellow is worth his salt if he minds an occasional bruise or cut.

* * *

> I do not give a snap for the good man who can't fight and hold his own in the world. A citizen has got to be decent of course. That is the first requisite; but the second, and just as important, is that he shall be efficient, and he can't be efficient unless he is manly.[2]

Now the New York police commissioner, Roosevelt was hell-bent on using his influence to square away football in the public mind, but more immediately to get Harvard and Yale back to playing each other. After the bloodbath at Hampden Park, the universities were at a standoff, not just in football but in all the major sports. Yale men wanted formal apologies for the insults hurled at Hinkey, but they were not forthcoming. Boston journalists questioned the ethics of Yale men, and Yale loyalists called their accusations the baseless complaints of sore losers. Adding kindling to the flames, a New Haven journalist claimed that Harvard advisors had told players to " 'do up' Butterworth at Springfield." The alleged proof was a letter left crumpled in a hotel room that a maid supposedly handed over to authorities. In disgust, Yale men urged Camp to drop Harvard permanently and seek long-term agreements with Cornell and Penn instead.[3]

Camp conceded that teams other than Harvard had gotten more competitive since his playing days, and yet Harvard and Yale's love-hate relationship made a clean break hard to contemplate. Whereas the 1893 Brown-Yale game netted the Financial Union $263, Yale's share of the split receipts that year with Harvard was a staggering $14,274.[4] The Princeton-Yale game came close to the same profitability ($13,506), but nothing matched the intensity of the Harvard-Yale rivalry, which generated more national interest than any non-Thanksgiving or intersectional contest ever could. And hence Camp breathed only a small sigh of relief in the immediate aftermath of '94. Although he looked to have saved college football, he failed to save its greatest rivalry. The big game was not to be in 1895 or 1896.

Reporters wondered why Camp could not swoop in and smooth over tensions as he had in the past, unaware of his personal anguish at the time. During weeks of the Harvard-Yale standoff, his parents were both frighteningly ill. Their long-time boarder, a teacher in Leverett Camp's school, contracted typhoid, and soon the Camps exhibited the symptoms as well. Leverett barely recovered, and Ellen died after a ten-day struggle in 1895 at the age of sixty-two. Living next door to his parents, Camp could only watch helplessly as his mother suffered. His attempts to soothe them while representing the major sports teams in failing negotiations had tapped him of energy. Admitting that the strain "was getting burdensome," he took a break from diplomacy, stepping away from the Advisory Committee to have yet another run at Stanford in the fall. Although friends hated to see the Yale eleven proceed without him, they agreed that the diversions and climate of California were what he needed to regroup.[5]

None of this, however, quashed Roosevelt's sense of urgency about reconciling the nation's two most elite colleges for football in the fall. He proposed that half a dozen Harvard men go to New Haven to patch up their differences and agreed to join the delegation if Camp also could find a way to be there. But feelings were still too raw on either side, and Camp was on his way to the West, where editorialists opined about the failings of Eastern college men: "Veteran leaders of Yale seem to be no more than shadows and memories in these piping times of letter writing on the etiquette of football. As if the gridiron were the waxy floor of a dancing school for little girls. . . . Harvard must apologize for confessing that Yale pounded her in the game of last fall! What next? Say 'beg your pardon' whenever a Harvard rib gets in the way of a Yale toe, or 'Pray excuse me while I have my collar bone adjusted?' "[6]

Roosevelt agreed that the Harvard-Yale moratorium was a slippery slide toward effeminacy. Since he had first witnessed Camp play in 1876, he had thought long and hard about the man-making qualities of football. Not only did he endorse the game in private letters to Camp, he publicly embarrassed Harvard men for not playing tougher. At the Harvard Club in Washington, he spoke out against Eliot's condemnation of football: "I decline to subscribe to the doctrine of the sacredness of the human arm or leg," he railed. "What matters a few broken bones to the glories of football as an intercollegiate sport? . . . I am the father of three boys. I do not know whether they are going to make athletes in college or not; but I will say right here that if I thought any one of them would weight a possible broken bone against the glory of being chosen to play on Harvard's football eleven I would disinherit him!"[7] To Roosevelt, the reconciliation of Harvard and Yale meant more than gate receipts; it was a saving of face essential to the manhood of college elites.

To his relief, a man on the Harvard side facilitated an eventual truce—someone not typically a maker of peace, but rather a scholar of war—Lorin Deland, inventor of the flying wedge. Camp and the Harvard strategist shared a mutual admiration that led to a friendship that soon extended to family vacations together and fruitful collaboration. The men appreciated each other's tactics and desire to improve football for the game's sake, regardless of the rivalry. During the Harvard-Yale moratorium, Camp showed up in Cambridge to watch the Harvard-Princeton game and generously offered Deland advice. "Watch this play closely; *it is going to be a touchdown for Princeton!*" he predicted. Princeton then proceeded to push the ball twenty-four yards for the score. Deland begged to know what Camp knew; Camp told him it was simple: He could see that one of Deland's substitutes looked anxious, and he saw that the Princeton quarterback had noticed him too and pegged him as a man to exploit. It is a game of glances, he told Deland; the best players read the eyes and body language, like anything else. "Every opinion was conditioned with wonderful foresight," Deland marveled. "He saw every possible development and contingency."[8]

That year, Deland and Camp collaborated on a book on football training and strategy, one that emphasized brains over brawn, sportsmanship, long runs, and kicking—all to counteract the bad press of the previous year. Drawing up a contract with Houghton Mifflin, each man agreed to split the writing of chapters, as well as the royalties. But it was Deland, a former publisher, who was most involved in the book's production, his wife Margaret drawing its illustrations. "I am almost living at Houghton & Mifflin in these days," Deland informed Camp in early October 1896. "I want that book on sale a thousand miles away from Boston at eight o'clock in the morning on Saturday, October 31st, and this means an awful lot of hustling from now on." Deland sent out thousands of circulars to players whose names he got combing the sports pages. The book was simply titled *Football*. With Camp's name on the cover, it needed little else to recommend it.[9]

The press speculated wildly about whether Camp and Deland's collaboration would reignite the Harvard-Yale rivalry. Indeed, during the course of their working together, Deland divulged information about the mindset of the Harvard Athletic Committee. "Does Yale want a foot-ball game with Harvard this fall?" he asked Camp. "All I shall require is that [Captain] Murphy, for Yale, will send a line to [Captain] Wrightington from Harvard, asking him if he will play a game of football at such a place, on such a day. . . . I have already gotten this thing through the Athletic Committee so that it now hangs on only a single condition, namely: that the Athletic Committee may wish to have the season close on the 21st, and not keep it open a week later. . . . All this must be kept in the strictest confidence."[10]

Deland revealed that Harvard's Athletic Committee was ready to reconcile, as long as egos were soothed. Camp was willing to meet privately and tried to be discreet when he traveled to Cambridge in

February 1897, but the press traced his movements. His assistant at the clock company supposed he had left for Boston the night before to spend the weekend with the Delands, but the next day, it was announced that Camp had been in Cambridge to broker peace.[11]

There was no word on where the undergraduates stood on the negotiations, yet Camp made sure that the new five-year agreement allowed them to control scheduling for all the major sports. In return, Yale gave up any prospect of playing in Springfield; Eliot wanted contests on college grounds, with the exception of boat races in New London. The colleges would split gate receipts down the middle, though they would be substantially less now that games were barred from Springfield. No doubt, the arrangement hastened along the building of Harvard's Soldiers Field in 1903 and the Yale Bowl a decade later to accommodate more paying spectators. Harvard's Athletic Committee insisted that a graduate from each college serve on a body of arbitration; not surprisingly, Camp was selected for Yale. In theory, he would deliberate with the Harvard representative and have authority to bring in a third party to settle disputes, though he never found reason to do so.[12]

"Mr. Camp's manly diplomacy finally won the day," a local paper declared. The truce did not come a moment too soon. Although Yale men had played other opponents in 1895 and '96, their football receipts were two-thirds of what they had been in 1894. In the void, men claiming to be former players came out of the woodwork and went on national tour as the "Yale Consolidated." Camp thought the team an embarrassment. In *Harper's*, he insisted that these men were professionals and impostors, desperate to capitalize on the Yale name by playing where less-than-savory audiences would not know that they were not certified footballers. With Harvard back on the schedule, he hoped that the nation's best rivalry would again take center stage and that the impostors would slink away, which they did. "Thank the Lord you are back again looking after Yale sports a bit and that you have succeeded in undoing the mischief," a former teammate wrote him in relief. All seemed right again when Yale football netted more profit that fall than in the past two seasons combined.[13]

All the dust of the Harvard-Yale moratorium had settled by the summer of 1897—the summer when Camp's daughter Janet was born.

Alice thought it should have been a carefree time, with the Harvard-Yale standoff over and clock company profits on the upswing. But for Walter, it felt more like an unsettled calm after three tumultuous years of scrutiny, frustrating negotiations, ministering to sick parents, and spin control of the press.

To help Alice recover from the delivery of her baby, the Delands invited the Camps up to Kennebunkport late in the season for relaxation in the milder climate. Alice recovered remarkably well; it was Walter who complained of pain. Go on your walks and ride your bicycle to clear your head, Alice urged him: but this time, exercise did not make him feel better. This pain was different than any suffered on the gridiron, he told her. It was a vague sensation, something that persisted because it was brought on by stress. Alice kept a watchful eye on him, as everyone else doted on his newborn daughter. Although Walter had become a master at masking his anxieties from the rest of the world, his wife knew how they ate at him. As a gridiron mother, she protected him however she could.[14]

Camp proved an effective peacemaker in sport; now, if only he could prove his mettle in war. Nearing forty years of age, he had only vicarious experience of war at best. He was two when the Civil War began, six when it ended. If he had any memories of its glory or devastation, he likely confused them with images that others had etched in his mind; fact and fiction blurred to create a portrait of the soldier he wanted to be, had he had the opportunity. What boy coming of age in the 1870s and '80s did not idolize his veteran father or uncle, or put himself in the shoes of the great Oliver Wendell Holmes, who described the horror of war and the heroism brought forth from it? "In this snug, over safe corner of the world we need it," Holmes said of war in 1895.[15]

Older Americans preached that a strong government relied on the fraternal spirit of its male citizens, and this spirit was in jeopardy as veterans like Holmes passed on responsibilities to the battle-uninitiated. Theodore Roosevelt contended that the "soldier-hero" would curb corruption and feminization in political life. As women started gaining limited voting rights in the states and clout in municipal reform, the need for manly leaders intensified, elite men warned—and a real war was in order to create them. Clark University psychologist G. Stanley

Hall was one of many experts calling for a martial spirit in American males, even in peacetime, as an antidote to race suicide.[16]

Like Hall, Roosevelt, and William James, Camp was also obsessed with war and its moral and physical equivalent when real war could not be had. Answering Hall's call for boys to hone their survival skills in paramilitary organizations or through competitive outdoor athletics, he proclaimed playing football on college campuses an imperative for national defense. In 1893, Camp wrote in *Harper's* that football was "doing for our college-bred men, in a peaceful way, what the experiences of war did for so many of their predecessors. . . . It is perhaps that likeness of football to war that so stirs men's hearts. The same physiological alterations occur in a great athletic contest such as the Harvard-Yale foot ball game as come in anticipation of mortal combat."[17]

While a handful of American men demonstrated their prowess in the 1896 athletic confrontation known as the modern Olympics, a more widespread experience appeared to be in the offing as tensions brewed in Cuba and the Philippines. Indeed, Civil War veterans could not wait for younger generations of American males to be tested in the Spanish-American War. Some charge that this was a skirmish manufactured for imperialist designs. With the closing of the Western frontier, white men's fantasies of conquest had been thwarted until they asserted their dominion over nonwhites in Guam, Puerto Rico, and Hawaii and pushed their commercial and political interests into Latin America in the name of the "white man's burden."

Whatever the official rationale for war, it was clear that young men yearned to conquer: more of them volunteered for military service in 1898 than the 125,000 that President McKinley had called for. At the end of sixteen weeks of fighting, the U.S. suffered 345 combat-related deaths. Even with the 2,565 men who fell prey less gallantly to disease, it seemed a small price to pay to reunite Northern and Southern white men against an outside enemy and to reinstate American manhood for the rest of the world. Hence the reason why, perhaps, John Hay called the conflict "a splendid little war."[18]

When the thirty-eight-year-old Theodore Roosevelt resigned as assistant secretary of the Navy to organize the First Cavalry Regiment, the Rough Riders, his preferred recruits were footballers and cowboys—two sides of the same manly coin, in his mind. He praised

General Leonard Wood for his prowess both on the gridiron and in battle. One recruit, Dudley Dean, he recognized immediately for his part in snatching victory from Yale in the big game of '90. Although Roosevelt's cavalry saw only brief combat in the battle of San Juan Hill, it displayed enough military heroism to propel him into national politics. He became a shoo-in for the gubernatorial race in New York, followed by the vice-presidential slot on the Republican ticket. Unlike college-educated "dudes" with patronage appointments, he finally demonstrated the physical courage he had dreamed of showing on the gridiron.[19]

Roosevelt saw football as synonymous with what Thorstein Veblen termed "the martial spirit." Veblen observed that this "warlike prowess" was far more apparent—because it was far more functional—in men of the leisure classes, who yearned for tests of honor to distinguish them. Frederic Remington was typical, someone who had longed for the man-making effects of both football and war since his college playing days. He had cattle-ranched, set out to track the infamous Geronimo, and been a stone's throw away from the fighting at Wounded Knee. With Harvard graduate and novelist Owen Wister, he stayed for long stints in the lawless, often womanless West in search of adventure and regenerative masculinity, painting and writing about cowboys until he finally got his long-sought war correspondent's post in Cuba. "We are getting old," he wrote Wister, "and one cannot *get* old without having seen a war." Like the mythical West or the gridiron, war provided a chance to demonstrate mastery over danger, adversaries, and pain. His oil renderings of the Rough Riders charging San Juan Hill helped to create a modern masculine myth, even if these were scenes plucked from his imagination.[20]

Thanks to Camp and his fellow sportswriters, newspaper reportage had so commonly described football as metaphorical war that Americans forgot whether terms like "advance," "attack," and "in the trenches" originated on the gridiron or on the actual battlefield. Writer Stephen Crane admitted that when he imagined Civil War battles for *Red Badge of Courage* (1896), he presumed the psychology of football and war to be the same; he had played the former at Syracuse before covering football in the *Journal*. Richard Harding Davis, who had established the Lehigh eleven before covering Princeton-Yale contests, also came to view his task as a correspondent in the Spanish-American War like his reportage of big games. It was all so ironic: men finally participating in real war yet making sense of the experience in terms of football, rather than the other way around.[21]

Yale undergraduates were also swept up in the fervor of war in 1898, 150 of them volunteering for the Yale battery, and thirty-five more in other units. At a mass meeting in College Street Hall, Bernadotte Perrin, professor of Greek, sounded like Camp when he reminisced of being "born too late to take part in the Civil War"; he had hoped for, and now found, a cause to "stir our souls as the souls of the men of sixty-one had been stirred."[22] War was a timely diversion for Yale men, since their gridiron warriors were not playing up to standard. Expectations had run high. Before the season, Camp handpicked nine starters to train in Kennebunkport, where he stayed with Deland, only to suffer gastritis that put him out of commission. It was a rare occurrence foreboding even rarer things to come. While Yale won the first seven games of 1898 by a cumulative score of 146 to 11, the team lost its last games against Princeton and Harvard. Compared to the last fifteen seasons, this one was a failure.[23]

Speculation abounded in New Haven that Camp's absence on the practice field was the reason for the aberration, and that he needed to be brought more actively into the fold. Although Yale was fairly well represented on his All-America lists that year, with tackle Burr Chamberlin and guard Gordon Brown on the first team, for the first time, the first string also included a fullback from the University of Chicago, Clarence Herschberger. His quarterback Walter Kennedy made the second team, as did men from schools other than the Big Three and Penn, such as Allen Steckle and William Cunningham from Michigan, Pat O'Dea from Wisconsin, and "Brute" Randolph from Penn State. On the third team, there was even a halfback from as far west as Nebraska.

Camp acknowledged men whom Whitney had been clamoring for him to notice, but former teammate Ray Tompkins wondered if the lists of 1898 All-Americans indicated a disturbing trend. Had Camp's dissemination of disciples jeopardized Yale's supremacy in football? Maybe it was time for Yale to have a professional head coach of its own, he suggested, one that would work fulltime for no other purpose than to build up the eleven and keep his strategies to himself. For all this time, the Elis had relied on graduated players returning to campus to coach as volunteers, albeit with Camp's counsel; perhaps the time had come for more continuity and fulltime instruction.

"We must have a head coach and thus follow the footsteps of Harvard, who has beaten us twice since '76," Tompkins urged, adding that anyone but Camp filling these shoes would cause "open revolt." Camp had been asked to coach for money before, turning down compensation at Stanford on "ethical grounds," as he did yet again when offered $5,000 for a mere six weeks of instruction. Still, Eugene Richards thought he could entice Camp to accept a salary in New Haven if he were given a prestigious faculty appointment. Alumni went to the administration to see if an offer could be presented.[24]

It was hard to deny the rapid progress of other teams under paid, full-time coaches. Stagg, Williams, Woodruff, and other disciples had taken pages from Camp's book and perfected his craft to field competitive squads. The conditioning, the inspirational talks, the drawing of x's and o's were all part of their repertoires too. But teams were also emerging under coaches with no direct ties to Yale at all; homegrown experts were starting football traditions of their own. One of the greatest standouts by the turn of the century was the head coach at the University of Michigan, Fielding Yost, who started as little more than a "mucker"—a bought man—when he left West Virginia as a player mid-season to join Lafayette. Despite his unsavory beginnings, he turned into a respected football statesman and developed his "point-a-minute" offenses without the help of Yale men. Sportswriters described him as Camp's younger, Southern equivalent, a seeming gentleman, albeit without an Ivy League pedigree. He was a stickler for conditioning, and his pep talks were classics. Like Camp, he refused to speak to the press before games. Everything he did was designed to create a psychological edge.[25]

Other paid men, like Glenn "Pop" Warner and John Heisman, showed their abilities to innovate when they wrote Camp asking for clarifications of rules so they could drum up new plays that challenged their boundaries. According to British standards, these pioneering coaches may have been cheaters, with their penchants for trick plays; Camp thought them innovators and tactical specialists who advanced the game by forcing clarity of the rules and rapid evolution. With their Yankee ingenuity, they set training schedules and team diets and researched the best equipment, proving Camp's contention that football was a cerebral game. Their work grew so specialized that they soon hired specialists to work for them—trainers, masseurs, and equipment makers—just to keep up with the competition. Camp received letters from men who proclaimed themselves "position coaches," looking to advance from less prestigious athletic departments to Yale. Now a whole brigade of medical men, training table cooks, outfitters, and publishers made a living off the industry of football.[26]

Still, more often than not, when a marketer or editor needed an expert on football, he turned to Camp and paid him handsomely. *Encyclopedia Britannica* hired him to write entries on football, while Doubleday called on him to edit a series on outdoor sports that included football alongside volumes on yachting, shooting, and lawn tennis. Camp was also an unofficial agent for the "House of Spalding," as were YMCA director Luther Gulick, and the amateur-sport bureaucrat James Sullivan, as president of Spalding's highly profitable American Sports Publishing Company. Camp wrote for Sullivan's Athletic Library Series and printed updated rules, reviews of seasons, and portraits of players and teams in Spalding's annual football guides. He included stat sheets for colleges and prominent highs schools, articles on football ethics, and, of course, lists of All-Americans.[27]

The Spalding guides also included catalogs featuring the latest lines of football gear. At the turn of the century, the standard-issue football sold for four dollars, the letterman sweater for six; "Varsity Union Suits" varied in price, depending on their grade of leather, canvas, down, or moleskin. Socks and shirts came in a range of colors in stripes or solids to represent the big universities, and cleats ranged in price depending on whether they had calfskin or reinforced sides. Taking Camp's mantra of specialization to heart, Spalding marketed uniforms for quicker backs or more lumbering linemen, and adapted headgear, nose masks, shoulder saddles, and flak jackets for the different positions. Shin guards, mouth guards, ankle supports, elbow and shoulder pads, and jock straps were becoming standard in gridiron battle, and football pants now came with lightweight padding at the hips and knees.[28]

Spalding executive Julian Curtiss found his friendship with Camp beneficial when it came to selling his expanding equipment lines. When he developed a new shin guard, for instance, he showed it to his friend to make sure it conformed to Rule Three, Section Three of the football code, which forbade the wearing of "projecting, metallic, or hard substances." Spalding held off on production of head harnesses in 1902 until Camp could influence legislation on protective headwear. The sporting goods company marketed to casual players and high school leagues too, since many of them conformed to IFA guidelines and looked to the college game for guidance. In return, Camp was able to outfit Yale athletes at a discounted rate, and Curtiss offered him first dibs on the newest golf equipment, his-and-her bicycles, and skates and sleds for his kids.[29]

Despite his deals with Spalding, Camp continued to have some equipment made in New Haven, however, to keep an edge on the competition. After failing to design his own spikeless shoe, he turned to artisans on Chapel Street to make shoes, headgear, and harnesses. Yale men enjoyed the benefits of shoe spikes arranged in patterns for better traction, and pads were affixed to their bodies, rather than to the clothes themselves. Bruises and sprains were wrapped in surgeon's plaster and electrical tape, the thought being that this would allow more flexibility of movement than the overly quilted uniforms Harvard men wore. Outfitting had grown so systematized in New Haven that an injured Yale man had only a day to wait for custom equipment; Camp kept measurements and injury histories on file for when the need arose.[30]

It was glaringly apparent to the Yale undergraduates who turned over every four years that Camp was the well of wisdom to tap if they wanted to perpetuate their winning traditions. And thus even as they maintained official power, they turned to him to handle everything from training regimens to game plans, the overflow of ticket requests, and the unloading of streetcars at big games. He was the much-needed continuity in athletic management and shaped institutional memory in his conveyances to younger men. "I appreciate more & more how greatly I was helped by the hint talks which you gave me," a graduating manager wrote him. "It might be a wise thing for you to drop a few words to the incoming managers & captains." Little did he know that Camp had been doing just this since 1882.[31]

All seemed to run smoothly in Yale athletics, but stresses in Camp's personal life continued to take their toll. On an exceedingly cold February day in 1899, a fire broke out in the home he was renting for his family on Beach Street in the Savin Rock section of West Haven. Firefighters surmised that an overheated furnace was to blame for an estimated $10,000 in damage. New Haven Clock Company executive Frank Morgan owned the home that went ablaze in the light of day, luckily when no one was inside to be engulfed in the flames. Firefighters could not save the structure, but Camp played down the economic and emotional losses, telling reporters that most of his cups and trophies had been stored elsewhere and were not damaged.[32]

Leverett Camp had transferred property in Meriden to his son two years earlier, but Walter preferred to stay in New Haven, moving his family over the next several years to Howe Street, then Everett Street, Orange Street, and eventually, a prestigious address on Hillhouse Avenue. Although the Camps found respite nearby at their summer residence in Pine Orchard, the females of the house felt less sanguine about the loss of their possessions. Janet, a mere toddler, recounted how the fire "burned up . . . My little shoes & stockings—all my dresses . . . My dollies & my books." For a time, Camp thought Alice might be "on the verge of a nervous breakdown."[33]

It gave her some solace immediately after the fire to live with her brother Graham and his family, but it was hard not to notice Sumner's physical decline. When Camp was an undergraduate, he had revered Sumner for opening his mind. Mental force and an imposing physical presence had made Sumner seem the most virile man on the faculty. But undergraduates' perceptions of him changed after he turned fifty and suffered bodily collapse. Doctors diagnosed him with a "nervous illness," and for two years, he was so much an invalid that he could no longer teach. The man who preached self-sufficiency now accepted the largess of former students like Cornelius Vanderbilt and Henry Holt, who contributed to a fund created to pay for Sumner's living expenses as he took his leave from Yale.[34] When he recovered well enough to return, he was noticeably weakened. On the eve of the new century, he stood a slighter figure at the lectern; his mind was intact, but his physical presence commanded less respect than it used to.

This was clear when he faced a roomful of undergraduates after a spring weekend. Previous classes of men once hung on his every word, but not now; when he began to lecture, chatter persisted underneath the rustle of newspapers, which were forbidden in his lecture rooms. Previously, a disdaining look from Sumner prompted men to fold them closed and pass them to the ends of the rows, where they remained until class was over. But on this day, Sumner's condemning looks did not stop the rustling of papers, almost all of which were turned to the sports page.[35]

Within a decade, coverage of sport in the *World* alone had increased six times, and in the *Sun*, fifteen.[36] In his annual "Review of the Football Season," Camp ruminated on the bonding that occurred between father and son in the fall as they devoured the coverage of collegiate teams. Football was simple enough to be understood quickly, and yet its intricacies gave boys endless fodder for discussion that Camp proclaimed proof of their analytical minds. Yale undergraduates were especially driven to read the sporting news because their team was featured so regularly, giving them a sense of priority in the nation's affairs. Such was the mindset emboldening them after Sumner gave them the evil eye.

In an example of art imitating life, novelist Richard Holbrook conjured up nearly the same scenario facing Sumner in *Boys and Men* (1900), a book he subtitled *A Story of Life at Yale*. Paying only half attention in morning services, a varsity player walks out of chapel and purchases a paper. He takes it into his morning lecture and is consumed with reading about himself until a professor casually asks him to put the paper away. In the real-life scenario, Sumner showed less tolerance. The entitlement displayed before him was more than a learned man of simple means and habits could take. His colleagues also complained of "the coughing and hawking," the "contagiousness of the idiotic laugh" in morning chapel that made this batch of undergraduates seem ruder than their predecessors.[37] He motioned again that he was waiting for silence, but papers kept flapping in front of the faces before him. So he finally spoke:

"When I wish to speak through newspapers, I do it by correspondence." He paused until his sarcasm was understood. The front rows
snickered, but the chatter resumed. "I was to lecture to you young
gentlemen on the danger of taxing the strong for the benefit of the
weak. . . ."

The indifference persisted, so Sumner turned snide:

You pay no taxes. You are as yet neither weak nor strong, for you
are dependents. Your first test will be earning a living, your next
marriage. You think you will succeed in both. I can tell you that
statistically considered not four in ten of your marriages will be truly
successful. They will fail . . . because you are too ignorant of the real
values of living to make them succeed. Gentlemen, you will not find
that statement in the newspapers you are reading.[38]

Sumner's students drowned out his moralizing. Whereas he once
stirred undergraduates to action with words, now words seemed impotent in light of action. More and more, undergraduates saw their
academic and extracurricular worlds as separate, the latter prevailing;
they did not want the gentlemanly erudition Sumner offered. Sumner's
graduate student Albert Keller lamented how much undergraduates
now misunderstood the gist of the man's ideas, for his Darwinism had
never been justification for cruel indifference. Keller swore that Sumner
"would have been the first to lift the drunkard out of the gutter." Sure,
he believed "the sot was where he belonged, but he couldn't be left
there." As blind believers in survival of the fittest as natural law, younger
Yale men apparently disagreed.[39]

Under doctor's orders, Sumner grudgingly acquired a bicycle to ride
for rehabilitation. It was, Camp later recalled, "in the days of the high
wheel," and the novice rider took an inevitable header while riding
it. "Ah ha Professor, I see you have become a football man," joked a
bystander who saw Sumner in his sling. "Not at all," he replied. "I
have the symptoms, but not the disease." He boasted in vain that the
last time he bothered to catch a football game was Thanksgiving of
1876. When someone tried to draw him into conversation by asking
what his brother-in-law thought about recent football matters, he grew
obviously irritated; younger generations of Yale men seemed far more

interested in Camp's kind of expertise than in his own. "What do I know what Camp thinks. Get him in here and he'll tell you. He can say plainly what he thinks, and isn't afraid to."[40]

This was true about any number of topics, not just football. Now a self-proclaimed expert on golf as well, Camp collaborated on a book called *Drives and Putts*, as well as a much larger history of Yale for the college's bicentennial. Coauthored by *Yale Alumni Weekly* editor Lewis Sheldon Welch, *Yale, Her Campus, Class-rooms, and Athletics* (1899) was a 700-page tome in which, as the title suggests, Camp got the final word. His contribution to the manuscript was the exhaustive, if not disproportionate, coverage of the last few decades of Yale's rise to athletic prominence. The college's sporting tradition read like a creation myth, with Camp as the decided creator.[41]

As the century drew to a close, Camp stood as assistant treasurer of a thriving clock manufacturer and the newly appointed director of Peck Brothers, a local plumbing supply company to which he had family ties. Now too, the powers at Yale had a mind to formalize his position within the administration. Before the Harvard standoff, there had been clamor to elevate Camp to "chair of athletics" and pay him a $3,500 salary, the equivalent of Sumner's. President Timothy Dwight stopped short of supporting the measure, but when former Bonesman Arthur Hadley replaced him in 1899, he gave Camp the title "Director of Athletics" and a seat on the University Council alongside the deans of the college. Camp was not a member of any individual faculty, Hadley clarified; he was head of a department, analogous to an independent dean.[42]

A sense of tradition wafted in the air that November of 1899. Camp organized a commemorative football match between former greats of the Yale gridiron and the current eleven and capped off the week by meeting Theodore Roosevelt at the train depot in New Haven. The former leader of the Rough Riders had arrived to speak to Yale undergraduates on football and manhood, as he would again three years later, as the president of the United States. Camp could not think of a more virile last impression to leave with college men as they left the nineteenth century and entered the twentieth.[43]

Halftime

The Yale Man at the Turn of the Century

THE YALE ELEVEN OF 1900 was a team for the ages. It won all twelve of its games, outscoring its opponents 336 to 10. Camp named seven of his starting eleven to the All-America first team, three to the second team, and the remaining starter to the third. While the Yale crew spent more than it made and the baseball nine made only marginal profits, football netted more than $43,000 in receipts. Over blue point oysters on the half shell, alumni feted their "Team of the Century" and toasted its graduate advisor, who was referred to in the dinner program as "The Man Behind the Gun." Indeed they believed that Yale's gridiron success had everything to do with the fact that Camp was leading the proverbial charge.[1]

A New York judge from the Class of '71 made a toast: "At last Yale is permitted to have something surpassing even fellowships and funds—the teaching, the experience, the diplomacy of a man who represents all that is best in the university spirit. . . . Now we can say, with the boy who stood on the burning deck: 'Why should I fear when Walter's at the helm! We are willing to be nothing but Camp followers!'"[2]

Camp approached the podium and waited for the applause to die down so he could shift attention to Gordon Brown, the graduating captain of the championship team. Brown was a 6' 3", 192-pound guard who, with his light eyes and dark hair, was handsome in the conventional sense. Men respected him as the leader who maintained diplomacy with Harvard and brought his team victory. He had spent many nights in Camp's living room talking strategy, hanging his game-day decisions on his mentor's every word. He believed that his defensive line had been impenetrable because he had implemented Camp's plays to perfection.[3]

The audience beamed at the two men in front of them—Yale captains twenty years apart. Both had reputations for a superior work ethic on the gridiron, though Camp thought Brown's drive remarkable given his privileged birth. A Groton man and nephew of tycoon J. P. Morgan, Brown did not have to pull up his bootstraps to fall in with the right connections. And yet, despite the hours he put into crew and football, he was one of the top three men in his class, earning the respect of faculty and classmates alike. Looking at Brown standing at the podium at the pinnacle of his athletic glory, Camp felt paternal affection and a tinge of nostalgia. Brown had supplanted him as "man about campus."[4]

And yet as both a varsity letterman and a member of Phi Beta Kappa, Brown was a rare breed, especially now that sport and society life loomed so much larger to his peers than academic accolades. Between 1861 and 1894, only eight Yale valedictorians were snubbed by the senior societies; between 1895 and 1902, all of them were, suggesting that scholarship carried less and less social currency. The faculty viewed Brown's class as one of the least academically minded in recent memory. Gone were the days of coming to New Haven to become men of letters; at the turn of the century, undergraduates were more interested in honing the art of power. Men rejected the religious and intellectual leadership of their forebears for the corporate strategies of modern managers. The faculty scholarship committee sensed it, lamenting that "hard study has become unfashionable at Yale."[5]

One literature professor saw it as battle lines drawn: "Plato versus John Rockefeller, Shakespeare versus Benjamin Franklin, Milton against the stock exchange." Whereas 9 percent of students had gone into business in the Class of '49, 40 percent chose that path in 1891. By 1900, there was an overwhelming sense that things extracurricular were more important for instilling the institutional loyalty and competitive ethos of the work world to come. Recitation offered a man little, but clubs and football taught him everything.[6]

Thorstein Veblen criticized the extent to which scholarship was "made subordinate to genteel dissipation" in New Haven.[7] Fraternities, eating clubs, and sports dominated a Yale man's thoughts because they fostered the social connections he presumed necessary in a post-college world dominated by insiders. Owen Johnson, who graduated with Gordon Brown in 1900, vouched for as much in his novel *Stover at Yale*. On a train en route to New Haven, freshman Dink Stover meets an upperclassman, who schools him on Yale's social terrain:

> This college is made up of all sorts of elements. . . . And it is not easy to run it. Now in every class there are just a small number of fellows who are able to do it and who will do it. They form the real crowd. All the rest don't count. Now, Stover, you're going to have a chance at something big on the football side; but that is not all. You might make captain of the eleven and miss out on a senior election. You're going to be judged by your friends, and it is just as easy to know the right crowd as the wrong.

* * *

> You might think the world begins outside of college. It begins right here. . . . Now know the game, go in and win.[8]

"Win"—the charge of the Yale man. Camp uttered it in practice and in the stands, as well as in his writings. He insisted that a real man would rather "tear out the grand central ganglion of his nerves before you could make him enjoy losing." In New Haven, the determination to win was propagated more successfully through sport than in the literary societies on campus, and hence the one extracurricular organization to thrive alongside athletics was the campus YMCA, which had more than 1,000 members by 1901, no doubt because its brand of Muscular Christianity encouraged wins on the athletic field. By the turn of the century, the dominance of Yale's major athletic teams was apparent: The crew defeated Harvard in twelve of sixteen contests in the 1880s and '90s, and the record of Yale baseball from 1880 to 1898 was 247 wins, 95 losses, and 3 ties. The track and tennis teams consistently dominated in the Northeast, while minor sports like basketball (1895), hockey (1896), golf (1898), cycling (1898), swimming (1901), and wrestling (1903) gained popularity in Yale men's quest for glory. Camp had more of a hand in organizing these squads and funneling profits from football to fund them than anyone, causing one dean to proclaim, "The College is wholly given over to athletics."[9]

Once, William Graham Sumner had admired Yale's "forgotten student"—the man who paid his way to become learned for knowledge's sake. Now, he wondered where this student had gone. After 1900, undergraduates wore the entitlement of the nouveau riche and preferred the physical manhood and winning ways of his brother-in-law. Yale men of the new century were self-proclaimed "doers" rather than deep thinkers, and Camp seemed to be a doer like no other. Already the treasurer of the New Haven Clock Company, he had a proven record of producing profits when company president Samuel Galpin died in 1902 and the board of trustees charged him with running the company. He vowed to modernize production and reduce costs like a good efficiency man would, and he stayed in the black by revamping the watchmaking department. Yale men looked at his successful business record and believed that his manhood spoke for itself. It showed in the muscularity of his body, wins on the gridiron, company dividends, and on any sports page. Camp's manhood was modern because it was conspicuous.

And hence Richard Harding Davis declared Camp the most important man in New Haven: "Everybody tells you this indirectly when they speak of Camp," he wrote in *Harper's*, "and I was somewhat impressed with the fact that a streetcar conductor came to his house and informed him that a car was waiting for him and his guest at the corner, a block below. It took his guest some time to find their glove and veils and overcoat, and so, 10 minutes later, the car conductor arrived again, and with apologistic mien asked if Mr. Camp's 'party' would keep him much longer, as there were at the time six cars blocked, and each car loaded to the roof with students and towns-people going to the game. That is a specimen of public veneration that is of much more worth than a bronze statue." The only man Davis could think of who was more important in New Haven was the president of Yale, and frankly, he could not even remember his name.[10]

If undergraduates did not model themselves on Camp, they venerated all associated with the athletic universe he had created. Even he noted that they stood in awe at the annual election of captains for the major teams: When "the athletic Gods of the place spoke," their peers "listened like mortals who had been admitted to Olympus for a few brief moments." Henry Seidel Canby, an undergraduate turned literature professor, admitted that, upon entering Yale, he had thought the arrogance of the big men on campus intoxicating. "I longed to get rid of my suitcase with its irrelevant books, and into a sweater which I saw to be obligatory—to dress like them, be like them. . . . They were the 'Strong Silent Men' I had read about in the newspapers, the football and crew heroes, calming the crowded field by the full-breasted dignity of the white letters on their blue sweaters."[11]

Next to these athletes stood heroes of a more subtle kind—"slighter figures in tiny top coats with upturned collars, who seemed to exercise an equal authority." They were the athletic managers—"the powers behind college life," Canby was told, "the real masters of this new state." At the turn of the century, the manager of the Yale eleven was, fittingly, Percy Rockefeller, son of the oil magnate, who took his place in the family business after graduation. With profits and an image to manage, he found Yale football an ideal apprenticeship, but his sway in Yale football did not end with graduation. Camp's heightened influence brought about a redistribution of power, allowing an alumnus like Rockefeller to dictate how university resources would be spent long after he left New Haven.[12]

Not surprisingly, the biggest priority after 1900 was building a bigger football stadium. Harvard raised more than $300,000 to construct Soldiers Field for 30,000 spectators, and Camp estimated that he would need double that number of seats to honor all alumni requests for tickets in New Haven. He did not think it would take long to raise the necessary funds, given the interest in Manhattan alone. The key was convincing investors that winning on the gridiron and winning in business were indelibly intertwined. "Finding a weak spot through which a play can be made, feeling out the line with experimental attempts, concealing the real strength 'til everything is ripe for the big push, then letting drive where least expected, what is this, an outline of football or business tactics?" Camp asked. "Both, of course."[13]

The Paynes, Whitneys, and Vanderbilts all approved of Camp's lessons in the modern corporation called football, joining with other alumni and aligning with undergraduates to spruce up clubhouses and expand gymnasiums rather than contribute to the building of science labs per faculty wishes. "Like children wanting one more exciting story before bedtime, the alumni wanted victories," Canby recalled—especially on the gridiron.[14]

It was becoming a cliché to refer to Yale "brawn" and Harvard "brains," or Harvard "reserve" versus Yale "spirit." Whether this was viewed a good thing often depended on one's proximity to New Haven. Harvard philosopher George Santayana described the feel of the Yale campus as "boyish," which made it "American—not to say Amurrcan." Since the Civil War, the nation's institutions of higher learning had been steadily morphing into research universities. Yale resisted the trend—not in name, since it became a "university" in 1887, but in practice; administrators held fast to the mission of "gentlemanly training." While its football thrived, admission requirements continued to emphasize defunct languages—all when Harvard modernized through practical instruction and electives. As Harvard expanded its graduate offerings, Yale maintained focus on classical undergraduate schooling, with athletics a centerpiece of its character-building mission. "Yale is in many respects what Harvard used to be," concluded Santayana. "The essential object of the institution is still to educate rather than to instruct, to be a mother of men rather than a school for doctors."[15]

In his final assessment, Camp would have replaced "mother" with "father" and not acknowledged his part in the confused state of campus culture. In the New Haven air wafted a concoction of innovation and tradition, athletics and classics, elitism and democracy, things not so easily reconciled. While Camp's Financial Union seemed the epitome of modern corporatism, it also appeared to be a twentieth-century innovation nestled inside a bastion of nineteenth-century values and outmoded rules. As much as Yale men fashioned themselves as the future captains of industry, there was still a lingering sense that higher education should cultivate a certain kind of man—one who, in practice, mastered a gentleman's C over workaday skills. Animosity lingered between the kinds of men Yale administrators wanted to make and what Yale men wanted to be. Footballers like Gordon Brown seemed both Victorian gentlemen and masculine beings in the modern sense—a crisis of identity that Camp also would not escape.

p. 278.	p. 78.
William Palmer Allen,	Auburn, N. Y.
John Arnold Amundson,	Rochester, Minn.
Edward Manross Bentley,	Ellenville, N. Y.
Walter Chauncey Camp,	New Haven, Conn.
Edmund Frank Green,	Oakland, Cal.
Walter Jennings,	Fairfield, Conn.
Alfred Bull Nichols,	New Haven, Conn.
Henry Choate Ordway,	Hampstead, N. H.
Wilbur Parker,	Cleveland, O.
Sidney Catlin Partridge,	Brooklyn, N. Y.
William Allison Peters,	Wilkesbarre, Pa.
Doremus Scudder,	Brooklyn, N. Y.
Edward Curran Spencer,	St. Paul, Minn.
Harry Waters Taft,	Cincinnati, O.
Walter Crafts Witherbee,	New York City.

The official program of the "Concessionary Game" that inspired Camp, as a high school senior, to attend Yale football practices and try out for the varsity squad in 1876. *Yale Football Programs. Manuscripts and Archives, Yale University, New Haven, CT*

The official list of the fifteen men tapped for Skull and Bones from the Yale Class of 1880. *Pamphlets of the Skull and Bones Society, The Russell Trust Association. Manuscripts and Archives, Yale University*

The 1879 Yale football varsity captained by Walter Camp, now able to grow his distinctive facial hair. *Yale athletic photographs, ca. 1850-2007 (inclusive), (RU 0691). Manuscripts and Archives, Yale University*

William Graham Sumner, the Yale professor who pioneered the field of American sociology, propagated Social Darwinism, and coined the term "the Forgotten Man." In some circles, he became better known as the brother-in-law of the Father of Football. *Images of Yale Individuals, ca. 1750-2001 (inclusive) (RU 0684). Manuscripts and Archives, Yale University*

One of the few images of Alice Sumner Camp, the much younger sister of William Graham Sumner and Camp's wife and coaching assistant. At the twenty-fifth anniversary dinner of the Yale Championship team of 1888, the commemorative program referred to both Alice and Walter Camp as head coaches. *Walter Chauncey Camp papers. Manuscripts and Archives, Yale University*

Alice Sumner with her mother. *Walter Chauncey Camp papers. Manuscripts and Archives, Yale University*

The Yale varsity of 1894 practicing the debilitating "flying wedge," invented two years earlier by Boston businessman Lorin Deland, Camp's friend and one-time writing partner. *Yale athletic photographs, ca. 1850-2007 (inclusive) (RU 0691). Manuscripts and Archives, Yale University*

Camp on the Yale playing field with Mike Murphy, the man he hired in 1888 to serve as athletic trainer to Yale athletes. The more athletic directors saw the benefits of specialized training in Yale athletes, the more valuable a commodity Murphy's knowledge became. *Images of Yale Individuals, ca. 1750-2001 (inclusive) (RU 0684). Manuscripts and Archives, Yale University*

An advertisement for the New Haven Clock Company's Yale Watch. The name of the watch was an obvious homage to the prestigious college in New Haven, where the clock company was based. But it also seized on the connection consumers might make between the most winning college football team in the nation and its long-standing adviser, Walter Camp, who, by now, was NHCC president. *Collier's*, January 27, 1906, v. XXXVI, p. 5. *Courtesy of the General Research Division, The New York Public Library, Astor, Lenox, and Tilden Foundations*

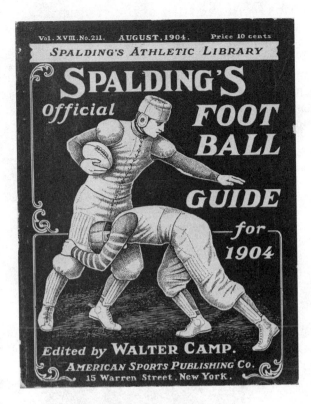

Vol. XVIII. No. 211. AUGUST, 1904. Price 10 cents

SPALDING'S ATHLETIC LIBRARY

SPALDING'S

Official **FOOT BALL GUIDE**

for 1904

Edited by **WALTER CAMP.**

AMERICAN SPORTS PUBLISHING CO.
15 Warren Street, New York.

Spalding's *Official Foot Ball Guide* for 1904, which included articles written by Camp as well as listings of the men who made up the Intercollegiate Football Rules Committee and All-America teams. *Walter Chauncey Camp papers. Manuscripts and Archives, Yale University*

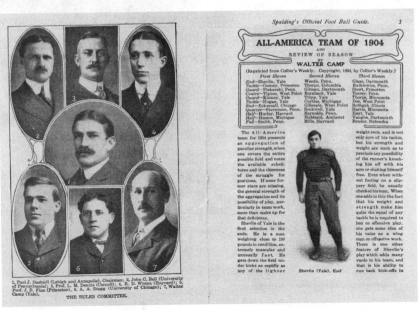

Spalding's Official Foot Ball Guide. 3

ALL-AMERICA TEAM OF 1904

AND
REVIEW OF SEASON

BY
WALTER CAMP

(Reprinted from Collier's Weekly. Copyright, 1904, by Collier's Weekly.)

First Eleven	*Second Eleven*	*Third Eleven*
End—Shevlin, Yale	Woods, Penn.	Glaze, Dartmouth
Tackle—Cooney, Princeton	Thorpe, Columbia	Butkiewicz, Penn.
Guard—Piekarski, Penn.	Gilman, Dartmouth	Short, Princeton
Centre—Tipton, West Point	Roraback, Yale	Torrey, Penn.
Guard—Kinney, Yale	Tripp, Yale	Thorpe, Minnesota
Tackle—Hogan, Yale	Curtiss, Michigan	Doe, West Point
End—Eckersall, Chicago	Gillespie, West Point	Rothgeb, Illinois
Quarter—Stevenson, Penn.	Rockwell, Yale	Harris, Minnesota
Half—Hurley, Harvard	Reynolds, Penn.	Hoyt, Yale
Half—Heston, Michigan	Hubbard, Amherst	Vaughn, Dartmouth
Full—Smith, Penn.	Mills, Harvard	Bender, Nebraska

The All-America team for 1904 presents an aggregation of peculiar strength, when one covers the entire possible field and notes the available substitutes and the closeness of the struggle for positions. If some former stars are missing, the general strength of the aggregation and its possibility of play, particularly in team work, more than make up for that deficiency.

Shevlin of Yale is the first selection in the ends. He is a man weighing close to 190 pounds in condition, extremely muscular and unusually fast. He gets down the field under kicks as rapidly as any of the lighter

weight ends, and is not only sure of his tackle, but his strength and weight are such as to preclude any possibility of the runner's knocking him off with his arm or shaking himself free. Even when without footing on a slippery field, he usually checked his man. When one adds to this the fact that his weight and strength make him quite the equal of any tackle he is required to box on offensive play, one gets some idea of his value as a wing man on offensive work. There is one other feature of Shevlin's play which adds many yards to his team, and that is his ability to run back kick-offs in

Shevlin (Yale), End

1, Paul J. Dashiell (Lehigh and Annapolis), Chairman; 2, John C. Bell (University of Pennsylvania); 3, Prof. L. M. Dennis (Cornell); 4, R. D. Wrenn (Harvard); 5, Prof. J. B. Fine (Princeton), 6, A. A. Stagg (University of Chicago); 7, Walter Camp (Yale).
THE RULES COMMITTEE.

Yale All-American icons from the turn of the century

Walter "Pudge" Heffelfinger and Thomas Lee "Bum" McClung were national celebrities after graduating as All-Americans in the early 1890s; after coaching the Berkeley rivals of the Stanford team Camp coached in 1892, 1894, and 1895, these men used their football fame to make names for themselves in business and politics. McClung, most notably, went on to become the Treasurer of the United States. *Yale athletics photographs, ca. 1850-2007 (inclusive) (RU 0691)*

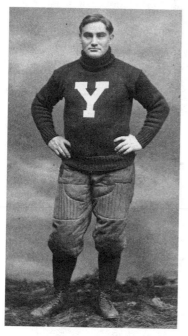

Three-time All-American Jim Hogan exemplified the emergence of Irish and immigrant players on Yale and other elite college squads. He, like others, proved enterprising, turning a profit while he played. *Walter Chauncey Camp papers. Manuscripts and Archives, Yale University*

Ted Coy, perhaps the last truly great player of the legendary Yale squads, was thought to be Camp's inspiration for his first football novel, *The Substitute*. *Images of Yale Individuals, ca. 1750-2001 (inclusive) (RU 0684). Manuscripts and Archives, Yale University*

NEXT!
'A' president who ''does'' things.

Drawn by Charles Lewis Bartholomew, likely late in 1905, this cartoon of President Theodore Roosevelt depicts a "doer," hell-bent on fixing football, ameliorating labor strife, and demonstrating international supremacy all at once. Indeed, Roosevelt thought that a uniquely American brand of virility, cultivated through playing football, was essential to his "big stick" diplomacy and bully pulpit reform. *Prints and Photographs Division, Library of Congress, Washington, DC (LC-DIG-ppmsca-37840)*

Camp at fifty, as the esteemed president of the New Haven Clock Company and Yale's coach of coaches. His influence over the Yale eleven would diminish from here, as Yale's football preeminence waned. *Images of Yale individuals, ca. 1750-2007 (inclusive) (RU 0684). Manuscripts and Archives, Yale University*

Camp works on technique with Yale player Francis Knox in 1907. His preference was to be present at practices with Yale players, but when his work with the New Haven Clock Company forbade it, he coached from afar by inviting coaches and team captains to his home in the evening to discuss strategy. *Pictures of Yale Athletics, ca. 1850-1980 (inclusive) (RU 0691). Manuscripts and Archives, Yale University*

Theodore Roosevelt Jr. is escorted off the Harvard practice field in 1905. His father thought injuries both inevitable and necessary on the path to effective manhood. *Theodore Roosevelt Collection, 570.R67t-012, Houghton Library, Harvard University, Cambridge, Massachusetts*

Walter Camp reuniting with his daughter, Janet, in May 1913, while she was a finishing school student overseas. *Walter Chauncey Camp papers. Manuscripts and Archives, Yale University*

Walter Camp at old Yale Field with his son, Walter Jr., in 1912, when injury brought Walter Jr.'s college football career to an abrupt end. *Images of Yale Individuals, ca. 1750-2001 (inclusive) (RU 0684). Manuscripts and Archives, Yale University*

Three-time All-American and millionaire lumber scion Tom Shevlin on Yale Field, serving for a second time as emergency head coach following Camp's departure and Yale football's steady decline. Weeks after the failed season of 1915, Shevlin succumbed to pneumonia and died suddenly. He was only thirty-two. *Yale athletics photographs, ca. 1850-2007 (inclusive) (RU 0691). Manuscripts and Archives, Yale University*

A panoramic view of the Yale Bowl on the day of its inaugural game, November 21, 1914. In front of more than 70,000 spectators, Harvard dominated the home team by a score of 36-0. *Photograph collection of Brian K. Welch (RU 0666). Manuscripts and Archives, Yale University*

Walter Camp and Walter Camp Jr. in uniform during World War I. At the same time Camp Sr. supervised athletic programs in the Navy camps, Walter Jr. administered athletic programs as an aide-de-camp at Fort Hancock. Unlike his father, Walter Jr. eventually saw combat overseas. *Walter Chauncey Camp papers. Manuscripts and Archives, Yale University*

Camp with Senior Service Corps executive members Col. Isaac M. Ullman, president of the New Haven Chamber of Commerce, and former U.S. President William Howard Taft, in 1917. *Walter Chauncey Camp papers. Manuscripts and Archives, Yale University*

The New Haven Senior Service Corps (SSC) doing drills led by Yale athletic director W. C. Anderson. Former U.S. President William Howard Taft is in the center of the front row. *Walter Chauncey Camp papers. Manuscripts and Archives, Yale University*

Paul Robeson, an All-American in 1917 and 1918, worked in earnest on the gridiron and in the classroom so as not to incite the ill will of white administrators, teammates, and journalists. At Rutgers, he also lettered in baseball, basketball, and track. Camp thought Robeson, like Jim Thorpe, was one of the greatest athletes he had ever seen. *Paul Robeson papers, Special Collections and University Archives, Rutgers University Libraries*

The national weekly *Leslie's* featured the Carlisle Industrial School's football squad on its November 4, 1897 cover. In the foreground is Billy Bull, the Yale graduate Camp chose to be Carlisle's head coach. The caption accompanying the image (quoted on page 226) reveals white readers' mixed feelings about Native American players, who fascinated them and fueled their anxieties about "overcivilization" at once. *Courtesy of Archives and Special Collections, Dickinson College, Carlisle, PA*

Camp's "Daily Dozen" consisted of four sets of three exercises: hands, hips, head; grind, grate, grasp; crawl, curl, crouch; wave, weave, wing. Here, Camp demonstrates "grate." *Walter Chauncey Camp papers. Manuscripts and Archives, Yale University*

Walter Camp at fifty-eight, in 1917. He took great pride in being able to loosen his tie and demonstrate his Daily Dozen, reportedly without breaking a sweat. LC-DIG-hec-09211, *Library of Congress Prints and Photographs Division, Washington, DC*

A young Walter Camp takes a swing. Golf, Camp's favorite leisure activity, provided the fresh air and light aerobic exercise he thought American men needed after the age of forty. In the early 1920s, he championed the lowering of golf course fees and the creation of municipal courses to make golf available to more American men. *Walter Chauncey Camp papers. Manuscripts and Archives, Yale University*

1925, the year of Camp's death, marked the professional coming out of University of Illinois back Harold "Red" Grange, who left college to pursue the lucrative football contract and endorsement deals that Camp had publicly shunned, yet played an undeniable role in creating. LC-DIG-npcc-15254, *Library of Congress Prints and Photographs Division, Washington, DC*

Completed in 1928, the gateway to Walter Camp Field at Yale was paid for largely by donations from 224 college and 279 high school athletic departments around the country, in honor of the man remembered as the quintessential "Gentleman Athlete." *Yale University buildings and grounds photographs, 1716-2004 (inclusive) (RU 0703). Manuscripts and Archives, Yale University*

THIRD QUARTER: MANHOOD TESTED

7

Camp's Boyology*: The Making of Eligible Men

WALTER CAMP LOVED TO TALK to and about American boys. He gave football pointers to the student athletes of Lawrenceville Prep and straight talk to Boy Scouts about living healthfully, often refusing all speaking fees except for the cost of travel. He served on the board of the National Friends of Boys, because administrators were convinced of his positive influence. "Boys will talk more unreservedly to me than to you," he told a room of New York schoolmasters, and some admitted it was true. Edwin Milton Fairchild, founder of the Character Education Institute, presumed Camp's knowledge of boys to be so absolute that he sent him an outline of an upcoming speech, asking if he had accurately described the "boy temperament" in the midst of athletic competition.[1]

Like a true expert, Camp spoke about boys in definitive, rather than speculative, terms, often in the form of easily digestible aphorisms:

- If your boy does not feel badly when beaten he will never in sport or life work hard enough to become a winner.
- Don't let your boy get such a maximum of old man's caution that he reduces to a minimum the young man's courage.

---

*"Boyology," the study of male adolescent psychology, was coined by YMCA boy worker H. W. Gibson. See Kett, *Rites of Passage*, 224.

- Education and discipline may make a good boy but you will have to add pluck and initiative if you would make him a success.
- If nature thought a real passion for wisdom was good for your boy she would have put it in him in place of his admiration for physical strength and courage.
- If you fail to take an interest in your boy's sports you can no more get hold of him then you can pick up a globule of mercury.
- Better make a boy an outdoor savage than an indoor weakling.
- A feminine mind will never make a foot ball player; it is an intensely masculine game.
- When the old Greeks began to chisel their statues of Apollo with less muscled and more rounded limbs, altering their standard of masculine beauty to a more luxurious effeminate softness, their age of decadence had already begun.[2]

His sound bites were effective amid the recent clamor about American males. Social scientists and medical men were utterly preoccupied by them, an indication of their collective insecurity about manhood in the industrial age. So many works of the Progressive period—John Ellis's *The Deterioration of Puritan Stock and Its Causes* (1884), Brooks Adams's *Law of Civilization and Decay* (1895), Madison Grant's *The Passing of the Great Race* (1916), to name just a few—questioned the white male's ability to stave off race suicide to retain a sense of superiority in the world.

Empirically speaking, there was reason to worry. Census figures showed that the American frontier was closed and that more American males now lived in cities, working for others behind desks rather than self-sufficiently or doing physically demanding tasks. Without Indian wars or preindustrial labor, Anglo-Saxon males lacked the hardening rites of passage that proved race superiority in earlier times, so experts feared. Harvard men Dudley Sargent, Theodore Roosevelt, and Henry Cabot Lodge sounded alarms about the entropy of American males and the consequent demise of "the race," encouraging Anglo-Saxon men to build stamina, muscle, and courage through dangerous forays in the wilderness or in imperial contests, if not on the high seas, then the dissipating frontier. *Being a Boy* and *The Court of Boyville* are yet other works in which Camp's contemporaries harkened back to simpler, more physical forms of experience in reaction to the luxuriating Gilded Age.

In the collective mind of white elites, the fictional Tom Sawyer or Huck Finn stood as the antithesis of the effeminate boy—polite, but not a do-gooder, respectful of his mother, but eager to leave home for adventures and tussles away from her apron strings. With wild instincts unsuppressed by the four walls of the house, he was a strenuous man in waiting. Outdoors, he staved off homosexuality (or suspicions of it as he bonded with other males) and learned physical courage, as well as the merits of democracy, freedom, and fair play. For boys stuck in cities, Camp said that baseball diamonds and football gridirons sufficed as terrain on which to undergo such manly transformations.[3]

Just as Brooks Adams discerned evolutionary stages in the development of civilizations, psychologist G. Stanley Hall saw them in the development of American males, describing boys as appropriately primitive in youth and "civilizing" over time. According to Hall, a white boy's development replicated the trajectory of his race: He relived the adult stages of primitive ancestors and hence stayed boyish longer than did males of races whose potential to evolve was limited. His notions accommodated new realities; as roads to financial independence grew less certain, he imagined new paths to manhood on which prolonged stints of mischief, financial dependency, or schooling for white-collar work were expected. Hall referred to this longer layover between boyhood and manhood as adolescence, and he called it a necessary stage for any boy who hoped to be effective in the modern age.[4]

Camp agreed with Hall that physical horseplay was part of a boy's healthy development, a necessary evolutionary stage passed through before becoming superior to other races and genders. American youths needed to play and run wild in all-male environments before becoming upstanding, responsible men. Like Hall, he saw boyhood and manhood as stages along the same virile path. And like Hall and Sigmund Freud, he viewed violent struggle as instinctual, cathartic—a natural and necessary part of boyhood. Confronting violence early in life developed physical and moral courage, allowing one to master adult pressures without falling into nervous collapse.

The American boy, in his rhetoric, had "a strain in his blood coming down to him through rugged ancestors that g[ave] him that unquenchable lust for uncivilized places." Rather than defy it, he urged boys to cultivate it, if not primarily through football then through outdoor activity generally. Camp became a proponent of the theories of Joseph Lee and Henry Curtis, pioneers of the playground movement, as well as William Forbush, author of *The Boy Problem*, echoing their ideas on the merits of play in the physical education movement. Nevertheless, he insisted that football figured ideally into adolescence as the mechanism facilitating roughness and discipline that propelled boys into manhood better than anything else.[5]

Where Camp's views were more tempered than Hall's was on the issue of eugenics. Camp proclaimed himself a "rational" or "moderate" eugenicist, in that he did not believe in limiting the reproduction of a class of "unfit" people. Heredity was not the sole transmitter of traits, as he saw it; environmental factors, including education, could also bring about race improvement. In the case of humans, unlike animals, strict scientific law was not the sole predictor of how one would fare in life; individual effort mattered more in his estimation, and he was proof. He did not think football should only be played by boys of superior stock, in other words, because he was convinced that football made superior stock over time, even if it took generations. Such was the mindset of a self-made man.[6]

Although Camp pontificated on the problem of the "tom-boy" now and again, the problem of effeminacy in sons was direr in his mind, its early signs needing immediate attention so they would not take permanent hold. He blamed doting mothers and absentee fathers, the former instilling undue caution in a boy and the latter neglectfully letting it happen. "Fear and timidity have no place in the boy's mental make up, for they rob him of boyhood's most precious privilege," he insisted. "Boys should be reckless; they must be if they are to attain the full physical development which is their birthright." This was a birthright more easily realized if fathers tussled with their sons from time to time.[7]

In *The Young Man and the World* (1905), like-minded Senator Albert Beveridge decided that going to college was good, but not at the risk of falling into the trappings of "over-refinement." Civilizing—emasculating—agents bore down on white boys in indoor spaces, he feared; they came in the forms of book learning and cultured women, whose tendencies were to turn sons into priggish Fauntleroys, emotional and scared by nature, confrontation, or the sight of blood. Playing football was the most effective way to make a youth "accustomed to hard knocks," Camp affirmed, as well as to build up his courage.[8]

This was courage he thought innate, but it needed to be coaxed to the surface by a mature male figure—if not father, then a father-like figure who neutralized the emasculating forces in a boy's life. Upon the exclusively male terrain of the gridiron, Camp insisted that another male figure reign supreme—the coach—a surrogate father to boys, to mitigate the feminizing forces of modern life. W. Cameron Forbes, grandson of Ralph Waldo Emerson, called football coaches the "greatest men on earth" before becoming one himself at the turn of the century. He denied his Harvard players timeouts and medical attention, all to thwart their emasculation, buying into Camp's contention that football coaches imposed strenuousness that turned boys into men.[9]

Camp recognized that American males in the modern age had diminishing control over social rules, political systems, and financial outcomes. So he gave them solace, telling them that they could at least bring order into their disorderly bodies, build them up and tone them just so, and feel a degree of *self*-control, if nothing else. He venerated the physically self-possessed—be they boxers, the scantily clad body-builder Eugene Sandow, or physical culturist Bernarr Macfadden, with his Greco-Roman physique. And yet his All-American was perhaps the most widely embraced iconic man's man of his time, perhaps because his traits were so conspicuously on display. In the modern culture of consumption, his attributes were externally acquirable rather than inconspicuously internalized. Though Camp encouraged boys to have moral courage that was not always seen, he also insinuated that their inner strength counted for little if it was not displayed outwardly on the physical body. The YMCA endorsed his secular notions about sport because they adhered to his same dual premise: that manliness coalesced in the physical body, and that superior strength and stamina was a reflection of superior character.[10]

Because muscle was so conspicuous, it sometimes appeared as though Camp were heralding brawn at the expense of brain; in the new century, he often said as much. To a room full of educators in Philadelphia, he told the cautionary tale of his class valedictorian at Yale, William Montague Hall, a man who reportedly studied too much to go outdoors. After graduation, friends tried to bring color to his cheeks by encouraging him to take up sport, but he died five years later, under-exercised and overworked; excessive brainwork had tapped him of nerve force, at least according to Camp's diagnosis. "There were other men in my class who thought perhaps too much of athletics," he admitted. One was thrown out of Yale twice, but Camp explained that the man had since made his fortune and with it sent hundreds of boys to college: "Nature does not make any marks against the athletic fellow who doesn't make good at college. She gives him his opportunity to make good in another line that's more fitted to his abilities." If educators were unconvinced, Camp's example punctuated the point: Athleticism, not scholarship, had made him a household name.[11]

No game was better for American youths than football, Camp insisted, but, he stressed, it was a game only for the young. It was too rigorous for males in their thirties and forties; when the time came, these men would have to shift to other virile activities to maintain their vigor. As an editor for *Outing*, as well as for the sport, travel, and adventure department of *Collier's*, Camp encouraged older men to continue engaging in outdoor tests of fortitude. "It is a rare stunt . . . when a man goes naked into the Maine woods . . . and comes out alive, clothed in furs, and fatter than when he went in," he lamented. "All of us *ought* to be able to do that. . . . Only the trained athlete can do to-day what every man in primitive times had to do, in order to reach his twentieth birthday." When he wrote this, Camp was likely referring to the Boston illustrator Joseph Knowles, who, at forty-four, walked away from his urban existence to attempt survival in the woods of Maine. Knowles played out the romantic dream of Camp and his generation, liberating himself from the iron cage of the office and the trappings of civilization as if he were Tarzan in the flesh.[12]

In making pleas for older urbanites to return to preindustrial rigors, Camp echoed editorialists in *Forest and Stream, Sports Afield*, and *Outdoor Life*, as well as Theodore Roosevelt in his Boone and Crocket Club and adherents of the arts and crafts and country life movements. And yet, Camp the editor solicited pieces on woodland biking and alpine skiing as he sat at lavish tables at Delmonico's with his publishers Robert Collier and Condé Nast. More and more these days, he could only shed the trappings of his effete indoor world vicariously.[13] He rarely had time to be the outdoorsman of his youth, but he endorsed the Boy Scouts of America (BSA) in hopes of helping more boys know his childhood experience. The militaristic organization had grown out of Sir Robert Baden-Powell's international movement, and like British rugby, it now allowed American males to flex their proverbial muscles. The BSA fostered discipline, self-efficiency, and Anglo-Saxon expansionism. Much like the Sons of Daniel Boone, with which it merged, the Scouts claimed to rekindle powers of the savage and combat emasculating "spectatoritis" in city youth. Camp became a recruiter of scouts and scoutmasters; BSA executives thought no one better to "appeal to the boy instinct" and to stand as a role model for them.[14]

Treating young boys like strenuous men in waiting, Camp prepped them for the gridiron in writings for Harper's Young People book series, the BSA's *Boys Magazine*, *The American Boy*, and *McClure's* youth's department. His stories for *Youth's Companion*, *The Congregationalist and Christian World*, and *St. Nicholas Magazine* celebrated bonding in all-male worlds in which virility was cultivated and reassuringly preserved; and like the adventure tales of Jack London, Zane Grey, and Owen Wister, his works appealed to the cult of the primitive as they prescribed athletic manhood.[15]

Camp agonized over the ending of the short story "The Best Way to Win": Should Fred resolve not to play in the big game on moral grounds? Would he be acting in the best interest of the team if he did? As careful in scripting his manly lessons as he was in choosing All-Americans, Camp fit seamlessly into a genre of sports fiction for boys that had been thriving since the 1890s. Protagonists were typically humble, honest, and shunning of muckers and "dudish" or affectatious clothes; antagonists were poor sports, "stuffed shirts," and bullies; and heroes held to creeds of honor, spirit, fair play, and never quit. Ralph Henry Barbour, author of *The Half-Back* (1901), *Captain of the Crew* (1901), and *The Crimson Sweater* (1907); Edward Stratemeyer; Ralph Paine; former player T. Truxton Hare; and dozens of others were faithful to this formula.[16]

And yet, the most successful franchise belonged to Gilbert Patten (pen name Burt Standish), creator of All-American Frank Merriwell (1896), one of the most morally correct fullbacks that the fictional Yale ever produced. He was a straight shooter and all-around athlete who pitched, rowed for the crew, ran sprints and the mile, pole-vaulted, high-jumped, and threw the hammer. Injury never deterred him, and he always found a way to win the big game. Patten chose a name for his protagonist that epitomized the Yale athlete: "*Frank* for frankness, *merry* for a happy disposition, *well* for health and abounding vitality." Although Patten insisted that Merriwell was too perfect to be based on a flesh-and-blood player, people presumed he was a fictionalized version of Camp in his heyday, since he resembled him down to the position he played and the sportsmanship he espoused. (George Brooke, author of *The Story of a Football Season* [1907], admitted that his "Walter Campbell" was less thinly veiled.)[17]

Originally printed in *Tip Top Weekly,* Merriwell's escapades were made into dime novels by Street and Smith and sold vigorously for two decades. Patten wrote 208 novels and sold an estimated 500,000 copies of the Merriwell stories a week. Camp figured that there was no one better than himself to also cash in on this literary market. Having never left the college athletic experience, he claimed that his sports fiction would be more authentic than any other.

And so, with Arthur Stanwood Pier's *The New Boy* and Barbour's *Forward Pass,* Camp's *The Substitute* appeared in October 1908. There was no one better suited than the man who worked tirelessly on the scrub team to ready starters for the weekend game to convey the importance of pluck, sacrifice, and team spirit. Camp's protagonist Dick Goddard, a boy leaving prep school to attend Yale, makes a name for himself in athletics—first on the freshman eleven and in time on the varsity. In the world he enters, peers refer to each other by last names or body types and put on poundage for social collateral. The opening scene is a sports banquet at Goddard's prep school. Fairfax, the current captain of the Yale eleven, talks to the graduating seniors, and Goddard hangs on his every word:

> Yale is in earnest, in deadly earnest. . . . It makes men of you, and makes men of you fast. . . .
>
> Yale men always play to win. That is the code. Play fair, but play hard, and never give up. If, after all, you get whipped, keep your mouth shut; accept the issue, but determine to reverse it another year. . . .
>
> When a man tells you not to care about winning, what difference does it make, you let him alone. American boys and good American men don't take anything that way. . . .

Believe in your own men and your own abilities, and then when you go down to New Haven you will become one of that great body of Yale men who have made the term "Yale Pluck" synonymous the country over with bulldog courage and determination that cannot be shaken off.[18]

Commenting on Camp's recent novel, a friend surmised that the character "Thompson" was "pretty clearly Ray Tompkins"; "Hinman," Frank Hinkey; "Blaine," Frank Butterworth; "Warner and Willis," Wallis and Winter. Camp undoubtedly took inspiration from already mythologized Yale men. His books were marketed as inside glimpses of what really occurred behind the scenes, making them necessary guides for aspirants to Big Three athletics. The founder of the Crescent Athletic Club assured Camp that his son would "read [*The Substitute*] preparatory to going to New Haven," and a coach at Newark Academy presented each of his players with a copy.

G. Stanley Hall contended that men rediscovered their lost passions in the primitive emotions of their sons, and according to Camp's contemporaries, *The Substitute* brought sublimated feelings to the surface: "There is no book of the kind that is in the same class, except *Tom Brown*," one raved. "Those football talks & that blocked kick had my pulse going about 140." Another exclaimed that *The Substitute* "was bully! . . . I made myself Goddard from the start and lived with him. . . . I read all my boy's books. . . . None of them have the intense interest of the 'Substitute.' " An editor of the *Yale Alumni Weekly* felt sorry for any fathers "so emaciated and bloodless, or so far removed from the interests of their younger days" that the book did not stir them to action.[19]

Camp's daughter Janet remembered orders for *The Substitute* coming in for years, and libraries rebinding copies to meet demand. Appleton seized on its success and published five more novels: *Jack Hall at Yale* (1909) continued the story of *The Substitute*, while *Old Ryerson* (1911) was, in one reviewer's summary, a tale of the evolution of a "a 'dig' to a champion wrestler." *Danny Fists* (1913) told of a hot-tempered prep boy who gets his nickname for sparring with peers. Danny's mother worries that she is raising a thug, but dad is less concerned, figuring that as long as Danny is able to shake off hard feelings after brawls, he is a boy with promise. This fictional pater's tolerance of interpersonal violence was increasingly apparent in the real world of prep schools, where bare-fisted brawls were now assumed to be an indication of virility developing as it should. Danny's father presumes that his son will master self-control when the time comes; in his absence, Yale coaches channel Danny's fighting virtues into controlled and effective aggression. *Captain Danny* (1914) and *Danny the Freshman* (1915) soon followed, holding up the Yale fighting spirit as a universal asset for American males.[20]

Marketers lauded Camp for striking the perfect balance by writing stories that parents approved of as character-building and that interested their sons. One reviewer declared that any prep school dorm without a copy of *Jack Hall* was likely "occupied by a dig or a mollycoddle." With so many football novels to choose from, the *Dial* advised parents to opt for Camp's before all others. Of course, one commentator, noting that Camp did not "pretend to literary art," noticed too that females were conspicuously absent from *The Substitute:* "Parents are not allowed nearer than the sidelines. Professors are kept in the bleachers. Here you shall find prep school teams, freshman teams, scrub teams, varsity teams, coaches and trainers, nose guards, shin guards and moleskins and nothing else." Apparently, Camp thought girls and grinds had little to teach the red-blooded American boy.[21]

Camp did not promote the Danny books as vigilantly as *The Substitute*, perhaps because he did not actually write them. Appleton arranged to have them drafted by William Heyliger, who later became a successful novelist in his own right, and for Camp to approve the final manuscripts. Heyliger checked in with Camp to make sure that his descriptions of Yale life were accurate. "If you have anything that will fit into the general plot—Glee Club, Junior Prom[,] or anything like that, why send it along and I will try to have it fit someplace," he wrote Camp. "I could use a map if I had it, something showing the location of the different places of Yale interest. When do Freshmen select captains for the nine, after a few games have been played, or before the opening game?"[22]

Meanwhile, Camp signed a contract with Hurst to write six 60,000-word manuscripts in short order, assuredly with profit in mind. This level of productivity would have been daunting had he not engaged the services of a less busy man—Yale athletics ticket manager

Everard Thompson. Camp may have done little more than approve storylines for main character Frank Armstrong, a Yale athlete like his others. When the first four installments of the series sold fewer than had been hoped, he took half of the initially agreed-upon royalties and grew offended when editors asked him to assume some of the expense of publicity. Because he did not think the books measured up to his literary standard, he published them under the pseudonym "Matthew Colton," in order to not tarnish his name. It was hard for Armstrong to stand out when he could not be billed as the creation of the "Father of Football." Perhaps the series also suffered because Hurst marketed Frank Armstrong alongside inventors, aviators, Boy Scouts, Navy men, statesmen, and outdoor adventurers, to say nothing of an array of collegiate athletes.[23]

Occasionally, Camp received fan letters asking how closely Jack Hall, Dick Goddard, or Danny Fists resembled real flesh-and-blood Yale men. This was becoming a difficult question to answer, since it was getting harder to identify a typical type among real Yale players. There was three-time All-American Tom Shevlin, for instance, the scion of a millionaire lumber executive. His wealth and physical prowess were as newsworthy as his football, stories abounding about how he boxed against the formidable Jim Corbett and cavorted around New Haven in expensive clothes and cars. He reportedly paid the expenses of classmates anonymously, like a swashbuckling angel in football togs.[24]

Then, too, was Shevlin's captain, a man of more humble beginnings named Jim Hogan, also a three-time All-American. Camp praised the Irishman for working his way through college as he played ball and courted investors of the Yale Bowl. Despite the rigors of the football season, Hogan remained in the top third of his class and was voted "the man who had done most for Yale" in 1904. He was proof that players who courted blueblood investors need not be blue-blooded themselves. Together, he and Shevlin perpetuated a fiction of classlessness at Yale that Camp seized on in his novels, for his success stories appeared to be privileged boys who did not rest on their laurels, or poor boys who pulled themselves up from nothing.[25]

Yale did not admit black students, as Harvard did intermittently, but more working-class and immigrant men found their way to the campus after the turn of the century. Whereas 87 percent of undergraduates came from elite New England families in 1800, that percentage was halved in 1900, in a student body ten times larger. More Yale men were self-supporting, sometimes making ends meet by serving in dining clubs or tutoring in the dorms. Canby noted that his students still teased the bloodless "grinds," but now they had special contempt for "greasy grinds"—their ethnic variation. Italians, Armenians, an occasional Chinese, and Eastern Europeans (namely Polish Jews) now sat in his classes. In fact, Jewish students formed their own fraternity at Yale, the nation's first, though they labeled it nonsectarian to avoid anti-Semitic attacks.[26]

The more frequent appearance on campus of nonconformist "freaks"—the sons of bohemian artists who had been schooled in Europe—and "potential homosexuals" also belied Camp's image of the Yale All-American. Often, these men committed no crime other than exhibiting "adult intellect" in Yale's "society of adolescents," Canby noted, eschewing fraternities and football for chemistry. They had broken unspoken codes, playing the violin, spouting radicalism, knowing about art, wearing silk pajamas, or keeping their hair long when they were not football heroes needing to protect their ears.[27]

On the gridiron, Camp could not ignore the formidable presence of Germans and Irishmen whose parents had immigrated earlier in the nineteenth century and assimilated well enough to send their sons and grandsons to Ivy League schools. After the turn of the century, the Yale eleven fielded its famed "Irish line" featuring Jim Hogan, John Kilpatrick, and Ned Glass. Boys across the country admired their climb to gridiron greatness. One eighteen-year-old of German background told Camp of his ambitions to leave Kentucky to go to Yale, as Hogan had, confessing, "As I have to pay my own way through I would like to go through on my athletics." First-generation Polish and Italian immigrants had reacted ambivalently to rising American sports, but their sons saw sports as an in—as access to the privileges of American life. College football was a fast track like nothing else.[28]

Indeed, the spirit of athletic competition started opening doors at Yale for men who had not come from privilege. And as they proved to be competent in the athletics that mattered most to their peers, the social climate of campus invariably changed. "Veils of glamour in older countries have protected rank and wealth—especially in those college aristocracies nearest to our own," Canby noted, referring to Cambridge and Oxford. "Not so with us. They were stripped away from our young plutocrats. After the sons and heirs who might have formed an American aristocracy of wealth and privilege had been shuffled in the college competitions with the shrewd children of parvenus and the good baseball players whose fathers were Irish policemen, cards were redealt in new social categories."[29] Men were coming to Yale to live a distinctly American dream, one for which the gentleman's code of English sport no longer applied. Winning mattered more to them—less because it brought honor than because it moved them up the social ladder.

Standing between two classes—the privileged and the self-made—and identifying with both when the need arose, Camp seemed ambivalent about the trend. Although most of his fictional characters were from elite backgrounds, he also created Jack Hall, an undergraduate without pedigree but with the work ethic and athletic ability to excel. More and more, this was the kind of man Camp acknowledged as heroic, All-American, and manly in the new century.

But occasionally, there was a bad egg. If former players inspired Camp's fictional heroes, the center of the team of '91, George Foster Sanford, was the antihero about whom Camp rarely spoke, let alone wrote. Sanford was then and forever after a problem child—talented but unscrupulous, and thus an embarrassment to his former coach. His eligibility had been suspect in 1893 when he played ostensibly as a law student but attended class so rarely that the dean called for his disqualification from the team. Sanford's ethics came into greater question in 1899, when he accepted $5,000 to coach at Columbia. Unlike the contracts of other former players, this one made Camp uneasy; the money was exorbitant because Columbia's athletic department figured that Sanford would divulge more about Yale tactics than Camp would ever approve, and they were right. Camp's worst fears materialized when Sanford coached Columbia to its first victory against Yale that fall. The *Evening Telegram* reported that Sanford's men "outrushed, out-tackled, outgeneraled and outplayed at every point." Camp's coaching had been used against him.[30]

But gentlemen lost with dignity, and Camp was a gentleman. He congratulated Sanford in the press, although privately, he turned on him. The problem was not just that Sanford beat him; Camp was pretty sure that he did it by violating the amateur code. Rumors swirled that Sanford recruited men using financial inducements and placed these recruits on a student roster so that they looked like undergraduates. When Columbia president Seth Low asked Camp to sign a statement verifying that he thought the players on the Columbia roster were legitimate, Camp strategically refused. While it looked vindictive to blow the whistle on Sanford's ring himself, Camp quietly pointed Columbia administrators in the direction of members of the board of governors of the Knickerbocker Athletic Club, who knew details about how Sanford acquired his quarterback and other questionable players.[31]

Investigations confirmed that at least four Columbia players had their tuition paid and that others dined at the team training table free of charge. Columbia officials had seemed largely not to care about the situation until football managers announced that the team was $400 in the red. In fact, the captains of Columbia's other sports charged that Sanford's salary and his inducements to players had bankrupted the entire athletics department. Suddenly, it was corruption that could not be ignored.[32]

Inspired by the faculty of the Western Conference to purify sports across colleges, Brown University president George Munro had convened representatives of Eastern schools in 1898 for the purpose of instituting stronger amateur guidelines. Every institution of the modern-day Ivy League was represented in Providence except Yale; Camp insisted that there was no reason to attend when Yale athletes did such a fine job of regulating themselves. Under his advisement, Yale had adopted "the strictest set of eligibility rules of any of the colleges," he assured President Hadley. And thus, without him in attendance, representatives at Brown drew up a list of recommendations for bringing balance back to campuses, including stricter faculty control of playing schedules and entrance requirements, transparent student transfers, and the banning of off-season practice and training tables.[33]

In the end, the Brown guidelines were never formally enforced, perhaps because following them would have made it harder for schools to be as profitable and victorious as Yale. Still, it gnawed at Camp that the conference participants did not acknowledge his earlier efforts to set eligibility guidelines. In 1882, for instance, he had proposed that member institutions of the IFA not allow men to play in championship games for more than five years, not coincidentally after he had personally played in them for six. Eventually, he called for proof of men's enrollment and satisfactory academic performance in full schedules of coursework, and he had Yale men sign affidavits attesting to the fact. He proposed making freshmen ineligible for the varsity until they had a year of academic work behind them. No Yale man, in other words, would be able to simply walk on campus and play for a team. By insisting on full academic schedules, he hoped to shrink the "galaxy of graduates" on rosters. He called it the "Undergraduate Plan."[34]

Of course, the Brown meeting would not have occurred had Camp's guidelines found universal acceptance. In practice, each university created its own rules and lobbied for them at IFA meetings. It became commonplace to see talented players at one school suddenly appear at another. Sometimes they attended classes, but often they did not; they were "tramp players," essentially selling their wares. Caspar Whitney lamented that men in the West were bought and sold like cattle, refusing to admit that the elite schools in the East had started the trend. In early days, Harvard men accused Princeton of being the greatest offender of eligibility guidelines, leading to sentiment for a "dual league" in Cambridge and New Haven for a time.[35]

Harvard and Princeton men were both known to visit the prep schools to snatch up talent before others could. Camp took the higher road, or so he claimed, telling his football captains not to stoop to offering inducements. And yet he turned a blind eye when Mike Murphy made unofficial excursions to Exeter, and Exeter men appeared in New Haven the following fall. The elite prep schools also funneled players into the college game who were already in their twenties, making Stagg far from unusual when he started for Yale at twenty-seven. A man on Woodruff's Penn squad was reportedly in his thirties, with a family to feed. Even Yale's golden child Jim Hogan, twenty-three when he finished at Exeter, was given tuition, scholarships, a vacation to Cuba, and the right to sell cigarettes on campus during his All-America years.[36]

So, true enough, Camp made gestures to curb professionalism—and yet it thrived right under his nose. The cases most out in the open did not occur in football, at least not yet, but rather in baseball, where playing for money had already been institutionalized. The advent of the Cincinnati Red Stockings, the first paid nine, in 1869, was followed by the organization of the National Association of Professional Baseball Players in 1871, the National League in 1876, and the competing American League in 1901. Still, athletic directors maintained the fiction that college men were not paid to play baseball. They denied knowing that collegiate athletes often changed their names to compete in the off-season, if not in the pros, then in the summer resorts of the White Mountains or down South for hotel and club teams.[37]

In theory, Camp thought the baseball diamond was a perfectly acceptable place for a young man when he was not in the classroom and that nothing was wrong with paying his expenses. The dangerous precedent was set when he received compensation above and beyond making him square. To avoid the slippery slope, Camp's official stance was that men should play for no compensation whatsoever—not room, board, or money—to be eligible for a college team. The ban also applied to men who took handouts before college, often before they knew they were breaking the amateur code. Camp issued statements against summer baseball year after year, as did Stagg and prominent athletic directors, but the abuses never ceased. The truth was that eligibility rules were harder to enforce as more of the nation's college athletes were boys without trust funds, students who worked on family farms or held jobs to pay expenses while they participated in college sports.[38]

Camp's sensitivity to the socioeconomics of the situation was apparent in an article he wrote for *Century* in 1901, as he described a typical scenario: A college hopeful waits tables at a summer resort and the proprietor hires him for his athletic prowess. He gets room and board to play baseball after his shift, and soon gets a cut of the gate receipts. "Even before he ha[s] reached college he [has been] contaminated with the touch of professionalism," Camp noted sympathetically. The man who played summer baseball was the same man who was seduced by recruiters and ate for free at the training table. "[We] have well high driven those who love sport for its own sake to turn to the English system of caste as the only one likely to keep the sports really the sports of gentlemen," he wrote with seeming regret.[39]

Cultural biases and class-conscious fears shaped much of the debate on the finer points of professionalism. Caspar Whitney likened the amateur athlete to the aristocratic Lord Greystoke—a gentleman hardened by the physicality of his primitive environment, yet a gentleman no less. The professional athlete, meanwhile, he viewed as his cultural antithesis: a powerful ape not yet accommodated by the civilized world. As for Camp, he found himself in the impossible position of having to plead the ethicalness of a snobbish philosophy of amateurism when a professional element generated profits and wider interest in college sports. Rather than denounce obvious abuses, he often resorted to delineating between good and bad strains of professional behavior. It was not always a bugbear, he explained in *Outing*: Take for instance the work of umpires and referees—examples of paid specialization for the better. All was well, he argued, as long as students were never corrupted.[40]

Camp liked to say that professionalism was less prominent in football than in baseball—that gentlemanliness still prevailed in his game—but his insistence on this point looked like willful ignorance after a while. Semiprofessional elevens had sprouted up first in Pennsylvania and Ohio, and collegiate men knew how to tap them if they were not tapped to play for them first. Non-collegiate clubs like the Orange and Crescent in Manhattan and the Boston Athletic Association (BAA) even played against Big Three teams, while the Olympic and Reliance Clubs played collegians of the California Football League. Camp distanced himself from the professional game by writing exclusively about college ball, but he was surely aware of college men playing on club football teams. One of the first who cashed in was none other than Yale's Pudge Heffelfinger, who played for the Allegheny Athletic Association as early as 1892. For a single game, he was paid $500 under the table; a Pittsburgh club had offered him $250, but he thought the offer too low to risk jeopardizing his amateur status.[41]

Camp did not speak publicly about Heff's transgression, and yet it not so coincidentally occurred the year Camp lobbied with renewed intensity for stricter eligibility guidelines at Yale. Undergraduates passed his freshman rule, requiring enrollment in classes fulltime before playing on a varsity team and limiting players to four years of varsity play. Transfers from another college had to show sufficient grades for a year before being considered for a varsity sport. Yale also adopted Camp's undergraduate rule in 1893, to be renegotiated in 1894. The move was highly strategic since Yale's law program was an undergraduate department. Some of Harvard's best players, notably black center

William Henry Lewis, attended the graduate law school, and hence would be ineligible under the same guidelines. A Yale man called the undergraduate rule "a dandy" that would "hit Harvard in fine style" if adhered to. Camp called it self-regulation at its finest.[42]

His zealous efforts made Yale men appear above the taint of professionalism, but all the while, Caspar Whitney was scrutinizing Yale rosters for violators of the amateur code, and definitely finding a few. In 1900, he had evidence to prove that members of Yale's baseball and crew teams coached and played for hotels the summer before, and he threatened to publish what he knew if Camp did not clean up his house. So Camp refurbished the school's eligibility rules and distributed them to prospective athletes at prep schools. In 1901, the *Boston Post* printed the headline "Yale's New Rules: Amateur Requirements Made More Strict in Interest of Purity."[43]

Apparently, Camp did not distribute the rules widely enough. James Sullivan, president of the AAU, lamented that "in many parts of this country to-day among school-boys no attention is paid to the amateur definition." And then there were boys who paid attention but were confused, like Bert Jenkins of Harvard City, Michigan, who wrote directly to Camp: "I am coaching this city's football team, for a certain amount, and I play with them—but in my contract I have it understood that if I should play with them after coaching to do that as a favor—not for money. Does this make me a professional?" A teen named Francis Hoffman wrote Camp explaining that he had played on a factory nine and accepted a portion of the gate receipts. Although he had not previously considered going to college, he had now changed his mind and wondered if he was eligible to play at Yale.[44] Even a college administrator asked Camp for clarification:

Last year this man, a Freshman, played with the Cheyenne Baseball Team as a pitcher and worked his way in the RR Shops at the time. In one of the games he performed a star play which saved the Team from defeat. The people in the Grand Stand were so delighted that they passed around a hat and the sum of $7.50 was thrown to him from the Stand. He boyishly took it thinking that it was alright and with no idea at all that it might be construed as pay by rival College Football Teams later. . . . We wish to do the square thing and accordingly desire your opinion.[45]

Camp had bad news for these prospects, especially now that violations in the Big Three made national headlines. Harvard's Athletic Committee had suspicions about a Yale man named Dirk Sheldon, who had connections with the NYAC and possibly coached a school team for money before coming to New Haven. More consequential allegations followed regarding Yale guard Ned Glass, who had played previously at Mercersburg Academy. At a towering 6' 4 ½" and 211 pounds, Glass was intimidating and a shoo-in for the All-America team. Although he was in good academic standing, Harvard men discovered that he had played at Syracuse University before going to Mercersburg; Harvard argued that, according to Camp's own guidelines, Glass's previous college experience made him ineligible to play at Yale for another year.[46]

Yale captain Charles Gould refused to see how the rule applied in Glass's case, given his more recent prep school enrollment, but Camp knew that it looked hypocritical to press the issue. He advised Gould to bench Glass, at least for the big games against Harvard and Princeton, which Gould accepted with great reluctance. A prominent Yale graduate in Boston agreed that there was no other choice from a public relations point of view: "It is pretty hard to lose Glass, I agree, especially when Harvard has a graduate of Bates and a graduate of Northwestern on its team, both of whom played one or more years on university teams before coming to Harvard, and especially when they are playing three men twenty-eight years of age. . . . But they have the luck to be inside the rule, though outside the spirit, and we have the ill luck, as I understand it, to be outside the rule and inside the spirit."[47]

An opportunity for retaliation came just before the Harvard-Yale game. Camp received information regarding the big, twenty-eight-year-old Harvard tackle Oliver Cutts. According to informants, Cutts had been an athlete at Bates for three years, took a position at Haverford Prep teaching math, and then entered Harvard Law School. Apparently, while at Haverford, Cutts also took payments for boxing lessons, making him a professional and thus ineligible for collegiate football.[48] Today, his activities would not disqualify him, but the N4A had established back in the 1880s that remuneration for athletic activities of any kind—playing, betting, or coaching—was professionalism that disqualified. Cutts's salary as a math instructor was never questioned; Yale athletes also tutored to cover expenses. But athletic coaching was different. Camp always insisted that his instruction of Yale men was proper because it was unpaid—a sort of patriotic service to the school. Cutts's coaching, however, even of sports other than football, tainted him then and forever after, as if professionalism were an incurable disease.

Camp pounced on what he knew. He claimed that unsolicited evidence poured into his office, including a course catalog listing Cutts as an instructor in physical culture and a bill for his services as a boxing trainer of schoolboys. In 1899, Cutts apparently received $15 for lessons he gave at 75 cents per half hour. Some of this information was leaked to the press, but Camp made sure that he did not look like the one who leaked it. Behind the scenes, he sent men to Cambridge to talk to Ira Hollis, the engineering professor who headed the Harvard Athletic Committee, hoping Hollis would be grateful for the discretion and would bench Cutts himself. When reporters asked Camp for his opinion on the case, he would not comment, and he asked players not to do so either. Meanwhile, Hollis claimed to have looked into Cutts's standing and turned up nothing.

Cutts played in the big game, and Harvard proceeded to destroy Yale that weekend by a score of 22 to 0. And then, remarkably, Cutts's memory of said payments was suddenly jarred. He remembered the money he earned for athletic training, but said he thought nothing of it at the time because he was ignorant of the rules defining amateur status. Yale men thought the timing of his confession convenient, but of course, so were their allegations.[49]

All the public cordiality hid the fact that relations between Harvard and Yale were fraying again, just as their five-year athletic agreement was up for renegotiation. Hollis invited Yale managers and captains to Cambridge. Camp politely declined for the undergraduates but agreed to come as their liaison. He had convinced Yale managers to form a committee on athletic intercollegiate relations, and though it was undergraduate in majority and installed by vote at a mass meeting, it empowered him, and only him, to carry on negotiations with colleges. To President Hadley, he admitted that he had come up with the new machinery to preserve the look of "undergraduate management, and yet at the same time not run too great risk of wreck on the rock of some single individual who reached the office [of manager], but who was not competent to fill it." Once again, he had masterminded a way to have pull in the name of student self-governance.[50]

Camp arrived in Cambridge by train on February 14, 1902, and dined with Hollis at the Hotel Touraine. They spoke about mending fences, but Hollis was perturbed by reports coming out of New Haven that he acted like a despot and that Yale men wanted him to resign from the Harvard Athletic Committee. He ranted on until midnight; Camp could not soothe him. The next morning, Camp wasted no time, laying out terms for another five-year agreement, which he represented as the wishes of the Yale undergraduates. Hollis would not agree to anything without a formal conference between graduates and faculty, a position that he swore was endorsed by Harvard undergraduates. Camp doubted that was true, but he waited patiently for faculty approvals of the new athletic agreement, which finally came in March.[51]

The new contract did not end debate on how to define an eligible athlete, which became a problem when Yale graduates confirmed once again that Harvard was fielding a questionable player, a center named Emmett King. Affidavits surfaced from men who claimed they played with him in Indiana for four years before King entered law school and played for Harvard. A Yale graduate even presented Camp with evidence of King organizing a team in Indiana that played other teams for profit.[52]

The King case and others forced Camp to meet with representatives from Harvard and Princeton to hammer out a formal eligibility policy to which the Big Three would adhere. Camp stipulated that players on major teams be limited to undergraduates, strictly construed. He wanted to be able to take contested cases to a board of arbitrators, but Harvard preferred that cases go through its Athletic Committee. Back and forth the parties went until several key guidelines were approved. College degree holders were barred from play, as were first-year men until they took a full year of courses and passed examinations well enough to advance with their class. The undergraduate rule allowed only men in the general college and scientific schools to play on varsity teams. "Special" students were not eligible unless vouched for by a dean. Four years of varsity play was the maximum time allowed any man, and years were counted cumulatively between institutions. These rules went into effect in September 1906.[53]

While Camp debated eligibility, his former wayward player Foster Sanford attempted a return to Yale football. He met with Yale secretary

Anson Phelps Stokes in Manhattan and seemed a reformed man, confessing that Columbia's generous salary had corrupted him, but now he was cured. If he would not be permitted to coach at Yale, he wanted to serve as a trainer for its major teams. Stokes was willing to consider it if Camp was amenable, but former Yale All-American Vance McCormick urged him not to be, blaming Sanford for tainting Columbia football "with professionalism and rowdyism." "The only football he knows is 'mucker' football, just what we're trying to get away from," McCormick railed. "At West Point last year I heard him in the dressing room coach[ing] our centers to slug. I hope you will use any influence you have to prevent Yale being disgraced with such an instructor." Many alumni seconded McCormick's sentiments.[54]

Sanford had become the poster child for professionalism gone amuck in college football. It did not much matter that he was a competent coach, or that other men could have just as rightly taken a place on the poster. Stokes gave Sanford the polite snub that Camp asked him to give, but Sanford still tried to return. Occasionally, he left his office at the New York Life Insurance Company to ride up to New Haven, hoping that if he could not coach, he could at least take his turn as an assistant or trainer. But Camp made sure that Sanford was banned during public practices and games. The headmaster of St. Mark's School assured Yale authorities that, while mentoring his students, Sanford's "conduct and conversation with the boys was of the right sort." However, he allegedly attended a Groton game without announcing himself to the home coach, causing men to accuse him of scouting.[55]

Nearly every coach in the Northeast, including Camp, scouted routinely, but when Sanford appeared at games, it seemed scandalous. He had become the scapegoat for Yale's indiscretions, an example usefully hauled out when charges of dirty play came dangerously close to tarnishing Camp and his men. With perseverance, Sanford found coaching jobs at Northwestern, Virginia, Army, and finally at Rutgers, where he was well compensated and respected. Camp praised his work for other teams but shunned him in New Haven, because there, men did not pay players or get paid to coach—not officially anyway. As the rest of the country headed down the road toward professionalism, Camp saw to it that Yale appeared to be above the fray.

8

Make Men, but Do Not Break Them, 1903–1906

PUBLICLY, CAMP SEEMED NOT TO budge in his adherence to the tenets of amateurism. But his attitude toward the rules governing play on the football field was more flexible. The college rulebook went through regular revision, for better or worse. Camp responded graciously to feedback he received from coaches, alumni, players, and fans, which came in face-to-face meetings and in hundreds of letters sent to him from across the country. He thought all this interest in the game a good thing; it told him that people cared enough to make football evolve to fulfill societal needs. Because football changed, it would always be relevant.

Football was now viewed by many as a moral imperative in American life, a game that generated physical and emotional outlets for players and spectators, as well as patriotism for alma mater that Camp and college officials approvingly called "esprit de corps." As campuses grew more diverse, football united students under a common banner; Camp thought it the purest form of democracy. The president of Western Reserve University agreed that there was no more wholesome instrument for ending "indifferentism" on campus, and he could not deny that football brought prestige and profit. In Camp's hands, football players appeared to sacrifice nobly in the name of lofty ideals, and yet nothing fueled commercialism in the university more than football matches that brought thousands of paying customers to the stands.[1]

In response to the growing concerns of game officials, in 1903, the rules committee revamped the college playing field, turning the familiar gridiron into a waffle iron for a time. It was not a change that Camp heartily endorsed, but the additional markings helped to track a quarterback's movement east and west as well as north and south—at least until the rules limiting the quarterback's movements changed again and hash marks came into use. In the spirit of experimentation, Camp tried this solution until better suggestions came along. John Heisman, who had coached at Oberlin and Auburn and had just left Clemson for Georgia Tech, told Camp following the season of 1903 that he thought the squares on the field distracting. He recommended instead that the quarterback be allowed to cross the line of scrimmage as long as he went anywhere outside the second man from the snapper on the rush line. This would do away with the need for cross lines, he explained, while making it easier for the referee and runner, since they tended not to have their eyes focused on the ground. Camp thanked him for the suggestion and said he would take it under advisement.[2]

Heisman had other ideas too, good ones, it turned out, ones that were already being considered by the Southern Intercollegiate Athletics Association, regardless of the rules in the Northeast. He proposed making it mandatory that seven men assemble on the line of scrimmage, for instance, as well as giving medical advisors the power to stop play to tend to injured men on the field. To Heisman, these were not minor adjustments, but imperative solutions to a problem much bigger than distracting chalk lines. In his coaching experience, he had yet again witnessed an unacceptable number of men being maimed on the football field.

Heisman was hardly alone in sounding alarms: Camp received mail in droves, sent by concerned bystanders wanting more safety legislated into football, at both the high school and college levels. If they had not personally witnessed severe injuries, his correspondents were unnerved by press reports of death tolls ratcheting up since Camp had been asked to make adjustments to the rules in 1894. Football reportedly caused thirty-five deaths directly or indirectly in 1903, in addition to eleven cases of paralysis and over 500 "severe" injuries to college and high school males.[3]

Under the headline "The Pathology of Football," a journalist noted the frequent occurrence of tenosynovitis, dislocation of the xiphoid, and hematoma of the ear in practices and games; and high school athletic directors worried about the long-term effects of injuries on bodies that were still growing. One athletic director in Missouri told Camp that the sentiment against football was mounting in his section of the country and that he liked Coach Stagg's idea of a separate, safer set of rules for high school boys. Contributors to the *American Physical Education Review* reiterated that this was a matter of urgency, since 78 percent of American high schools now had football squads. More boys were playing under Camp's guidelines than those regulating any other extracurricular activity.[4]

Camp agreed that younger boys needed protections, as they were not yet physically ready to be made men through his game. But an athletic director in New York told him that regulations at the high school level would prove to be insufficient, given the abuses he had witnessed. There were postgraduate men playing in the high school ranks, he reported. Some of them did not have grades good enough to attend college, and yet prep schools gave them scholarships to play football against younger students. "A boy of 16, weighing one hundred and twenty pounds is compelled to play against men of twenty-two,—three,—four years of age." Would injuries be less severe, he asked Camp, if boys were physically matched?[5]

The deluge of stories in the press about death and maiming on high school gridirons suggested that he had a point. In 1903 alone, boys reportedly died of broken necks and backs, concussions, fractured skulls, ruptured arteries, and internal injuries. Camp said he was concerned, but he also harkened back to the time when English papers had included men killed in saloons after games in their tabulations of American football fatalities. The important thing to note, he emphasized, was that death and serious injury were not occurring at the big colleges and universities, where men were presumably so well conditioned that injuries did not befall them.[6]

Big Three respondents for *Football, Facts, and Figures* generally supported this theory back in 1894, but in 1903, medical professionals poked holes in Camp's elitist logic. In the *Boston Medical and Surgical Journal*, physicians revealed a startling number of injuries to Harvard players the previous fall: Of the 150 men on the squad, only seventy played throughout the season, the rest forced out by injuries. Men suffered broken bones and damage to knees and ankles, as well as the permanent loss of teeth. More shocking were the frequent concussions, which were detected more often by medical professionals on the sidelines than by the players themselves. Players minimized these injuries after the season. One reported that he had recovered "except for a slight loss of vision," while another admitted "a slight dullness in the side of his head" and "a bloodshot eye," but thought himself no worse for the wear. They accepted their injuries as collateral damage and wore them as badges of honor.[7]

Camp would have approved; keeping a stiff upper lip was proof that a boy was being made virile by football. His medical proof came in the form of reports by Dr. William Lee Howard, who confirmed that the game's physical rigors were positively transformative: "As a physician who daily sees mental and moral instabilities—the result of indifferent fathers, coddling mothers, and complacent teachers I say to college authorities: Place no barriers subjectively or objectively, against football." Former Harvard man turned Senator Henry Cabot Lodge agreed that the gridiron provided a necessary amount of physical punishment—"the price which the English-speaking race has paid for being world conquerors." At Yale, Professor Eugene Richards continued to extol football's man-making effects; as more undergraduates came from cities, he believed the game "the best antidote to the dudish spirit" in this "effeminate class" of men. His views were seconded by Yale President Arthur Hadley, and at Brown, President W. H. P. Faunce agreed that men "ought to have one 'rough' game in college."[8]

Although Camp had important college administrators and faculty on his side, others emphatically disagreed about the merits of football. University of Wisconsin historian Frederick Jackson Turner thought it too brutish to be man-making, despite Camp's claim that Turner's own thesis on the closing frontier proved football was a social imperative. Camp called his game a safety valve for male animalistic tendencies that could no longer be channeled into conquering Native Americans and settling the West. But Turner doubted that football was an ideal replacement, witnessing firsthand how it led to student truancy, gambling, and hooliganism in Madison, much as it had in 1894. Shailer Mathews of Chicago's Divinity School did not mince words when he called football "a boy-killing, education prostituting, gladiatorial sport," echoing college presidents during the football crisis ten years earlier.[9]

Former player Fred Murphy, now a Yale team physician, warned Camp that the medical reports out of Harvard were creating havoc at medical meetings and fueling his critics. It was only a matter of time before they would create a public-relations nightmare from which football would not recover, he told Camp, so "get in the first blow." Murphy's data on Yale men seemed to suggest that he patched up players perfectly well, with no long-term adverse effects, so Camp made sure his statistics were widely distributed. But encouraging news out of New Haven could not drown out what was reported around the country. Even compared to boxing, football looked savage as written up in the nation's sports pages. A special dispatch to the *Times* reported on a bill legalizing four-round bouts of boxing in New York, the decision to pass it rationalized by studies confirming that the ring was safer than the gridiron. Senators cited only four deaths in boxing in 1904 compared to twenty-six in football, which, they reminded, was played only three months a year.[10]

These were the damning stories that brought football apologists out of the woodwork, many of them turning to Camp first and foremost to help build a defense for the game. Desperate for exonerating statistics, a former football player turned local journalist in New York State asked Camp,

Will you please tell me how many men in the United States played football during the fall of 1902[?] What is taking in High Schools, Town teams, etc. also the number that were killed, and if possible will you kindly tell whether they were white, or colored, did they play on school teams, or on town teams, and whether they understood the game or not[?] The reason that I am asking you these questions Mr. Camp, is this. Somebody wrote a piece on football, and put it into our county paper, they ran it down about as hard as they could, and compared it with prizefighting. I should like to put a few facts before the public, and show them that the most accidents occur in games played by town teams or where the rougher class play, such as drinking men, an[d] men without principle.[11]

The data this journalist sought varied greatly from one reported study to another, and Camp's empirical evidence was selective. One report estimated that a serious injury or death had occurred in one of every 400 boys who played; another determined the ratio to be closer to 1 in 7. Edwin Dexter, a professor at the University of Illinois, helped Camp stave off hysteria with his ten-year study that put football in a better light. After analyzing data from fifty-eight colleges, he determined that only 2.9 percent of football participants suffered serious injury at the collegiate level. Comparing 31,000 insurance claims filed over the previous five years, he also ascertained that horseback riding, baseball, swimming, wrestling, bowling, hunting, tennis, canoeing, and gym work were more dangerous than football. Camp printed the reassuring numbers in the 1904 edition of *Spalding's Official Foot Ball Guide*.[12]

When Dexter had solicited Camp for data on Yale's injured, Camp had assured him that the only injuries on the books were "trifling" and would remain so because competent trainers and graduate coaches supervised his men. Nevertheless, in 1904, he quietly kept his own tally of injuries in the collegiate game and became startled. Week after week, men proved unfit to play in games, not just at Illinois, Wisconsin, and Michigan, but at Harvard, Princeton, and Yale, where he insisted the men were fitter. Although most injuries were minor, the sheer number was disturbing, some teams suffering five or six injuries in a single week. An English acquaintance suggested to Camp that American football might be more compelling if the "armor" and medical equipment on the sidelines had not become such a distraction: "Why is it that the Field itself so oft resembles a Hospital? Is not the very appearance of the American player a severe criticism of the American game?"[13]

Former Harvard player J. Mott Hallowell forced Camp to address the trends when he published a critique of football rules as they stood. In the *Yale Alumni Weekly*, Camp itemized proposed amendments in response, his most radical being a reconsideration of the yardage required for a first down. If men had to cover ten yards in three tries, instead of five yards, he thought the game would open up, thus reducing injuries caused by pile-ons and dirty plays that officials could

not see when bodies were close together. He had offered the suggestion back in 1894, and it had fallen on deaf ears, but now football men
pondered it thoughtfully. Stagg liked the ten-yard rule, and Fielding
Yost of Michigan thought it practicable between the twenty-five-yard
hash marks. Others thought it wiser to do away with Camp's coveted
interference or expand the quarterback's arsenal of plays. Heisman and
Henry Williams wondered if the best solution was simply to allow the
forward pass.[14]

The forward pass: For all Camp's foresight and innovation, this was
the one play he worried would alter the complexion of football too
radically to be taken seriously. It was not a play that required high
skill, in his opinion, and he worried that it allowed luck to factor too
much in the outcomes of games. Gains in yardage could happen acci-
dentally with the forward pass, or be made by smaller, less physically
robust men who had not endured the character-building, one-on-one
struggles on the line. He did not think players earned aerial yardage
with hard work. Touchdowns could become, as he put it, "miracles,"
flukes, anti-science—rather than the consequence of ordered, reasoned
workings of the machine. Men on the rules committee agreed that
"alter[ing] the basic scientific principles" of football "would prove a
very bad mistake." "We have been educated up to battles of the giants
and we will never be satisfied with the scrimmages of the lightweights,"
a Penn rule-maker told the *Pittsburg Press*.[15]

Nevertheless, when Camp spoke to football men in Chicago in
1904, it was apparent that a more open style of play, allowing for more
speed and general interest for the spectator, had already caught hold
in the West, where resentment against the Northeastern oligarchy was
palpable. Since the previous football crisis, Westerners felt that the
rules committee largely ignored their concerns. In 1895, they asserted
independence by forming their own sectional committee, which
allowed for more faculty control of athletics. The Big Nine—Purdue,
Northwestern, Chicago, Iowa, Wisconsin, Minnesota, Michigan,
Indiana, and Illinois—prided themselves on focusing on what was best
for the student rather than the amateur, worrying less about payments
to players than whether or not they showed up for class. As a result,
players were less obsessed with winning, they argued, and hence
resorted to fewer acts of brutality that maimed and killed.[16]

Camp sensed that facets of the Western game were not going away, especially since Southerners had adopted a similar point of view. The shifting tides had already led him to incorporate some Big Nine regulations into the football rules and to select Michigan's Willie Heston for the All-America team. Yost urged him also to consider Stagg for the rules committee. Camp agreed that it was a needed peace offering. With Stagg in the mix, he could curb complaints that the rules committee had grown elitist and out of touch.[17]

And so it happened. Now the committee consisted of Paul Dashiell of Navy as chairman, Camp as secretary, Louis Dennis of Cornell, John Fine of Princeton, John Bell of Penn, Stagg, and William Reid, the new twenty-six-year-old head coach of Harvard. Camp remembered young Reid from his years coaching in California, when Reid's father managed to get Camp to coach his son's secondary school eleven for a single afternoon. Camp's visit left an impression, for the reedy Reid bulked up, went on to Harvard, and developed into one of the best backfield players in the game. Having broken with the tradition of graduate coaches, the Crimson hired Reid for an unprecedented $7,000, half paid by the university and half by alumni. Harvard men charged him with achieving for Harvard the successes that Camp had achieved at Yale.[18]

But Reid was in a precarious position. To some extent, his decision to be on the rules committee had been based on self-preservation. Herbert White, a former Harvard football manager, had telephoned Reid to tell him that the Harvard overseers had secretly voted to abolish football. Reid's reaction was to immediately gather his assistants and draft a letter to the Harvard Athletic Association that expressed strong criticism of the game as played, called for radical change, and presented him as a true reformer. The letter had its desired effect, thwarting a ban, at least temporarily.[19]

It became clear, however, that other members of the rules committee were less motivated than Reid to make radical revisions—or even meet to discuss them. After many failed attempts to coordinate schedules, the committee finally gathered in the spring of 1905. All agreed that a more open game was desirable, but Camp opposed limiting the offense or defense too dramatically, and he swayed the rest. Someone proposed that men back up farther off the line, but Camp, Stagg, and Bell would not hear of it. Camp proposed his ten-yard idea, but his colleagues worried that it would force them to tweak other rules too profoundly. Frustrated by the stalemate, John Bell motioned over and over for the committee to adjourn, so it did at half past three in the morning, with nothing accomplished. The rumors were true, Reid told Eliot. The rules committee really was "a tool of Camp's," and he thought it should be abolished.[20]

Reid did not know when the committee would meet again. Stagg went off to a water cure in Indiana, and Camp, who was busy coaching the Yale nine that spring, announced that he was leaving on a six-week business trip to England. Caspar Whitney was appalled at the committee's inaction, charging that members seemed to harbor "schoolboy resentment against those who love Rome more than Caesar." It "has again demonstrated its unfitness for either the responsibility of legislating for the players, or of the trust of the college world," he complained, and he criticized Camp for not resigning in protest. Camp defended himself, insisting that he was a true reformer who was just not being heard. "Somewhat over a year ago [I] advocated the opening of the game by the introduction of the rule making it necessary to gain ten yards instead of five in three attempts," he explained. "The suggestion was not accepted."[21]

"Talk is pretty cheap," Whitney responded. Knowing that his colleagues had no interest in his ten-yard rule, why had Camp not floated a more viable plan? More to the point, why did Camp's committee fear radical reform in the first place? Obviously, teams with representation in the IFA—Harvard, Yale, Princeton, Wesleyan, and Penn—had perfected a style of play and wanted rules to conform to it to keep control within their privileged ranks. But John Bell betrayed a deeper reason when he confessed to a reporter that his hesitancy to legislate roughness out of the game was tied to fears of emasculation. The underlying truth was that the very ruggedness of football was what made it useful to college men. Now into the second term of his presidency, Theodore Roosevelt concurred: "We cannot afford to turn out college men who shrink from physical effort or from a little physical pain," he told reporters. His proof that physical courage made leaders was his cabinet—Secretaries Shaw, Taft, Moody, Cortelyou, Morton, and Metcalf—a lineup of former college athletes and gridiron men.[22]

Roosevelt insisted that as one of the few rugged activities still available to urban boys, football had to have its place—the nation's future leadership depended on it. And yet he thought reform of dirty play was in order, less because such conduct caused damage to men's bodies than to their characters. Having just ended a war in the Far East, mediated between France and Germany over Morocco, approved the Food and Drug Act, and negotiated an end to railroad rate disputes, he had turned the White House into a bully pulpit of Progressive paternalism. Unlike the rules committee, his reputation was not for elitism or inaction. And so in October 1905, he invited Camp to lunch at the White House with Edwin Nichols and Reid of Harvard, and John Fine and Arthur Hildebrand of Princeton. Camp brought Yale's current graduate coach, John Owsley, with him to round out the Big Three, and Roosevelt also invited secretary of war and Bonesman William Howard Taft, a good-faith gesture to Yale men. Taft was out of town, so Elihu Root, secretary of state, attended the meeting instead.[23]

Roosevelt wrote his son Kermit at Groton: "Today I see the football men of Harvard, Yale, and Princeton, to try to get them to come to a gentleman's agreement not to have mucker play." The meeting was especially urgent now that Teddy Jr. was trying out for Harvard's freshman team. On the morning of October 9, the Big Three representatives sat around a table in the White House dining room, Camp to the president's immediate right. "Football is on trial," Roosevelt began. "Because I believe in the game, I want to do all I can to save it. And so I have called you all down here to see whether you won't all agree to abide by both the letter and spirit of the rules, for that will help." He added that he was personally aware of instances of coaches encouraging men to commit fouls that put opponents out, as long as officials did not see them. It would take just one incident, a high-profile death on the gridiron, he reminded them, to lose public favor and banish football for good.[24]

Camp appeared to listen intently before yet again proposing his ten-yard rule as a panacea. He made his case to no avail, but no one had better alternatives. Roosevelt waited. Then, having to tend to presidential matters, he left his guests to work out their differences on the White House porch. They talked for two more hours and then adjourned, having little to show for themselves. Knowing that they would need something for the morning editions, Camp drafted a public statement on the train ride home:

> At a meeting with the President of the United States it was agreed that we consider an honorable obligation existed to carry out in letter and in spirit the rules of the game of football relating to roughness, holding and foul-play and the active coaches of the University being present with us pledge themselves to so regard it to do their utmost to carry out these obligations.[25]

There was no mention of rule changes in the statement, and yet Roosevelt telegraphed Camp to tell him that he heartily approved. George Sawyer, a Yale man who had been in Washington during the meeting, expressed frustration to Taft afterward that Camp's ten-yard proposal was ignored: "I think a strong word should come promptly in favor of Walter Camp's rule, and incidentally, that he should have the credit due to a gentleman and a conscientious, high-minded, far-seeing man who anticipated the present criticism and was stubbornly resisted in the Rules Committee." To this Yale man and others, Camp's conduct was above reproach.[26]

Reid, however, thought Camp acted less nobly at the White House, describing him as "slippery" in his polite but firm denials of having knowledge of, let alone responsibility for, dirty play on the gridiron. Privately, Roosevelt asked Camp why the forward pass remained off the table, to which Camp responded:

> Those who wish to open the game . . . fritter away their energies in manifold suggestions, forward passing, placing men in prescribed squares and a dozen other things. . . . If Reid would join me in fighting for the ten-yard rule we could carry the thing through, and that would mean the opening of the play, the elimination of all concealed acts, the opportunity for more men of average or even light weight, the lessening of the more serious injuries like those to the head and spine which come from close play. . . . But this means a struggle with the present players and coaches and I shall certainly need help, even at home, to convert them.[27]

That weekend, Roosevelt heard that his son had been "laid out" on the Harvard practice field. Teddy Jr. emerged from a pile with a bloodied face from a cut to his eye. Weeks later, he stood his ground on the line against Yale freshmen when his nose was smashed, causing him to need reconstructive surgery. Harvard fans complained that he had been singled out. As he should have, Roosevelt responded; his son was the smallest player at 130 pounds, and hence the weakest link on the field. He assured Camp that Teddy Jr. had not been dished an uppercut or treated with malicious intent. Such were the casualties of battle, and they hardened the men who suffered them. Teddy Jr. had no gripes, Roosevelt reiterated. Like his father, he could take his licks like a man.[28]

Although the American president objected little to the present state of football, many American college presidents complained that the statement out of the White House conference was too tepid. They could not deny that football had the power to advertise and make money for their institutions, but the commercialism around the game and the deaths and maimings were problems too serious to ignore. B. P. Raymond of Wesleyan railed against football's "hippodrome features," while Henry Pritchett of MIT lamented "the extreme development of athleticism" in college men. Joseph Swain of Swarthmore decided that the root of evils was the collegiate man's obsession with "mere winning." Even Brown University's President Faunce, a supporter of Camp, spoke out against "the severe training, the desperate encounter, the staking o[f] large sums of money on the result, [and] the exaltation of the athlete as the finest product of the college."[29]

If these college leaders were identifying larger deficits in the American character, they were desperate to point fingers at a singular cause. All men were not the trouble, they qualified, just the athletic ones; and not all athletes, just the college ones; and not all college athletes, mainly the football players; and not all football players, just the ones close to the game's legislating body; and not even all of them, just the primary one pulling the strings, who was, without question, Walter Camp.

Columbia's Committee on Athletics convinced President Nicholas Murray Butler that Camp's "self-perpetuating, non-representative, pig-headed, oblivious to public opinion and obstinate" rules committee was ultimately at fault for football's misdirection. President Benjamin Ide Wheeler of Berkeley agreed in a lecture to undergraduates: "The great trouble is that the game is in the hands of a self-appointed, self-organized committee of rules. I refer to Walter Camp and his associates. They have promised reforms, but have done nothing." Charles Eliot concurred that Camp "controlled the existing irresponsible committee," and did it largely by mandating that all amendments to rules require unanimous votes. "The trouble with him seems to me to be that he is deficient in moral responsibility," Eliot added condemningly. "I should never have had any faith in his superintendence of football reform, inasmuch [as] he is directly responsible for the degradation and ruin of the game."[30]

On this point, the presidents of Harvard and the United States could not be more opposed. Whereas Eliot wanted football rescued from Camp's grip, Roosevelt believed that reform had to come from the one man whose influence on the game had been wholesome and manly all along. Before the Harvard-Yale match of 1905, the *Evening Mail* acknowledged the standoff: "Eliot advocates using a meat axe on the American game and chopping it out altogether. President Roosevelt believes that football officials should swing a big stick, enforce the rules and save the grand old sport." But that weekend, a big stick was not in evidence for the 43,000 fans who watched Harvard lose. Assessing the reasons for Yale's narrow victory, a Boston reporter decided that Camp's men withstood more physical punishment, even if they did not necessarily play with more skill.[31]

Harvard men were sore after the game, and not just physically. One play against them was particularly egregious: Yale had punted the ball, and Harvard's Francis Burr called for a fair catch on Yale's forty-yard line. Yale Captain Tom Shevlin tackled him low and fairly, but teammate James Quill rushed in and allegedly punched Burr's face with a closed fist while Burr was unable to protect himself. Reportedly, the blood spurting from Burr's nose was visible from the stands, though Yale men invariably saw it differently: Quill slugged no one, they insisted; Burr's face happened to be in the way of a perfectly timed, open-handed tackle.

The official, Paul Dashiell, apparently agreed, because he did not penalize Quill. Harvard fans ran to the sideline to insist that Reid lodge a protest. Yale Coach Jack Owsley thought them a bunch of whiners, but Camp was careful not to respond out of turn, since Dashiell's involvement complicated matters. Harvard had protested his appointment as the game official, but Camp told Yale captains to refuse a replacement; now his insistence looked dubious. Roosevelt called Dashiell to the White House to discuss the incident, and Camp held an inquiry to smooth feathers. It was yet another public-relations nightmare, the likes of which Camp had not seen since the bloodbath of '94.[32]

No amount of spin control could obscure the fact that the weekend had been especially punishing on college and high school gridirons. The press had already reported sixteen deaths in football games over the past six weeks, adding three more to the tally that Saturday. Athletic directors at both the college and high school levels wrote Camp, pleading for something to be done. "The usefullness [sic] and the very existence of the game of football is seriously threatened," feared a director in the Cleveland public schools. When all was said and done, twenty-six players died playing football in 1905, more of them high school boys than college men. Seven suffered abdominal injuries; four, spinal injuries; five, concussions; five, fractured skulls; two, cerebral hemorrhages; two, fractured ribs that bore through their hearts; and one, acute peritonitis. Congressman Charles Landis was appalled, calling any sport that required physicians onsite no sport at all; cock-fighting was a "Sabbath School game" in comparison. The death of Union College's Herald Moore that weekend stirred the most comments, since it occurred so close to the hotel where Camp and his committee ineffectively deliberated. Moore's cerebral hemorrhage occurred in a pileup of bodies in a season-ending game against NYU. University Chancellor Henry MacCracken declared an immediate ban of the "homicidal" game.[33]

Camp was once again vilified in the *Evening Post*, this time by editor Oswald Villard. Meanwhile at Harvard, the national panic over football fatalities brought out sentiments that had been stewing for years. Eliot made Camp appear to be beneath contempt in publications from Boston and Cambridge. The inaction of his rules committee, he explained, was symptomatic of a more profound anti-intellectualism and tolerance for violence that Camp encouraged on the field, in the stands, and in society at large. He had created a Spartan mentality in New Haven, in contrast to Harvard's preference for the Athenian. A contributor to Harvard's *Graduate Magazine* concurred that the intellectual devolution of Yale coincided with the years in which football and Camp had taken greatest hold:

WALTER CAMP'S CONTRIBUTION: Will the historian of American education, when he comes to write the history of the years from 1870 to 1905, be able to point to any single important contribution made by Yale to either educational or administrative progress? The adoption of the elective system, the abolition of compulsory worship, the development of postgraduate instruction, the establishment of the case system in the study of law, the conversion of the professional schools into graduate schools—not one of these great reforms originated at Yale; and only tardily, with great reluctance, have some of them been partially adopted there. But that historian cannot fail to give Yale full credit for organizing and maintaining the most remarkable athletic system ever seen in an American or English university. He may ask in vain for any conspicuous discovery in science, for any vital book, for any advance in educational method which Yale can claim in the past decade or two; but the modern game of football developed by Walter Camp, is the one great contribution made in New Haven in recent years to the world's progress and the intellectual and spiritual uplift of mankind.[34]

Former Yale player Ray Tompkins told Camp to take heart. "Colleges and universities that dislike Yale are fanning this flame. . . . You, of course, know there is no difference in opinion among Yale men about you." Indeed, a New Haven paper charged "that the animus of the attack c[ame] from institutions that have been licked out of their boots by the superior football genius of Walter Camp." Spalding executive Julian Curtiss told Camp that he thought college presidents "were acting like a lot of hysterical old women." Still, Camp felt the sting of their words. He offered to resign from his athletic posts, but President Hadley would not hear of it. In fact, he met with Alice to draft a plan for her husband's next confrontation with the rules committee. He wanted Camp to demand that the ten-yard rule be adopted, or threaten to secede in the name of real reform.[35]

Camp lobbied for his rule one last time, as well as for more restrictions on high tackles, protection for fair catches, and shortened playing time. Alas, the committee stagnated with indecision, until others forced its hand. Columbia University's council issued a public statement in late November: "The manifold evils flowing from the game of football are too serious and too deep seated to be dealt with by any process of amendment or reformation of the game." Football, in its view, cultivated "a general demoralization of student and public sentiment" and "the subversion of intellectual and moral ideals," and thus had to be abolished on campus for now and the foreseeable future. Reporters wired Camp immediately, wanting his response to Columbia's actions, but he said nothing. Undergraduates protested and Wall Street alumni filed petitions to resurrect football at Columbia, but administrators were unmoved. In their eyes, players had perpetrated crimes as minor as cutting class and as severe as manslaughter in the interest of winning. Eventually, Northwestern, MIT, Stanford, Baylor, and Berkeley joined the ban.[36]

NYU Chancellor Henry MacCracken called together men from thirteen Eastern colleges on December 8 to vote on whether to ban or reform football for 1906. Reform won marginally, so MacCracken invited representatives from sixty-eight Eastern and Western institutions to the Murray Hill Hotel three weeks later to discuss what forms it should take. Hadley neglected to send a representative from Yale to the conference, never betraying the extent to which he consulted with Camp on the matter. Men from Brown, Princeton, Cornell, Johns Hopkins, and Trinity also did not attend, seemingly in solidarity with Camp and the rules committee. For all his ranting against football, Charles Eliot also chose not to send a representative, citing his preference for handling problems internally. Although he thought Camp a despot, he was not prepared to relinquish control of athletic affairs to smaller institutions.[37]

At the Murray Hill Hotel, MacCracken called the rules committee a "Tsarist regime" in need of "Bolshevik overthrow." Because Yale seemed to benefit most under the current rules, it was easy to peg Camp as the worst tyrant among them. The *Times* reported that he had convinced the committee yet again not to abandon the one-man veto rule, allowing for "one-man domination with Walter Camp in the position of dictator." Nevertheless, Palmer Pierce, a West Point captain who emerged as leader of this new body and the AAU, proposed that rather than overthrow the old committee and lose the benefit of Camp's wisdom, a new committee merge with the old.

Pierce dispatched seven men to Philadelphia, where Camp and the old committee planned to meet. Football veterans E. K. Hall of

Dartmouth, Henry Williams of Minnesota, and Charles Daly of West Point were joined by representatives from smaller, Western schools for the uncomfortable confrontation. When the new rule-makers asked Camp and the old committee to share the burden of football reform, Camp was politely standoffish. This was not a decision he or his colleagues could make hastily, he explained; they would need formal permission from their institutions, and that would take time. The new committee agreed to wait.[38]

If a coup was taking place, Camp wanted the record to show that he had never ruled with an iron fist; his leadership had not been forced upon a proletariat of universities, but had in fact been sought by them for decades. If this were true, a West Point man challenged, than why would Camp have an axe to grind with men from smaller schools now asking to share the power? Sacrifice your vanity for the common good of the game, he pleaded. "The public has lost faith in your committee."[39]

Two weeks later, the old and new committees held separate meetings at the Netherland and Murray Hill Hotels. Now a trainer at Penn, Mike Murphy tipped Camp off that Reid would make a power play, and he did, resigning from the old committee to join the new. Reid had already convinced members of the old committee to relent and support reforms wanted by the Harvard Athletic Committee. After the Burr-Quill incident, Roosevelt had gently nudged Dashiell to go along with the coup to end Camp's unanimous rule.[40]

Stagg wrote Camp from the Mudlavia water baths: "Chicago favors Amalgamation. I would like you to act for me using your best judgment." At this stage, Camp had no choice but to concede control. The new committee offered to ease the transition by having three men from the old body and two from the new serve as the amalgamated committee's executive board. With that, Camp joined the others to form the American Intercollegiate Football Rules Committee, or the amalgamated committee of the Intercollegiate Athletic Association, known after 1910 as the National Collegiate Athletics Association, or NCAA. Reid, not Camp, served as secretary, and E. K. Hall was the chair. Camp remained editor of the rules, and Easterners largely continued to fill the executive seats.[41]

Camp seemed to be conciliatory, but in New Haven, he spoke out of the other side of his mouth to quell fears that reformers would strip manly rigor from his game. At a banquet hall, he assured alumni that brutality in football had been "greatly overrated," while also reiterating that physical danger was inherent in any manly game. "All last year there were at Yale only twenty-four accidents," he reported, "of which seventeen were nothing worse than sprained ankles." President Hadley took the podium in solidarity: "We believe that football rules should be framed as far as possible by football experts. . . . We are content to leave that matter in the hands of Mr. Camp."

With that, cheers spontaneously erupted. "Yale is determined to play football as she believes it should be played," wrote a reporter defending Camp. "If the rest of the country wants to play jackstraws that is the business of the rest of the country. Princeton and Pennsylvania and many other colleges seem to hold similar views, and Yale has no fear of lonesomeness." In the Eastern establishment, there was little support for the "McCracken powwow" or for leaving football rules in the hands of "pigeon-livered professors," who, one reporter carped, had "no more idea of the game than the average woman."[42]

In the press, Camp had avoided signs of a power struggle, but he privately took desperate measures to diminish the influence of the new rule-makers. Pierce asked Hadley to join the IAA (NCAA), and Camp convinced Hadley to refuse. Pierce's committee demonstrated "as complete a centralization of power as I have seen," Camp railed, reminding Hadley that the old Brown conference started out along similar lines and failed. Adhering to the laissez-faire philosophies of his brother-in-law, he vowed that athletics, like economies, would right themselves in time. In the meantime, forty-nine colleges and universities joined Pierce's organization, including Penn and Chicago in 1907, and Princeton and Cornell soon afterward. Harvard and Yale defended their autonomy in an uncomfortable union for now. Their Jeffersonian opposition to "Pierce's oligarchy" was convenient, if not ironic, having been happily Hamiltonian when they had controlling interests in college sports. The *Times* noted that the Big Two grew defensive of tradition with "the growing strength and virility of the Intercollegiate Athletic Association." But the Big Two became a clinging One, once Harvard joined the NCAA in 1910.[43]

Although Yale did not join the NCAA, Camp was a member, albeit a reticent one, of its amalgamated committee, which divided in 1906 into subcommittees on open play, brutality, and the establishment of a centralized board of officials. Camp sat on the subcommittee on open play with Reid and Hall, figuring that this was where he could best make his case for the ten-yard rule. He won his rule—at the expense of accepting the forward pass, but he figured that the pass would never become a formidable weapon, given all the restrictions placed on it. Quarterbacks had to throw from at least five yards behind the line of scrimmage, and the ball had to cross the line within five yards to the left or right of the snapper. A pass could be used only once per set of downs, and it could not result in a touchdown. If it crossed the goal line on the fly untouched, it was a touchback; if it was caught over the goal line, it also was a touchback. Offenses were penalized for incomplete passes so severely that Camp presumed few teams would attempt to complete them.[44]

After several contentious meetings, the amalgamated committee announced a comprehensive set of reforms in April 1906. More than thirty changes were made to the old code: Along with the ten-yard rule and forward pass, men making fair catches were required to signal their intentions by raising their hands above their heads while advancing toward the ball; opponents were to let them catch the ball unaccosted or be penalized—a nod to the Burr-Quill incident. To minimize slugging on the line, players had to have both hands and feet up to or within one foot of the line of scrimmage, or one foot and the opposite hand within one foot of the line in a crouched formation. To prevent momentum plays, at least six men had to line up on the line and stay still until the ball was snapped. The referee blew the whistle and called the ball down once any body part of the receiver, except hands or feet, touched the ground.

Camp finally had his neutral zone and penalties against hurdling and tripping. To reduce physical exhaustion, the game was also shortened to two thirty-minute halves, and captains could request three timeouts per half without penalty. The officiating crew expanded to a referee, two umpires, and a line judge, who were given more power. Men who kneed, elbowed, kicked, or struck another player's face with the heel of the hand were penalized. Tackling out of bounds or below the knee resulted in a fifteen-yard loss for the offending side, and "unsportsmanlike conduct," such as hurling abusive language at opponents or officials, resulted in suspension for one game; two suspensions resulted in suspension for the season. Camp conceded to these punishments when men could not regulate themselves.[45]

So, yet again, Camp thwarted a ban on his game. A headline declared him "Still 'It' In College Football" as he continued to edit the annual rulebook and establish the centralized board of officials. As the most readily identified member of the amalgamated committee, he was dispatched across the country to explain the new rules. Coaches and officials convened at venues like the Beach Hotel in Chicago to witness his command of the technicalities of the new game, as if he alone had masterminded the changes. Apparently, they were effective. At season's end, the *Sun* declared him the "patron saint of Foot Ball," whose ten-yard rule reduced injuries by 50 percent.[46]

But would he rebound from this crisis as he had the last? This time, the attacks were personal and wore him down when his resilience had already been tested. Along with fires at the manufacturing facilities of the New Haven Clock Company, Camp's cousin Charles, the Yale football hero of '76, succumbed to complications related to diabetes, dying at the age of forty-nine. Soon after, Camp sat vigil at his father's sickbed until he too passed away and left his son without a living parent. Illness also struck Alice, who underwent surgery, and little Janet had dangerously high fevers after having her tonsils removed. "We are all rather disgusted that she does not make headway faster," Camp confided to a friend in a rare moment of disclosure. His anguish in these months was also compounded by the unexpected death of one of his sales agents in London, who suffered fatal injuries in a car accident. As he dealt with negative press out of Boston, Camp helped the man's family return his body to New Haven for the funeral. Indeed, the crises he faced in 1905 extended far beyond football, yet he remained stoic, remarkably in control.[47]

9

Rewriting the Gridiron Narrative, 1906–1912

DURING THE FRANTIC MONTHS OF football reform, Camp had kept up correspondence with University of California President Benjamin Wheeler, hoping to win him over to his views. In theory, this should not have been hard. Wheeler was a self-proclaimed supporter of athletics; as an undergraduate at Brown, he had rowed and played baseball, and in the 1890s, as chair of the faculty athletic committee at Cornell, he supplied Camp with laudatory remarks for *Football Facts and Figures*: "The game as a whole tends to the production of manly, earnest character, to the throttling of pettiness and peevishness, and to the establishment of habits of punctuality, or a sense for discipline and authority, or a readiness for cooperation." Reading this, Camp figured he had a valuable ally.[1]

But Wheeler's tune changed by 1905. Disillusioned with football as played and with the makeup of the rules committee, he aligned with Stanford President David Starr Jordan and declared his unwillingness to let students play football as it was governed. He urged Arthur Hadley to join the opposition, compelling Camp to write him in earnest. Camp swore to Wheeler that he was not the self-serving regulator he made him out to be, and that he would even go against consensus opinion in New Haven if it meant saving his game. It was unlike Camp to grovel at the knees of college presidents, but there was much at stake. When he had coached at Stanford in the 1890s, the Berkeley match attracted crowds rivaling those in New York on Thanksgiving. In Camp's mind, California's embrace of football had been the ultimate proof of its arrival.[2]

When Camp asked Wheeler to consider some of his proposed rule changes for 1906, Wheeler told him there was no point. The problems he perceived in football were intrinsic to the game, he told Camp, and he prophesied that it would cease to exist as a college sport in ten years. Camp asked him why he thought so. Because, Wheeler told him, English rugby was a superior game. In fact after watching an exhibition of it, Wheeler thought it "better for academic use." The Stanford president concurred that football could never be anything more than "Rugby's American pervert."[3]

But rugby lacked the American game's definitiveness and planning, Camp argued. It relied too much on luck and individual play. The team ethic should be emphasized in the training of modern men, Camp insisted. But Wheeler was unmoved. He preferred rugby because it was not so complicated to necessitate highly trained officials at all times, making it refreshingly accessible. It could be played spontaneously by a group of boys anywhere, not merely a selection of highly trained, muscle-bound men in college arenas. "A man can play in the afternoon who expects to study in the evening. It is a game which a man can play without being in gladiatorial training. It is a game which a man can play without having been made through long practice a part of a mere machine. A player retains his individuality; he must think for himself all the time. . . . This makes men alert, it keeps them versatile in the play, it keeps them as personalities instead of reducing them to cogs and cams." Wheeler did not believe that the bureaucratic man could be effective if he did not have a moral compass of his own, and he did not think the American game taught boys to have one, as it encouraged mindless conformity and rogue brutality.[4]

It was ironic that Wheeler thought a game played by English gentry more democratic in its opportunities and appeal, but to him, American football was too involved to build character on a mass scale. He calculated a mere seventy-five undergraduates at Berkeley who had made the team over the course of football's first decade on campus, from a pool exceeding 4,000 men. "Take off the headgear and the nose guards, and the thigh padding and the knee padding, and introduce the Association game for light men and runners—indeed for the average man," he pleaded. "Then let the student mass descend from its enthronement in sedentary athletics on the bleachers and get health and fun and virility out of the heartiest and manliest of our sports." It was hard for Camp to refute Wheeler's claims about rugby's accessibility. Even at Yale, average-sized undergraduates presented him with a petition to make association football a minor sport to receive funding from the Financial Union. The petition was signed by nearly seventy men who wanted to play not for Yale glory, but rather for the simple fun of it.[5]

Wheeler's perspective made sense, given his purpose to cultivate Western men. The success of his nascent university relied on his buying into athletic traditions and male role models of another kind, ones that could be made to reflect the rugged individualism of the Pacific Coast rather than the privilege he had left behind in the East. With no war currently in the offing and the relegation of Native Americans to the region's reservations, the martial quality of Camp's game was not useful for Wheeler, so he railed against Camp's effort to shape football into military spectacle:

> Two rigid, rampart-like lines of human flesh have been created, and behind the latter is established a catapult to fire through a porthole open in the offensive rampart a missile composed of four or five human bodies globulated about a carried football with a maximum of initial velocity against the presumably weakest point in the opposing rampart. The 'point' is a single human being. If it prove not to have been the weakest to start with, it can be made such, if the missile be fired times enough. Therein lies the distinctive American contribution to the Rugby game.[6]

In March 1906, Wheeler warned Camp that Berkeley's banning of the American game was imminent and that Stanford, Southern California, St. Mary's College, and the University of Santa Clara were joining in his experiment with English rugby. Of the other West Coast schools, only Pomona, the University of Nevada, the University of California at Santa Cruz, and a few California high schools answered Wheeler's call to make the change, and that gave Camp reason to hope. Popular reaction to rugby was mixed in the West. Many observers thought rugby effeminate, with its lack of hard tackling; players seemed less virile with their shorter pants and lesser heft. Especially vocal was Harvard Coach Bill Reid, who grew up in California and vowed that he would bring the American game back to his state. And yet, the first Berkeley-Stanford rugby matches in 1906 brought in substantial gate receipts. Some local sportswriters thought the game compelling, since it was quicker and open, while others expressed discomfort with the "foreign" sport replacing their red-blooded American game.[7]

Camp seized on these patriotic sentiments to make pleas for football in *Collier's*, much to the chagrin of John Morgan, an Englishman who wrote countering editorials in 1908. He charged that Camp, in making his case, exaggerated the number of fatal injuries caused by the rugby scrum. "Deaths from injuries have been less frequent in the last two years in the American game," he conceded. "Yet, after all that is said and done the cold glaring *fact* remains that small as this number is[,] it is *still* four times and probably five times more than the total fatal accidents caused in English rugby." Camp's response was far from contrite. He insisted that he had taken his data from the official rugby rulebook of Australia, where officials abandoned English rules on the grounds of safety. As to the charge that he was desperate to propagate football, he smugly replied, "It seems to have a fair hold as it is."[8]

By now he was certainly not wrong. Despite rugby's adoption in the Far West, 1,500 college football matches were scheduled for the fall of 1908. Still, it disturbed this Englishman that Camp emasculated rugby to prop up his game, and that other sportswriters followed his lead: "I have too often seen in American sporting journals that English Rugby was a parlour game, a ladies' game played in conventional style with eye glasses and monocles with the 'Ah pardon me, would you kindly oblige me by letting me pass with the ball, so beastly strenuous to push through don[]'t chew know.'" As much as Camp wanted the reading public to think that football made men stronger, strategic, and specialized, this commentator thought football players were walking contradictions—men "of science" who acted out of primitive emotion; gentlemen of good breeding who acted as if they were raised by wolves: "Not long ago I read in an American Journal an account of a match twixt rival colleges—the supposed centre of culture[,] gentlemanly arts[,] and learning—in which players punched each other, one brutally kicked while in the melee[,] another with two teeth knocked out, another narrowly escaping having one of his optics gouged out[,] and one actually had his thumb bitten through. Oh, my! What a gloriously fine spectacle of '*scientific football*'."[9]

Camp's writings had made it appear as though Americans had invented athletic competition, but the Englishman thought that they had more or less corrupted it, annihilating the British ideal of fair play. Camp admitted that Americans transformed British athletics, but only for the better. He recalled in his youth watching the men of Yale compete against English crews and deciding that, while the Americans were novices in the sport, all they needed was time before they blew the competition out of the water. Standing on the riverbank, he honed in on their strokes—the English one, long and slow; the American one, high and rapid. He supposed that the differences reflected vastly different sensibilities, for while it was bad form to defeat another crew too definitively in England, in America, no one gave points for style or faulted a man for trying hard or winning big.[10]

He was beginning to understand the differences as grounded in the very function sports served: In England, they were the conspicuous display of the wealthy—and hence *how* one played defined the man. In America, that might have been true for a brief time; but in the modern age, participation in sports seemed less a confirmation that one had already arrived than a means of getting there. Hence the outcome mattered more.

Disagreeing with the very premise, Morgan ridiculed Camp's description of American boys putting on their "fighting" faces to play his game. It was poor form, pathetic, as was the American obsession with football dime novels and paraphernalia. Other Englishmen told Camp that they had no patience for the start-and-stop pacing of American football, failing to appreciate the narrative tension built into its pauses and clear delineations of possession. Camp liked to think that he had given football its heroes and villains, a sense of building, climax, and denouement, as well as timely moral lessons. He wanted football to be a parable on how to be effective men, but Englishmen thought the story a sham.

So Camp ended his love affair with English sport. In the pages of *Outing*, he declared that the difference in the attitude of British and American men was no more apparent than in their respective brands of football—"athletics for fun" versus "athletics to win." He described a Yale game as "an organized and fanatical war," with teams "trained like armies," while at Oxford and Cambridge, men played casually for a few friends who "stopped in to see them and clapped a good play." Camp surmised that the English used the ideal of "sportsmanship" as "an excuse for laziness or as a cloak to cover lack of preparation." "This marked decay in athletic success may indeed foreshadow even to the British mind a decline," he condemned. To him, sport had to be more than simply enjoyed.[11]

If Camp told truths American men wanted to hear, President Jordan of Stanford preferred the lessons of rugby and wrote Eastern college presidents of its resounding appeal on the West Coast. In the four years since abandoning the American game, he claimed that injuries had been reduced and smaller players stood out as exceptional talents. Skill had beaten out size, he insisted, because rugby was a sport, not a battle, "played not in armor but in cotton knee breeches." Like Wheeler, he thought that a game that simulated war was troublesome. He was a pacifist, oddly because he was a eugenicist. To him, football, like war, stripped a nation of its best stock by killing it or grinding it down until it lost effectiveness. Since taking Camp in to coach in 1892, he saw that football had preoccupied his students too completely. Rugby "does not seem to produce the same obsession," he told Camp. "The game is distinctively a sport which men can play for pleasure and without coaches."[12]

Although injuries to limbs were as likely in rugby as in football, Jordan maintained that the danger to the nervous system and internal organs was substantially less, largely because rugby did away with interference. He thought that once Camp allowed men to travel off sides, he had opened the floodgates to mass play and low tackles. Regrettably, he had also encouraged the domination of professional coaches now that football was played like a chess match, with men contriving moves from the sidelines. Whereas rugby encouraged players to think for themselves, Jordan believed that Camp had created teams of mindless thugs, the professional coach now the only brain among them. "I do not regard the element of certainty—the condition under which the general or coach arranges the whole plan of battle beforehand[—]as a desirable element in intercollegiate sports," he wrote Camp. "In Rugby as in baseball a man is trained to seize chances as they rise." Camp politely accepted his point, even if what Jordan thought desirable, he thought random and utterly unscientific.[13]

If Jordan conceded anything, it was that his own son had "not taken kindly to Rugby," for he was too heavy to make the Stanford team. Camp noted and seized on the demoralization of big men like Jordan's son, as well as American rugby players who suffered blowout after blowout against international teams. Seven years after their switch to rugby, an "All-America" squad made up of the best players in the Bay Area managed to score only three points against the New Zealand All-Blacks' fifty-three. An Englishman in California wrote Camp with highlights and scores of the matches overseas, reporting that a combined team of players from Stanford, Berkeley, and Nevada traveled to Australia and New Zealand to play club squads in 1910 but could not muster a win. The same scenario played out three years later, leading a reporter for the *San Francisco Call* to wistfully wonder, "Will California Produce Rugby's World Champions?" The continued drubbings caused fans to doubt if, at its core, rugby could ever be an American game. If so, why had American men not yet dominated it?[14]

Wheeler and Jordan soon discovered that no matter how hard they tried to enforce British rules and customs, American tendencies started rearing their heads in collegiate rugby. American players were bulkier than their international counterparts, and they focused on facets of the game that most resembled the crushing features of football. Teams started calling for changes to the rules—more tackling, a seven-man scrum, fewer players on the field—in attempts to make the game more palatable to both themselves and fans.

Professionalism also crept into the game Wheeler declared impervious to commercial forces. The beauty of rugby, he once stated, was that it was a pastime, not a vocation; a sport, not a spectacle. And yet, to gain an edge, California undergraduates now spent summers in Australia to glean techniques from better teams. They played the professional non-collegians of the Olympic Club, the San Francisco-based Barbarians Club, and the Los Angeles Athletic Club, who had also turned to rugby in hopes of carving out a niche of superiority over Eastern men. Berkeley soon recruited graduate students and international players and offered them financial inducements, leaving Wheeler to woefully wonder if there was a game that American men could not corrupt. Camp waited patiently, confident that Western men would not follow "false Gods" for long.[15]

Within a decade, all the college administrators of the West came around as Camp had predicted; rugby fizzled out, and American football returned to the campuses that banned it in 1906. Still, he blamed Harvard's Charles Eliot for the temporary waywardness of Western presidents. As the most influential college president in the country, as well as Camp's most vocal critic, Eliot was the one man for whom Camp had true disdain that could not, for the sake of football or the Harvard-Yale rivalry, be openly expressed. And thus, while Eliot attacked Camp's character in the Boston press, Camp's offensives were veiled and more passively aggressive. At the same time college rugby was being launched in California, he had seized an opportunity to respond to Eliot's vitriol, not with fighting words but with jokes intended to emasculate. At a banquet celebrating the fortieth anniversary of the Yale Alumni Association of Boston, he stood at the podium and read off a mock list of rules that would have been enacted in 1906, he quipped, had Eliot reformed football his way:

The field must be soft.

> . . . a fire must be built on the 15-yard line before the game, in order that all frost may be thawed out.
> . . . Over the entire field there must be a layer of cotton batting two inches thick. On this must be placed a carpet three-quarters of an inch thick. . . .
> . . . No player shall have more than $2 in his clothes. If he does he is in danger of being rated as a professional. . . .[16]

Yale men thought Camp's list hilarious, but his jokes went over less well in the Boston press: "Walter Camp's recent 'wit' . . . was a ludicrous exhibition of Camp's weakness of position and an attempt to divert attention from his responsibility for the faults of the game which have become apparent," exclaimed a reader of the *Advertiser.* "Under Camp Yale had Hinkeyism and this has clung to her for years—now in the last year she, under Camp, had her Quill. . . . And then the Yale team goes home and elects for captain for next year the player who was ruled off the field for slugging."[17]

Camp had let down his guard and blown off steam, and his timing could not have been worse. His detractors were already scrutinizing his every move, not just as a rule-maker but also as Yale athletics' financial advisor. Despite the crises in college football, the Financial Union's surplus had nearly doubled in a decade, exceeding $106,000 in 1905. Less than transparently, Camp had been depositing the surplus into a reserve fund consisting of four separate bank accounts in New York and New Haven. Now an older Yale alumnus, Clarence Deming, insisted that Camp had some explaining to do. Where had this massive surplus been hidden before, and how had Yale been accumulating and spending its profits through the years? Deming guessed that the money was not going toward academics and said as much in *Outlook* and the *Evening Post*. He noted that profits made in Yale sports in one year alone could pay the salaries of thirty full professors, but instead, professional baseball coaches and trainers received salaries that were the envy of academic faculty. Although Yale still did not officially have a paid head football coach, Camp now drew $5,000 in salary from these profits, when full professors made $3,500 a year.[18]

Had Deming looked into the athletic programs at Chicago or Harvard, he would have seen that there, too, football profits brought in revenues second only to tuition payments. But Deming made Camp an example. Where were these salaries hidden in the financial statements, he asked? The crew coach's salary was covered under "boathouse maintenance," Camp explained. The Financial Union covered the salary of the team trainer, as well as Camp's pay as Union treasurer, under "maintenance of the Yale Field."[19] Deming probed further:

"Is it true that Union funds were used to tutor students in jeopardy of falling behind?"

"Yes."

"Did the Union pay for trainer Mike Murphy's trip to Cuba to restore his health?"

"Yes."

"Did football captain Hogan accompany him?"

"Yes."

"Were expenses paid for both?"

"Yes."[20]

Camp answered as if he had nothing to hide. Still, Deming wondered how the surplus had been kept a secret. Camp told him that he purposely did not list accumulated profits in his annual reports, but that Eugene Richards and other faculty members were aware of these figures. If undergraduates knew of these monies, they would be incentive for extravagance, he reasoned. He prudently saved for large expenditures, such as upkeep of the university boathouse and maintenance of the wooden stands at Yale Field, which were going to cost tens of thousands of dollars to replace now that they were falling into disrepair. He wanted the undergraduates to learn thrift and discipline, so he was modeling responsibility. He reminded Deming as well that Yale's surplus accrued without graduate donations. Whereas alumni gave state-of-the-art stadiums to Syracuse, Princeton, and Harvard, Yale men relied largely on gate receipts they generated themselves. It was self-sufficiency of the highest order.[21]

Still, given the scrutiny, Camp thought it best to reduce his pay. Already his salaries had been reduced to $3,750, but now he asked to shave off another $500, "$250 on the University side and $250 on the Financial Union side." Again, Hadley would not hear of it, and New York alumni questioned Deming's motives for trying to tarnish Camp's reputation. Campus reporters lauded Camp's business savvy over the previous fourteen years, calling the surplus proof of his careful management. He was using profits to pay down the debt on Yale Field and broker land deals for the Yale Bowl, to overwhelming support in New Haven. Members of the Yale Corporation thought Camp such an asset, in fact, that they awarded him an honorary master's degree in 1908, the highest honor they could bestow on someone with a bachelor's degree.[22]

But no one could deny that the recent audit also brought some unsavory practices to light. There was, admittedly, incomplete accounting for where all the profits had gone, leading to speculation on the part of Stanford's President Jordan that Yale was paying its players. Already it was clear, he told the *Times*, that Yale and Chicago offered scholarships for athletic ability. Camp denied this outright but could not explain away the expenditures on hotel rooms, theater tickets, and rounds of drinks and cigars at establishments in Boston and New York over the years. Yale secretary Anson Phelps Stokes also evinced concern when he uncovered a liquor bill for over $400 accumulated by alumni coaches at the New Haven House. "It would create a very bad outside impression if this charge for coaches['] drinks appeared in our accounts," he told Camp. Clearly, he wanted it to disappear.[23]

Publicly, Yale administrators minimized the fiscal abuses, and yet they were sufficiently concerned to form an investigative committee to determine their extent. They insisted that the inquiry was no concession to faculty control and that they hoped to use the findings merely to offer undergraduates suggestions for recalibrating their priorities. "Self-purification is a far more wholesome process than suppression from above," insisted Theodore Woolsey, the chair. But his committee could not deny the startling findings. Although players appeared to be official students on the books, they missed an unacceptable number of classes. Gate receipts were exorbitant, and grandstand tickets for the Harvard-Yale game were prohibitively priced for those who worked their way through college. Along with more liquor and hotel stays, the investigation turned up receipts for overpriced "equipment." While the Financial Union still officially did not pay graduate coaches in football, it paid handsomely to entertain them, smacking of the inducements that Camp had always condemned.[24]

In the Midwest, such excesses had been taken as proof that athletics needed to be brought under faculty control. James Angell, president of the University of Michigan, had assembled Big Nine representatives to pass some of the most drastic athletic reforms in the country: They limited a collegian's athletic career to three years, and graduates and high school boys were barred from playing in college games. Organized training was no longer allowed before the school year began, and the season was limited to five games played by Thanksgiving. Freshman teams were prohibited from playing other schools, and to curtail fiscal extravagance, ticket prices were set at fifty cents apiece and the training table abolished. Standards of scholarship were enforced and the professional coach removed. The "team advisor" now had to be a regular member of the faculty who received compensation commensurate with that of his academic colleagues.[25]

Getting rid of the "coach" in this way may have been an exercise in semantics. Nonetheless, the Big Nine showed earnestness in trying to avoid the slippery slope of which Deming had foretold, one that had culminated in a paradox in Yale athletics: "On the one side are the strenuous physical effort and discipline which in many respects are good," Deming explained. "On the other side are the mercenary spirit, the wastage, and the luxury which are in all respects bad." He lamented the "temptation to masked professionalism, to the sacrifice of scholarship in athletic excess, and to the giving of undue dominance to the verb 'to win.' "[26] More and more, the consensus was that Camp had pushed the rock that started the avalanche for the rest of college sports.

A friend publicly defended Camp, insisting that it was his "love of football and his business judgment" that made him "overlook the fact that overwhelming popular patronage has injured every sport which it has ever touched." Yet another otherwise sympathetic journalist could not help but condemn the results of Camp's obsessive work for the game: "[His] length and expertness of service ha[ve] given rise . . . to one of the most frequently heard of criticisms against both Mr. Camp and Yale. Many assert that he has turned the game from a sport into a business. Other institutions, in order to play on even terms with Yale, have been obliged to follow his methods. Year after year the thing has been developed into more and more of a science, requiring more money, more time, more attention." Even Yale trainer William Dole, whose father and brothers had also been trainers, disparaged the athletic culture under Camp: "We have outgrown the old English ideal of amateur athletics. We no longer indulge in sport for sport's sake but because it pays. This commercialism is our disease."[27]

All along, Camp had insisted that sport left in student hands was an experience that disciplined, and that Yale football was an ideal training ground for the corporate leaders of the country. But now, one had to wonder if self-regulation was possible. Privately, even Hadley had come to Camp concerned about athletes who seemed to train obsessively during the season, only to be in drunken stupors immediately afterward. Had they grown soft on over-indulgence? Yale men had insisted that their intense athletic culture promoted character, but Harvard philosopher William James wondered whether it cultivated individual personality. Given the priorities Camp had set at Yale, James concluded that men of individual genius would feel more "richly fed" in Cambridge.[28]

Camp was not surprised that Harvard men questioned Yale's "must win" mentality, but critics slowly came out of Yale too. In 1907, undergraduate J. Howland Auchincloss weighed the Yale man's ability to "push his way along in life" against the individuality he relinquished in a collective quest to succeed. While a Yale man turned his football captaincy into a future as a captain of industry, Auchincloss decided that the Harvard man had "a better chance to follow his own salvation." The Yale man's preoccupation with corporate identity, team spirit, and competition did not, in his conclusion, lead to success that was more profound.[29]

Even Yale's gymnasium director William Anderson expressed concern to Camp about the negative impact of team sport on undergraduates. His records indicated that plenty of average men wanted to improve their fitness, and that they showed interest in wrestling, boxing, fencing, and bowling. But they, too, sacrificed for "the team"—the Yale eleven especially—since they had to defer to athletes who had the run of the locker rooms, the pool, the pulley machines, batting cages, courts, and practice fields. What about the non-specialist, Anderson asked the Gymnasium Advisory Committee, the man who did not compete to win but to cultivate his body for his own sake?[30]

No one put campus values to task as publicly as Owen Johnson, the Yale graduate of 1900 who serialized fictional accounts of Yale life in *McClure's* before packaging them as the bestselling novel *Stover at Yale* (1912). On the surface, protagonist Dink Stover's coming-of-age tale resembles Dick Goddard's in *The Substitute*, as he leaves Lawrenceville Prep with ambitions to become a football star and Bonesman. But the tone of the novel subtly turns. Johnson ultimately portrays Stover's classmates as juvenile in their social preoccupations, and football as a business in which the quest to win counteracts any benefits derived from it. While Frank Merriwell is arguably a young Walter Camp, Johnson presents a more cynical portrait of a figure believed to be Frank Hinkey. One of the more rebellious students in the book—a literary man, not an athlete—condemns the managerial cliques of Yale, calling the university a "social clearinghouse" rather than a "school for character." Stover's democratic values are challenged, his individuality stifled, and Johnson alludes to the athletic professionalism that Camp publicly shunned yet quietly fed. Camp's reaction to *Stover at Yale* was gracious but ambiguous, reminding the public that it was fiction after all.[31]

It did not help that Johnson cast doubt on the moral and ethical value of football as the press scrutinized its long-term physical effects. Months before *Stover at Yale* was released, the seemingly invincible Yale All-American Jim Hogan died of Bright's disease at age thirty-three. Equally shocking, months later, Gordon Brown, captain of the "Team of the Century," died of complications of diabetes; he was only thirty-one. Three years later, Lee McClung, former treasurer of the United States and Yale Captain of '91, died in London of typhoid. He was a bit older at forty-four, but even his death begged the question: Did football tap bodies of vital energy to stave off disease? Camp had heralded these men as the fittest on the gridiron and encouraged boys to emulate their training. McClung boasted that no injury had ever stricken him in his undergraduate years, but critics now wondered if he and his fallen compatriots had overexerted themselves and paid the price. Given the successes of the teams on which they played, it looked as if they might have been spent too much for the good of the collective machine.[32]

Camp had been using Anderson's research in the Yale gymnasium to argue that the opposite was true, that the rigor of college athletics was good for longevity. Tabulating mortality rates for all Yale athletes and non-athletes over a fifty-year span, Anderson determined the death rate for varsity lettermen to be more than 5 percent lower than for the general undergraduate population. His overall conclusion: "Yale athletes do not die young."[33]

Had he published his results four years later, he would have had to include Hogan and Brown in his fatalities, however, as well as the obese Frederic Remington, who died of complications from appendicitis at the end of 1909. Remington had always been large, and he packed on the pounds after leaving New Haven. By age twenty, he weighed 220; by twenty-eight, 230. After returning from Cuba in the Spanish-American War, he weighed an uncomfortable 295. His wife nagged him to trim down, which he did in fits and starts, taking weeks-long expeditions out West to shed pounds in bouts of "violent exercise." After he made his fortune, he bought a horse, but recreational riding did not help him lose weight. He ate rich foods and loved his scotch and cigars. The man romanticized cowboys, but never relinquished the habits he learned in the urban Northeast, where his life was consumed by consumption. His accumulation of size was only outdone by fellow Yale man William Howard Taft, whose 300+ pounds was the stuff of headlines by his presidency's end.[34]

Statistically speaking, American men were getting bigger, and football players disproportionately so. Having rejected the sinewy "greyhound" look of crewmen of the nineteenth century, a handful of gridiron men, including Heffelfinger, reached 200 pounds by 1890. Twenty years later, All-American James Walker dwarfed Heff at 6' 3" and a meatier 250 pounds. Although his size was not the norm, he was not off the charts, his mesomorphic build becoming the masculine ideal. A study in 1907 revealed that Yale tackles averaged 202 pounds, significantly beefier than the average undergraduate, who stood between 5' 7" and 5' 8" and weighed 137 pounds.[35]

Camp told aspiring players that there was utility in added girth around their shoulders, necks, biceps, and chests. To hold off opponents, he encouraged future linemen to build tree trunks for thighs. The muscular body he idealized was not passively inherited, but rather achieved through work. A case in point was the physical culturist Bernarr Macfadden, to whose form gridiron men aspired. Players read his books and watched his literal self-making, which was measurable in profits and physical metamorphosis. At Harvard and Yale, gym directors filed data on incoming freshmen and charted their burgeoning manhood through the gains in circumference around their body parts. Camp provided growth charts for schoolboys in *American Boy* magazine, encouraging adolescent readers, like football players, to measure their manhood in inches and pounds.[36]

But the problem was that after college a man's training invariably trailed off and heft traveled to his midsection, where there was no perceptible use for it. Sportswriters wondered what Camp's culpability had been in creating the fat ex-athlete, and to Camp it hardly seemed fair. The fetish for bulk was widespread, yet he was chastised for starting the trend and not stopping it. David Starr Jordan indicted him too, charging that Camp had been exclusionary in developing a game that most American boys were too small to play. Camp defended himself; he was, after all, the only one interested in creating a game for fat boys in the first place. Before football, the hefty boy "had no field in which he could shine, and hence too little incentive to exercise," but Camp liked to think that he gave him a chance to feel the physical and psychological effects of becoming an athlete. A writer in the *Times* called his focus on big boys pathetic, but Camp took credit for being mindful of male bodies that society had ignored. The center and guard positions were the fat boy's salvation, he proclaimed. By opening sport up to thousands, he had been as inclusive as Jordan had hoped to be with rugby, yet failed.[37]

That winter of 1910, Camp was suffering this criticism as he mourned Remington and was soon to say goodbye to yet another Yale legend, this time, his brother-in-law William Graham Sumner. His degeneration had been gradual, but no less thought provoking, for Camp wondered if Sumner's decrepit state had been the price exacted for years of intellectual, rather than physical, overwork. Though Sumner had long stopped smoking and drank more tea than alcohol, he had put in twelve-hour days to remain a prolific scholar well into his sixties. He had since relinquished his bicycle for gentler walks around New Haven, which he liked to take alone; he felt self-conscious around younger men, given his lumbering pace.[38]

Sumner had suffered a stroke in 1907 while brushing his teeth, and his right hand was nearly useless thereafter. He tried to conceal his frailties, even presiding over the American Sociological Society and presenting a paper at its 1909 Christmas meeting in New York. While there, he suffered another stroke, and Camp sat at his hospital bedside rather than attend his usual rules meetings. Sumner had kidded about all the social calamities he predicted were coming that he would, thankfully, not have to live through now. And yet he left a sizable blank book labeled "SUBJECTS," which contained ideas for the essays he had yet to write: "Parasites of Human Society" . . . "What is a Scholar?" . . . "The Moral Right of the Man who has met all the regular demands of the Society on him to Peace and Quiet. . . ."[39]

The Sumner whom Camp had come to know was gentler than the imposing lecturer of Yale. Most of his undergraduates never knew how much he hated to see suffering, even as he rationalized its existence. Among his mourners was an Irish housemaid whose sons' education he had quietly paid for. His favorite dinner companions were not his colleagues, but their children, in whose presence he seemed to melt.

Although he and Camp often worked at cross-purposes, over time, they had built up mutual respect. Camp cited Sumner often to give his athletic philosophies scholarly mien, and Sumner asked his famous brother-in-law for signed footballs as gifts for the children of his graduate students. He admired Camp's energy and work ethic and praised the high tone of his fiction. Only months before he died, he had asked his former student, William Howard Taft, to consider Camp for a position in his presidential administration. He could think of few men more effective for modern times.[40]

It was not the first suggestion that Camp might be well suited to politics. He had been approached in the past about being the Republican candidate for mayor of New Haven, but any fantasy he had of throwing his hat into the political ring was fleeting. Camp's dream was to leave his mark in sport, not policy or watchmaking, and thus another tome on football was overdue. In the midst of compiling small pieces like *Football Don'ts* for the Outing Publishing Company, he rearranged material already written in *Century* and published it in 1910 as *The Book of Foot-ball*, the cornerstone of a collection that made up Walter Camp's Library of Sport.[41]

The frontispiece of previous books featured Camp in the togs of his playing days, but this one opened with a formal portrait borrowed from the halls of the Crescent Athletic Club. He looked to be a true elder statesman—the only man who could write with continuous memory of American football in all its phases. Whole sections of *The Book of Foot-ball* were devoted to the evolution of rules and legendary All-Americans, creating a lore that made football seem long embedded in the national past. He situated the game's origins in classical times, tracing its evolution to Renaissance Europe until it reached the Britons, was fine-tuned by Americans, and perfected at Yale. Just as the American Constitution was a living document, amendments to the rules of football made it a living game. Camp was founding father and modern expert of a sport that confirmed American exceptionalism.[42]

The book was a public relations vehicle as the death toll in football ratcheted up yet again. By the end of 1909, a disturbing thirty-three players around the country had died by playing football, a marked rise from thirteen the year before. Whitman College abolished football after players suffered injuries against Washington State. In a

Georgetown-Virginia game, Archer Christian died of head injuries, causing Georgetown to discontinue football for the season and the Virginia legislature to consider making playing football a criminal offense. Also damning was news of the paralysis of Navy's Earl Wilson after a game against Villanova, the death of Wabash's Ralph Wilson in a match against St. Louis University, and the demise of Eugene Byrne, an Annapolis cadet, in a high-profile match against Harvard. The press turned to Camp for comment. He reached out to his contacts to glean details about the incidents and begin the damage control.[43]

Members of the amalgamated committee implored Camp to speak to President Taft so that he would not kowtow to public pressure and ban football at the military academies. But Yale player turned physician Josh Hartwell forewarned Camp that this new crisis might not be so easily thwarted. The injuries he was seeing in his practice caused him great concern, because they appeared to be due, in his estimation, to "accidents inherent in the game," and not "avoided by a change of rules." He told Camp: "I am constantly being consulted by parents as to the advisability of their sons playing the game, and I confess, that at the present time I feel rather loath to take the responsibility of telling them to take the risk."[44]

Debate over abolition or radical reform reared its head once again. This time, however, Camp would not have to contend with the disapproval of Charles Eliot. After forty years, the Harvard president stepped down from his university post, his departure marking the end of his public condemnation of football. His replacement, A. Lawrence Lowell, met personally with Hadley and Camp and proved to be a man more amenable to building consensus. Princeton President Woodrow Wilson also was willing to brainstorm solutions rather than condemn football, though privately, his head coach William Roper told him that he thought reform impossible as long as Camp held sway over the rules committee. From his perspective, the amalgamation had not thwarted Camp's power; legislators old and new seemed content once again to defer to his whims, which always played to Yale's "bucking game." Yale performed best when allowed to push and pull the ball carrier, Roper contended, and the rules still allowed for it, despite the overhauls of recent years.[45]

Camp, of course, saw things differently. "I am only one of fourteen on the Rules Committee," he lamented to Yale men. "I cannot *make* them listen to reason." When the committee met to make changes in February 1910, some called for more restrictions on mass play, while others claimed the more open game—with its flying tackles, pass interference, and unprotected punt receivers—caused more injuries. While Camp admitted that the forward pass was safer in some instances, he also claimed that it caused ends to suffer brutal punishment as they waited unprotected to receive the ball; teams were using six to eight backups just to get through the season.[46]

Still, the decline in deaths in 1906, '07, and '08 indicated that the new passing game could be safer with a few adjustments. Deaths in 1909 occurred three times more often to high school boys than college men, making Camp wonder if physical maturity and conditioning were factors. Was it coincidence that no official fatalities occurred at Harvard, Yale, Princeton, or Penn, where he presumed men were trained to perfect pitch? Cadet Byrne's death in the Harvard game was preventable, he argued, since witnesses told him that they could see Byrne struggling with exhaustion before his fatal injury occurred. University of Virginia President W. A. Lambeth concurred that the two deaths he personally witnessed on the gridiron were due not to brutal play, but to exhaustion.[47]

So Camp emphasized a point that he had made less effusively in 1905: that only the fittest could play safely, and high school boys had more physical and emotional developing to do. Mike Murphy also went on record, saying that he had come across schoolboys, but frankly also young undergraduates, who were not yet ready for the strenuous competition of the college game, and that a player's physical and mental readiness must be better assessed before he is allowed on the field. Camp was sufficiently convinced to hold back his own son's entrance to Yale one year to give him more time to develop, despite his muscular six-foot frame. More parents of high school seniors were holding back their sons on similar grounds, though in Washington, D.C., and Manhattan, they soon did so for naught. Deciding unilaterally that schoolboys' bodies and minds were ill-prepared for football, administrators banned the game in public schools altogether.[48]

That Murphy's expert opinion was reprinted on sports pages across the nation was proof that athletic training had become a respected specialization in its own right. But there was something else implicit in Murphy's comments to the press, a mixed message that both condemned and extolled the violence of football. While he admitted that there were too many instances of exhausted or unfit players on the field, he also implied that the blame lay with coaches, not the players. Not only did Murphy think it normal for boys to want to play through injury, he thought it should not be discouraged. Eugene Byrne was an unfortunate case in point, since his duties as the substitute captain compelled him to stay in a game he was unfit to play. But as the general, he was never going to leave his men in battle. This unspoken rule was so deeply ingrained that coaches thought better of suggesting otherwise. According to this implicit pain principle, one was most manly when living by dangerous creeds.[49]

Camp also romanticized playing through pain with his heroic depictions of men concussed and fractured in big games. Red-blooded males preferred action to the sidelines, he insisted: "How can a man, whose blood is warm within, sit like his grandsire carved in alabaster? . . . No amount of accumulated caution has ever had much of any effect upon this ever-bubbling spirit of youth." G. Stanley Hall and other self-fashioned boy experts resoundingly agreed that such was the nature of healthy American males. It was foolish to discourage them from exhibiting the pluck that would make them successful men. Editors of the *Yale Alumni Weekly* to legislators in the Southern Intercollegiate Athletics Association added to the consensus view that injury and death in football should be minimized by taking decisions to pull players from games out of the hands of players too courageous to do it themselves. Along with mandating physical examinations before each season, football officials started making athletic directors responsible for detecting and removing exhausted and injured men on the field, absolving players from the responsibility of it.[50]

According to a Boston paper, such recommendations were to the relief of local mothers, who appreciated the game's influence but also feared its potential to maim. One mother said that she would not deny her sons the opportunity to play, because then they would not be perceived as "sissies," but she felt better knowing that others would protect them when they would not protect themselves. A female contributor to *Outlook* explained that mothers, like fathers, viewed football as a rite of passage for their sons, but wanted a game that was somewhat controlled—by older, more cautious men. In its ideal form, football would be that dose of harshness that, like a vaccine, built up a boy's tolerance, without ultimately doing him in.[51]

Statisticians noted that more serious injuries occurred at the ends of halves, when players were winded and vulnerable. Lambeth thus recommended that the game be divided into shorter quarters, and Heisman wrote Camp seconding the idea: "In boxing we have three minute rounds and at the end of that time the contestants rest up for a minute. Is football any less arduous than boxing?" The rules committee thought not, recalibrating the collegiate game into four fifteen-minute quarters, punctuated by rest times and a longer hiatus at the midpoint. The game clock would stop to accommodate the treatment of injured and exhausted men on the field, and the onus was on older coaches, trainers, and athletic directors to see that players got proper medical attention. Teams made official appointments of surgeons and beefed up the staff of medical assistants. The new guidelines lent legitimacy to the role of the trainer as never before. Not only did he tend to the injured, he taped them and positioned protective gear in such a way as to prevent injuries that would force men to leave games before they were ready to surrender.[52]

The rules committee made minor adjustments to the body-on-body contact allowed on the field. "Flying" or "driving" tackles were outlawed, and it was now mandatory that seven men per side line up on the line of scrimmage. Men could no longer push or pull teammates carrying the ball or engage in "interlocking interference," to Camp's chagrin, and onside kicks had to travel twenty yards before an attacker could pursue a ball carrier. The game was opened up even more when the five-yard restriction on the quarterback was removed, allowing him greater freedom to pass. Penalties for incomplete passes were also eliminated in support of the aerial game.[53]

None of this pleased Yale men, given the style of play they had perfected. They complained, especially about the expansion of the forward pass, which essentially neutralized their most effective weapons. Anticipating the new culture of caution that would result from the changes, a New Haven journalist announced the "End to Football Heroics." Pa Corbin, the center of Camp's famed team of '88, wondered if the complexion of college football had changed too profoundly. It was, he ranted,

> a far cry from the football of word and sign signals, snapping the ball by foot, continuous forty-five-minute halves, one to three games a week, thirteen or fifteen games a season, no substitutions without injury, no neutral zone, free to use hands and arms, free ball, flying tackles, only one man necessary on scrimmage line, mass plays, "V's," flying wedges, hurling, "guards and tackles back" formations, absolute playing responsibility of captain or quarterback[;] to this over-legislated, over-restricted, over-supervised, fifteen-minute-quarter pink tea, neutral zone, dead ball, curtailed tackling, hamstrung hands, helmets, armor menace, puppet, sideline managed, commercialized, basketball, Lady Luck spectacle.[54]

Camp also worried that the game had lost virility, but he was determined to keep the man-making narrative of football intact—and the appearance that he had control over it. There was no denying the popularity of the aerial game, and the public was convinced that openness was safer, whether it actually was or not. He resigned himself to alterations in football's heroic narrative to appease a public that at times was admittedly troublesome.

As a result, fatalities decreased in 1911, but so did the scoring. Aside from the forward pass, the changes of the last few years favored defenses, so in 1912, Camp lobbied for rules that allowed for more continuous action. To make it easier to get into the end zone, he supported the creation of a fourth attempt at first downs and a ten-yard shrinking of the field. The value of touchdowns also increased from five points to six. Less enthusiastically, he also agreed to do away with legislation that limited forward passes to twenty yards. Longer passes could be thrown more easily now that the regulation football was redesigned to be more aerodynamic. If Camp was dissatisfied, he did not say so in the papers. He was relieved that critics no longer saw the need to abolish a game that had value for American males.[55]

Back in 1906, when the forward pass had first become legal, Camp had grudgingly designed a few aerial plays for the Yale eleven. In the Harvard game that fall, he instructed Paul Veeder to go back as if to dropkick, but when he received the ball, Veeder, according to plan, ran sideways, eluded the Crimson forwards, and launched a throw to a man who stood alone near the goal line. Camp's play made national headlines, and for the next two years, his passing strategy looked more effective than that of his opponents.[56]

But his reputation as an innovator of the aerial game was short-lived. In the longer term, Yale did not take advantage of the forward pass to the same extent as teams in the West and the South. Every year, he made pleas to do away with it, in fact, only to find himself swimming against the current. A bout of food poisoning caused him to be absent for the vote that retained the forward pass in college football and even reduced penalties against it when incomplete. Yet again, in 1911, the play was on the chopping block, but Southerners on the amalgamated committee allied with representatives from the Midwest and threatened to secede if the "cavalry" of their offense were eliminated.[57]

The fate of the forward pass foretold the steady decline of Camp's influence over what was considered a new, improved brand of football. The programs that were building offenses around passing were steadily not the Big Three but the smaller schools that had nothing to lose by scrapping the mass game and starting from scratch. Coaches came out of the woodwork insisting that they had used the forward pass more effectively and sooner than Camp, but did not have his celebrity to prove it. Eddie Cochems at St. Louis University, for one, alleged that he had already been drilling his quarterback for the season when the forward pass became legal, and hence his team outscored opponents 407 to 11 once it was. By necessity, the smaller players of the Carlisle Indian Industrial School had also adopted pass plays as a means of getting around larger defenses. The true innovators of the forward pass were not Camp's disciples, but disciples of his disciple Stagg, who began a hiring-out program that rivaled Camp's when Arkansas and other teams asked his graduates to coach forward pass plays. One of those coaches was Notre Dame's Jesse Harper, who imparted the value of forward passing to his quarterback Gus Dorais, who used it to defeat mighty Army in 1913, starting a football dynasty for Midwestern Catholics that the Big Three Protestants could not match.[58]

Journeying across the continent selling timepieces and football, Camp had managed to catch games between some of these lesser-known squads now and again. He wrote about them occasionally, yet Westerners wondered if his lip service was meant merely to appease. When it came around to making his All-America picks, he still chose overwhelmingly talents closer to home, perhaps because he still knew them best. Men from the West and the South complained in *Collier's*. One fan recommended that Camp "take Horace Greeley's advice and go West and learn something about what is going on out there among the Western Athletes"; another lambasted Camp for his "monumental stupidity": "Why cannot you supposedly erudite Eastern foot-ball critics do justice to Western football players?" A Wisconsin man thought it curious that Harvard, Princeton, and Yale were still referred to as "Big" colleges when it came to football: "The Western universities with enrollments up in the five thousands seem to have no All-American material, while the small Eastern colleges with enrollments in the hundreds abound with All-American stock." Commentators in the South thought his omissions of their players equally curious.[59]

It was hard to fault Camp for not sizing up players thousands of miles from home. Already he filled up his schedule with games in the Northeast, scouting and covering matches for the papers. Football historian Parke Davis sympathized with his predicament in 1912: "When Walter Camp invented the All-American football idea . . . it was possible for a single observer to study all of the material in action against one another. . . . Today there are 300 college and university football teams in the United States presenting a field of material in excess of 10,000 men. Manifestly, it is impossible for a single observer to see more than twenty-eight of these elevens in action and these cannot be the right elevens since some of the most formidable teams do not play one another."[60]

Even if Camp wanted to compare talent across regions, few teams crossed boundaries to play each other. Occasionally, Michigan played Cornell, or Chicago went to the far West, but the general rule was still that Eastern teams stayed East, emboldening them to feel superior well after that was the case. That said, during the football crisis of 1909–10,

Camp had traveled to the South to watch winter practices under some of his proposed new rules, and for years he had conferred with informants around the country, who submitted reports to him about teams and players. Clifton McArthur, a member of the Oregon House of Representatives, for instance, kept him abreast of developments in the Pacific Northwest, and when he missed games, he referred Camp to sports editors at the *Oregonian*, who in turn sent Camp conference all-star picks and copies of the Portland and Seattle sports pages.[61]

When an informant touted talent, Camp followed up with inquiries to coaches of opposing teams. Early in the fall, he used scouting reports to whittle down a list of about one hundred All-America prospects, crossing off men as the season progressed. Once it came time to decide honors for first, second, and third teams, he tried to scout the men himself, traveling hundreds of miles if necessary. Even so, there remained talent he did not know about. The game was growing too quickly to see it all.[62]

Since his selection of Clarence Herschberger to his first team in 1898, players from schools west of the Alleghenies had made his lists here and there. Willie Heston of Yost's "point-a-minute" team was his choice for halfback in 1903, and the Chicago quarterback Walter Eckersall made the team in 1905. "Mother" Dunn, a center, appeared on the first team from Penn State the following year, followed by the Michigan center Germany Schultz in '07 and the Michigan guard Al Benbrook in '09. The year 1910 was a breakout one for Western players, as the third team included men from Nebraska, Oregon, and Washington State, in addition to players from Illinois and Vanderbilt. Still, fans around the country complained that Camp ignored their local heroes. "They haven't the prep school training, but their aptitude both for fight and physique is greater," a Washington man said of local players. "The sacred confines of Yale and Harvard may contain a good deal of football knowledge, but not all of the football ability."[63]

Camp was not surprised when local sportswriters started publishing their own All-Regional and All-America lists; there were nearly a hundred published by 1910. Local boosters claimed that the Eastern establishment had banished truer innovators to the West and the South, where they developed a game that was faster and made individual talent conspicuous. The fakes, the end runs, the passes, and other weapons in the Western arsenal put less of a premium on size, more on athletic ability, and eventually appeared to be more effective than the Ivy League preference for ball control, conservative kicking, and mass formations. Eastern men apparently started to agree, for in a reversal of trends, they borrowed Western coaches and plays. Camp even adopted Henry Williams's offensive maneuver, the "Minnesota Shift," in New Haven. A headline in the Northeast announced in 1911: "Small Colleges Shake Up Prestige of Big Elevens. Open Game Has Seriously Assailed 'Aristocracy' of the Gridiron."[64]

The forward pass would be the democratizing force that steadily stripped Camp of his authority and Yale of its prestige in football. It brought forth a new style of player who was quick and no longer necessarily bulky, whose masculinity was shown in his stamina, rather than brute force. Westerners and Southerners started to insist that they had more of the traits of potential All-Americans, embodying Camp's virile ideal better than any Harvard or Yale man who had not worked his way up from nothing. "There is too much belly to most of your Eastern footballers," an Oakland man told Camp.[65] Given the shifting tides, he could not entirely disagree.

FOURTH QUARTER: MANHOOD RECONSIDERED

10

Realizing Real All-Americans in the 1910s

THE PROFILE OF THE ALL-AMERICAN changed faster in many American minds than in Camp's annual picks for *Collier's*, but even those changed in time. Take his 1913 selection of the boy who came from Norway to become, as it turned out, one of the most renowned All-Americans of the twentieth century. The boy's father, a carriage builder, hoped to peddle his wares at the Chicago World's Fair in 1893, and came to the United States alone before sending for his family. Knute Rockne knew no English when he arrived with his siblings in New York and settled in a Chicago neighborhood inhabited by Irishmen and Swedes. It was on the gritty streets of this immigrant enclave, rather than the fields of a Northeastern prep school, where he began playing football, unaware of Camp's technicalities or amateur ideals. He sided with Swedes in street matches, but found "a couple of bruiser-like Italians" to join his squad. Everyone got so used to pummeling each other that cops insisted only players with nose guards be allowed to wade through the crowds after their pick-up games.

At thirteen, Rockne weighed 113 pounds and played on the scrub team of Northwest Division High School. It was not a Yale man, but South Side standout Walter Eckersall, who became his inspiration. Whereas privileged youths went straight onto Ivy League practice fields, Rockne took his time entering the college ranks. He washed windows and delivered mail until he saved enough to enroll in undergraduate courses. He had his heart set on the University of Illinois but settled for Notre Dame, where he was a Protestant among four hundred Catholics. The university allowed him to work off his room and board as a janitor in the chemical laboratory until, at age twenty-two, he tried out for the freshman team. At this point, he was introduced to his most influential mentor—again, not a Yale man, but a tramp athlete named "Foley," at least at the time. He had "roamed the country, overflowing with college spirit, regardless of the college," Rockne joked, playing under aliases and learning the harsh realities of the collegiate game. Living "foot to mouth, so to speak," he made Rockne less naïve about the business of football. At twenty-three, Rockne wore his lettered sweater "without too much intoxication."

The Norwegian whom Camp considered for his All-America squad experienced an America utterly different from the one most All-Americans before him had known; football was his ticket to their privileges. Whereas the national prestige of Yale once made football a reputable sport, football was going to turn Rockne's obscure Midwestern school into an institution with national fame, and him into a celebrity coach. "How a youngster from Voss, a hamlet in Norway . . . could find himself in his mid-twenties captain of a typical, mid-Western American football team . . . is a typical American story," he later reflected. His, not Whitney's or Camp's, was the proverbial dream for the modern man. But he had Camp to thank for infusing football with the heroic meaning that made his dream come true.[1]

When Camp had come around to selecting the bronze-complexioned Jim Thorpe for his All-America team in 1911, nearly every sportswriter in the East and the West was in emphatic agreement. "He combines every quality of football skill," affirmed the *New York Item*, and the *Herald* called him "close to perfection." Thorpe excelled at the positions of running back and kicker, though his strength and speed gave him the ability to play any position he wanted. Camp chose the Native American from the Carlisle Industrial School for his All-America team once more in 1912, declaring that Thorpe exhibited "the greatest individual prowess of any back on the gridiron."[2]

Americans had read only months before that Thorpe proved his superior athleticism in international track-and-field competition, when he won the pentathlon and decathlon at the Olympic games in Stockholm. The Swedish king shook Thorpe's hand at the medal ceremonies and reportedly told him: "Sir, you are the most wonderful athlete in the world." Thorpe was humble and remained so when he returned stateside in August. At parades in his honor, he stood in embarrassed silence; with a Panama hat hanging over his eyes, he chewed gum nervously as white men sang his praises. In Carlisle, Pennsylvania, the superintendent of the Indian Industrial School looked at Thorpe and Louis Tewanima, a Hopi Indian who had won silver medals at 5,000 and 10,000 meters, and decided that they were "real Americans": "Their forefathers were on the reception committee which welcomed to this soil and this glorious New World the famed first settlers who arrived here on the Mayflower," he creatively recounted, and ended his tribute with a letter from President Taft, who called Thorpe "the best type of American citizen."[3]

The revisionist history was likely startling to the Sauk and Fox Indian whose people had been forced onto a reservation out West. Thorpe's family was unusual; they had mastered English and wore Western clothes. Most others they knew lived a catch-as-catch-can existence devoid of interaction with whites. Indian agents and school officials once called young Thorpe a misfit. Now they considered him a role model for American youth—his athleticism apparently made the difference. A Missouri journalist referred to him as "a real, bona fide thoroughbred and registered American, not of imported but of aboriginal stock." Amid rampant immigration to American cities, this was intended to be a compliment of the highest order.[4]

Thorpe's glory on the international stage stirred up romantic visions in Camp as it probably did for any sportswriter in 1912. Until then, Europeans had figured that the athletic traditions of Americans were essentially English; they considered baseball to be the bastard son of rounders, and football the brutal stepchild of rugby. But Thorpe's athletic prowess in Stockholm proved that American men—and football players in particular—were the most effective males in the world. That Thorpe was a Native American in the most literal sense and an All-American in Camp's sense was proof that the American parts of football—the ones that Camp did not borrow but invented from scratch on home turf—made the superior man. Having served the national Olympic Committee, Camp was eager to promote Thorpe as the emerging face of American sport for the rest of the world to see.[5]

Thorpe's boyhood had been a collection of the experiences Camp had sought out for himself as a boy and wanted for the white youths coming of age in modern times. He had run wildly outdoors chasing rabbits and foxes until he had speed and endurance surpassing that of white boys his age. He weathered the elements, often barefoot, riding horses and paddling in boats he made out of hollowed tree trunks, surviving on fish he caught and berries he gathered.

Whereas Camp would have praised his self-sufficiency, Indian agents thought Thorpe a savage lacking discipline and direction. His father sent him to the Haskell Institute for Indian youths in Lawrence, Kansas, where he was supposed to learn a trade and self-control. School officials cropped his hair and dressed him in military uniform, punishing him corporally when he did not do what he was told. He felt liked a caged animal and fled from Haskell several times. Mercifully, Indian agents accepted him at Carlisle, a place that many of the Haskell boys talked about with reverence. It was where Indians had been molded into some of the best football players in the nation, beating white men handily at their own game. Sixteen-year old Thorpe arrived at Carlisle in 1904, a mere 5' 5" tall and 115 pounds; when he left in his mid-twenties, he was nearly 6' tall and a muscular 185 pounds.[6]

Camp played a role in Thorpe's athletic stardom, for it is doubtful there would have been a Carlisle athletic program, let alone an athletic director who trained Thorpe for greatness, had Camp not made it so. His connection to Carlisle can be traced to the 1890s, when the school's director, Richard Henry Pratt, consulted him about starting a football program. A retired cavalry officer, Pratt had convinced the federal government to use an abandoned military barracks to house and "assimilate" Indian children into white society. Through his school, he hoped to prove that savagery was not innate, that an Indian could be civilized—Americanized—if taken from the reservation and put in an environment in which military discipline and industrial training had their predicted transformative effects.[7]

These were years in which whites were inundated with images of Native Americans in dime novels and Wild West shows. Frederic Remington attempted to portray them in a more authentic light, and yet, popular images were often of men more prone to treachery than honesty. The "trickster" was a familiar figure in the oral culture of Native Americans, displaying wit and guile. White Americans also conjured up images of Indian tricksters, but interpreted their deceptions as more sinister or, at the very least, ungentlemanly. Pratt hoped to debunk myths about Indians' deceit and laziness and to prove that a "new Indian" was on the scene. On the field behind the main schoolhouse, the boys of Carlisle already played shinny, a game that primed them for the bruising play of football. What better way to "kill the Indian, save the man," Pratt figured, than by letting them compete against whites in their man-making game? This was, in essence, a form of "muscular assimilation."[8]

Pratt allowed the older boys to scrimmage with students at nearby Dickinson College, until Stacy Matlock, a Pawnee, broke his leg and Pratt reconsidered. Only months after the massacre at Wounded Knee, students crowded into his office and pleaded to be allowed to play again; they had prepared the fields and wanted formal instruction this time. One student bought into Camp's thinking to make his case: "Long ago, it was said that the Indian could not understand civilization. . . . The only way I see how he may reoccupy the lands that once were his, is through football, and as football takes brains, takes energy, proves whether a civilization can be understood by the Indian or not, we are willing to perpetuate it."[9]

Pratt asked for Camp's counsel as debates over football's brutality were coming to a head in 1894. The game was undeniably violent, and whites expected violence from his primordial charges. Would the press attack him, he wondered, "for developing the original war instincts and savagery of the Indian?" While white men's physicality had found its uses and outlets on a mythical frontier, the physicality whites presumed in Indians was different; it was not deliberate or channeled, they imagined, and thus they held it as a strike against them.[10]

Camp understood that it might be frightening to let "savages" unleash their unbridled energies on the grounds he had made sacred for white men, but he also believed that football had the ability to teach *all* men how to harness their aggression and channel it productively. Cautiously, Pratt placed conditions on his boys playing football. They were to conduct themselves as gentlemen at all times, never slugging opponents or coming off as less than civilized, even if the white players did not act in kind. He was aware of the hypocrisy, but he knew what his students were up against. By virtue of playing football, they would be visible in ways other Native Americans never would. Their behavior on and off the field would be scrutinized, much as Camp's had been as the architect of a violent game.[11]

Pratt's designs on a national championship were remarkable considering the football material that stood before him. His students may have been hungry to play, but they also looked just plain hungry. They were scrawny, some outwardly exhibiting signs of tuberculosis picked up since their more frequent interactions with whites. This was not a squad made up of prep school boys who had been groomed to play the college game. Only several hundred students at any given time were the right age and gender for football, and most who looked the part were off campus earning wages in the school's hiring-out program. These boys did not view themselves as college upperclassmen or undergraduates, since they trained in industrial or agricultural work that made classes and rankings immaterial. The Carlisle girls learned stenography and domesticity, while the boys learned how to blacksmith, plow, or operate machines. The end goal was self-sufficiency in the Jeffersonian sense.[12]

And yet Camp did for Pratt what he had done for athletic directors around the country, sending him Yale graduates who would instill in the Indians the discipline and technique his game required. Vance McCormick had just graduated as a national champion when Camp sent him to coach at Carlisle in 1894. His persistence was admirable, given that he was teaching fundamentals to boys who did not have the equipment, uniforms, or physical build of collegiate players, or even a command of English. He took solace in the assistance of Billy Bull, Yale's famous dropkicker, and in the Indians' willingness to learn. He noted that his charges had a raw ability to run, kick, and dodge. They were eager to test themselves against white players and soon got their chance at Bucknell, Lehigh, Dickinson, and the local YMCA.[13]

Former Yale guard William Hickok replaced McCormick as coach in 1896. From the start, his players resented him. He was a conspicuously wealthy Anglo-Saxon who did not have McCormick's noblesse oblige. This was evident when the Indians finally got their chance to play Yale at the former Polo Grounds in Manhattan. A correspondent for the *World* anticipated the contest as one between men who "represent[ed], physically, the perfection of modern athletes and intellectually the culture and refinement of the best modern American life" and "the aborigine, the real son of the forest and plain, the redskin of history, of story, of war." Some of Yale's wealthiest alumni occupied the box seats, while fans of the Indians yelled imitation war whoops along the sides of the field. That Hickok coached and also officiated did not bother anyone until he called back Carlisle's Jake Jamison after a touchdown run; no Indian heard the whistle he allegedly blew.

Fans jeered Hickok, and the Carlisle players left the field in protest. One reporter speculated in half jest that, enraged by the injustice of it, the "Redmen would whip out their tomahawks and simply scalp the sons of Eli in their tracks." Pratt made his way down to the sideline from a box where he sat with his host, the New York benefactor Russell Sage, and urged that his men go back on the field. This was a fundraising opportunity, and his men had a gentlemanly reputation to uphold.[14]

Though the Indians lost, they received a resounding ovation, and reporters wrote of the botched call as yet another case of Indians being wronged by white men. The *New York Sun* likened Hickok to a crooked Indian agent, while an acerbic Rochester reporter supposed, "If we have a right to rob the Indian anywhere, we certainly have a right to cheat him out of football games." Sportswriters also pointed out that, despite the calls, the Indians had remained in self-control. Caspar Whitney praised them for their high level of play after only a few years of learning the game, as well as for their sportsmanship. Writing for the *Journal*, Stephen Crane put himself in the minds of the stately "aborigines" as they prepared to play Harvard the following week: "They have stolen a continent from us, a wide, wide continent, which was ours, and lately they have stolen various touchdowns that were also ours. . . . The white men line up in their pride. If sacrifice of bone and sinew can square the thing, let us sacrifice, and perhaps the smoke of our wigwam camp fire will blow softly against the dangling scalp[s] of our enemies."[15]

Crane was hardly the only observer enthralled by the Indians' civility and imagined savagery. Before the Yale-Carlisle game of '97, the *Herald* described the Indians' nose guards and shoulder pads as war paint and the football as their "totem." Players were transformed into the noble savages of a Cooper novel—gentlemen and children at the same time, as well as come-from-behind heroes held up over men for whom privilege had been a birthright. Under Yale's Billy Bull, *Leslie's Weekly* described them as "the most interesting feature to-day in the foot-ball world. Their condition is so amazing that they play from beginning to end without appreciable loss of strength. Almost without armor, they move with dash and quickness unequaled by any of their opponents. When the university men call time, so as to patch up wounds, take refreshments, and catch breath, the Indians throw handsprings and turn somersaults." The *Journal* described a crowd roaring "with hoarse delight" when the rusher Metoxen came up from a pile of Yale men, clothes torn, "half-nude." Unaffected by civilization, he was a man in his natural state. Reportedly, "not one of the pretty Yale girls took her eyes from the scene."[16]

It was not lost on Camp that most of the 10,000 spectators who had come to see the Yale game in '96 wanted Carlisle to win. It was easy to sympathize with mistreated Indians, gridiron and national under-dogs. Because the de facto effect of the Dawes Act had been to relegate many of them to a form of second-class citizenship, whites felt less threatened by them than in decades past, and even rooted them on. Carlisle students traveling with their team did not seem to object to the stereotyped whooping calls as shows of support, since they were signs of shifting tides, indications that Yale athletes represented a social elite that did not represent the American fan—or the American man, at large. White cheers might not have been, however, a show of racial acceptance as much as everyman solidarity.[17]

Camp liked to think of the Indians as little diamonds in the rough. He maintained that their lack of elite school training was an asset in the end, because they obeyed their white coaches, rather than forming their own ideas. He thought that the Indians' self-possession was indoc-trinated rather than innate, having been drilled into them by the white man. The red man was a "born tackler," he admitted, and yet "more mercurial in football than his brother the pale face." Although his jour-nalistic coverage of Carlisle was never explicitly racist, his commentary was racially charged. Sometimes he, too, referred to Carlisle scores as instances of "taking scalps."[18]

Yale man John Hall replaced Billy Bull as the Carlisle coach in 1898, and finally, a non-Yale man replaced him in 1899—a Cornell man in fact, whom Camp recommended not only as football coach, but as Carlisle's athletic director. Glenn Scobey Warner's paternal influence had earned him the nickname "Pop" in his playing days. He had no qualms about lending his expertise to the highest bidder and agreed to come to Carlisle for a generous salary plus expenses. In this and other ways, Warner was Camp's antithesis. He allegedly womanized and cursed profusely through the hand-rolled cigarettes he held in his teeth. Having already coached at Iowa State and Georgia, he had proved that he knew when to employ Eastern methods or abandon them for new ones. His wing plays, screen passes, and tackling dummies were innovations that eventually led sportswriters to wonder if he were more innovative than the "Father of Football" himself.[19]

That said, Warner had his doubts when he first met the Carlisle men on the practice field. They looked sickly, he told Pratt, as though they were trying out for beds in hospitals, not spots on a varsity squad. Only one Carlisle team in the next thirteen averaged more than 170 pounds per player, forcing Warner to configure strategies that emphasized speed and deception over size. Out of sheer necessity, he made his men some of the greatest shifters and forward passers of the early twentieth century.[20]

Nevertheless, Warner had had preconceptions about Indians being lazy and prone to quitting, and he berated them—until they proved him wrong. In time, he saw that the Indians were quick learners who showed stamina he had not seen in white men. While they seemed to have a nearly inhuman threshold for pain, they proved to have a very human intolerance for his cussing, some even walking off the practice field in a stand against his abuse. He came to see that they had "real race pride and a fierce determination to show the palefaces what they could do." "It was not that they felt any definite bitterness against the conquering white, or against the government for years of unfair treatment," Warner reflected, "but rather they believed the armed contests between red men and white had never been waged on equal terms." A Sioux player insightfully explained to him that every time white men won, it was called a battle; when Indians won, it was called a massacre.[21]

Carlisle won eight games in Warner's first year of coaching, losing only to Harvard and Princeton. Camp ranked Carlisle fourth in the nation by 1900 and chose running back Isaac Seneca for the All-America first team, tackle Martin Wheelock for the second, and quarterback Frank Hudson for the third. Whereas Yale men remained reluctant to test their mettle outside the Northeast, the Indians traveled anywhere white men were willing to play them. With no home field, they took trains to Cambridge, California, and anywhere in between, even facing off against high school and club teams. White spectators found them remarkably resilient, given the wear and tear of their grueling schedule, and they whipped up a following wherever they went. Carlisle seemed well on its way to national stardom, and yet Warner suddenly left the team in 1904. He was offered a job to coach at his alma mater, and he thought it an offer too good to refuse.[22]

Camp was given the task of finding a Yale-trained coach once again, and he put the Indians in the hands of George Woodruff, followed by All-American Ralph Kinney and center Carl Flanders in 1906. The Yale reign ended when Warner returned in 1907; the revised rules of 1906 were largely the reason, for now he could exploit the Indians' quickness and the penchant he had already detected in them for the aerial game. Warner taught players to throw a spiral, gripping the ball on its laces to give it better spin. Quarterback Frank Mt. Pleasant emerged as a star, capable of launching deep passes for sizable gains.

That season, Carlisle defeated Penn, then Syracuse, and eventually Harvard. A Philadelphia reporter observed that Carlisle's passing was a "beauty to watch . . . natural instinct on the part of the Indian." Opponents noticed Warner's transformed tactics—not merely the forward passes, but the body blocks, feigned handoffs, low line charges, runs around the ends, flea-flickers, and reverses to compensate for his men's lack of heft—and concluded that the game was becoming "Indianized." Indeed, some of the hand signals used by the quarterback were indigenous sign language adapted to the gridiron. Camp could not deny that the "Carlisle system" created a more exciting game of high-speed chase than anything he had seen before.[23]

And yet, Warner's speediest player sat on the bench in 1907. As much as Jim Thorpe had potential, Warner thought him undisciplined. Although he had plucked Thorpe from track and field, Warner could not come to terms with Thorpe's careless demeanor, and so he made him watch and learn under the tutelage of halfback Fritz Hendricks and second team All-American Al Exendine. Finally, Warner let Thorpe loose in 1908, and he led the Indians to a 10-2-1 record before earning a spot on Camp's All-America third team. Warner figured that Thorpe was a shoo-in for the first team in 1909, but wanderlust struck again. For two years, Thorpe puttered around, whereabouts unknown, before showing up in Oklahoma, where Warner's assistant coach retrieved him.[24]

The two seasons that followed proved to be Carlisle's best, but the sweetest of all the victories occurred in November 1912 against Army, in a match billed as the best offense versus the best defense in the nation, as well as the ultimate battle between red man and white man. No fewer than nine future generals played for Army that afternoon. Warner alleged that his players felt no fear; he merely reminded them that their opponents, imposing as they were, were the pale-faced sons and grandsons of the military men who fought and killed their ancestors. Apparently, it was all the inspiration they needed. In the words of the *New York Times*, "Thorpe and his redoubtable band of Carlisle Indian gridiron stars invaded the plains of West Point . . . [and] outclassed the Cadets as they might be expected to outclass a prep school." The Indians defeated Army 26 to 7.[25]

Camp had been standing on the sidelines at West Point, one of the 5,000 spectators at this historic game. Afterward, he headed back to Manhattan, sharing a rail car with the Carlisle players. It was clear, he told them, that Army had been blindsided by Warner's double-wing formation, and the Indians explained that they chose this meaningful game for its debut. Camp asked why quarterback Gus Welch called plays so quickly, before sizing up the defense before him. "At Yale we don't play that kind of ball," he told them. Thorpe explained that speed was the point; they had to keep opponents confused since they did not have the size to outmatch them.[26]

Camp formulated theories to explain the Indians' success. The sheer athletic prowess of individuals like Thorpe certainly elevated the team, but it also seemed that the Carlisle players, as well as the Indians at Haskell for a time, picked up the nuances of football quickly because they resembled aspects of the games they had played as children. He also sensed that, unlike their white opponents, the Indians completely submitted themselves to the team; there was never a question about giving up individual glory to sacrifice for the whole.

But the most crucial reason he thought them effective was that they had lived more ruggedly than white men, and it showed on the gridiron. In their experience of physical toil, he claimed, they also developed thick skins and resolve. Camp lamented that white boys no longer played "Cowboy and Indian" as they used to, because it had forged hardiness in progenitors who had played it for real. His feelings toward the Carlisle Indians were complex and sometimes contradictory, as were his ideas about manhood. He wanted American men to be both modern and primitive at the same time. His romanticizing of the savagery of the Indian, like his promotion of football, was an antidote to the decadence of the modern age.[27]

But Carlisle's greatness was short-lived, Warner having much to do with its rise, as well as its rapid decline. He had modeled his fiscal administration on Camp's and soon suffered the same criticisms. In 1907, he had netted more than $50,000 in profit for Carlisle's athletic department. Some of this money went to the building of athletic facilities, as well as the school's Indian art program. But athletic directors at competing schools started inquiring into how much money he spent on recruitment, hearing that Carlisle men received payments or, at the very least, better room and board than other students. As at Yale, receipts turned up showing that Warner paid for players' tutoring and entertainment. Bill Reid charged Warner with recruiting from the Sherman Indian School in California, for no other purpose than adding athleticism to his eleven. Under the aegis of the federal government, Warner was reputedly engaging in an egregious form of professionalism.[28]

Warner denied buying his football talent and swore that his players were bona fide students. They went to classes for half a day, worked the other half, and reserved a mere hour before supper for practice, he insisted. But the truth was more complicated. Because Carlisle was a training school, not a college, some players had lived on campus for a decade, unaware of the concept of the undergraduate, let alone the undergraduate rule. On occasion, players had been "employees" of Carlisle, Warner conceded, but the line between worker and student was hazy at an industrial school. College administrators told Camp that, as long as Carlisle had been classified as a college for athletic purposes, they thought its players should adhere to the same eligibility requirements of any college team. They too might have shared Carlisle's success, after all, if they had full-grown men (who did not need to demonstrate the academic competence of collegians) on the field for six- and seven-year stints.[29]

Should Indians be held to the same standards of gentlemanly honor as white men? Camp pondered this question often. He noted that even if opponents ignored Carlisle's eligibility violations, they could not excuse Warner's men for playing the Massillon Tigers and the Canton Athletic Club, teams unapologetically in the business of making profit. Major W. A. Mercer, Pratt's successor as superintendent, swore to Camp that he would never have assented to his boys playing professional squads had they not misrepresented themselves: "It is because of our high regard for you and your connection with the football world," he told Camp, "that I desire to have you and all lovers of the American game understand that we desire to maintain only the status of a college or school team."[30]

After 1907, Warner vowed in good faith to follow the NCAA amateur guidelines "so far as practicable," which meant relegating the Indians to four years of varsity play with strictly amateur teams. "Not a single protest has come to Carlisle from a university or college that [has] met the Indians," he boasted. As the coach of arguably the best team and player in the nation, he was desperate to put any controversy to rest.[31]

But what Warner claimed was not entirely true, as Camp had already discovered. His players did in fact stir protests, and Warner's penchant for trick plays was largely to blame. Once, before a game against Harvard, Warner had an elastic lining sewn in the jersey of Charles Dillon, a Sioux guard. During the contest, quarterback James Johnson received a kickoff; with the Carlisle men huddled closely together, Johnson snuck the ball into Dillon's shirt, securing it under the hidden elastic. Dillon darted left and down the sideline as if he were running interference for another ball carrier. The Harvard defense charged other men meanwhile, who were holding their stomachs as if they had the ball. After Dillon reached the end zone, he took the ball out from where Johnson had lodged it, much to Warner's delight. Harvard Coach John Cranston complained that Carlisle had resorted to the lowest form of deception. They scored because they behaved like stereotypical Indians.[32]

Camp reluctantly weighed in, describing the play as something "perpetrated," like a crime, but also likening it to a hand signal or body fake: a legal and cunning maneuver. The incident would have likely faded into memory had others of Warner's trick plays not come to the attention of the rules committee. The Indians were known, for instance, to "play possum" during pregame warm-ups, feigning injuries they did not have. Princeton and Syracuse men reported back to Camp that the Indians sewed pouches into the fronts of their jerseys, making it look as though they were carrying balls that did not actually exist.

Camp was sympathetic; it was hard to be critical when Warner had merely taken to heart what Camp had proclaimed in his books—that nearly all was fair in metaphorical war. Harvard Coach Percy Haughton decided to match Warner's deception by painting footballs the color of Harvard jerseys, and Warner could not quibble; such were the deceptions of soldiers in battle, as long as no rule forbade them. Instead, he upped the ante in a game against the University of Chicago, thwarting the rule against catching a ball out of bounds by sending his player out of bounds, around the opponent's bench, and back in bounds again to make a legal catch.[33]

Although Warner's reputation was not damaged by his exploits, the same could not be said of his players. In trying to make them winners, he unwittingly fueled what whites thought they knew about Indians: that shifty play suited their trickster temperaments. Sportswriters chalked up Carlisle wins to their brute Indian-ness: On the gridiron, they proved cunning and vengeful, as history had proved in wars against whites. Some reporters forgave their shortcomings; they were red men, after all. How could they be expected to internalize the white man's sense of honor?[34]

But now, reporters also watched their every move, as Pratt once worried they would, both on and off the field. Carlisle players were confronted at train depots and in hotel lobbies, their speech and table manners carefully monitored and reported. Journalists played into stereotypes, conjuring up hostile comments that Indian players allegedly uttered in broken English during games. Whether Indians appeared to have usurped the traits of white men or were depicted in popular caricatures, they rarely were portrayed as fully dimensional men with identities of their own. Sympathetic or not, nearly all media coverage suggested that Indians had civility to prove. By 1910, Warner was asking Camp to help him defend his player Wauseka (also known to whites as Emil Hauser), whom reporters had lambasted for assaulting an official. He told Camp that his player merely pushed the man's chest in self-defense, but the press painted a picture of a red man wild with rage.[35]

Camp responded by giving the Carlisle students pep talks that generated publicity and boosted morale. He agreed to serve as advisor to Carlisle's Athletic Association, hoping to help Warner navigate the pitfalls of eligibility and public relations. But his efforts were useless in light of what happened next: The Indian Rights Association drafted a report to the Commissioner of Indian Affairs alleging that Warner pocketed athletic profits and paid players with gifts from the athletic fund. An assistant coach came forward, admitting that Warner kept a schedule of monetary awards for touchdowns and blocked kicks. It was also revealed that he paid to publicize the Indians in towns where they played, and that he recruited from reservations, despite his earlier denials.[36]

Then Carlisle's problems with alleged professionalism went from bad to worse. During the investigation of Warner, a Worcester reporter discovered that in the summers of 1909 and 1910, when Thorpe had gone missing from Carlisle, he apparently had been in North Carolina playing semiprofessional baseball for fifteen dollars a week. When questioned about it, Thorpe did not deny the allegations. He did not know at the time that he was returning to football, he told reporters, and he did not understand how accepting money to play one sport would forever tarnish his amateur status in another.[37]

Perhaps he should have taken cues from white players who used aliases when they accepted money, but Thorpe did not receive the "eligibility talk" in prep school. In a letter to the AAU, Warner argued that Thorpe's summer baseball had nothing to do with his training for the Olympics two years later, but the AAU made an example of him and stripped him of his Olympic medals. This punishment sent a clear message to the American public: Thorpe was no amateur, and certainly not the kind Camp had glorified at Yale or through his other

All-America picks. He was an athletic specimen who lacked the character of a gentleman.

But did the American public care at this point? Although Thorpe had been shunned by the arbiters of amateurism, fans seemed willing to forgive him for his indiscretions, yearning to see him, if not in college football, then on some athletic stage. From there, he transitioned almost seamlessly into professional sports, and Warner helped him by contacting baseball teams and offering him to the highest bidder. In 1913, the New York Giants agreed to pay the fan favorite $5,000 a year. Thorpe took the money and then bounced around, playing for the Cincinnati Reds, the Giants again, and finally the Boston Braves, before playing for triple-A squads in Akron, Toledo, and Portland.

During his baseball career, Thorpe helped former University of Illinois football player George Halas pioneer a professional football league, what became the National Football League or NFL, agreeing to serve as its first president. At the age of thirty-four, Thorpe organized a franchise called the Oorang Indians. The roster included actual Native Americans, some of them former teammates at Carlisle, who now went by names like "Bear Behind" and "Wrinkle Meat" and performed war dances with tomahawks at halftime. Thorpe played Indian now like he never had on the reservation, this time cashing in on the All-American-ness his ancestors—not Camp—had given him.[38]

Although Thorpe played up stereotypes he should not have had to accept, the man who fell from amateur grace remained a hero and bona fide athlete for decades beyond what Camp could have hoped for when he stopped playing college football in the 1880s. Like Knute Rockne's, Thorpe's story reveals the shifting complexion of the All-American in the popular mind. When Camp first invented the iconic figure in 1889, he did not intend to separate him from his idealized collective, the All-America team. Yet even then, fans often presumed that the men Camp selected were not selfless team players as much as the best individual performers in any context. Unwittingly, in selecting All-Americans, Camp created warriors who served as role models for the man-versus-world conditions of modern life. As icons of individual excellence, All-Americans seemed to have conquered the rat race, giving vicarious worth to the men who watched them.[39] Thorpe was struck down by the powers that be, but he brushed himself off and kept going. Americans loved that his talent could not be denied.

Camp did not stay in control of the narrative he wrote for football and its players. It grew in many, sometimes contradictory, directions. And yet, he was the one who had made the game malleable from the start, insisting that its ability to evolve would make it a national institution for the ages. As more American males took up his game, they used football to shape new ideas about athletic heroism, ones that transformed Camp's own.

Take yet another example of Camp's adapting to the times: his selection of African American running back Fritz Pollard for his All-America team. Pollard was not the first African American to earn the distinction; Camp had selected Harvard center William Henry Lewis to the first team in 1892 and Minnesota's Robert Marshall to the second team in 1905. But Camp did not appear to be fully receptive to non-white, non-Big Three talent until Pollard, along with Thorpe and Paul Robeson, a Rutgers player, forced him to reconsider what All-American-ness entailed.

Camp could not help but pay attention to Pollard in 1916. He had been looking through the letters of his football informants and found one written by a law clerk praising the Brown University back. "I know that prejudice exists among the followers of athletics in Yale University against the Negro," the writer acknowledged. "I hope that you will allow no feeling of race or prejudice to govern you in your selection of an All-America team this year; that you will give credit where credit is due; and that you will put Mr. Pollard where he rightly belongs—first."[40]

After observing Pollard himself, Camp agreed that his Olympic-grade quickness had become the marquis feature of the Brown offense. At a lithe 158 pounds, Pollard slipped in and out of holes before men were even aware of his presence. Camp chalked up his effectiveness to a crossover move Pollard did with his feet, allowing him to make forward progress even as he faked movements from side to side. After Pollard's stellar performance in New Haven, Camp had made sure to watch him play against Harvard and Colgate and swore that this "veritable will-o'-the wisp" was the most elusive runner he had ever seen. Even without the letter of endorsement, it seemed a no-brainer to select Pollard as a 1916 All-American.[41]

Pollard appeared on the collegiate scene at the right time for his shifty brand of play. The legalization of the forward pass had opened up the ground game and allowed his sidestepping to become a formidable weapon. His size was less of a liability than it would have been, now that speed was such an asset. Pollard's was the changing face of football increasingly acknowledged by the father of the game. He did not play for the Big Three, nor was he white or well-to-do. This specimen of gridiron manhood was shaped from altogether different material than it had been over the past forty years.

Like Rockne's, Pollard's ability had been honed on makeshift fields in Chicago, where his German immigrant neighbors called him Fritz. The name stuck, though his parents preferred the name they had given him, Frederick Douglass, after the abolitionist orator who had inspired them at the Columbian Exposition of 1893. Pollard was born the following year, the seventh of eight children, into a relatively affluent family of African Americans who, on his father's side, had fought in the Civil War. His mother's side was tinged with white and Native American blood that led to her children having skin of assorted shades of brown. The one trait all the Pollards shared, however, was athleticism. Fritz's sister was a champion sprinter, his brother Luther was an all-around interscholastic athlete, and all the boys played football. Leslie was the brother Fritz looked up to the most, and when he went east to play football at Dartmouth in 1908, Fritz vowed to follow in his footsteps.[42]

Princeton men had lodged protests when they discovered that Dartmouth had a black player, but this did not deter Leslie Pollard or the younger brother who looked up to him; as a rising high school star in baseball, track, and football, Fritz was confident, perhaps naïvely, that his talent would hush the racist naysayers. The truth, however, was that Fritz had more obvious limitations than his brother did. He was darker-skinned, which did not bode well in the lily-white Ivy League. It was true that a smattering of black men had played collegiate ball in the Northeast by the time Pollard entered high school. There was William Henry Lewis in the 1890s and William Clarence Matthews, the Harvard end of 1904, for instance, and Amherst fielded a few black players. But more times than not, these players were light-skinned, and several were known later to have passed as whites when they played.

Another apparent liability was that Fritz Pollard was exceedingly small. When his brother Hughes tried out for high school ball, he weighed over 200 pounds. Fritz, in stark contrast, packed less than 90 pounds on his sub-five-foot frame in his sophomore year of high school. It was not yet helpful to be small on the gridiron, much less on the Chicago streets, given the racial violence that occurred on both. With the migration of Southern blacks to the city, competition with ethnic whites was intense for menial jobs, as well as for positions on area football teams. Chicago high schools were integrated, but Pollard got used to men playing a little dirtier against him. His size and skin color made him a target, so his brothers taught him to lie on his back and bicycle kick violently to prevent men from piling on and maiming him after plays. He suffered punches and slurs, but he was able to take care of himself.[43]

In high school, he became an All-Cook County halfback, and college football loomed large in his ambitions. This was still a pipe-dream, however, since only thirteen black players made the rosters of teams at traditionally white colleges before 1900, and only twenty-seven more did so by 1914. Close to home, the only team that had recruited black players was Northwestern, but its football eleven was fledgling. Stagg had once accepted a black player at Chicago, only to ban any more. Michigan and Illinois let blacks enroll in courses, but they could not play on athletic teams. Minnesota appeared to have a better track record as home to the second team All-American Robert Marshall, despite the eugenicists in its administration. Oberlin, Beloit, Drake, and Coe had also fielded black players in spurts over the previous twenty years. But Pollard chose the program closest to home, Northwestern, and showed up on the practice field unannounced. When the dean realized that Pollard had no intention of taking classes, he asked Pollard to leave.[44]

Pollard went on to play semipro ball in several Chicago neighborhoods, jumping from team to team depending on who was offering the best pay. He described his teammates as factory stiffs, making twenty cents an hour, sixty hours a week, and blowing off steam on the field, often at his expense. Team managers were known to take up collections in the middle of games, strategically when home players made stunning plays, and Pollard made quite a few. Aside from an occasional slur from the opposing teams' stands, there was little indication that fans had a problem with him. The only time he tried to obscure his racial identity was when he posed as Charlie Lone Star to play on a Native American Wisconsin team. After the Indians won, Pollard joined his teammates in downing communal jugs of booze in the end zone.[45]

Pollard knew a proletarian brand of football, one Camp had likely seen in some form back East, but whitewashed as something else. It was football that abandoned the bourgeois values of college amateurs. Fans were hedonistic, and so were the players, who were unabashedly paid. Two of the clubs Pollard played against, the Decatur Staleys and the Racine Cardinals, became the Chicago Bears and Cardinals, charter members of the NFL.[46]

It is hard to know what fueled Pollard's ambitions to go on to Ivy League football at this point. If he wanted the honor of being perceived as an amateur, there were highly organized squads at black colleges, and in fact, his brother Leslie was a coach of one at Lincoln University. The first game between black institutions had taken place in 1892 between Biddle (later Johnson C. Smith) University and Livingstone College, followed by a game two years later between Howard and Lincoln, which started a Thanksgiving rivalry matching Yale and Princeton's. Tuskegee, Atlanta, Wiley, and other black institutions took up football in the South, and attendance records indicate that an emerging black middle class came to view football as a means of respectability for its men. While Pollard was in high school, black college administrators reacted to exclusion from the NCAA by convening the Colored Intercollegiate Athletic Association (CIAA), and soon the black press selected its own All-America team.[47]

Most of the first coaches of black collegiate football had been recruited from the Northeast: Matthew Washington Bullock, who coached at Atlanta Baptist, was, like Leslie Pollard, a Dartmouth man. Howard coaches Charles C. Cook and Edward Gray had gone to Cornell and Amherst, respectively. Perhaps wrongly, Pollard saw this as an indication of where real excellence was made. He was less inspired by "Terrible" Floyd Terry, who played brilliantly but in virtual anonymity at Talladega, Meharry, and Howard, than by white All-Americans and the notorious Jack Johnson, the black boxer who defeated white Tommy Burns to become the heavyweight champion of the world.

Johnson was, without question, the most widely known African American athlete of his day. White journalists, including Camp for the *World*, covered his exploits, particularly the fight in which he beat "Great White Hope" Jim Jeffries in 1910. Whites throughout the nation were shocked at his audacity, but Pollard was awed by Johnson's ability—not just in the ring—to shake the white power structure at its core. In the all-important athletic arena, Johnson flaunted his physical prowess and wore his rejection of racial inferiority on his sleeve. His come-from-nothing story intensified the anxieties of white Americans already threatened by the migration of blacks from Southern to Northern cities. His fame, as well as his notoriety, gave young Pollard an appreciation of both the possibilities and consequences of being victorious. A black athlete could make money for his prowess, but he could also appear too "uppity" for his own good. In the North, where a less flagrant Jim Crow system kept him at bay, a black athlete was wise to adhere to a humble code of conduct both on and off the field.[48]

Still, eager to compete against whites on *their* playing field, Pollard followed his brother to the Northeast. He showed up at Brown University mid-semester and was allowed to stay as a special student, on the condition that he took Spanish and French in summer school. But he had no intention of meeting the academic guidelines that Camp and decades of athletic committees developed. When it was clear that he was academically ineligible at one university, he simply moved on to another. From Brown he moved to Dartmouth—then Harvard, ever so briefly, thanks to the intervention of William Henry Lewis—and then to Bates, before ending up again at Brown. In effect, he was a ringer—a man who let himself be a borrowed gun—and he saw no lack of honor in it. Graduating with academic honors was irrelevant, because college was a steppingstone to an athletic career. Football, in other words, was not the means to a profession. It *was* the profession of his dreams.

Pollard's brother Leslie had taken up a collection and told him to use it to make a fresh start, so in 1915, the twenty-one-year-old took himself off to high school to earn language credits to re-enroll at Brown in the fall. He coached track too, since his financial situation was dire, having just married the mother of his baby son. Because Brown did not accept married students, he hid his situation by having his wife and child stay with friends. Unlike the majority of his white teammates, he did not have the luxury of spending extra time on the practice field; he was a working family man. He had opened a pressing service for Brown students and a tailor shop on Narragansett Pier to put food on the table as he played collegiate ball.[49]

The only blacks some of Pollard's teammates might have seen in all of 1915 were those onscreen in *The Birth of a Nation*, and they were played by white actors in blackface. There were fewer than 2,000 students at black colleges in the entire United States, and fewer than fifty blacks enrolled at traditionally white institutions. At Brown, Pollard was one of two, making him a curiosity to some and an interloper to others. Several blacks had played football at Brown before—Edward Stuart in the 1890s, and Herbert Ayler, a lineman who died of injuries a few years before Pollard arrived.[50] And yet, Pollard's teammates had mixed reactions when he first appeared for practice. "Christ, a nigger," a Southern player muttered when Pollard walked into the locker room. Another teammate's father, a Tennessean, threatened to pull his son from the squad if Pollard were allowed to play. Although he was allowed, Pollard got the oldest practice uniform and was given shoes too big for his feet. He showered alone and seemed to be forgotten when he lined up to pick up his game uniform and was told they did not have one for him. In a moment of vulnerability, he absconded to a corner of the locker room to cry in self-pity.[51]

The one ready friend Pollard made was a third-string quarterback named Clair Purdy, a Roman Catholic who warned that "Catholics and Niggers" were the last people white Protestant boys would allow to play. Still, Pollard persevered on the scrub team until he could no longer be ignored. It was hard to deny his talent, even if some teammates were put off by his cockiness; it made him look as if he thought he was their equal, and so, like Jack Johnson, he was given occasional reminders to the contrary. A few tried to maul him in practice, but he was too elusive to be stopped. He gained acceptance only when his quickness made Brown a contender for the national title.[52]

Camp saw Pollard play in the Yale Bowl that November. A few rare black students in Yale's school of religion had come to the gymnasium to see the Brown player that the press described as "burly" and were surprised to see a far less imposing figure. One of the students, William Ashby, thought the Yale line "would murder this little man" and sat on the visiting side in solidarity.[53]

The Yale home turf had been historically unwelcoming to black players. Back in 1889, upon hearing rumors that Camp might put a Negro on the eleven, a prominent alumnus begged him to reconsider— "The men are *black* and *blue* enough now," he half joked; had he been fully joking, perhaps the first black player would not have waited to appear at Yale until after World War II. In 1915, Pollard had to enter the field through a separate gate to avoid incident, but once he got on the field, his speed prevailed. He returned punts for sizable gains, and ran for thirty-two and twenty-three yards from the line of scrimmage. Fans shouted, "Catch that nigger! Kill that nigger!" Two Yale men tried to pin him in a flying tackle, but Pollard could not be stopped. Brown defeated the mighty Blue 3 to 0, and Pollard improved on his performance the following year, leading his team to a 21-to-6 victory on Yale's home turf.[54]

For all the glory he achieved in New Haven, Pollard later expressed bitterness about his playing in the Bowl. He had never felt so "niggerized," as he put it. Camp never reconciled the racism of his alma mater, perhaps because he never reconciled it in himself. He was the ambassador of a game in which non-white men were becoming players of note, even All-Americans, thanks to him. His frequent donations of books and money to black schools in the South suggest that he supported the goal of race uplift much the way he did at Carlisle or as espoused by Booker T. Washington—with a mind toward vocational training and cultural assimilation. But he never did call out Yale players who refused to play against blacks. When he selected William Henry Lewis as an All-American in the 1890s, his players infamously pulled out the Harvard center's hair on the line of scrimmage. Although he often spoke of football ennobling "the race" in generic terms, in front of audiences of white men, he specified that the manhood he sought to ennoble belonged to Anglo-Saxons. He described Yale spirit as democratic in his writings about poor men making good in New Haven, and yet none of Dick Goddard's friends were black, and none of his fictional blacks were athletes.[55]

In the NAACP's magazine *The Crisis*, Pollard's picture appeared on the "roll of honor" alongside that of another black football player four years his junior—Rutgers' Paul Robeson. Those who watched the intense matchup between Rutgers and Brown in 1916 would never have guessed that Robeson and Pollard were friends. They had met at the Narragansett Piers, while Pollard was tailoring the clothes of vacationers and Robeson was waiting on their tables. They played baseball and music together and found that they had a lot in common: Both were highly decorated collegiate track athletes and baseball, basketball, and football players on squads of less talented white men. But what eventually set them apart in a class all their own was Camp's selection of them as first team All-Americans.[56]

If Robeson ever had aspirations of going to Princeton, the college of his hometown, he knew better than to apply. He had the grades, but local blacks experienced Jim Crow segregation and associated with the university only as servants and laborers. Princeton's reputation for racism was arguably worse than Yale's, since more of its students were Southern whites with grudges. The only department to admit blacks was the divinity school, and the players on its athletic squads were known to employ especially brutal methods against blacks on opposing teams. As a Dartmouth halfback forbidden to play Princeton with the rest of his squad, Pollard's brother Leslie could attest to the hostility firsthand.[57] Although Robeson's father and brother attended Lincoln University, Paul earned a scholarship to Rutgers and went there. If he had not attended that all-white school, Camp would not have noticed him and been able to name him an All-American.

Whereas Pollard came off as cocky, Robeson was a modest utility man, playing left end as well as tackle, kick-off man, and punt receiver, if that was what was asked of him. At a robust 6' 2" and 210 pounds, he had the heft to be useful almost anywhere on the field. Having grown up in suburban New Jersey, he had long understood that being understated played well with whites. No one ever accused him of being uppity or not knowing his place; he shrugged off his accomplishments sheepishly. But like Pollard's, Robeson's presence on the athletic field was often only politely tolerated, if not outwardly shunned. In high school, his baseball teammates had had to protect him from opposing players who tried to mob him on the field. Robeson kept his head down and won his academic scholarship to Rutgers. There, he also chose doggedness over Pollard's flash, relying on power and discipline more than speed.[58]

Robeson's ability to harness control pleased his father, a minister, who raised him to do as Booker T. Washington told all uplifting blacks to do—to be "a credit to the race." This meant "lean[ing] over backwards to be a clean player," his father told him. "You can't afford to break any rules." Robeson swore that not once in his football career did he ever use his hands illegally, even as players did around him. He protected himself by tackling a little bit better than the others, breaking orange crates with his forearms to prepare for games.[59]

On some level, he had internalized an understanding of the logic that G. Stanley Hall and other boy "experts" had been propagating for years. The football field was presumably where the garb of civilization could come off for white boys, to let their primitive selves find expression. But black boys were assumed to be primitive enough. Their physicality, if superior, was not an indication of superior character, but rather compensation for inferior (less evolved) intellect. In their endeavors to reassure whites of their civilizing intentions, blacks had to rein in their brutish tendencies and reveal power only in the most controlled and deliberate spurts. Robeson worked hard at shaping his game to make whites feel better about his physical prowess. He did not gloat or contest calls and showed almost no expression on the field. In return, one sportswriter described him as a dignified presence, indifferent to the racial taunts hurled at him. Another thought his "self control, his gentlemanly instincts and his ability as an athlete made those who had been baiting him seem like pygmies by comparison." But there were also reporters who would never see civility in a black man. In the *Times*, one described the same Negro who shook hands after games as a vicious perpetrator of violence.[60]

Robeson never complained that on a campus of five hundred students, he was the sole black man and forced to live alone. On the nights of football banquets, when his peers convened at hotels where blacks were not allowed, he made other plans without making a fuss. Students and faculty thoroughly liked him for "acting right," but on the gridiron, his acceptance had been harder to earn. On the first day of practice, a teammate slugged him at the scrimmage line and broke his nose; while still on his back, another player jumped on him, knees first, and dislocated his shoulder. He was bedridden for ten days, before coming back and playing so physically that teammates started holding him in greater esteem. His perseverance came from knowing that his football career was larger than him. "I was the representative of a lot of Negro boys who wanted to play football and wanted to go to college," he later explained. "As their representative, I had to show that I could take whatever was handed out."[61]

But quietly he seethed. Once—only once—when he had been a freshman trying out for the team, he let anger momentarily get the best of him: "I made a tackle and was on the ground," he remembered:

A boy came over and stepped hard on my hand. He meant to break the bones. The bones held, but his cleats took every single one of my fingernails off my right hand.

That's when I knew rage!

The next play came around my end, the whole first-string back-field came at me. I swept out my arms—like this—and the three men running interference went down, they just went down. The ball-carrier was a first-class back named Kelly. I wanted to kill him and I meant to kill him. It wasn't a thought, it was just a feeling, to kill. I got Kelly in my two hands and I got him over my head—like this. I was going to smash him so hard to the ground that I'd break him in two, and I could have done it.

But just then the coach yelled, the first thing that came to his mind, he yelled: "Robey, you're on the varsity!" That brought me around.[62]

Players claimed that the coach had put them up to the abuse to find out what Robeson was made of. Ironically, Robeson came to see this man as a mentor and powerful ally. He was the rehabilitated Foster Sanford, the man who had become persona non grata at Yale for breaking Camp's amateur codes but who had since cleaned up his act, even in Camp's eyes. Sanford would come to defend his star player when fans yelled racist epithets and when Pullman conductors sought to remove him from the team's railroad car on road trips—but it took time. In October 1916, the players of Washington and Lee had refused to play if Robeson took the field. To play against a black man was to violate the tenets of white supremacy and bring dishonor to Southern players, as many Southerners believed. Because travel arrangements had already been made, Sanford succumbed to administrators' requests to bench his star player, who felt utterly betrayed.[63]

If Sanford's concession seems shocking, such "gentlemen's agreements" had grown common once interregional play gained momentum in the 1910s, with Northern squads even honoring segregationist policies on their home turf. Only in the late 1920s did they begin to contest these lame gestures of sectional reconciliation made at black players' expense. That said, Sanford refused to honor West Virginia University's request to bench Robeson later in the 1916 season. Robeson played brilliantly, as his opponents feared he would, though several shook his hand at the end of the game.[64]

Robeson moved on to Columbia University law school and became a renowned musician, actor, and activist. Pollard's path was arguably more muddled. After his All-America season, he fell perpetually behind on his tuition and assignments. Brown administrators forgave much of it and seemed not to care about his playing and boxing for money. John D. Rockefeller funneled funds his way to help him pay rent during the season. Meanwhile, alumni asked if he would tour around the country to speak for hire, even presenting him with a car that President Faunce asked him to decline.

It is unclear whether he did, but it did not matter, since he had other hustles. His son described him as "an operator" who lent himself to the highest bidder, because he could. Camp's selection of Pollard for the All-America team won him status that made him legitimate to white business partners. "It helped me in business because people trusted me," Pollard confirmed. "It gave me recognition wherever I went and cleared the way for me many times." All-America status had the same effect on Robeson in New Brunswick. Before it, he had been excluded from banquets; afterward, he was often the guest of honor.[65]

Pollard's and Robeson's experiences prove that Camp's All-American remained a model of ideal manhood, even as the model was expanding to include a handful of Catholics, Jews, ethnic whites, and non-white men who were once socially ineligible for the distinction. Unlike Jack

Johnson who was shunned in the white press, Pollard was celebrated as a heroic figure: "The larger public may take a wholesome satisfaction in the fact that a clean football player, an intelligent amateur, has succeeded an unsavory pugilist as the foremost athlete of his race," exclaimed the Chicago *Herald*. Camp's choosing of him said everything the white press needed to know, no further scrutiny required.

Pollard left Brown for military service in World War I; his former football accolades won him an appointment as physical director of the Army's YMCA unit at Camp Meade. After the war, Pollard continued down the slippery slope of professionalism, coaching and playing in Akron, Milwaukee, Hammond, and Providence before coaching a black basketball team in Philadelphia and Lincoln football, hiring Robeson as his assistant. Black men had not been part of the first industrial and mill town professional football teams of the 1890s, but now a few pro teams proved more welcoming of blacks than college teams were. Charles Follis was the first black pro, followed by Haitian-born Henry McDonald (Oxford Pros) and Charles "Doc" Baker just a few years before Pollard joined Akron. Pollard became the sixth black man to play professional football, and the first to coach and quarterback in what became the NFL.[66]

For a time, black men could make a living—and in Pollard's case, an exceptional one—playing team sport in a league that was formed just as American women were winning the right to vote. Professional football did not ban blacks or Native Americans outright, for now; Pollard played alongside whites (though he was barred from dressing with them in the locker room) in a game that had blue-collar affiliations. College administrators continued to call the pro game unsavory, and yet Pollard knew plenty of white college players who assumed aliases to get paid by the NFL. Professional sport was not yet an acceptable part of a white college graduate's self-making, but this changed; blacks were nowhere to be found on professional teams between 1934 and 1945, not coincidentally because pro football gained legitimacy in big-city markets and finally turned into an honorable pursuit for white college graduates.[67]

It took a world war to set these wheels in motion, for only then would college elites find themselves playing together with working-class men on service football teams that rendered Camp's amateur code moot. And yet, even before then, on the eve of World War I, Pollard already showed that there were athletes who had not internalized Camp's same sense of amateur honor, treating Camp's code as an obstacle to be worked around, not a mantra to live by. Unlike other mythical All-Americans, he boasted of his earnings and thought wealth the best indication of his success. He lived the dream of boys with no access to Yale or banking dynasties: If one could not pull up his bootstraps to graduate college, there was an athletic arena in which successful manhood was makeable. After his playing and coaching days, Pollard cashed in on his mild celebrity by starting up a black tabloid and a Harlem film studio. His ways on and off the field were those of a modern entrepreneur.

Camp took notes and made adjustments—not just to his game but also to his notions about manhood. He began to concede that professional ball was not *always* bad, and not just for minorities and manual workers. In fact, he confessed to understanding the impulse to go pro after college and be compensated for it. Who could blame the college graduate whose glory days had ended, yet who desperately wanted to have "another go at it" if he could, he thought.

More so than most of his Yale classmates, Camp identified with the plight of the self-made man forging his own way in college afterlife. Building a business and literary career along with his physique made him, like Thorpe and Pollard, a Horatio Alger success story. In the 1920s and '30s, writers of football pulp began dreaming up fictional protagonists who relived boyhoods through the professional game. In these shifting narratives, adult men did not automatically age out of the rites of passage that made them heroes, and their athletic earnings did not taint their athletic glory, as amateur purists once said they would. Although Camp continued to spout off old-school views about sport for pecuniary gain, his example belied his rhetoric. Football had been lucrative for him. Like more of his All-Americans, he was a man of the commercial age.[68]

11

Changing of the Guard, 1910–1916

AT FIFTY, WALTER CAMP STILL felt spry, yet while watching him on the sidelines of a Michigan game, one reporter decided that he looked more like a mature English gentleman than an athlete. He showed up at football contests with a fuzzy slouch hat over his balding head, and he carried a cane; he did not need it, but the accouterment completed his distinguished look. His mustache, though pronounced, no longer obscured the wrinkles forming around his mouth. He played golf to relieve the tensions of rule- and watchmaking, all the while thinking about the long-term effects of gridiron play. Were motorcars, rich diets, and sedentary, stressful jobs causing his generation to degenerate? While he pondered this question more than most, he refused to abandon his cigarettes. When he was in college, only "dudes" and "fops" smoked cigarettes rather than cigars, but he had since taken on the habits of the younger crowd, as had most men of his college days.[1]

Between 1872 and 1909, the record of Yale football was a staggering 324 wins, 17 losses, and 18 ties. The last team of this run went undefeated and was captained by the Bonesman and fullback Ted Coy, a specimen of physical culture loved by the camera. With his light, wavy hair and beautifully proportioned 190-pound frame, his signature running style resembled piston rods shooting forward; he was presumably Camp's inspiration for the novel *The Substitute*. Five of his teammates joined him on the All-America roster in 1909, and three others made the second team. According to the *Times*, the Financial Union spent more than $46,000 to cover their medical bills, hotel stays, equipment, meals, and rubbers (the then-used term for masseurs). Apparently, it was worth it, because no one had scored against them the entire season.[2]

But the success of 1909 was never replicated again. Over the next five years, Yale football spiraled to depths never seen before. The first signs of decline were subtle. In 1910, the Elis' record slipped to 6-2-2. One of the victorious teams that year, Brown, had not beaten Yale before; the other, West Point, only once. Yale won by a mere two points over Princeton that season and tied Vanderbilt, not scoring a single touchdown in either game. Tying Harvard in the final match of the year, 0-0, Yale gave Crimson Coach Percy Haughton the confidence to think that its era of domination was ending. Only one Yale man was on Camp's All-America first team that year; a more respectable three came out of Harvard.

Camp had anticipated the changing tides back when Harvard first abandoned graduate coaches and invested in Bill Reid. The continuity of the arrangement yielded results, and after systematizing football operations, Reid was replaced by Head Coach Joshua Crane, followed in 1908 by Haughton, former captain of the Harvard Nine, who confirmed that the professional model generated wins. The *World* described him as a new hybrid role-player—Harvard's "boss stevedore," its "gentleman and scholar," its "dollar-a-minute coach." He was methodical, a stickler for fundamentals. With his $8,500 salary, he was the fulltime, tactical mind on the sidelines that Camp could never be. Haughton was rugged yet refined—"red-blooded" and "blue-blooded" at the same time. Like a chess master, his mind was always moves ahead, and he exploited the special abilities of players as if they were pawns to be deployed. He also learned from past mistakes; using photographs of previous games, he showed his men what they did wrong so that they would never do it again.[3]

Camp's acceptance of the swifter game with the rule changes of 1910 had upset many supporters in New Haven, since the grittier ground game had always been Yale's strength. He reacted to complaints by trying to be a hands-on presence on the practice field, yet he remained frustrated by the players' "clumsy form" when it came to maneuvers designed for the new rules. The players blocked as if there had been no changes in the code, and so he personally demonstrated the newly legislated limited use of hands. He spared what time he could to be on the field, but friends started telling him of rumors. Many of the graduate assistants thought there was no point in coaching to rules that they presumed would be overturned, and there were also influential alumni in Manhattan who wanted Camp out of the way. In the week before the Brown game, Captain Daly was not practicing the plays Camp designed, and coaches did not come to his door the Thursday night before the match. It showed that weekend; rather than execute the shifts Camp recommended in his game plan, the players stuck with simpler, unsuccessful line-plunging plays.[4]

On the field, Yale was losing its way, suffering an identity crisis between old and new and stagnating as a consequence. Camp chalked up the problems to his steady loss of influence and the contradictory advice handed down to players by the graduates showing up to coach in New Haven. Traditionally, when each team captain graduated, he became the unpaid head coach the following season, advising the team as Camp unofficially advised him. But the novice coach was steadily getting steamrolled by outsiders. Tom Shevlin wrote Camp with alarm: "With the boy head-coach system[,] unless the head-coach is smart enough to use the best football brains that Yale has developed, it will not be able to compete with the Harvard system with a man like Haughton running it."[5]

Ray Tompkins wondered if the time had come for "a one man power" to hold the reins, a man with more expertise in coaching than new graduates. He wanted what already existed in Yale baseball and crew and what Camp had facilitated elsewhere—a seasoned specialist who was focused on a single sport because he was paid to be. It was time, he told Camp, to become the "chief of the staff"—not just by tradition, but formally so.[6]

But younger graduates wondered if Camp's czarist tendencies had not been the reason for Yale's stagnation in the first place. Was it time to run Yale football like a corporation, managed by networks of younger graduates? Camp always said that "too many cooks spoiled the broth," and his supporters agreed; history proved it best to stick with his singular master plan. And yet, over the next few years when he offered his expertise to captains, they declined his help. "I don't propose to do anything but keep my mouth shut, grin, bear the stories that 'Haughton has at last beaten Camp' etc., but I do want our captains who were so strongly with me in times past to know what is the situation," he told Tompkins. "We defeated Harvard year after year with monotonous regularity, then because a fool captain and young head coach will have no help . . . all the past is at once forgotten."[7]

Now, after all this time, there were Yale men who actually seemed to resent Camp's power in Yale athletics. As a Boston journalist put it, he had been "Caesar in the football world and, like Caesar, he fell from his throne, stabbed by the very men he had made great." Camp had been the one representative from athletics on the University Council, all the while serving as treasurer of the Financial Union and Yale Field. Since his graduation thirty years earlier, there had been few instances when he was not elected chair of the Athletic Committee or did not act like a de facto chair because students asked him to, and yet now, graduates made it known that they wanted his power diminished. Edwin Oviatt, editor of the *Yale Alumni Weekly*, expressed that graduates were ready for a change. Though Camp had too much national prestige to be removed entirely, it was hard for Yale alumni to endorse the salaries attached to his appointments when they believed he had grown complacent. "Mr. Camp stands in constant and imminent danger of facing a graduate rebellion," Oviatt warned. "His friends would be powerless to help him."[8]

Alumni who thought they knew better than Camp said that the game had passed him by; some even called him a "fossil" behind his back. Future Camp biographer Harford Powel observed that Camp had stiffened around the younger men, reserving his good humor for old friends, rather than ingratiating himself with new ones. It was probably true, since he was annoyed with the self-important men coming up in the ranks. Their heads swelled from the attention of the hero-worshipping press, even though they were rarely as good as past players. Rather than add to the hype, Camp downplayed their individual feats to focus, as always, on the team. He found it hard to be jovial around "jealous, envious men," as he characterized them, but tried to keep opinions to himself, venting his frustrations only to old comrades. "Our present deplorable situation c[omes] from a reliance upon the belief that committees of busy men not living in New Haven c[an] be relied upon to run our athletic affairs," he confided to Vance McCormick. The captain "consult[ed] with Tom, Dick and Harry at any old time, or, still worse, any man who had an afternoon off." For the first time, Camp felt utterly unappreciated.[9]

So he began severing ties, first stepping down from the Financial Union and gradually breaking away from football advising. The Yale press office released statements expressing regret over his resignations, as if they had not been coaxed behind the scenes. All-Americans Ted Coy, Billy Bull, Ned Glass, and Carl Flanders flocked to New Haven meanwhile, trying desperately to right the ship. Many graduates did not want to overthrow the Camp system, but to reinstate it, since they knew it to work. Shevlin, who left his lucrative lumber business late in 1910 to coach the team as he thought Camp would, asked Camp to draw up strategies from a distance. He turned the team around well enough to upset Princeton and tie Harvard at the end of the season, but Yale had a long way to go before it regained its former glory.[10]

Former All-American Wally Winter lamented that the current squad resorted to "trick (so-called in-side) football," and he urged Camp to rush in to enforce "the rudiments." Samuel Morse, former Yale captain and future developer of the Pebble Beach golf resort, read of the disturbing trends from California and could not be silent: "I have watched with growing uneasiness the lack of system which is so evident in our present method of coaching," he wrote Camp, "and wish with all my heart that we could go back to the old method which almost invariably landed us at the top of the pile. . . . That you were acting as grand adviser to the whole was what, in my opinion, enabled us to accomplish so much."[11]

An opportunity for Camp to reinsert himself into team decisions came as undergraduates called for a restructuring of the athletic administration. The Sheffield School of Science had grown since Camp's undergraduate years, and its men wanted more say in athletic affairs. The drafting of a new constitution for Yale athletics gave them this power in 1912; now, two of the four major sports managers were to come out of Sheffield. Rather than the major sports teams having separate administrations, they merged into a single body, the Yale Athletic Association, which, in addition to managers and captains of the major and minor teams, included five graduates and the president of Yale's Minor Sports Association.

Although the *Times* reported that the restructuring of Yale athletics was something Camp had promoted in order to phase out his own participation in athletic matters, that was not what resulted in the end. A clause in the new constitution stripped power from the football captain by giving a new football committee the authority to approve head coaches. Camp was soon the elected graduate on this body, as well as the chair. With the merging of major sports into the Yale Athletic Association, the Financial Union was formally dissolved, and its property between Chapel Street and Yale, Maltby, and Central Avenues, previously held in Camp's name, was transferred to the Association for the Yale Bowl. Camp was voted temporary treasurer of the body, then chairman, and then permanent treasurer. For all the regime changes, he remained central to the finances of Yale athletics.[12]

After New Year's of 1913, former captains and coaches met following a banquet at the Hotel Taft to outline coaching scenarios for the fall. Some of these Yale graduates speculated that Camp might lobby to make himself or his former star player Frank Hinkey head coach, but he endorsed the appointment of former player Howard Jones. Unlike the previous graduate coaches, Jones was to be paid. According to the *Yale Alumni Weekly*, he would not be a professional in the negative sense; his compensation would be modest, for time taken away from his occupation. He was older and wiser than captains just one year removed from playing, and hence in theory would be above the infighting of graduate coaches, yet subject to the will of the graduate committee. Camp hoped he would have the legitimacy of a Haughton, without his hefty price.[13]

Jones was receptive to the defensive strategies Camp suggested, but the season proved to be lackluster. Yale went 5-2-2, suffering losses to Colgate and Harvard. Nelson Talbott was the only player who appeared on Camp's All-America list; the only other teammate destined for fame, Archibald MacLeish, would earn his renown for Pulitzer Prize-winning poetry, not his athletic prowess. It was not clear whether more talent was coming to New Haven. "Yale has not had a first class back since Ted Coy and Steven Philbin left," a graduate complained from Kansas City. It pained him to see other teams better utilize the forward pass.[14]

Frank Hinkey replaced Jones in 1914; Camp was confident that he would work with him "in perfect sympathy," as he had in the 1890s. Hinkey signed a three-year contract at $5,000 a year, not generous by Harvard's standards. That March, Camp feted him at the Waldorf-Astoria in front of 1,100 graduates, many of them the financiers of the Yale Bowl that would open in November. In total, the steel and reinforced concrete structure cost $750,000, much of which Camp obtained by making graduates shareholders and promising them season tickets. He had abandoned the strategy of merely accumulating gate receipts, but it seemed worth it for a structure that accommodated 70,000 people, including 249 press seats. The *Yale Courant* called the Yale Bowl "America's supreme contribution to the great stadiums of the world."[15]

On opening day, 150 trolley cars and 43 special trains transported 77,000 fans to watch Harvard blow out the home team 36 to 0. Although Yale went 7-2 in 1914, not a single Yale man made Camp's All-America first team; only Maurice Brann and Harry LeGore made the second, and Alex Wilson the third. A New Haven sportswriter surmised that Harvard's formidable presence on the first team (five players) had much to do with Haughton's regime resembling Camp's of former years: "Yale lost her greatest asset when Walter Camp was ignored. . . . Harvard by this change was able to gradually outstrip Yale in the science of football. . . . The record shows that as Mr. Camp's grasp on Yale football was relinquished, Yale football gradually deteriorated until it is where it is today. The men who Mr. Camp taught here have gone out and made good all over the country as coaches, while Yale has been throwing away the teachings of the man who guided Yale football and made it supreme for many years." In the *Atlantic Monthly*, Lorin Deland described the components responsible for prior Yale wins: 20 percent, he surmised, had been player contributions, 35 percent coaches and captains, and 40 percent the "coaching of coaches," which had been exclusively in Camp's hands. Deland concluded that Camp had "forgotten more football than some of the men who coach to-day have ever known."[16]

And yet, Robert McCormick, the Scroll and Key man who headed the *Chicago Tribune*, confided to Camp that he thought the problems in

New Haven also stemmed from something deeper, namely the emasculated culture of the campus itself. Undergraduates no longer had virile influences, he carped, either on or off the field, and consequently, they lacked the pluck to win games. Camp conceded that Yale footballers were not the men they used to be. Now, when their grades slipped, they hired tutors as a quick fix and did not necessarily work harder. Rather than train rigorously, they waited for coaches to conjure short-cuts to success. They spent more daylight hours indoors, often in clubs, seeming to have "lost their individual initiative." Camp lamented to the football committee, "We can only partly do the job, unless the spirit of the community turns virile."[17]

Once, Yale men played for glory; now, even Camp admitted how often they were bought and sold. He supposed that they were not to blame. Many were the sons of men driven in motorcars to their office buildings on Fifth Avenue, where they honed their Machiavellian guile; or they were the sons of factory hands with no other way of attending college other than by brokering a deal and selling out. More and more, he received letters from agents of prospective athletes who assumed he would be party to their unsavory deals: "We have with us the son of Mr. Wm. J. Carter, of our firm. . . . We are writing the four leading colleges in the East and the best offer you can make will secure this young man." No one was embarrassed by such transactions anymore. Professionalization—the bad kind—had taken undeniable hold in New Haven, and players were unabashed and pampered guns for hire.[18]

The moral corruption was apparent not only within the university. Walter Jennings warned Camp about published photos of Yale athletes looking less than well groomed, a blunder he figured Haughton too conscientious to let happen in Cambridge. "The game of football is considered rough and ungentlemanly by a great many," he wrote Camp, "and when a picture like the one of [Captain] Ketcham is sent broadcast through the country, the idea of roughness is well exemplified and suggests a hard class of men are the ones who play it." Meanwhile, the headmaster of the Hill School wrote Camp damningly of Yale freshmen: "We all expected a manly lot of fellows and a clean, pleasant game, and their behavior was not that of gentlemen, or good sportsmen." Players threw their head guards to the ground in protest of the officiating.

Princeton freshmen confirmed that they too had not confronted less honorable opponents.[19]

Yale players no longer seemed to be young men of character, but how could they be? For all Camp's talk about the man-making lessons of self-regulation, they had become the puppets of their handlers. Coaches, promoters, trainers, and managers regulated their every move until they could not regulate themselves. Robert McCormick worried that it did not bode well for the varsity teams to come. In 1914, he sent Camp a newspaper clipping of a poem called "The Grad's Lament"; less than subtly, it told of the emasculation that older Yale men thought was taking place in New Haven:

> In the days of yore Yale's football
> Was very tough and crude.
> They used to treat old Harvard
> Like so much breakfast food;
> And rolling down to Mory's
> The sweatered seniors came,
> Roaring with booze and vict'ry
> After the Harvard game.
> But now the sons of Eli
> Are gentle and refined,
> When Harvard makes a touchdown
> They try hard not to mind.
> When stepped upon by Colgate
> Yale students never swear,
> Some go and plunge in Oolong,
> Some go and do their hair.
> I love such sweet refinement
> All rudeness I abhor;
> I hope Yale wins the tatting
> From Vassar and Bryn Mawr.
> But when it comes to football
> I think I'll save my bets,
> Lest some coarse Harvard person
> Should slap New Haven's pets.[20]

Yale football seemed a dynasty in decline—just as Camp's son was trying to make a name in it. It was his unfortunate timing to be arriving at Yale as the last great team, the team of 1909, was graduating. People called Walter Jr. "a chip off the old block"—a competent student, but an athlete at the core. Dad had pulled him from Hopkins to attend the Westminster School in Simsbury, where he bulked up for college ball. As a 172-pound high school sophomore, he was already bigger than most of his opponents, yet a reporter surmised that Walter Sr. would want him to put on another thirteen pounds before he weighed in at Yale, and he did. Like his father, he was a natural punter, the best on his high school team, but Camp managed his son's career carefully: Walter Jr. had already suffered a broken collarbone before stepping foot on a college gridiron, which meant that he needed to be both hardened and cautious. Local journalists could not resist what looked to be a tale of "like father, like son," but Walter Jr. was likely conflicted about the pressure to live up to his dad's successes. Camp's feats as a college player were now the stuff of legend.[21]

As it turned out, Walter Jr. had only a season and a half to make his mark on the college game: Adhering to eligibility rules, he did not play on the varsity his freshman year, and after a fairly auspicious start to his sophomore year, a sprained ankle forced him to the sidelines and prevented him from earning a varsity letter. His back gave him problems in 1911, but as a junior, he was determined to make the varsity squad. He did "brilliant work" in the Brown game, scoring Yale's only touchdown on a plunge through the line. Coaches saw glimmers of the evasive play that his father invented, as he nestled closely behind the interference of the shift play to slip through tackles for gains. A contest against Colgate was the high point of his career; he contributed to nearly every score of the 23-0 victory, and then gained more yards on the ground than any other Yale back in the final five games of the season. It was a good last impression; no one quibbled when his father chose him for the All-America second team to end his junior year.[22]

When the time came to choose a captain for his senior year, Walter Jr. did not put his hat in the ring. Some speculated that his decision was made at Camp's request and that the reasons were personal. His father's struggles with coaches may have been the unspoken problem, but there were other factors contributing to his less illustrious career. His father had delayed his entrance to college one year, despite his formidable size, because, deep down, he worried that Walter Jr. lacked the toughness that greatness required. "Boys of tender age who are overgrown are more inclined to injury," Camp reasoned. "He needed more maturity, and I insisted that he have it." Worried that his son's comfortable suburban existence had stunted his physical fortitude, Camp sent him to Canada in the summer of 1911, and the summer after that he spent six weeks with Shevlin at Lake Minnetonka, to be put through outdoor rigors.[23]

Doubts about Walter Jr.'s resilience were answered in his senior year, when he proved more breakable than his father had been. Rather than train vigorously in spring practice, he had surgery for chronic nasal trouble. Although he was expected to recover quickly and be the starting halfback and distance punter, just before the season, he was hospitalized for neuritis in his back and shoulder. He hoped he could build up his strength before the first game, but he remained ten pounds under his playing weight. The neuritis returned to plague him. By November, he abandoned training and left the squad.

Walter Jr. had rowed his freshman year and then stopped; he had played baseball, but only on intramural teams. He tried to involve himself in campus activities his father never tried, including oratory, playing Woodrow Wilson in a mock debate against William Howard Taft. But none of this made him exceptional. There was no competing with Dad's legend on the gridiron, or in anything else that mattered at Yale.[24]

During his junior year, his parents had entertained lavishly during Promenade Week at their house at 34 Hillhouse Avenue, the old Benjamin Silliman estate, later bought by future college president Charles Seymour and then sold to Yale. The Camps lived in the mansion at an ideal time to take advantage of its grandiosity: Janet would soon be a debutante taking callers, and Walter Jr. was nearing Tap Day just as boys from the Harriman and Vanderbilt families were being considered for the university's secret societies. The release of Owen Johnson's *Stover at Yale*, with its less-than-subtle critique of campus culture, however, had cast a pall on the Tap Day proceedings. For the first time, the *Hartford Courant* came out against the ritual as "cruel" and "pitiless." "Johnson's . . . saying right out that the awe and reverence for the senior societies at New Haven was a cramping and blinding worship of institutionalism had evidently not been lost on the college audience," reported a correspondent. Bystanders did not show up to watch the tapping ceremony in the numbers they had in the past.[25]

Times were changing, but Walter Jr. was a Bones legacy who stood among the hopefuls weathering the downpour on the green late that May afternoon in 1912. Camp Sr. watched the scene from a window above the grounds. Just before the five o'clock bell, men from the junior class gathered around the old tree between Durfee Hall and Battell Chapel, cheered and jeered at by the bystanders who collected at windows and rooftops of nearby halls. Several undergraduates had climbed up the old tree, poised to announce the selections. At the stroke of five, society men emerged from their headquarters and walked toward the mass of hopefuls in four-minute intervals. When they found their initiates, they slapped them on their backs and instructed them to go to their rooms. The taps came faster, and the remaining men wore looks of desperation. Walter Sr. left his dry perch to watch from the ground, and in a rare loss of composure, "dashed forth from the crowd, water dripping from his hair and a buff polo coat hanging to his back like a wet rag," according to the *Times*. Walter Jr. got a slap, and a cry went out from the old tree. He had been tapped for Scroll and Key.[26]

Was Walter Jr. rejected by Skull and Bones? If his father knew, he kept it quiet, the way he had learned to be about all fraternity business. Walter Jr.'s chum William Averill Harriman went Bones, as did George Cortelyou, the son of the president of Consolidated Gas. Jesse Spalding, the new football captain, went Keys, while Douglass Bomeisler, the All-American, did not get tapped at all. Another man who went Keys was the soon-to-be-Broadway-legend Cole Porter, who never got closer to the gridiron than writing the Yale fight song. One has to wonder whether his brothers were aware of his homosexuality and hence of how far their acceptance of alternative forms of manhood had come.[27]

The Tap Day of 1912 revealed a shifting configuration of social power at Yale. Amid mounting losses on the gridiron, it was a subtle refutation of football players as "men about campus." In 1913, most of the sophomore class protested Tap Day, requesting that it not get the publicity it had in years past. Owen Johnson's *Stover* had struck a nerve, creating the first open revolt against the society system. Younger

students complained that the selection process was rigged by prominent families, hardly a meritocracy, and that the secrecy surrounding
it created undue stress, hence outliving its purpose. The hero cited by
the protesters was Johnson's fictional Brockhurst, a renegade who noted
that the architecture of each society hall was suggestive of a dungeon—
"the prison of the human mind."[28]

As a consequence of the shifting sentiments, Tap Day in 1913 proved
to be a more humiliating experience for the soon-to-graduate Walter
Jr. than it had been for his father thirty-three years earlier. When he
emerged from the Keys' sacred tomb to tap his man on the campus
green, as he had been tapped the year before, he was actually teased;
chants of "Here comes my daddy, now" echoed around the old tree,
where he seemed to wander for a prolonged period of time because
he could not find his man. Eventually, a spectator perched on a tree
branch above him joked that his man must have "stepped out to lunch."
Apparently, the cachet of being tapped and told to go to one's room was
greatly diminished, if not gone.[29]

So ended the reign of Camp II at Yale. After graduation, his father
pulled strings to have him considered for a deputy commissioner position with the Parks Department in Boston. Despite the approval of
other commissioners and a good word put in by former President Taft,
the mayor ultimately chose a man with more relevant experience. The
newly minted graduate managed to find his way into the street railway
business instead, using his engineering degree to control traffic for the
Connecticut Company.[30]

Smitten with a local girl, Walter Jr. likely had few regrets about
remaining near home. By all accounts, his betrothed, Frances English,
was a perfect catch. A card-carrying Colonial Dame and the grand-
daughter of a Connecticut governor, she had bloodlines of the right
sort for an aspiring society man proposing to marry her. Since making
her debut several years back, she had turned heads with her stage role
in *The College Hero*. The *Herald* called the amateur actress "one of the
most beautiful and vivacious and talented of New Haven Society . . . a
leader in the college set." Alice was overjoyed when Frances and Walter
Jr. got engaged that September with plans to wed the following fall.[31]

The Camp estate was "wonderfully arranged" for the four hundred
guests Alice invited to tea in Frances's honor that October. From the

chrysanthemums in the music room, to the roses and dahlias in the library, and cosmos and snapdragons in the drawing room, no detail was overlooked. Frances wore blue brocade with fur trim, and Alice wore a gown of black charmeuse and white lace, the bodice cut in the "new blouse effect" to appeal to both the married and younger sets. A contributor to the society page noted that it had been "some time since a New Haven woman [gave] an entertainment for her son's fiancée." Alice spared no expense for the events leading up to what promised to be the most talked-about wedding of the social season.[32]

That summer, Alice took a respite from all the planning to accompany Walter to Europe. There was clock business in London, as always, but Walter also made time to golf, watch boxing, speak on American sports at the Savoy, and attend an induction ceremony as an honorary member of the American Universities Club. The Camps visited Janet at finishing school in Lausanne before leaving for the Olympic conference in Paris. With the death of James Sullivan, the American Olympic Committee lacked leadership, and Camp tried to fill the void. Increasingly, he inserted himself into the world of amateur athletics outside the college gridiron, laying the foundations for his activity on boards governing boxing and tennis in the 1920s.[33]

When the Camps returned to New Haven, the football season was beginning, but their house was abuzz with talk of food and flowers for the receptions preceding Walter Jr.'s wedding. In mid-October, hundreds gathered for the nuptials at St. Paul's Episcopal Church, followed by a reception at the Lawn Club. According to the local press, the only event exceeding its grandeur that season was the opening of the Yale Bowl.[34]

Watching his son marry made Camp forget about the troubles of Yale football, but the bliss did not last. Three months after the wedding, Walter Jr. had moved with Frances to Willow Street and was enjoying an afternoon of golf when he was struck with writhing pain. He was taken to the emergency room of New Haven Hospital, where doctors diagnosed him with appendicitis that required immediate surgery. Alice was en route to the hospital to be with her son, but her limousine collided with a wagon in the road, the impact throwing her to the side of the car and straining ligaments in her back and neck. After hosting a most spectacular wedding, Camp now found himself sitting vigil at two hospital bedsides.[35]

Walter Jr. recovered, while Alice was physically never the same. Friends subsequently described "New Haven's most popular woman" as "an almost constant sufferer," making it hard for her to host Janet's coming-out events with the same vivacity of the previous fall. Watching his wife's deterioration made Camp more mindful than ever of healthful living for the long term. And why was it, he also wondered, that his son had suffered illness and injuries that he had not experienced at his age?[36]

As he nursed his loved ones back to health, he thought less about conspicuous muscle and more about the internal constitution. The prevention of disease and avoidance of injury preoccupied him, and he tried his hand at designing protective athletic equipment, starting with elbow guards for golfers that he developed with Julian Curtiss. The project dovetailed with an article he was writing for *Vanity Fair* with efficiency expert Frank Gilbreth, who was performing motion studies of golf swings. More and more, Camp advised men over forty to take up the low-impact sport, writing about golf nearly as much as the younger man's game of football.[37]

In these months, Camp arose at 6:30 each morning to try to accomplish all that he needed to. Although he spent less time in Yale athletics, he had fingers in many pies, most of them literary. Harford Powel claimed that, by now, he was one of the three or four highest paid nonfiction writers in the country, and indeed, the vast amounts of material published in his name likely made this true. The Newspaper Enterprise Association paid him honoraria for regular pieces, as he sold columns to the *New York American, Chicago Examiner*, and various syndicates. He continued to write for *Collier's, Youth's Companion*, and other national publications while compiling material for his Century series. While he wrote bridge-playing manuals, he also penned the brief *Football for the Spectator*, which he dedicated to Janet. She remembered her father retreating upstairs to his sitting room after dinner during these busy months, working feverishly on his columns as she made her evening phone calls.[38]

At this time, Camp was also in negotiations to publish his most comprehensive work to date: a history of American athletics. Robert Appleton was interested in publishing it but wanted something less sweeping: a history of intercollegiate athletics perhaps, which could be sold in commemorative colors. There was no time to lose, as athletic pioneers were dying off, and the current generation was eager to hear their stories while they were still alive.[39]

These projects allowed Camp to remain peripherally involved in Yale athletics as he stepped down from more positions. He retired as treasurer of athletics and chairman of the Yale Football Committee, claiming that he needed to spend more time at the clock company's production facility. Labor problems led to a five-week machinists' strike, during which, ironically, Camp's disgruntled employees raised funds for their cause by collecting gate receipts at football games of their own.[40] With so much on his mind, he decided in 1915 to resign as chairman of the Yale Athletic Association, severing all official ties with university athletics. A letter Alice wrote football committeeman Vance McCormick suggests that even as she suffered her own ailments, she worried about her husband and thought his resignations a good thing:

> I've seen him sacrifice every personal feeling on the chance of saving a team here from disaster, and I have controlled my own indignation at the attitude of the captain or coaches, because football is to Walter like a child to its parent.
>
> Now, with your committee in charge, Walter can look on with satisfaction and will of course be glad to help always, if his help is sought, but his days of anxiety and worry over the situation must be over. I will not have him harassed day and night by the responsibility for conditions which ought never to have been reached. I have never said all this to him but Janet and I have said "Don't" steadily. . . . You will think me selfish and disloyal, but Walter comes first, and I have looked forward to a period of freedom from anxiety for so long that I am happy to have succeeded in withdrawing him from one contributory cause.[41]

Alice provides rare insight into Camp's suffering in sacrifice to football. He hid his feelings, much as he told gridiron warriors to sublimate physical pain; and in his case, the gridiron mother finally intervened. Although Camp was still a member of the University Council, for the first time in nearly forty years, Alice made sure that he had no role in Yale football. Captain Alex Wilson told reporters that this did not preclude Camp from contributing as a coach to the coaches from time to time, but the official resignations remained a cause of concern in the press. For a quarter century, Yale's athletic policy had essentially been Camp's. He had left the Financial Union with a $125,000 surplus. Who would manage these profits now that he was walking away? Sheffield Professor Robert Corwin agreed to take his place in the Yale Athletic Association, but given that Camp was the only person who had ever kept the books or handled intercollegiate negotiations, Corwin was not sure how to proceed.[42]

Camp still had more shocking announcements in 1915. Having served on every configuration of the rules committee since 1878, he decided that it was time to step down from it as well. He had been the one who suggested forming a graduate committee on rules and appeals and saw to the publication of rules every year for decades. Though members of the committee had come and gone and organized under the aegis of the NCAA, new legislators had still taken comfort in his steady presence. The thought of making decisions without him proved so daunting that one colleague respectfully protested his stepping down: "To say that the game of football would suffer a great loss if the Rules committee accepted your resignation is a platitude. . . . Your presence—AS LONG AS YOU LIVE—is absolutely necessary on the Committee!" At a meeting at the Hotel Biltmore, Dashiell, Stagg, and Parke Davis read tributes to their retiring colleague, and Percy Haughton admitted that his successes of late had much to do with watching Camp's every move. Henry Williams related the story of a time when his family was vacationing on Martha's Vineyard and word came of Camp's arrival on the island. Little boys ran shouting in excitement because the visitor was the undisputed "Father of Football."[43]

Camp was humbled by their words, so much so that he accepted an ambiguous status on the committee as an emeritus member. From there, he agreed to serve a little more, then a little more, until finally, he agreed to be secretary once again. Despite his intentions, he thus never truly shut the door on the rules committee, or on advising at Yale, for that matter. As much as younger men wanted his power diminished, they also passed motions to make him "ex officio" on committees, and he was too gracious to refuse.[44]

Still, his resignations, be they brief or undone, forever changed the modus operandi of Yale athletics and ended the rules committee's amalgamated structure. Upon his departure from the Yale Athletic Committee, he had told his successors that their reign of rogue regulating should end, and they voted to request NCAA membership. That year, Camp traveled to Chicago to attend the NCAA's ninth annual meeting. Representatives from more than one hundred institutions now convened, many of them awed by the miniature machinery Camp wore on his wrist, the latest of New Haven Clock Company innovations. He stood as a human billboard, but he was also there to be conciliatory. The days of Yale leading the football universe were over. Now, he had the difficult task of facing it.[45]

The nadir of Yale football in 1915 proved that this was true. For the first time, the team lost to a Southern squad, Virginia. Captain Alex Wilson had come to resent Hinkey's mismanagement so much that he called him out in front of the team when he could no longer ignore Hinkey's drunken rants. Old-timers confirmed the rumors of Hinkey's drinking for Camp, one describing him as "perfectly unreasonable after beginning." Wilson urged the football committee to force Hinkey out, and graduate coaches filled his shoes until Shevlin swooped in to try to rescue the team, as he had in 1910.[46]

Yale eked out a win against Princeton in the second-to-last game of the season, but that was the only success the team could muster, losing to Harvard in its final game, 41-0. The loss seemed to demoralize Shevlin completely. Over the course of the season, he had lost weight and he looked depleted; now, at season's end, he had become clearly ill. He contracted pneumonia the week of Christmas and died before New Year's Day, 1916, at the age of thirty-two. His passing marked the lowest point in the Yale football program. Five team members had been barred from games for playing paid summer baseball, and the team record was a lackluster 4-5, with no first team All-Americans.[47]

Yale graduates turned to the football committee and begged for changes. Cupid Black, captain for 1916, recommended for the head coach position his old mentor from Exeter, former Yale quarterback Tad Jones. The committee knew Jones well; he was the younger brother of former Yale coach Howard Jones and, in addition to once being class president and captain of the baseball nine, coached the Yale back-field for a time. Since his playing days, Jones had found religion; he permitted no swearing and pushed the disciplined austerity that suited Camp completely. Camp gave his blessing to a three-year contract that would pay $6,000 a year, and Jones asked Camp to join his staff. Camp was standoffish. Alice wanted him to stay away, he explained, and the directors at the clock company had an aversion to his "becoming offi-cially attached to the football again." But then, in a letter to Vance McCormick, he also left a door open: "You can use me all you like in the advisory capacity, and you must all come out and have your meet-ings at my house where, if you will, we can build up in a really conge-nial atmosphere the old-time spirit and plans."[48]

It was not long before Camp was roped into assuming a role on the "special football committee of reorganization," though he repeat-edly insisted that he was merely "an advisor." One of his first priorities was calling together the Corporation, the Athletic Committee, alumni advisors, the Board of Deans, the college president, and writers for the *Yale Alumni Weekly* to present a united front of support for Jones and his regime. Players were awestruck one day to find Lonnie Stagg on the sidelines at practice; to reinvigorate the team, Camp had brought in his big gun. Despite early refusals to come to spring practices, Camp started developing the men. "I became aware of the two most luminous and gleaming eyes I have ever seen in a man's face," quarterback Chet LaRoche recalled one afternoon. "I was almost paralyzed when I real-ized that Walter Camp was looking at me and speaking to me. It was like being addressed by a god." Apparently, Camp had never fully lost his star status in the players' eyes.[49]

Soon, Camp was shoring up eligibility matters and acquiring protec-tive gear. He ordered the men to work on their conditioning through the summer, charting their weights and daily exercise regimens. The linemen were to time themselves regularly in the forty-yard dash, as the backs practiced fast starts and ball handling. Camp conceded that the game was increasingly one of speed and technique: More often than gym work, he assigned boxing footwork and playbook studying. Prospective players even had to pass a written exam to play on the varsity team in the fall.[50]

Tasks that Yale men had once performed behind the scenes in anonymity were now acknowledged and paid for. Camp helped Jones seek out the most competent position men he could find, negotiating three-year contracts for former players Paul Veeder and Arthur Brides, coaches of ends and linemen at Massachusetts and Chapel Hill. Gone were the days of the captain addressing the press; now, a publicity man managed reporters. Although Camp still conducted private meetings with the coach and captain, his interventions were better tolerated with the building of the "coaches house" on Wall Street, where graduate and paid coaches convened to view game films.[51]

The changes had an uplifting effect on the team. Yale rebounded with an 8-1 record in 1916, losing only to Pollard's Brown squad and outscoring opponents 182 to 44; matches against Carnegie Institute, Lehigh, Virginia Poly, and Princeton were definitive shutouts. The return to fundamentals was evident in team play, as well as the stand-alone performances of Cupid Black and George Moseley, first team All-Americans; Artemus Gates and Harry LeGore made the second team. Most satisfying was the victory against Harvard in a packed Yale Bowl, breaking the four-year losing streak against the Crimson. Percy Haughton offered Camp his congratulations: "I have always maintained that Harvard's victories in recent years were due to a great measure to Yale's unsound methods. But this year it was Greek meeting Greek—and the 'Big Fellow' won."[52]

Haughton's words were vindicating. For now, it appeared that Camp's new efforts had paid off, and yet Alice could not fathom why her husband would be willing to expose himself to more stress and disappointment. She had seen it all before—the exhilaration of victory and the finger-pointing in defeat. It was only a matter of time before he suffered at the hands of his critics, she warned, and implored Walter to move on before the anxiety took over again. She had seen his heartache in his private moments; in one crisis after the next, football had taken its emotional and physical toll.

But she did not understand what was also at stake. If Yale's football fortunes were tied to his counsel, Camp's sense of worth had also become inextricably tied to Yale's football legacy, which both emasculated and reaffirmed. To the man who truly felt as though he had fathered an entire game, he could not abandon the place where he did it. He grew resigned to accepting the criticism with the praise, making an easy break impossible. Alice was convinced that even if her husband never stepped foot on another gridiron, his game would eventually kill him. Football had long become his obsession and proverbial sword.

12

Preparing Men for Real Battle, 1917–1918

WITH YALE AT THE TOP of the Big Three again, thousands of graduates celebrated at the Yale Club in Manhattan, followed by a viewing of *The Century Girl* at a theater decked out in blue. Inspired anew to make the 1917 team, eighty undergraduates showed up for winter practice; they competed for spots until football preparations came to a sudden halt. Woodrow Wilson, the football enthusiast-turned-U.S. president, had been maintaining a stance of neutrality in the Great War, but after the sinking of the *Lusitania* and German submarine attacks on American vessels, public sentiment had shifted in favor of intervention. On April 2, Wilson declared war on the Axis powers and mobilized units of the Army and National Guard. He also called for Congress to approve universal military service to raise an army for the Allied cause. Within a year and a half, almost all the undergraduates hoping to make the Yale eleven had left New Haven as conscripted or enlisted men.[1]

Camp had believed all along that the United States would enter the war; in anticipation, his company had been stockpiling metal and drumming up ways to pack more clocks into less cargo going overseas, knowing that exports would likely be curtailed. But war raised other questions in his mind too. Was it an opportunity, a collective rite of passage that would toughen American men? Theodore Roosevelt had always insisted that isolationism produced more pansies than prosperity.

Football had been the best substitute for war in the meantime, Camp agreed, but nothing compared to real life-and-death combat for making men out of pampered boys.[2]

The Committee on Public Information also made war appear to be the antidote to effeminacy, with its posters of sailors riding torpedoes, as if they were cowboys on horseback. One poster's caption unsubtly urged men to enlist because the enemy was out to "Crucify American Manhood." That Wilson and Congress felt justified in deferring the passing of woman suffrage until after the war suggests that, aside from pacifist and feminist groups, Americans wanted war to reassert national manhood and consequently a sense of American primacy in the world.[3]

But were American males prepared? Military officials and physical educators-turned-preparedness advocates asked the question in 1914, assimilating lessons gleaned from the Spanish-American War. Roosevelt had insisted that his Rough Riders be athletic back in 1898, but the military did little to organize sports for soldiers in Florida and Cuba. The troops grew bored and ill as they awaited orders, some dying of the malaria, dysentery, and yellow fever that festered in the camps. Only during the ensuing occupation of the Philippines did military officials start encouraging baseball leagues to improve health and morale. Army Chief of Staff Leonard Wood noted that organized sports provided the added benefit of allowing American soldiers to feel superior to the seemingly less athletic men of the lands they occupied, and hence he spent the years leading up to World War I promoting athletic training as a complement to military drills. At least 150 hours of accumulated experience in such activity would aid soldiers in proceeding with "smartness" and "precision," he surmised, insisting also that nothing instilled toughness, teamwork, group loyalty, and cooperation more effectively than troops playing in athletic contests.[4]

Military preparedness had been on Camp's mind also that summer of 1914. In England and France, he personally witnessed some of the first casualties of the Great War and was concerned. In due course, he estimated that a third of the American male population would be summoned to aid the Allied cause, and thus asked in his columns, "How shall we prepare that third?" He agreed with preparedness advocates who thought it should be made "patriotic and fashionable to drill"; in that inaugural year of the Yale Bowl, he proposed that thousands of men take to marching in football stadiums when they were not otherwise in use. But he doubted that drilling was enough. Though it instilled discipline, it did not necessarily simulate the conditions that helped men overcome the fear of confrontation. Camp agreed with Wood that if a soldier were put in a position of having to fight to the finish, competitive athletics would better prepare him. And football, of course, was the best preparation of all.[5]

But studies on the war-readiness of American men foretold a disaster in the making. In May 1917, an estimated 10 million men were of conscription age (between 21 and 31 years old), and yet estimates held that 30 percent of them would be unfit for service. These projections were confirmed as men tried to enlist and were rejected due to bad hearing or eyesight, flat feet, weak hearts, and other inherited defects. For too many others, however, disqualification seemed to be preventable: They were simply undersized and undertrained. Camp thought that all Americans should think the statistics "a source of abiding shame." If his generation seemed overcivilized, his son's appeared to be far worse.[6]

Athletes were an obvious exception, but a disturbingly rare one. Even with the expansion of athletic programs on U.S. campuses, the NCAA reported that college gymnasiums improved the fitness of only a fraction of college men. Roughly 17 percent of male students participated in organized athletics by World War I, and fewer than half exercised at all. Mortality from diseases of the heart, blood vessels, and kidneys had increased 41 percent in American males between 1890 and 1910, and Yale gymnasium director William Anderson now confirmed similar trends in Yale alumni. Although undergraduates stood taller and "better-chested" than thirty years before, heart disease crept up on them after college. Anderson speculated that "overeating and drinking, overwork, worry and haste" were contributing factors, as well as insufficient exposure to exercise in the undergraduate years.[7]

The Muscular Christians of the YMCA had long called for a shift in focus away from specialized athletics to fitness for the average youth. "The students will not energize by proxy," a YMCA worker warned Camp. "Every man should play in a physical way . . . and none must be slighted for the sake of an intercollegiate banner." When Yale football was on the wane, Camp also started writing more on "universal

fitness," with *Outing* calling him an "impelling force" for the movement. He was hardly the first force, but with war preparedness in mind,
he boldly unveiled his new idea: "FITNESS FOR ALL," lobbying with
Eugene Richards to expand athletic facilities at Yale to accommodate
the students at large.[8]

Providing baseball diamonds, tennis courts, and football fields was
essential for students who had never benefited from rigorous exercise,
he explained. In the civilized world, boys had become "domesticated
tigers," forgetful of their primal tendencies. Their physicality needed
awakening; once freed to run, kick, and throw, their instincts "to do"
would kick in. Because athletic departments were cutting costs in
wartime, he recommended that undergraduates maintain the playing
grounds on college campuses: "One man might get his exercise by
pitching on the nine, and the other man get his exercise by mowing
and rolling the diamond." Sports could bring out boys' primal tendencies any number of ways.[9]

Although Camp was past his conscription days, he had no intention
of directing boys from the proverbial sidelines. Thanks to Raymond
Fosdick, he did not have to. A former Princeton man, Fosdick had been
collecting data for the Bureau of Social Hygiene in Manhattan when
Secretary of War Newton Baker asked him to do the same in the military camps. His study led to the recommendation that accommodations
for sports and leisure be put in place in the camps as a diversion from
more illicit forms of recreation. Indeed, the surgeon general of the Army
confirmed a venereal disease rate of 114 per thousand enlisted men in
1917, and 150 per thousand the following year. Although social hygiene
reformers teamed up with YMCA volunteers and military chaplains
to promote sexual purity, they could not curb the trend. And thus the
Army and Navy established commissions on training camp activities to
provide more wholesome outlets, especially athletics. General John J.
Pershing chose Princeton Professor Joseph Raycroft to direct athletics
for the War Department and enlisted the YMCA to manage athletics
among the Expeditionary Forces (AEF) in France. Fosdick, working for
Navy Secretary Josephus Daniels, appointed Camp director of athletic
programs for the Navy.[10]

In internal reports, Camp agreed that organized sports were a diversion from boozing, masturbating, and prostitutes, but publicly, his

emphasis was satiating the more powerful "play instinct" thwarted by war. As more college men vacated campuses for naval stations, he vowed "to bring athletics to them." "Unless youth has relaxation in the form of sport and recreation he either 'breaks down' or 'breaks loose,' with disastrous results," he warned. Casual "hit-or-miss athletics" would not suffice; organized team sport was not only ideal preparation for war, it was a way of letting American boys be what was best about American boys.[11]

Camp looked to former football players to head up athletic programs in the thirteen naval districts, choosing men like Billy Bull at Newport and All-American center Herman Olcott at Great Lakes. Hockey and basketball prevailed in the winter, baseball and track in the spring and summer, and football dominated in the fall. At the Pelham Bay station alone, 6,000 recruits played volleyball, and yet the utility of individual sports like boxing, wrestling, and jujitsu was also not lost on Camp, who encouraged instruction to prepare for one-on-one confrontations should they arise. With the help of Olcott, he standardized the boxing curriculum, ensuring that recruits learned how to administer left hooks and right crosses to the belly. Professional fighters demonstrated techniques at the camps until the overflow of interest required pugilists Johnny Kilbane and Kid McCoy to make instructional films. Water training was yet another activity Camp organized once he discovered that naval recruits did not always know how to swim.[12]

But what was to be done with the non-athletes in the ranks? For all those who embraced sports at the camps, there were still significant numbers of nonparticipants, not to mention those who did not pass the physical requirements of the draft in the first place. When the war ended and heroes returned, would the noncombatants feel the psychological toll of rejection, and would this lead to their greater moral and physical decline?

Camp was convinced that he needed a more expansive plan to deal with out-of-shape American males. Until now, the calisthenics used in the camps and military schools had been Swedish exercises that Camp regarded as "painful, useless, [and] energy-absorbing." American physical educator C. E. Hammett concurred that these were "artificial movements, devoid of any element of pleasure." Naval commanders complained that soldiers were badly depleted by them and were frequently admitted to military hospitals because they were too weak to rebound from minor maladies like chickenpox and measles. Camp thought long and hard about a better regimen that strengthened the heart, increased suppleness, brought color to the face, and could be transferable to nonmilitary men over time. Rather than "make a fetish of muscle," he attempted to create a program that worked the men without leaving them drained.[13]

And so Camp came up with a series of setting-up exercises he dubbed the "Daily Dozen." As the name suggests, these were twelve simple movements divided into four groups of three alliterative exercises: hands, hips, head; grind, grate, grasp; crawl, curl, crouch; wave, weave, wing. "They are to be done lightly and naturally," Camp explained, "more in the spirit of recreation and pleasure than with lips compressed, lungs heaving, and muscles tightly flexed."[14]

A military report called Camp's exercises innovative, "devised from the most scientific physical culture plans." At Hampton Roads, 4,500 recruits did them each morning to the accompaniment of the station band. "We have arranged a high platform where Gunner Watkins leads this drill . . . also a large sign on the same platform which alternates 'inhale and exhale,' which adds much to execution of the breathing exercises," reported the director. Photographs sent to Camp show a sea of soldiers in white performing the exercises in unison. By August 1918, his regimen was routine for 65,595 naval recruits, causing aviation divisions to ask that he devise a system for the flyers who spent hours in cramped cockpits without physical activity. "Football Man Would Prepare Aviators as Gridiron Players Are Instructed," announced the *Times.* "Mr. Camp . . . said yesterday that . . . the aviator is really a quarter back of the war's gridiron and that, therefore, it is most important to give the same care and attention."[15]

Back on college campuses, the War Department had established the Student Army Training Corps (SATC), and at Yale, athletic facilities had been converted for military preparation. An armory and stables went up near the Yale Bowl, a drilling facility behind the gymnasium, and Yale Field became a training camp. Students and faculty organized into aviation and boat patrol units and established a government intelligence bureau. Yale also housed four batteries that served as a nucleus for an artillery officers training corps.[16]

President Wilson called for collegiate sport to "be continued as far as possible," but NCAA Chairman Palmer Pierce, who also sat on the War Board, discouraged colleges from scheduling "spectacular games" in such somber times, as well as pre-season coaching and training tables, as the country pooled resources for war. Men of the Yale SATC could play football as long as they maintained standards in military and academic work and did not spend more than an hour and a half in practice three days a week. Athletes paid for their own uniforms and equipment, and the university council limited intercollegiate competition to military and freshman matches, which were discontinued with the outbreak of Spanish influenza in the fall of 1918. Because the campus was under quarantine, spectators could not watch them anyhow.[17]

Henry Williams reported to Camp that football practice at Minnesota was curtailed by the 4,000 SATC recruits drilling on his fields. Camp was resigned to similar interruptions at Yale, professing that military drills readied men for the big game, as the big game readied men for war. He was not surprised when college football players answered the nation's call to arms at rates disproportionately higher than the population at large. Whereas many professional athletes, such as baseball players Ty Cobb and Babe Ruth, and boxer Jack Dempsey, deferred or opted out of military service, the enlistment rate of college football players was, according to one newspaper, almost 100 percent. The departure of upperclassmen decimated college squads, including the Big Three. John Heisman noted decreased gate receipts in the South because of enlistments and the flu epidemic. "The sweater and the jersey have given way to olive drab," Camp reported. "Football signals have been replaced by the 'One, Two, Three, Four' of drill." Even coach Tad Jones had vacated campus to build military ships in Seattle.[18]

Players represented in *Football Facts and Figures* had nearly unanimously claimed that the gridiron molded them into leaders in politics and business. Now, Camp contended, as he had in 1898, that his game created natural leaders of war. In *Collier's*, he listed high-level military men who first tested their mettle on the gridiron. Their coaches, he argued, had taught them how to "forget pain, exhaustion and discouragement . . . lessons which ma[k]e so many thousands of our American college boys such a factor in this war." Football, as he idealized it, cultivated an attitude and way of being suited to the trenches: "Courage," "pluck," "brains and knack," the "ability to remain cool," "take coaching," use one's "physique to the best possible advantage," and "think quickly under trying conditions" were requisites for both. Football also readied men for the mechanics of battle; Camp likened the motions of linemen to trench charging and bayonet work, and he now touted forward passing as preparation for the throwing of bombs and grenades.[19]

An editor of the *Army and Navy Journal* took issue with what Camp claimed on several scores, arguing that the methods of football were outmoded when applied to modern warfare. Technologies such as the rifle changed the accepted logic of forming mass columns of men to advance, and hence he thought a game like soccer, with its open formations, better preparation for battle. But Camp's rhetoric won the day. He had so successfully conflated football and war that sportswriters worried, in fact, whether high rates of volunteerism among football players might put an end to college contests for good. Camp assured them that war would not replace football, but instead convince Americans of football's indispensability as a training ground for the nation's youth now and in the future.[20]

And these predictions started to come true. During the war, high school and undergraduate games remained popular despite limited resources and personnel, perhaps because football looked less like a schoolboy diversion and more like a patriotic gesture. Game officials cut their fees as schools donated receipts to the war effort. And no one predicted the extent to which enlisted men would come to play in training camps and AEF and fleet teams overseas. One game between Camp Devens and the Radio School of the Naval First District netted gate profits of more than $8,500 for the war cause. There was so much interest in football at the naval station in Newport that officials installed a training room and hired masseuses to rub the men down before matches. *Outing* noted that there had never been a time when more American males played the game. As concluded in the *Times*: "Football owes more to the war in the way of the spread of the spirit of the game than it does to ten or twenty years of development in the period before." A Seattle naval officer confirmed: "Football seems to unite the camp as no other form of athletics will."[21]

Despite Camp's frequent characterizations of soldiers as well-bred college volunteers, the fact was that most who fought in World War I were draftees (67 percent), and a disproportionate amount of those, compared to the overall population, were foreign-born or African American.[22] For the hodgepodge of collegiate and non-collegiate, immigrant, and non-white men that military units had become, football was a galvanizing force, serving as a common and unifying experience that was transferable to peacetime.

And thus war did not stifle football, as it had so many other institutions born of the Progressive age. Thanks largely to military conscription, war created wider exposure to football that expanded and democratized it beyond what Camp and college officials could have achieved. Twenty years earlier, the muddying of boundaries between elite and non-elite players might have disturbed Camp a bit, but in the patriotic fervor of war, he no longer differentiated between grades of men: "War, whatever it may have done in wrecking college schedules, has brought about a far wider dissemination of foot ball as a sport than all the exhortations of those who have advocated 'play for the larger numbers,'" he gloated. Indeed, service teams went to the Rose Bowl and Camp chose all-service squads during World War I. Some of his selections were former collegians and some were not, further diminishing his game's elitist image. Football, like war, had become a meritocracy of the modern sort.[23]

And for this modern meritocracy, Camp's depiction of heroism invariably had to change. In his 1914 review of the football season, he did and did not sound like he had when depicting heroes in decades past:

There seems to be a poignant regret that the present war waging in Europe does not furnish heroes for the popular fancy as did war in olden time. Perhaps that is why football has become such a craze[,] because it does always supply a hero. The All-America man confers even upon his town a certain measure of distinction. The girl in the grandstand you can rest assured is not frittering away her affections by distributing them over the entire eleven men as a team but is concentrating them upon her one hero. Americans are peculiarly hero worshippers, and a football-loving public oftentimes goes as wild over the player for his unselfishness in allowing another the use of the limelight as it does for the star performance.[24]

Americans cast their heroes in spotlights that overshadowed their teams. It must have been a hard admission, coming from a man who spent most of his life touting the merits of teamwork over individual glory. In this instance, Camp rationalized hero worship as an appropriate show of appreciation for individuals acting selflessly for the team—his way of dealing with the cult of personality that American sport was already becoming. In wartime, he could justify acts of individual valor as life-saving measures for the unit, and ultimately for the team known as the nation.

His writings over the years had created athletic heroes for a generation of American boys who lacked military idols, but during the Great War many of them paid the ultimate sacrifice. James Miller ('04), Andrew Ortmayer ('06), and Joseph Stillman ('15) were some of the fallen soldiers Camp had personally coached at Yale. Alex Wilson, football captain of 1915, was made captain of Company A, 59th Infantry, 8th Brigade, before being killed near Septarges Wood. In his tribute, Camp spoke of Wilson's military and gridiron exploits interchangeably, and elsewhere too, he referred to the heroism of athletes and patriots as one and the same: "A nation should be made up of people who individually possess clean, strong bodies and pure minds, who have a respect for their own rights and the rights of others, [and] in addition possess the courage, strength, and discipline to redress wrongs," he declared in 1918. "The true leader and the real sportsman possess a chivalry that protects the weak and preserves veneration and love for parents and country and believes in the physical strength necessary to make that chivalry effective."[25]

In wartime columns, Camp chronicled the local football stars who had accrued physical courage on the gridiron and applied it to war. There was Bert Baston, the All-American out of Minnesota, who won the Distinguished Service Cross for remaining with his men despite gunshot wounds to his legs. And the fallen fighter pilot Hobey Baker, the Princeton athlete that classmate F. Scott Fitzgerald transformed into a fictional hero in *This Side of Paradise*. Camp reserved his greatest tribute, however, for Johnnie Poe, one of six brothers who were second cousins of the writer Edgar Allan Poe, in addition to being gridiron standouts. After playing at Princeton, Johnny had mined in the camps of Nevada before moving on to the gold fields of Tonopah and the ranks of the State Mounted Police. He had herded with cowboys and Mexicans, coached football at Annapolis, and joined the Government Expeditionary Force in Alaska before enlisting in the Spanish-American War and serving the Black Watch Regiment of the Scottish Highlanders. Johnny Poe was a man's man. In Camp's hands, his thirst for adventure made his death in France a most appropriate and virile end.[26]

Camp also made heroes out of men like Edward Wylie, who served in the American Field Service thanks to his coach's glowing character reference. Wylie had played for the Yale scrub team because his low grades had kept him off the varsity. Camp decided that his academic performance was irrelevant to the work of war. What mattered was that Wylie selflessly took his licks day after day on the practice field to prepare the starters for games. Camp knew the warrior in the man because he had seen him under fire, he assured recruiters, viewing the battlefields of France as the next great arena in which Wylie could prove his worth to a team. Who would a soldier want next to him in the trenches, Camp asked: a valedictorian or a team player like Ed Wylie?[27]

Naturally, his endorsement also allowed Walter Jr. to assume responsibilities as an aide-de-camp at Fort Hancock, where he received commendation for administering athletic programs. The secretary of labor sent a note of appreciation to Walter Sr. for "having the assistance of father and son in bracing and remaking the men of the country." *Leslie's Weekly* and *Outlook* featured Walter Jr.'s athletic directorship, but it was not until he served in combat that his father's pride and envy overflowed. In a letter home, Walter Jr. related how he endured sleepless nights and shellfire that tore through houses and blew craters in roads. One harrowing day, he tried to escape from the Germans over bridges rigged to detonate. He swore that football had taught him to work through fear and stay focused. "When I was under fire I was perfectly able to control my actions," he told his father. Death had become "simply part of the game."[28]

While Walter Jr. was overseas, Frances took care of their infant son, Walter III, who had been born early in 1917. In a show of female patriotism, she also instructed Red Cross nurses in the art of preparing

surgical dressings, finally reuniting with her husband after he conva-
lesced at a base hospital in France and a debarkation facility on Staten
Island. He had been gassed several times, and there were subtle signs
that he was shell-shocked. Having just placed physical directors in the
convalescent camps, Camp noted the irony to the surgeon general of
the War Department: "I did not expect one of my earliest patients to
be my own son."[29]

And yet, as hellish as war was, Walter Sr. still envied Jr. for having
endured it. By all measures, his athletic work in the naval camps was a
success, but it brought Camp vicarious heroism at best. At fifty-eight,
he still felt untried. An editorial in the *Boston Post* summed up his sentiments: "Man of fifty finds that he is physically incapacitated for any
strenuous pursuits. He is exempt from military service, of course, but
sometimes he feels that he wishes he were in good enough trim to be a
solider. He wants to do something more than serve on committees or
subscribe to war funds."[30]

Another man who longed to be useful was Frank Gilbreth, the efficiency expert with whom Camp had collaborated on golfing articles
for *Vanity Fair*. In middle age, Gilbreth also wanted in on the action
overseas, even as he tipped the scales at 220 pounds, telling the War
Department that his expertise in motion study was useful not just
to golfers but to the Army Corps of Engineers. He received orders
to report to Fort Sill to make instructional films for handling guns,
and left his business, wife, and nine children behind. Likewise, the
famed escape artist Harry Houdini, ineligible for military service at
age forty-three, inserted himself into the war effort by teaching soldiers
how to rescue themselves from sinking vessels and the manacles of
German enemies. For all his death-defying escapades he was desperate
for the ultimate test of war, as was Edgar Rice Burroughs, the creator
of Tarzan. Also too old for service at forty-two, Burroughs did the next
best thing, joining the Illinois Reserve Militia and rising to the rank
of captain.[31]

Camp understood their quests for military glory; he too left behind a
family and business to take part in war. Hard times at the clock company
had deflated him, as lawmakers mandated that the metal and labor to
make timepieces be transferred to the manufacture of munitions. In
1917, his sense of inadequacy was also mixed with sheer exhaustion. He

had been unable to relax as war loomed, and now he watched men his age and executive rank work to collapse managing wartime industries and government agencies in their quests to prove their mettle. Camp sensed that even at this, they felt impotent compared to younger men fighting overseas. "I have placed my two sons in the service of Uncle Sam," a friend told him, "and am now looking around to see what the old man might do."[32]

It was unfortunate that military glory had been so elusive for his generation. The 1910 census indicated that just under eight million American men were between the ages of forty-five and sixty-five; assuming conservatively that 75 percent of his cohort was physically unfit to serve, Camp figured that nearly two million men could still be made into a viable reserve army if he organized one. Hence his Senior Service Corps (SSC) was born. Starting out by convening prominent men in New Haven in April 1917, he formed a squad designed to put his middle-aged recruits through their paces, just as conscripted men were being put through theirs. His means of training the men: drilling and adaptations of the Daily Dozen.[33]

This was no flight of fancy, he professed. If contingency called for it, older men might need to guard railroads, bridges, or munitions factories. "You cannot whistle physical condition back like a dog when you need it," he warned. "Every one of these men has a patriotic duty to perform in making himself physically fit for the work ahead." Convening a board of advisors that included Dudley Sargent and fitness experts from Princeton, Brown, Amherst, Stanford, and the YMCA, Camp also got President Wilson to stand in as honorary president of his organization.[34]

It was important that the New Haven squad look successful, since it was the test group Camp publicized to the nation. Starting with ninety-two recruits who ranged between 5'4" and 6'4", 116 and 265 pounds (William Howard Taft likely rounded out the higher end of the range, though he had managed to lose some 85 pounds since his presidency), Camp asked his men to track their weight and muscle measurements over the weeks of his instruction. For the next ninety days, they met three mornings a week to perform fifteen minutes of calisthenics, followed by forty-five minutes of marching that grew more rigorous over the days.[35]

At first, recruits complained that the pace of the hikes was too brisk. Camp told them to stick with it and be patient. "The walk began with level stretches and has now included some hill work," he reported several weeks in. "The men are already showing physical improvement under it, and those who, through the use of the motor car, had almost forgotten how to walk are finding the benefits of the sunshine and fresh air." "I feel that the drill & c has benefited me," one man confirmed, "—can do the march with very little fatigue—find my wind improves every day." Over the weeks, men reported shedding abdominal girth. One recruit's wife thought he walked more erect; another's tailor made adjustments to his suits for his "straighter and chestier" frame.[36]

Soon, Camp did not think putting men through their paces was enough. He sought a fuller military experience, collecting modest fees for army-style jackets, hats, leggings, and shoes for marching in the Memorial Day parade. As major of the "battalion," he assigned a quartermaster and adjutant, who assigned sergeants and corporals under them. As the group grew in New Haven, the men divided into four platoons; for each, a drill officer commanded them to fall in for calisthenics. The men separated themselves into double-rank formation, with each new column forming forty inches behind the last. Camp worried that his militaristic vision would not appeal, but recruits asked for even stricter adherence to the U.S. Infantry Drill Regulations. "I have found that men in the ranks will execute commands with more precision if they sense they are being 'commanded' (not requested) to execute this or that," a recruit confided. "They take no offense at being commanded with force and authority." Camp's close friends addressed him as their commanding officer until they were formally dismissed, playing out fantasies of soldiery to their fullest. One economics professor even asked if he could pack a revolver during drills.[37]

Coverage from the *Boston Globe* to the YMCA's national magazine lauded Camp's experiment in New Haven. The next step was to expand nationwide by having communities apply to create SSC units of their own. Membership merely required men to convene and provide proof of age and a doctor's consent to exercise. Once Camp's office received names for executive committees, secretaries, and physicians for units, applicants received their first set of standing orders to begin the drills.[38] Camp sent information to legislators and prominent businessmen, fraternity brothers, and men he had known through football. One of his letters went to an undergraduate manager he had met at Stanford in the 1890s, now an engineer and civil servant by the name of Herbert Hoover. His pitch was both patriotic and scientific, as he called middle-aged men to physical, but less than strenuous, action.

> If, in these days of preparation, you had an ordnance officer, who fired a gun, that was tested for but 200 rounds without heating, 500 times and this cracked it, what would you say of him? If you had a superintendent in a factory who doubled the number of hours he was running his automatic machinery and instead of doubling the amount of oil actually cut it in half and thus ruined the machines, what would you say of him? Are men . . . less valuable to us in this emergency than machines and guns, that we should burn them out for lack of lubricant and rest or physical conservation?[39]

Executives at General Electric and other national manufacturers requested Camp's exercise guidelines for their employees. The SSC also appealed to the sons of Civil War veterans and men like Silas Hurin, an Ohio judge and former Princeton man who remembered watching Camp play for Yale in the 1880s. He read about the SSC in *Collier's* and wrote Camp to find out if a unit had been started near him, since ones already existed in states farther west, including California. In one week alone, Camp received applications for units in 491 separate communities. Governors and mayors supported the SSC, as did Connecticut Representative John Tilson, who praised it on the floor of the House of Representatives.[40]

Camp was pleased to capture interest in Washington, for he had seen the physical toll of the war on friends-turned-public servants. Once, over dinner at the Biltmore, Fred Stevenson, famed crew captain of '89, confided that his creation of a wartime telephone service for D.C. officials had fatigued him beyond recovery. Camp saw the same exhaustion on the face of Vance McCormick that night at the Yale Club. The former All-American, now chairman of the Democratic National Committee, visited only briefly, having to return to Washington. Fred Allen, another former crew captain, left the club to return to war work too, Camp noting the "hurry and worry stamped on his features." The scene played itself out over and over throughout the spring of 1917. Camp rubbed elbows with the secretary of war, the assistant treasury secretary, and fellow Bonesman and tariff commissioner William Kent. All these men looked utterly spent.[41]

Camp voiced his concerns to Robert Garrett, a former Princeton man and Olympic discus thrower-turned-Washington insider: "Physical exercise and relaxation is the lubricant of the human machine, and if you think the Government can order Nature to change her methods you are mistaken," he warned. "Your loyalty to the country and that of the heads of the department at Washington and the Executives and Advisers in civil life is just as surely leading to disaster as though there were a signboard pointing to the examples of Parry of the Federal Trade Commission, and Senator Lane." Camp was referring to men who, according to his diagnosis, had recently succumbed to exhaustion: Parry had died a month earlier at fifty-three, and Lane, only the night before, with many linking his deterioration to criticism suffered after voting against the war. Camp counted seven U.S. senators who had already died in wartime months and wondered if moderate exercise would have made a difference. Washington officials needed an SSC unit, he told Garrett. "If it is done, these men will last through the long strain that is to come."[42]

Woodrow Wilson was lukewarm to making exercise mandatory in his administration. Known to play an occasional round of golf, he abhorred weight training and resented the extent to which his predecessor Theodore Roosevelt had turned presidential fitness into a topic of public interest. Wilson's Navy Secretary Franklin Delano Roosevelt, like his fifth cousin Theodore, had been a sportsman at Harvard before beginning his political career. He confided to Camp that men under him neglected their fitness because of their overtime hours. Like the secretaries of agriculture, labor, commerce, forestry, the interior, and the treasury, he asked if Camp would lead exercises for his men. Even the attorney general and secretary of war turned to Camp for counsel.[43]

So Camp established the most publicized of his SSC units in Washington—a cadre of advisors, cabinet members, and department secretaries that came to be known as the Walter Scamps. William Kent offered his home on F Street as the headquarters where Camp led his recruits. Inside the shrubbery of his east yard, the men began their calisthenics, and then Camp led them on a hike. At the foot of the 23rd Street hill, he would call for volunteers to run up the slope, and consistently among the willing was the younger Roosevelt, who raced a few competitive souls back to Kent's backyard.[44] Because the fitness levels of the men varied widely, Camp drew up personalized plans for each, such as this for Paul Warburg, a member of the Federal Reserve Board:

—weighs 153
—does his work easily
—his muscular perceptions are quick and generally accurate
—has natural knack
—High quality of control
—Ought to be an inch or two less around the waist to match up with his diagnosis
—Looking at his upper body one expects a smaller waist
—Not that he is stout—until he strips one would not notice this, but he ought to pull in those muscles
—His neck will bear a little setting back and probably that will accomplish the lifting of his chest and at the same time of those abdominal walls. His face shows the effect of certain mental strain, but nothing of serious menace
PERSONAL INSTRUCTIONS: You have gotten into the habit of letting your head roll a little by not setting those neck muscles, and this tends to let your chest forward. The work will not bother you and if you get that head up and chin in[,] your lungs will get more oxygen and you will be able to take in your belt a little.[45]

The Scamps moved from Kent's place to the rooftop of the Powhatan Hotel, where they drilled before hiking behind the Treasury Building. When the heat grew extreme, Camp commanded that they go light on the double quick. "The general principle that I am working upon," he explained, "is to increase endurance and resistive force and to conserve nervous energy so I do not take too much out of the men." His recruits knew nothing of the personal sacrifices he had made to stay in Washington. Alice was ill and had planned to leave New Haven with him for the milder climate of Maine, but Walter insisted that making leaders fit was a matter of national security. When he finally left Washington, Walter Jr. led the recruits in his place.[46]

It was a point of pride that no Scamp reported having to stay home from work due to illness that summer. "My work during the months of July and August has been unusually exacting on account of the war," Assistant Commerce Secretary Edwin Sweet relayed, "but your scheme of morning exercise has carried me through without a loss of an hour. . . . When I was weighed in I pulled down the scales at 153 pounds. The same scales informed me this morning that I lost exactly 3 pounds. This is nearly all abdominal and can well be spared." Sweet's preoccupation with his abdomen was Camp's too, since he thought it a telling indicator of modern indulgence. In his consultations, Camp urged men to distribute weight away from the midsection, toward muscles in the supportive areas of the neck, chest, and sides of the torso. The legs and arms were less of a concern in his older recruits, for whom he emphasized suppleness over size and stamina over strength.[47]

A few Scamps took his lessons to heart and became model specimens. At 6' and 190 pounds, Comptroller John Skelton Williams was one of his greatest success stories. "I am rather proud of a Phi Beta Kappa man with such physical development!" Camp boasted. Motivated by his gains, Williams continued to show up at the Powhatan Hotel every morning into the new year. But on January 2, 1918, he reported woefully that he was "the sole survivor" of the Walter Scamps.[48] Indeed, many recruits apparently became too busy with war work to make the morning sessions, but they were grateful for feeling better than they had in years. Some of the men were inspired enough to present Camp with a little ode:

> To Walter Camp
> Your drill has been a test of us;
> You've better made the best of us;
> You've much improved the rest of us;
> You've raised each sinking chest of us;
> You've much reduced each vest of us;
> You ever will be blest of us,
> North, South, East, and West of us.
> Signed,
> (With the Seal Attest of Us)
> The Walter Scamps.[49]

Camp liked to think that his Washington unit inspired other middle-aged men around the country. Home Guards, Civic Guards, American Defense Societies, Internal Defense Leagues, and other home-grown paramilitary units sprouted up, sometimes, to Camp's lament, at the expense of SSC units. A former Princeton man told him that in Morristown, New Jersey, there were "organizations galore," making it difficult to choose. Camp tried to convince him that the SSC was the only one that dealt with the aging body in a scientific way. His exercises were "carefully graded" so that older bodies would not give out. It did not matter "how plucky or well preserved may be the older man," he warned. "He must be handled as would the candidate for a foot ball team, taken through a careful course of preparation and gradually brought along to the pitch of what his powers can safely stand." Camp cautioned his men to limit cocktails, rich foods, and smoking (at least until the afternoon). In modern life, moderation was key. It became his mission to thwart modern men's path toward crashing and burning and to make them smell the roses—even if it took walking a brisk mile to reach them.[50]

13

Death and Democratization, 1919–1925

THE GERMANS AND ALLIED FORCES signed an armistice on November 11, 1918, putting an end to the fighting of World War I. In the four years of war, eight and a half million men perished and another twenty-one million were wounded or maimed; of those, 116,000 of the dead and 204,000 of the wounded were Americans. Although the outcome of the war was already starting to become apparent when the United States joined the Allied forces in the fighting, Americans liked to think that their intervention made the difference. Camp swore that it was American athleticism in particular that prevailed on the battlefield, attributing Germany's defeat to its soldiers having grown up with "practically no sports . . . no games which developed [their] imaginations and stimulated [their] personal initiative."[1]

In sharp contrast, American boys had learned through sport that losing was demoralizing, and thus not an option. Camp boasted that the British and French military brass envied his athletic programs so much that they asked for his help in adopting football and baseball to build morale and effectiveness in their men. "The head of the Chinese Legation of the George Washington wished me to help him introduce football into China," Camp told an army colonel. "How would you like to have four hundred million Chinamen made physically fit and aggressive?"[2]

The American military seized on the manly connotation of sport to prop itself up, while Camp seized on the Great War to make athletics look like the maker of manhood, and athleticism the advent and export of American men. He was smug in *Athletes, All*, his 1919 book dedicated to American boys:

> Not only have our fighters turned out to be effective, but the lessons of discipline, courage, and spirit inculcated on the athletic fields have been found to quicken very materially the processes of making civilians into soldiers. So much has this proven true and so impressive has the demonstration been that the American is now athleticizing (if one may use the word) all our foreign allies. True, England was the pioneer in athletic sports, but of late years much of the increased development and specializing has come from American sources. . . . It should be remembered that, after all, our boys were the ones who had these athletics in the very earliest days, even before they put on long trousers, and this educational development along these lines has told, as the evidence in this war soundly corroborates.[3]

Regardless of whether American athleticism won the war, the war was an undeniable boon to American athletics. More than three million men played intramural sports in the U.S. military, and many of them had never engaged in organized sports before. After the war, Americans enjoyed an invigorated economy and more leisure pursuits, and their consumption of sports became an indelible fact of the 1920s. Football's appeal only broadened as its connections with patriotism solidified—literally—as the building of Soldier Field in Chicago and Memorial Stadium in Champaign, Illinois, attests.[4]

In a culturally heterogeneous country, football unified fans and participants with its common set of manly ideals. Although Camp had observed an increasing number of boys of Irish and German extraction playing football at the beginning of the century, college rosters after the war reveal the most thorough democratization of the game yet. Its success among southern European and second-generation immigrant workers, Jews, and boys at state and Catholic colleges only quickened its transformation from an elite gentleman's sport to a multiethnic, cross-class, male rite of passage. The conspicuous absence of African

American players, who still only enjoyed a token presence on college squads, if not specifically at black institutions, was the most glaring exception to the rule. If football was helping to redefine American manhood, it was still a manhood predicated on whiteness, albeit more inclusive than before.[5]

After the war, Camp championed his game as always, but now he was also impassioned about building national manhood through athleticism broadly defined. "Universal fitness"—health and athletics for all—was patriotic peacetime work of the highest order. "The greatest race of the future," Camp now frequently cautioned, "would be the one that could send the most men to the top of the Matterhorn."[6] "The country needs every man and needs him at the best of his power," he warned in *Keeping Fit All the Way* (1919):

> This is a young nation. It began with the great gods of Life, Liberty, and the Pursuit of Happiness. And it fought a good fight in the War of Independence for Freedom and Equality. Then came the lesser gods of material success. They broke the nation apart. But it survived. Since the Civil War we have grown rich and fat, flaccid and spineless. We are like the great careless boy with a rich father; our crops and material resources symbolize the rich father who is able to pay for all his son's foolishness. And so the youth has never stopped to think.[7]

Camp painted a bleak picture but told readers not to fear; "underneath that careless exterior" of American boys was "muscle and character" that just needed some drawing out.

An opportunity availed itself in 1919 when athletes in the armed services competed in the Inter-Allied Games in Paris. Conceived as a friendly show of international unity, the competitions might have propagated the industrial mythos of the participating nations more than anything else. Still, Camp saw them as an opportunity to flaunt Americans' superior athleticism—an opportunity that quickly came and went. Americans were hardly dominant at the games, but Camp saw them as a mere prelude to the Olympic Games in 1920. With another year to prepare, an unprecedented amount of resources went toward producing a national team that demonstrated American exceptionalism and superiority. Camp's celebrity helped the national

Olympic Committee raise $300,000 to send a delegation to Antwerp that outperformed all others; the Finnish team was a distant second in the medal count. Before Jim Thorpe's successes of 1912, the American team was made up largely of college men from the Northeast. For Antwerp, however, tryouts took place in Philadelphia, Chicago, and Pasadena under the auspices of the military, making athletics appear patriotic and truly national.[8]

Still, Camp's goal of universal fitness was far from realization. Back in 1916, he had led the physical regeneration movement of the National Security League, writing five thousand mayors to support fitness in the name of war preparedness. Then, during the war, he devised standardized exercise programs for the Boy Scouts in the hopes of promoting fitness sooner in American males, before their physical maturation as men. Now, in the postwar era, he lobbied for a national Physical Education Bill that would allocate to the states approximately one dollar per school-aged child for athletic equipment, facilities, and salaries for qualified teachers. Although a national bill was not passed, twenty-eight states passed physical education legislation by 1921.[9]

Back at Yale, the new college president, James Rowland Angell, seized on Camp's wartime renown and made him a faculty member at New Haven's "School of Coaching," a "centre of athletics and recreational work for all classes." Camp had long promoted public health on local Chamber of Commerce committees, providing dance halls, playgrounds, and "wholesome recreation" for immigrant youth.[10] But the lack of battle- and production-ready bodies during the war moved him now to create outlets for adult wage earners too. He wrote a piece on "Industrial Athletics" in *Outing* and joined corporate leaders Charles Schwab, Coleman DuPont, and John D. Rockefeller to endorse these activities for the nation's workers. "If capital and labor are to understand each other they must talk the same language," he cautioned, and insisted that sports had become that language. For years, he had witnessed white- and blue-collar men coming together for the common goal of rooting for a football team. Now, in the *American Scandinavian Review*, he referred to American sports as "the broad folk highway": "More people march together contentedly and in democratic spirit along that highway than along any other of the roads trod by humankind."[11]

Sports crossed class and cultural boundaries like nothing else in Camp's experience. He had always seen playing fields as safety valves, and now he also thought of them as melting pots to which men of all means and most creeds should have access. The recently passed Daylight Saving Law made it easier for workers to play in twilight leagues after working hours, and he praised companies like International Harvester and Carnegie Steel for letting workers blow off steam on company baseball and track teams. Back when golf caught on in the 1890s, only the wealthy could afford course memberships. Now, Camp urged course managers to lower their fees as he championed the building of municipal courses to promote outdoor exercise across class lines. Taking cues from Sumner, he urged boards of private athletic clubs not to lose sight of the "Forgotten Man." He wrote *Football without a Coach* (1920) for the worker who savored football, but could not pay experts to coach him.[12]

No doubt the war quickened a transformation already evident in Camp in glimpses, the one that made him more interested in sports for the masses. And yet, while he seemed to embrace ethnic pluralism with his endorsement of industrial athletics, he did not shed all residues of cultural privilege. His rhetoric, while seemingly inclusive, was also tinged with anxiety about the unbridled energies of immigrant groups. His goal was "to make Americans through play," though his lessons need not apply to Asians, whom he ominously referred to as "the Yellow Peril" after World War I (or, as he once despondently called it, the "White Civil War"). His interest in sports for workers was also fueled by his need to stabilize the labor situation in his own production facility, and thus he hoped to uplift and pacify at once. "Baseball beats Bolshevism!" "Fans are better than fanatics!" His slogans were patriotic, but they were also desperate attempts to define the meaning of athletics in a society where traditional rules of social power were becoming a fading dream.[13]

Given the Daily Dozen's broad appeal in the Navy camps and to the middle-aged bureaucrats of D.C., it only made sense that Camp now share his exercises with the broader civilian public. Publishers, filmmakers, and phonograph record companies were eager to help—or at least cash in. "All this soldier business has made the entire population think more of its physical condition," Rufus Steele of the U.S. Committee on Public Information confirmed. To Camp, he pitched the idea of a two-reel picture called *Making the Nation Fit.* "I was impressed with your statement that the old-time athlete with swollen muscles is no longer a popular ideal," Steele commented. "I think we ought to show this man and then, by contrast, to show the smooth-limbed fellow with the rippling unobstructive muscles who so much better exemplifies the present day ideals."[14]

After Bernarr Macfadden and Eugene Sandow had made fortunes on bodybuilding regimens and equipment, Camp now critiqued the Herculean build they painstakingly developed—at least for post-collegiate men. "There was a time when we deluded ourselves with the idea that the physically-fit man was the man with the huge bulging muscles, and we were led to look with admiration upon the development of these prodigies and tried to be like them," he admitted. "[But] the war really brought the thing home to most of us. The muscled heavy man could not stand the strain as well as the supple enduring one. . . . What we want is suppleness, chest expansion, resistive force, and endurance. . . . These do not come from great bulging knots of muscle. . . . The real essential is, after all, the engine, the part under the hood, as it were."[15]

Camp boasted that his war work was the catalyst for new philosophies on male bodies, but in truth, his innovations were part of a larger shift fully realized only after the war. Fitness equipment companies started marketing "therapeutic" approaches to training, with contraptions that stretched the body, rather than built it up. The Battle Creek Health Sanitarium marketed therapies using vibrating chairs to cultivate muscle tone, not bulk, to prevent the stiffness that came with riding in motorcars and sitting at desks. Before the war, American men were urged to cultivate strength as their contribution to national character. Now, John Kellogg proselytized the religion "of being good to yourself," promoting psychic as well as physical health. Marketers pushed fad diets and stamina-building regimens that offered a personal sense of wellbeing, but Camp differentiated himself by insisting that he was not out to profit from fads. His proof was his decision not to copyright the Daily Dozen. "I know it will help people in private as much as it helped the naval recruits and the men in Washington," he reasoned, "and I don't want to appear to be one of those woolly-headed physical culturists. I would rather give it away."[16]

He said that profiting from the Daily Dozen would be taking advantage of his reputation in amateur athletics, and hence he made the ethical choice. It is more likely, however, that his benevolence had more to do with the fact that college trainers had used identical exercises to warm up athletes for years. His Daily Dozen, in other words, may not have been his as much as he wanted others to believe. Nevertheless, he appeared altruistic in comparison to associates like Izzy Winters, a Yale wrestling coach, who opened exercise institutes in the early 1920s that turned him into a fitness celebrity in his own right.[17]

For a time, Camp thought about opening an exercise institute bearing his own name, but decided ultimately to accept a modest fee to publish the Daily Dozen in *American Magazine* and in pamphlets for schools, businesses, and government agencies. Former college athlete William Almon Wolff claimed to grow so trim on the exercises that he offered to edit the version of them in *Collier's* and to pose for the accompanying photographs. Camp received a small royalty for the more than 400,000 copies sold before granting permission to Harper and Brothers to include the exercises in *Keeping Fit All the Way*.[18] Finally in 1921, the Reynolds Company published *The Daily Dozen* in book form. A caged tiger graced its cover—a less than subtle metaphor for modern man:

He dreams and roars and paces his life away, in the cruelly narrow limits of his prison. And yet he is not often sick. He is probably in better health than his wild brother in the jungle; he lives fully as long; he becomes the father of vigorous cubs. Tiger and lion in their cages, cat and dog in the almost equally artificial and cramping environment of our steam-heated city homes, are nearer to being as strong as their wild ancestors than we are to matching the physique and good health of men who live in the open.

Exercise is the answer. But does the tiger "exercise" with a dumb-bell in each paw? Of course not. . . . Caged animals have the same habits as domestic animals. They are always stretching and twisting their trunks, using the floors and bars of their cells to furnish resistance. . . . If a domesticated animal can do this, so can a domesticated man.[19]

The film version of *The Daily Dozen* echoed the same primal themes. As Camp narrates, a caged tiger fades into a man working in his office. The walls of his office then fade into prison bars, and then fade out into office walls again. A cartoon caveman climbs a tree to escape a wild animal, only to turn into that modern businessman who Camp less than subtly suggests has a primitive nature needing release. Modern man's overcivilized state was Camp's fixation in nearly all his postwar works. "We were all meant to earn our bread by the sweat of our brows," he explained.

> Instead of doing this, we have our food brought to us on a platter—many times too much of it—and we earn it with practically no physical effort or stretching of the muscles, but simply by work with our brains. . . . Civilization has brought us ease, comfort, luxuries. It has given us the automobile, and the telephone. It has heaped upon us time-saving devices, and with the time-saving devices it has stolen away from us physical activity. Too many men never think of walking, even moderate distances, if the motor car or trolley is at the door. Stealthily then this civilization is depriving us of that essential to good health, physical exercise and fresh air.[20]

The Daily Dozen was a significant part of Camp's fitness regime, but not all of it. Like a modern lifestyle guru, he tackled insomnia, fat burning, and other growing preoccupations of modern Americans. Constipation, in his view, was yet another ailment of civilization, the result of a failure to develop trunk muscles that used to be developed as a matter of course. He recommended outdoor activity at least ten hours a week, paid work no more than 295 days a year, and at least three weeks of continuous annual vacation, all the while performing the Daily Dozen. Taking inspiration from vegetarians, purists, and Fletcherites, who made the rigorous mastication of food the basis of a health program, he advised drinking six glasses of water a day, sleeping with the windows open, eating less meat after age thirty, using whole wheat in breads, and chewing starchy foods especially well. In his estimation, the "Salisbury meat" diet and others were baseless marketing ploys. His mantra was moderation and active, simplified living.[21]

Letters he received from across the country suggest that Americans trusted his advice:

> . . . I was an athlete in college ten years ago and now, although not exercising, am fit, except that there is a tendency to gain around the

abdomen. I now, in fact have what is called a nice little corporation. It is unbecoming. What shall I do to get rid of it?

* * *

. . . I am a commuter, forty-two years old. Occasionally in order to make my train I find I have to run fast for a hundred yards or so. I take no other exercise. Isn't what I am called upon to do to catch my train, enough in the way of keeping fit?

* * *

. . . Of late I have tried cutting out luncheon in the middle of the day. I am in a sedentary occupation. I feel better for it until just before 6:30 dinner when there is a gone feeling in my stomach. Am I doing well? I am fifty years old.[22]

One New York man claimed that the Daily Dozen turned him from a 200-pound "winded horse" into a "Greek God." Yet all too frequently, Camp also heard of bodies failing to withstand the rigors of modern life. Some of them belonged to men his age, but a shocking number were younger men who went to Ivy League schools and moved on to elected office and major corporations. They were doctors, lawyers, publishers—success stories in the conventional sense. Now their names were listed one after the other in the papers—in the obituaries.

"Why is the obituary column, which records only the men of great prominence[,] full of those who are dropping off at fifty or younger—men who should be doing more of the world's work, for another score of years?" he questioned. Camp soon wrote so often about this trend that Alice found it disturbing. Once, after a round of golf, he pontificated on the middle-aged men he had personally known who dropped dead right on the green and surmised that it was not the golf that killed them, but the hurry and worry they were trying to escape by taking up golf in the first place. As he observed during the war, his contemporaries remained undertrained and invariably overworked. "What excessive nerve strain comes from the pace at which you are living and the road you are travelling over?" he asked them.

"Men don't know how to match up or compensate for the conditions that hem them in like an iron cage."[23]

What distressed him most were the former high-level athletes on his lists of the prematurely deceased. Percy Haughton, for one, had dropped dead while coaching on the Columbia University playing field at forty-eight, and months later, Yale All-American Billy Bull died at fifty-six. Muscular Christian Luther Gulick was a less than ripe fifty-three when he succumbed to illness after visiting troops overseas; several years later, Frank Hinkey, the "Disembodied Spirit," succumbed to complications of tuberculosis at fifty-four. Hinkey's lack of longevity was no longer unusual for former Yale football players. Remington was only forty-eight when he died, and All-American Ted Coy was forty-seven.

Finely tuned athletes had fallen prey to heart disease, alcoholism, and life-style-related ailments in middle age. Camp wondered how much "violent strenuous exercise" was also to blame. He took the death of Theodore Roosevelt especially hard. Only six months Camp's senior, the former president had made it to age sixty before contracting the diseases in the Amazon that likely contributed to his death, but Camp had presumed the man indestructible. "I knew him well for nearly forty years, and I never knew him to shirk any duty, physical or moral," he eulogized. Camp had always considered Roosevelt, having conquered physical deficiencies to live strenuously, as a kindred spirit.[24]

Desperate to understand these cases of premature demise, Camp ultimately decided that they were instances of men breaking his golden rule. They had lived by extremes, working and playing intensely, belonging to country clubs that did not necessarily offer "country living," trying to fit in weeks of exercise on a single weekend afternoon, leaving their offices in Manhattan with golf clubs and returning Monday morning hung over and depleted. Stiff and sore, they spent the remainder of the week "resting up after their orgy of exercise."[25]

German Turners, physical culturists, and Swedish drillers did not have the answers for aging bodies. Camp believed that these men still needed physical rigor, but not to the degree of their youths. Instead of activities that winded and fatigued, he recommended a shift to tennis by thirty and golf by forty, in conjunction with his Daily Dozen. These activities stretched the body without the overexertion of violent sport or the deadening air of the gym. He told middle-aged men to walk to work and take extended lunch breaks to golf; the resulting productivity would more than make up for lost time. He welcomed diversions from money-making—the greatest stressor of his generation, in his estimation. Middle-aged men had fallen too readily into "worshipping the Golden image of wealth or power and turning their backs unceremoniously upon God Health." By middle age, they were paying the price.[26]

If he sounded sanctimonious, he seemed to follow his own advice to a tee. At the University Club in Pittsburgh, he took off his evening coat and in front of Pitt and Princeton graduates demonstrated "in strenuous detail the muscular movements he evolved." "Sometimes his shirtfront buckled and sometimes his pearl studs came loose," an observer noted, "but Camp went through his exercises from beginning to end." Indeed, age had not diminished his gait or golf swing, and he never seemed to perspire or be out of breath, even on humid days. His suits needed no altering over the years, since his body was still straight and taut; even the sure signs of aging on the throat were not apparent on him. No matter how deeply he sat in a chair, he was able to emerge from it without pushing himself up with his hands. And when he had to sit at a desk for hours, he did not writhe restlessly. He swore it was because he took time out for his Daily Dozen, even if it meant slipping into the office bathroom to do them.[27]

A *Herald* reporter described Camp in 1920 as "lithe, vigorous, with the poise and graceful movement of a well-trained well-conditioned boxer or wrestler." After Camp offered him a cigarette, the reporter could only wonder if smoking affected the health of this middle-aged man, ultimately deciding that it did not. Another reporter remarked several years later that despite his baldness, Camp looked relatively young. Golfing had given his face a "bronzed and weather beaten" look that made him "the picture of virile manhood." During their meal together at the Yale Club, he noticed that Camp refused coffee or tea, preferring a "milk and honey diet." And for the entire sitting, he smoked his cigarettes like a man—"plain . . . without gold tips or nuthin."[28]

Yale's gymnasium records suggest that it was not just the middle-aged needing Camp's health advice. Ninety-six percent of the freshman class of 1920 exhibited at least one of twenty-two classified physical defects due to lack of exercise: 315 had flat chests; 673, rounded shoulders. These numbers were likely typical in the public at large, which was what pained Camp the most. The average Yale man seemed physically exceptional once, especially the athletes, but growth charts that Camp made available in magazines across the country had inspired boys on farms, out West, and in working-class neighborhoods to add girth to their necks and chests more successfully than the men walking the green in New Haven.[29]

Yale athletes had been physically dwarfed, and it made a difference on the gridiron. Immediately after the war, the Yale eleven spiraled downward again, losing to Harvard and Princeton and also to unremarkable Boston College. Former player Al Sharpe had served as head coach until Tad Jones returned in 1920, signing a three-year contract for $20,000. Camp sat on the Football Committee, until Captain Tim Callahan asked him to step down. Vance McCormick planned on resigning in protest until he was also removed.[30]

This time, Camp seemed less hurt than resigned. Jones's hefty contract was just one more indication that his original vision of amateur sport had long faded, and it was time to move on. One sports page called it the end of an era, the "Natural Death of the Big Three"; more aptly, it was the rise of a mediocre Ivy League. Up to this point, Yale had contributed the most players to All-America squads with eighty-four; Harvard was second with seventy-three, and Princeton third with fifty-three. But Northeastern dominance was a thing of the past; Cornell was the last Ivy League school to win a national championship, in 1922. After one more stellar season under Jones in 1923, the Yale eleven fell back in the pack. "It has grieved me very much to see others passing us," Camp confided. The glory days of Yale football really had come to an end.[31]

This decline coincided with a sense of new priorities in New Haven, as the university experienced a cultural renaissance of sorts. Undergraduates John Farrar (1918), Thornton Wilder, and Henry Luce (1920) were just a few who contributed to it as Yale athletics waned. In these years, Janet Camp married graduate Thayer Hobson, a machine gunner for the U.S. Expeditionary Forces, who returned from war to manage the *Yale Daily News*, not to captain a gridiron eleven. The future president of the William Morrow Publishing Company was a departure from the athletic types to whom Janet had grown accustomed, as were the two Yale men she married after Hobson.[32]

Although she shared her father's talent for writing and authored books on the poet and painter Dante Gabriel Rossetti, Janet had no children to whom she could pass her father's torch on the playing field. Walter Jr. did not pass it either. Although he attended occasional Harvard-Yale games in his postgraduate years, he never got involved in Yale's athletic administration. Like his father, he started to go bald, but he made a conscious effort to carve out niches of endeavor in which his father had not cast an imposing shadow, turning ultimately to the financing of motion pictures. While dad played golf, Jr. played polo and slipped in and out of four marriages. His son, Walter III, played football for a time, but was an unremarkable player. His glory, like his father's, was better actualized in a world war.[33]

In the 1920s, players from Berkeley, Navy, Pittsburgh, Illinois, North Carolina State, Syracuse, Minnesota, West Virginia, and Georgia Tech captured Camp's attention for the All-America team. More and more he covered intersectional play, including Harvard's trek to Pasadena to play Oregon in the Tournament of Roses. Standing on the sidelines watching Chicago play Illinois, he admitted that he witnessed "more real football in thirty minutes than he had witnessed in the East all season." Colleges had plenty of talent on which to draw now that 91 percent of the nation's high schools had football squads that fed into the local college ranks.[34]

Covering teams from the Middle West, Rocky Mountain, Missouri Valley, and Southwest Texas Conferences, Camp hardly seemed surprised when 5,000 more spectators congregated in Waco than had once convened in Springfield for the biggest of the Harvard-Yale games. He reported that since football returned to California, Stanford's million-dollar stadium matched the size of Ohio State's, while the Coliseum in Los Angeles rivaled its Roman namesake, soon seating 100,000. Each region came to have a distinctive style of play that fueled regional pride: The Midwest perfected power-running, while the Southwest became known for aerial shootouts, and the Deep South, its well-honed defense.[35]

Camp could never have predicted that his simulated war for Ivy League men would suit and affirm the grandsons of Confederates, and yet, their aptitude for football was apparent when Heisman's Georgia Tech defeated Penn in 1917 in one of four straight national title matches. His territorial game had become civic religion in the South, a means of reestablishing manhood stripped since the "lost cause." Now that Southerners could no longer legally duel, football was the blood sport that perpetuated their code of honor. Fans envisioned the forward-passing quarterback as a modern version of the Southern cavalier, unruffled under pressure. Southern Progressives turned football into an emblem of the New South, since it reinforced the region's traditional values as it integrated Southerners into the industrial world of their Northern counterparts and gave legitimacy to their institutions of higher learning. When little Centre College of Kentucky defeated Harvard in 1921, men throughout the South saw the victory as redemption, an indication that they still laid claim to a robust brand of manhood in the new century.[36]

For a while now, Camp had not been able to boast that the nation's football brain trust emanated solely from New Haven. In his reviews of seasons, he gave kudos to the succeeding generation of men who pioneered roles as strategists of the college game—veterans like Warner, now at Pittsburgh, Yost at Michigan, and Heisman at Georgia Tech, as well as a new regime—Zuppke at Illinois, Rockne at Notre Dame, Bezdek at Penn State, and even Fritz Pollard at Lincoln, and former Carlisle Indian Al Exendine at Georgetown. Correctly, he had predicted that bidding for head coaches would lead to salaries "never before dreamed of." Now, as the modern coach developed plays, he also served as a role model and motivator, whose emotional makeup factored into Camp's preseason assessment of teams.

In 1923, Amherst President Alexander Meiklejohn pleaded one last time for rule-makers to relegate head coaches to the stands during games, but the public had come to embrace the coach so completely as a sideline and off-the-field influence that seasonal coaches were done away with across the board, replaced by fulltime specialists who paced the sidelines and practice fields year-round. Ironically, Camp, the unpaid coach of coaches, did more than anyone to give the paid full-time coach a venerated place in the lives of American men, portraying him as a cerebral strategist, a paternal presence, and—with his raison d'etre being "to win"—a distinctly American figure. To this day, football is considered a coach's game.[37]

While the professional coach gained acceptance, professionalism in other contexts continued to pose problems in postwar athletics. Serving on boards for international boxing, the Olympics, and the National Lawn Tennis Association, Camp witnessed athletes capitalizing on endorsements and media opportunities and stirring debate. In the early 1920s, he was asked to weigh in on the case of tennis great Bill Tilden. The president of the U.S. Lawn Tennis Association thought it unfair that Tilden made as much as $15,000 a year playing tennis and writing about it on the side. How could opponents compete when they had to hold down fulltime jobs, he asked Camp, who was in no place to judge. Although he no longer played football and was never paid to coach, the "Father of Football" had certainly capitalized on his athletic expertise. He paid lip service to the cultural preferences of English amateurs, but ultimately his values were those of the American marketplace.[38]

Once, reporters cornered Camp in a hotel and asked for his thoughts about the Chicago White Sox, who were accused of throwing the 1919 World Series for money. Did the "Black Sox" scandal portend similar problems in college football? In his willfully naïve way, Camp insisted it did not. Although he admitted that in college football the quest for victory had led to inducements, he saw this as a distant cry from intentionally throwing games. He still wanted to believe, or perhaps make it appear, that football did not share the commercial enticements that led to corruption in baseball. "Shoeless" Joe Jackson was, after all, an illiterate farm boy, and hence more easily seduced than a college man, he reasoned, as if the line between the amateur collegian and professional ringer had not been blurred in football for decades. By the 1910s, Illinois' Percy Graves held rights to concession stands that allowed him to profit at the very football games he played in, while Notre Dame players received $200 charge accounts. Even Stagg, one of the most vocal proponents of amateurism, now rationalized his use of tramp athletes to generate wins on the gridiron.[39]

Eligibility problems that first surfaced in the 1880s never subsided and grew worse because of the contradiction that Camp helped to create but did not acknowledge: that profitability was likely the most American thing about amateur football. Its magnetic pull led players, coaches, promoters, and fans to develop the professional game within and alongside the college one for decades, and the trend took off after World War I. Attendance at college games increased 119 percent in the 1920s, as gate receipts tripled. By 1926, an NCAA-commissioned Carnegie Foundation report on excess in college sports determined that professionalism was rampant in the nation's football programs. But there was little will to correct abuses in college football when gate receipts were the means to institutional stability.[40]

Although the Big Three went on to discontinue athletic scholarships and eventually spring practice and participation in bowl games, these measures seemed to be the convenient sanctimony of devolving teams. Schools in the South and West discovered that winning football brought in cash and prestige that made calls for athletic purity fall on deaf ears. Perhaps the more realistic response of reformers would have been to offer suggestions for managing football as a commercial enterprise. For better or worse, professionalization looked to be the American way.

Camp finally stepped down as chairman of the board of the New Haven Clock Company in 1923. The timing turned out to be timely. The Connecticut clockmaking industry would suffer sharp declines once new companies introduced customers to electric quartz technology in the coming years. With an eye toward retirement, he made sure that his life insurance policy was in order; and aware of his reputation for fitness, his provider waived age limit provisions in his singular case, declaring Camp at sixty-four "as healthy a risk as is possible to find." It was true, he was hard-pressed to remember the last time he suffered a cold or a headache. He presumed it was due to his living more temperately than most, regulating his physical and financial reserves so that he could enjoy his twilight years. He had made a point of spending less than he made and invested soundly, accumulating a nest egg that would have been worth millions today. He assured Alice that they could live comfortably for the rest of their days.[41]

In the fall of 1924, he trekked west to scout potential All-Americans in San Francisco and Seattle and was greeted with banquets, box seats, and standing ovations. In Los Angeles, he was an honored guest of Yale alumni at the University Club, and he proselytized fitness to 4,000 men at the Philharmonic Auditorium. He returned east to make an intercollegiate coaches' meeting soon after New Year's of 1925, but he ended up not attending; Alice was too ill to be left alone in New Haven. He was able to go to New York in March, however, to make annual adjustments to the college football code. Arriving at the Hotel Pennsylvania in his usual good spirits and with his collection of notes, he looked no worse for his worries at home. He was the oldest man in the room, but he swore that he hardly felt it; he boasted, in fact, that he was writing a book about feeling young after fifty.[42]

Not fifty years before, the rules committee had been comprised of men from a handful of schools in the Northeast. Now it included Camp, its longstanding secretary, and representatives from Princeton, Dartmouth, Chicago, Lehigh, Kansas, Washington, Georgia, Texas, and West Point. Even with the regional diversity, there was not the acrimony of years past. Into the night, the committee reworked rules without incident, deciding that a kick blocked behind the line of scrimmage would go to the recovering team and that the penalty for clipping would be changed from fifteen to twenty-five yards. The captain winning the opening toss would choose whether he wanted to receive or kick first, and offenses would receive five yards for defensive off-sides, without a loss of downs. The penalty for flying tackles was finally abolished; the passing game had rendered the rule obsolete.[43]

Camp and his colleagues returned to their hotel rooms around midnight, planning to tie up loose ends in the morning. But when they reconvened at ten o'clock, their secretary was not among them. Because Camp had all the notes, the meeting could not start without him. It was all too strange, so Princeton and Trinity coaches Bill Roper and W. S. Langford volunteered to retrieve Camp from his room at the Hotel Belmont. The front desk called up, but no one answered in Camp's room. After much persistence, a bellboy led them to his door and knocked, but no one answered. The situation was so unusual that they convinced the hotel management to have a carpenter remove a panel from Camp's room door. When the door was opened, there he was, their veteran secretary, still in his pajamas, lifeless in bed. A doctor confirmed that he had died in his sleep just hours before he was found.[44]

The diagnosis was a simple heart attack, only weeks before his sixty-sixth birthday. Although his colleagues still had minor matters to discuss, they were too shocked to continue the meeting. They adjourned immediately to assist with arrangements for the body. Alice was called but told to stay put at the apartment she and Walter had rented on Humphrey Street in their attempt to scale down. Walter Jr., who was living in Manhattan, joined the men in escorting his father's body back to New Haven, as news of Camp's death quickly spread. Colleagues traveling overseas were, ironically, huddled on the deck of a steamship discussing Camp's superior health when they received the wire announcing his demise. Friends who included heart specialists were baffled by the news; they had never heard him complain of anything that would suggest he had a blockage or a failing heart. Julian Curtiss swore that he was "the picture of perfect health . . . the last man in the world I would think was facing death."[45]

Weeks before, Camp had written warnings to American men about their propensity toward overwork. "[It] is like overdrawing your bank balance," he explained. "You will have to pay up the next day." And yet, his stoicism had concealed from everyone that he had been physically and emotionally worked over as badly as any bank president or civil servant he ever knew. The war had exhausted him as much as anyone, but he never slowed down afterward, even in retirement. He had made an art of hiding the strain of life, from others and himself. A friend noted that Camp had a "genuine horror of slipping into a rather lazy old age" and thus fought like mad to stave off mental and physical atrophy. Because it scared him to lose vitality, he kept moving—at a breakneck pace—to convince himself that he had not.[46]

The irony of his death was not lost on editorialists, who now questioned why Camp's "Own Medicine Fail[ed]." As did the deaths of other Yale footballers, Camp's opened up debates about the "athletic heart"—myth or unacknowledged condition? The director of the Life Extension Institute used Camp's example to urge older men "to go slow in the matter of exercise," for he had also seen the sudden death of the overscheduled engineer Frank Gilbreth only months before. Upon review of several recent deaths in "athletic men of affairs," a journalist for the *Philadelphia Evening Post* urged older men "to stop playing before play stops us!" The obvious comparison was drawn between Camp and Percy Haughton, both college lettermen in crew, baseball, and football who were corporate executives, athletic advisors, regular exercisers, and war volunteers, and who suffered recent criticism at their alma maters before dying less than three months apart. Several doctors concluded that in their cases, it was likely they had overtaxed their hearts during the rigors of college sports, only to pay the price later in stressful lives behind desks, building fortunes and football dynasties. Bernarr Macfadden mourned Camp's death in the *Graphic* but decided that it could have been prevented if the "Father of Football" had fasted and dieted like the self-proclaimed physical culturists whom Camp had always rejected.[47]

The year of 1925 was one of tremendous loss in the sports world. At Yale, Frank Hinkey, swimming star William Jelliffe, and basketball coach Joe Fogarty joined Camp on the list of the departed. In baseball, Americans lost the clean-playing, Sunday-school-teaching Giants pitcher Christy Mathewson and Charles Ebbets; and in boxing, junior lightweight Pepper Martin and twenty-three-year-old flyweight Pancho Villa. Bodybuilding legend Eugene Sandow died mysteriously at fifty-eight, while jockeys Paul Hurn and J. Berg suffered fatal injuries on the horse track. On college gridirons, at least twenty players died of injuries. Such was the apparent price for becoming the most athletic nation in the world.[48]

In the days that followed Camp's death, thousands of mourners sent telegrams and flowers to his residence. Alice requested that the funeral remain a private affair for family and friends. Two hundred people gathered for a service that began on Humphrey Street and ended at the family plot in Evergreen Cemetery. Along with some of Camp's closest friends in football, President Angell paid his respects, as well as a dormitory janitor who had known Camp since his undergraduate days. According to the *Times*, a few former teammates were in attendance, as well as an employee from the New Haven Clock Company—an older man who appreciated that Camp had never uttered an angry word. A year later, the papers reported that Camp's estate had been appraised at over $328,000; remarkably, only $12,500 of it appeared to be in company stock, the rest likely the sum total of his varied work in athletics. That he made his wife, and not his son, executor and sole heir of his fortune attests to the companionate marriage the Camps enjoyed for thirty-seven years. Despite her chronic ailments, Alice lived until 1934.[49]

The journalist Grantland Rice officially took over the selection of football All-Americans and did it devotedly until 1948. Meanwhile, the executive committee of the NCAA elected Tad Jones as Camp's replacement on the rules committee and formed a Walter Camp Memorial Board. Members pondered how best to pay tribute to a man who, when he was alive, worried perpetually that he would not be remembered as he wanted to be, or that the heroism he infused into his football stories might be lost if he let others write them. Likening his creation of football legends to the writing of Spartan history, he believed it important to make gridiron men appear as timeless heroes for American boys. Selfishly, he also wanted to be seen as a general to all Spartan generals, the man who saved American males from degeneracy by introducing them to his game.[50]

He would have been pleased by the homage paid to him in the *Bookman*, which called his ideal Spartan rather than Athenian: "The Morgans and the Harrimans created the big business ideal. The advertising pages of the great magazines and their clients have spread the gospel of toothbrush, mouth wash, soap, and luxurious bathing facilities. It was Walter Camp who created a symbol for men . . . of a trim, careful age." Heywood Broun surmised that thanks to Camp, the nation had grown obsessed with the best of the best—from the best footballers in the country to "the six best novels published in February." He had made Americans think in superlatives—in sports and everything else.[51]

Three years after his death, the legacy he would have wanted was very much intact with the building of the Walter Camp Gateway leading up to the Yale Bowl. Inscriptions on the four hundred feet of wall on either side of its colonnades list 224 colleges and 279 high schools that contributed to the memorial fund. At the dedication ceremony before a Yale-Dartmouth game, former football rules committee chairman E. K. Hall praised his former colleague:

> [Camp] understood as few men have, the American boy. His ruling passion was to see him develop into a man's man. He realized long before most of us, and while many were still carping at them, that in the playgrounds and athletic fields of America lies the surest hope for conserving and perpetuating the virility of this virile race. . . . He saw the athletic field as a crucible where the youth of the land is tested and tempered under the intense heat of fierce competition and physical conflict. A crucible where the poisonous elements are driven

off, and where other elements are changed into pure gold, and where entirely new values are fused into the boy's character.[52]

While the archway remains, the heroism once attached to Camp's work has faded from popular memory, as he has. Whereas most Americans a hundred years ago knew who he was, that is not true today. His rhetoric about team sport now sounds out of touch, but it was becoming so back then too. In 1910, he conceded that "individual personality" had become a hallmark of the "new football," and yet he sounded like a curmudgeon complaining about the "long swiper" in golf and "the long ball hitter" in baseball who single-handedly changed outcomes with a single stroke and became larger than his team in the public eye. It pained him that Americans went to the ballpark to see Babe Ruth hit homeruns, not to marvel at grittier team efforts. If boys once played football to acquire character, fans now watched it to consume the personalities. The growing penchant for celebrity profiles in the press indicated how much his game had become a form of mass entertainment, rather than an experience in itself.[53]

Camp witnessed the cult of personality take over in any number of ways after World War I: The titles of football films, novels, and board games indicated nothing about the team; the quarterback—the lone general—was the stuff of fantasy. When a film executive had asked him to edit a movie on sports legends in the early 1920s, Camp proposed a film on the Yale championship team of 1909; but producers wanted only a reel on the team's standout player Ted Coy. Camp was devastated, but the message was clear: The sport's hero was not a cog in the machine but the self-made individual—for he was the inspiring proof that success was achievable now that the rules of success had changed. Men like Babe Ruth represented the ideals of individualism and equality of opportunity that Americans celebrate, even though they sometimes contradict each other. In truth, Camp never reconciled these ideals either.[54]

Months before Camp died, University of Illinois tailback "Red" Grange tore up the field against Yost's Michigan defense, scoring four touchdowns in twelve minutes, without much help from his teammates. Grange was no quarterback, but a standout nonetheless. His escapades were written up in the dailies, fitting into narratives that shifted from the gladiatorial epics of the 1890s to tales of individual heroism. As early as 1902, select audiences could watch grainy, silent films of the big Yale-Princeton or Army-Navy contests. By 1925, Grange's drives were described by WGN radio commentators and seen by fans in nearly 90 percent of the 18,000 movie houses across the country. On film, he appeared faster than humanly possible, his anonymous teammates mere background in highlight reels soon amplified with sound.[55]

In Camp's heyday, even working-class men admitted sheepishly to playing football for money, but Grange had no qualms about forgoing his senior year at Illinois to sign a fat contract with the Chicago Bears. Only months after Camp's death, Grange had an agent and was cashing in on endorsements for chocolate and action figures. He did not apologize for playing football for gain rather than school spirit, for survival rather than honor—and, in fact, he soon started a team in the American Football League with promoter Charles "Cold Cash" Pyle, hoping to "get to the gate while the getting's good." Eventually, Grange transitioned into Hollywood films and sports commentating—first on radio in the 1920s and '30s and then television in the 1950s. Although football had afforded Camp expert status after college, he did not predict the opportunities football would create in related careers off the gridiron. As it evolved into pageant and media spectacle, professions evolved to accommodate new forms of consumption. Even Alice Camp's role as the female morale booster was formalized in the 1920s with the advent of attractive damsels on the sidelines, known forever after as cheerleaders.[56]

Walter Camp had trained men to be athletically minded and bodied so that they could run companies and run for office, not become professional athletes. But men like Grange made football their livelihood and public persona well after their playing days were over, and their success was appealing because birthright had nothing to do with it. Grange's humble beginnings hauling ice in small-town America were to be admired as the new stuff of legend, as football's representative class no longer seemed to be the elite as much as the wide-ranging middle class. Like Rockne's and Thorpe's, Grange's rise from nothing made him a greater hero in modern eyes than any man wearing a "Y" in Camp's novels, which is partly why no one reads them anymore. If there is one of Camp's inventions that has lingered, it is the All-American. In the year of Camp's death, Grange said, "If you weren't on the Camp team, it didn't mean a thing," and today, All-America status still carries distinction, even if it is rarely given to the Ivy Leaguers for whom Camp originally intended it.[57]

Player-turned-literary scholar Michael Oriard concludes that Camp, as "author" of a game originally intended for elite white boys, ultimately lost control of his text. Perhaps this is only partly true, for Camp was also conscious of turning football into a means of modern self-making. Aspiring boys came to play it with abandon because it had the ability to create a living, an identity, and stardom—and winning made the difference. Although Camp felt great pressure to keep up the ruse of English amateurism in college athletics, he ultimately rejected the ideal of ascribed status and acknowledged achieved status as truly American. "There is caste in sport," he admitted, "but neither birth nor wealth helps a man to enter." He liked to think that on the gridiron, a natural aristocracy prevailed. This is a part of his legacy that we would be wrong to forget. That working, immigrant, and non-white men started to excel in his game tells us that his vision of American manhood, while not initially inclusive, had the potential to become so, which is why it has endured.[58]

Postgame Analysis

THIS PORTRAIT OF THE "Father of Football" depicts a man against a backdrop of cultural crisis—crisis not always acknowledged or understood, but glaringly apparent in hindsight. It was a crisis of identity in white, Protestant men who once held dominion in American life but sensed cultural change coming. As women gained ground in higher education, paid work, and the political sphere, Camp reoriented the figurative playing field on which men and women competed in public life, and he did it by creating a physical playing field on elite college campuses where only men had access and their greater heft mattered here as nowhere else. In his rhetoric, female football spectators maintained the gender status quo by acting like helpless damsels or gridiron mothers who fawned over their warriors and yet recognized that they lacked the physical courage or size to emulate them.

The gridiron, as psychic and literal turf, was one of the few spaces left in the public sphere that Camp could designate as truly male. His definition of manhood, rooted in the physically powerful body, offset fears of emasculation in white American men, creating boundaries that women likely could never cross. And yet, for many minority and working-class men, this definition of manhood, rooted in the athletic physique, was not a boundary but rather an advantage in the end.

Of course, Camp's version of physical manhood was not universally accepted, and he too thought and lived like a man in transition, sometimes touting civilized manliness and primitive masculinity all at once. Those who met him remarked that he embodied both the emotional self-restraint of a Victorian and the physical vitality of a modern. And yet, Camp convinced a nation that unleashing the primal energies of boys in simulated battle would have a character-building effect. He made Americans think that old and new forms of manhood could be reconciled into an effective whole, since he was walking proof—an intellectual and an athlete, a moral and physical specimen, a gentleman and a man's man. Few Americans were more successfully or literally self-made.

Camp turned his gridiron into a panacea for the moral, physical, and psychological ills of American males. He appealed to boys' desire to play rather than ponder, and called it a natural instinct traceable to the conquerors of yore. Indeed, to lend legitimacy to his man-making game, he literally rewrote history, describing the Anglo-Saxon tradition as one in which rudimentary forms of football had a central, identity-forming place. Although his game had been spawned from British rugby, he conveniently recalled Puritan New Englanders kicking pig bladders after their Thanksgiving suppers. Football was American through and through, he insisted, and so was the superior manhood cultivated through it. Whereas American men once went to work, or war, or out West to feel worth, in the twentieth century, they had the gridiron—a space where men were warriors and winners.[1]

There was really no better proof of football's effectiveness than the powerful figures who became tied to it—from Presidents Roosevelt, Taft, and Wilson to the Rockefellers and Standard Oil scions. In 1912, Camp wrote about the pluck of a cadet who lined up against Jim Thorpe in the great Army-Carlisle game: future President Dwight Eisenhower. He liked to think that football made Ike's political future a foregone conclusion.[2]

Camp portrayed football, more than any other burgeoning sport, as providing the forced discipline, sense of danger, and physical hardening that white college men needed to retain power in the modern age. And yet, he also embraced football's democratization once it invariably occurred. It was not the only time he seemed to speak out of both sides of his mouth. He claimed that college football promoted amateur ideals, for instance, even as he was aware of the growing commercial influences in it. He also claimed to want to make football safer, though he allowed for roughness in its rules. Camp's ideas evolved and grew muddied with lived experience, and hence he occasionally appeared as a man of contradictions. To portray him otherwise would be to paint him in caricature, not as the complex person he was.

When Camp weighed in on football, his opinions were embraced but also contested—widely and publicly—making football one of the most revealing cultural phenomena of its time. These conversations reveal much about how Americans tried to define male success in modern life. Some chose to see it as something one was born into; others, as something one had to work at. Still, Americans have not reached a consensus about how much valor, righteousness, luck, strength, discipline, and cunning have had to do with it.

And yet, through football and Camp, a general shift in sensibilities comes into view: a turn from honoring nineteenth-century manliness to revering twentieth-century masculinity. During his life, Americans reimagined manhood as something externally demonstrated, having less to do with one's breeding than one's conspicuous physical body. While Camp was part of a larger impulse, he also stands apart as someone who worked doggedly on multiple fronts for fifty years to make his conceptions of manhood seem natural and American. That they persisted after his death is apparent in psychologist Lewis Terman's intelligence testing of junior high students in 1936, which confirmed that young Americans still thought football players more masculine than any other males. Such perceptions persist in a culture that tells boys that the alpha types among them belong on football fields, with female and effeminate admirers on the sidelines.[3]

Few Americans know that the All-American was an iconic figure of Camp's careful design, or that many of the debates rocking football today were ones he tried to resolve. Football enthusiasts remain defensive amid indictments of the brutality of the sport and, by extension, the efficacy of its virile lessons. Stories have been publicized in recent years revealing homophobia and misogyny in the locker room, and adolescent boys, desperate to show their manhood, refuse to take precautions to avoid concussion or other serious injury. Hazing is still an accepted part of the gridiron, as is the shaking off of disorientation after a blow to the head on the field. "Be a man and get back out there"—these are the words of coaches and the internal monologues of players desperate to show their grit—or as Camp would have said it, "pluck" or "sand"—on the gridiron.

Deaths on the football field forced Camp to act swiftly, to make adjustments before the public rejected his game. Today, concern about football's effects on brains and growing bodies has also led to rule and equipment changes. But football is so firmly entrenched in American culture that even the most radical reformers stop short of calling for a ban on the game altogether. Americans see less death and maiming on the gridiron than they used to. Now, most of the injuries football players suffer are minor and temporary, or quiet and lingering. Only later, when ex-players have suffered dementia and debilities that cannot be seen or proved as directly linked to football, have they questioned if it was worth their health to be manly on the gridiron.

Take former Pittsburgh Steeler Ralph Wenzel, who died in 2012. Only after a neuropathologist harvested his brain was it clear that repeated blows to his head decades before led to the chronic traumatic encephalopathy (CTE) that killed him. His brain damage was exacerbated during his seven years as a pro offensive lineman, but his history of concussion likely began in high school, when he first learned to live by the pain principle. He died by it too, and he is not alone; the suicides of former Chicago Bear Dave Duerson and All-Pro linebacker Junior Seau have been linked to the same brain malady. Neuropathology researchers at Boston University Medical School have seen dozens of brains like theirs in former football players and lament their gradual but gruesome degeneration.[4]

In 2011, NFL Commissioner Roger Goodell instituted stricter rules about defensive tackling in an attempt to reduce helmet-to-helmet injuries in the open field. Some have welcomed this and other modest attempts to mitigate debilitating contact in football. Pittsburgh defender Troy Polamalu, however, initially voiced his resentment of the new regulations, insisting that they took away his edge. Camp seems cut off from this conversation in twenty-first-century professional football, given that his work was in the college game and that helmets were not even required on the gridiron until fourteen years after his death. And yet, his specter still eerily lingers in the points raised. Goodell's pressure to institute change was the same Camp felt in the college game, and today's football apologists echo his concerns of one hundred years ago, insisting that the new regulations give ball carriers, who are getting bigger, more athletic, and more elusive, undue advantages over defenders, disrupting the sense of balance that makes football compelling.

Sports Illustrated's Tim Layden sounds melancholy about the lengthening list of rules that have put defenders on their heels, reckoning that they have "turned the pure takedown into a dying art." Polamalu is philosophical about the restrictions he is forced to play under: "When you start conforming to these rules, you take away the aspect of fear, and overcoming fear is what makes us men, you know? It's what challenges us. You take that away, you kind of make the game for everybody." He still sees the physical courage gained in the violent confrontations of football as man-making, as what makes him exceptional.[5]

Camp's greatest challenge was to institute change in football without compromising the character-building potential he claimed for it. In the twenty-first century, as we hear of proposals to penalize further unnecessary roughness, redesign helmets, test more for substance abuse, and treat concussions more seriously, we have to wonder how he would have weighed in. Would he have tried to patent the latest in protective equipment or thought that helmets detracted from the hardening lessons of football? Would the bigness and commercial hype of Super Bowl Sunday and college programs have repulsed him, or been his vision realized? Would draft day have looked like the selling-off of chattel? Would unionized college ball have seemed to be beside the point? Would he have thought fantasy leagues too vicarious an experience to have man-making value? Most profoundly, would he have thought that football still made men out of boys? The story in these pages puts a name to one of the most distinctive voices that ever whispered to American men, telling them that the athlete, the warrior, the gridiron hero is who they have always wanted to be.

NOTES

Unless stated otherwise, archival materials come from the Walter Chauncey Camp Collection (WCCC), Yale University Special Collections, Manuscript Collection 125, New Haven, CT. Many of the writings in his collection are undated, untitled drafts, and may be cited merely by the series (S), box (B), and folder (f) to which they belong.

Many of the nineteenth-century newspaper and magazine clippings used were reprinted in *The Lost Century of American Football* (Lost Century of Sports Collection, 2011) or came from unsourced clippings in the WCCC or the Amos Alonzo Stagg Papers, University of Chicago Archives and Special Collections, Chicago, IL and hence may not have complete citations.

Pregame Commentary

1. James Percy to Walter Camp, August 31, 1910, Walter Chauncey Camp Collection (hereafter WCCC), SI, B3, f87; Robert P. Bradley to St. Nicholas, January 4, 1889, WCCC, SI, B3, f88; Frederick Braman to Camp, November 22, 1893, WCCC, SI, B3, f89.
2. Theodore Roosevelt, "The American Boy," *The Strenuous Life: Essays and Addresses* (Mineola, NY: Dover, 2009), 77 (original article was published in *St. Nicholas Magazine* in May 1900).
3. St. Louis Club flyer [1915], WCCC, SI, B4, f112.
4. Harford Powel Jr., *Walter Camp: The Father of American Football* (Boston: Little, Brown, 1926), 32; *St. Louis Republic* in advertisement for Camp's books, WCCC, SII, B58, f413; Michael Oriard, *Reading Football: How the Popular Press Created an American Spectacle* (Chapel Hill, NC: University

of North Carolina Press, 1993), 35–36; John L. Miller, *The Big Scrum: How Teddy Roosevelt Saved Football* (New York: HarperCollins, 2011), 76.

5. Parke Davis eulogized Camp in the 1925 edition of *Spalding's Official Football Guide,* the publication Walter Camp edited for forty-two years. See WCCC, SV, B67, f15.

Introduction

1. Résumé in the Walter Chauncey Camp Collection (hereafter WCCC), SV, B66, f1.

2. E. Anthony Rotundo, *American Manhood: Transformations in Masculinity from the Revolution to the Modern Era* (New York: Basic Books, 1993), 168.

3. Aphorisms, WCCC, SII, B58, f418; Kathleen Valenzi, ed., *Champion of Sport: The Life of Walter Camp* (Charlottesville, VA: Howell Press, 1990), 98.

4. The nineteenth-century understanding of "middle class" does not match the current, catchall connotation. The industrial middle class of the nineteenth century was largely well-to-do by today's standards. Professional wage earners ("white collar" as opposed to "blue collar") might have called themselves middle class to distinguish themselves from men who inherited their wealth without working for it. Steven Riess, "Sport and the Redefinition of American Middle-Class Masculinity," *International Journal of the History of Sport*, 8 (May 1991), 5–22; Patrick B. Miller, ed., "Introduction," *The Sporting World of the Modern South* (Urbana, IL: University of Illinois Press, 2002), 4.

5. Allen Guttmann, *The Erotic in Sports* (New York: Columbia University Press, 1996), 62.

6. Résumé in WCCC, SV, B66, f1.

7. Harold Hornstein, "Golden Days with Walter Camp Relived by Daughter," *New Haven Register*, November 18, 1979, WCCC, SV, B72, f59; Harford Powel Jr., *Walter Camp: The Father of American Football* (Boston: Little, Brown, 1926), viii, 104–105, 196.

8. Robert Clancy, "Although Yale's Coach Sits on Michigan Bench, Notre Dame Has His Sympathy," November 1909, WCCC, SIII.

9. Frederic Remington to Walter Camp, April 3, 1894, Letters of Frederic Remington, MSS 8242, University of Virginia, Alderman Library, Charlottesville VA; Gerald Roberts, "The Strenuous Life: The Cult of Manliness in the Era of Theodore Roosevelt" (Ph.D. diss., Michigan State University, 1970), 134–162.

Chapter 1

1. "The Season Begins and Ends Today," *Harvard Crimson* (November 19, 1983), (http://www.thecrimson.com/article/1983/11/19/the-season-begins-and-ends-today/); Invitation to plaque unveiling, November 25, 1967, Walter Chauncey Camp Collection (hereafter WCCC), SV, B72, f57; Robert Anthony, 1980, WCCC, SV, B66, f1; Robert O. Anthony, *Finding Aid for the Walter Camp Papers* (New Haven: Yale University Library, 1982) 1, WCCC.

2. E. C. Camp to Camp, January 16, 1920, WCCC, SV, B66, f1; Norris Galpin Osborn, *Men of Mark in Connecticut*, vol. 1 (Hartford, CT: W. R. Goodspeed, 1906), 428–431.

3. "Death of Mrs. Camp," [1895]; "Principal of Dwight School" [n.d.], personal clippings, WCCC, SIII; Osborn, *Men of Mark*; Richard P. Borkowski, "The Life and Contributions of Walter Camp to American Football" (Ph.D. diss., Temple University, 1979), 2–3; Harford Powel Jr., *Walter Camp: The Father of American Football* (Boston: Little, Brown, 1926), 151.

4. Clifford Putney, *Muscular Christianity: Manhood and Sports in Protestant America, 1880–1920* (Cambridge, MA: Harvard University Press, 2001), 11–72.

5. "The Resurrection of Muscle," *New York Times*, April 30, 1860; Putney, *Muscular Christianity*, 11–44; Gerald Roberts, "The Strenuous Life: The Cult of Manliness in the Era of Theodore Roosevelt" (Ph.D. diss., Michigan State University, 1970), 52–77; William Winn, "Tom Brown's Schooldays and the Development of 'Muscular Christianity,'" *Church History*, 21, March 1960, 64–73.

6. Osborn, *Men of Mark*; Benjamin Rader, *American Sports: From the Age of Folk Games to the Age of Televised Sports*, 5th ed. (Upper Saddle River, NJ: Prentice Hall, 2004), 44, 85.

7. On Bennett, WCCC, SII, B33, f25.

8. "Foot ball at Yale," *Titusville Herald*, December 17, 1873; WCCC, SII, B33, f16, 24; WCCC, SV, B66, f1.

9. Henry Seidel Canby, *Alma Mater: The Gothic Age of the American College* (New York: Arno Press, 1975), 4–5, 17.

10. Lyman Hotchkiss Bagg, *Four Years at Yale* (New Haven, CT: Charles C. Chatfield and Co., 1871), 501, 515; Town and Gown Relations, WCCC, SII, B52, f321; B53, f332; B58, f408; class bully in f409.

11. WCCC, SV, B66, f1; Bagg, *Four Years at Yale*, 366; Steven A. Riess, ed., *Major Problems in American Sport History* (Boston: Houghton Mifflin, 1997), 112; WCCC, SII, B52, f328.

12. History of post-Civil War athletics in WCCC, SII, B60, f439.

13. Edward Mussey Hartwell, "On Physical Training in the United States," *Public Health Papers and Reports*, vol. 10, American Public Health Association, 1885, 27–35; "The Muscular Reform," *New York World*, August 21, 1860; Bagg, *Four Years at Yale*, 402–403.

14. William Blaikie, *How To Get Strong and How To Stay So* (New York: Harper and Brothers, 1879); Recollections of Yale Gymnasium in WCCC, SV, B66, f1.

15. E. Anthony Rotundo notes this shift toward a more competitive spirit after the Civil War in *American Manhood: Transformations in Masculinity from the Revolution to the Modern Era* (New York: Basic Books, 1993), 240; Richard O. Davies, *Rivals! The Ten Greatest American Sports Rivalries of the 20th Century* (West Sussex, UK: Wiley Blackwell, 2010), 4; Brooks Mather Kelley, *Yale: A History* (New Haven, CT: Yale University Press, 1974), 299–300; Lewis Sheldon Welch and Walter Camp, *Yale, Her Campus, Classrooms, and*

Athletics (New York: L. C. Page and Co., 1899), 551–553; on Yale sports history, WCCC, SII, B60, f444.

16. S. W. Pope, *Patriotic Games: Sporting Traditions in the American Imagination, 1876–1926* (Knoxville, TN: University of Tennessee Press, 1997), 5; WCCC, SII, B60, 444.

17. Teen excursions in WCCC, SII, B60, f436, f444.

18. Camp, *The Daily Dozen* (New York: Reynolds Co., 1925 [1921]), 17–18.

19. John Stuart Martin, "Walter Camp and His Gridiron Game," *American Heritage*, October 1961; Michael Kimmel, *The History of Men* (Albany, NY: State University of New York, 2005), 55; Rader, *American Sport*, 67; Powel, *Walter Camp*, 4–7.

20. "Hopkins Grammar School," June 1899, WCCC, SI, B14, f371; Hopkins, WCCC, SII, B58, f407; G. Edward White, *The Eastern Establishment and the Western Experience* (New Haven, CT: Yale University Press, 1968), 23.

21. Endicott Peabody, "The Boy and the Boarding School," 1908, WCCC, SIII; Putney, *Muscular Christianity*, 106–108.

22. Edward M. House, "Memories," WCCC, SII, B58, f407.

23. Powel, *Walter Camp*, 9–11, 21; Rotundo, *American Manhood*, 40–41.

24. "Reports from the Potomac Flotilla," *New York Times*, October 17, 1861; "Letter of Hon. Lawrence Branch to Constituents," May 15, 1860, *North Carolina Standard*.

25. David M. Nelson, *The Anatomy of a Game: Football, the Rules, and the Men Who Made the Game* (Newark, DE: University of Delaware Press, 1993), 25; Bagg, *Four Years at Yale*, 259–261; "Riot and Excitement at New Haven," *Norwalk Experimenter*, November 24, 1841; "Yale Foot Ball Game," correspondence of the *New York Times*, October 18, 1852; "The Annual Rush at Yale," *Iowa Algona Republican*, October 23, 1872.

26. Clipping from the Rutgers University *Targum*, November 1869, WCCC; Richard Goldstein, *Ivy League Autumns* (New York: St. Martin's Press, 1996), 4–6.

27. "The Annual Rush at Yale"; Martin, "Walter Camp and His Gridiron Game"; Nelson, *Anatomy of a Game*, 28–30.

28. "College News," *Boston Daily Globe*, November 6, 1875; Camp, "A Historic Game of Football," *The Youth's Companion*, November 29, 1900, 625–626.

29. On 1875 match, WCCC, SII, B32, f12; Thomas G. Bergin, *The Game: The Harvard-Yale Football Rivalry, 1875–1983* (New Haven, CT: Yale University Press, 1984), 4–6; "The Harvard-Yale Football Game," *Boston Daily Globe*, November 15, 1875.

30. On Baker, WCCC, SV, B66, f1.

31. John Whitehead, "The Class of '80 Left its Mark," *Yale Alumni Magazine and Journal*, June 1980, 8.

32. Anthony Rotundo maintains that in this period, "youths" were considered to be boys in their late teens who were often leaving home for the first time. Male "youth" lasted, culturally speaking, until the late 20s or 30s. See *American Manhood*, 55; Kathleen Valenzi, ed., *Champion of Sport: The Life of Walter Camp* (Charlottesville, VA: Howell Press, 1990), 17.

33. Camp on Hale, WCCC, SII, B53, f333; Walter Jennings to Alice Camp, March 24, 1925, WCCC, SV, B70, f54.

34. Diary excerpts, WCCC, SV, B66, f2; Kelley, *Yale: A History*, 283.

35. Welch and Camp, *Yale*, 427; John Addison Porter, ed., *Sketches of Yale Life* (Washington, DC: Arlington Publishing Co., 1886), 24.

36. Porter, *Sketches of Life at Yale*, 100–102, 225; Bagg, *Four Years at Yale*, 293–295, 527–528; Camp on Moriarty's, WCCC, SII, B58, f408; Henry A. Beers, *The Ways of Yale in the Consulship of Plancus* (New York: Henry Holt, 1895), 109–110.

37. Diary excerpts, WCCC, SV, B66, f2; Beers, *The Ways of Yale*, 94–95; Welch and Camp, *Yale*, 183, 427; Bagg, *Four Years at Yale*, 298, 521.

38. Porter, *Sketches of Yale Life*, 136–137.

39. Beers, *The Ways of Yale*, 194–195.

40. John L. Miller, *The Big Scrum: How Teddy Roosevelt Saved Football* (New York: HarperCollins, 2011), 96–105.

41. Robert J. Higgs, "Yale and the Heroic Ideal, *Götterdämmerung* and Palingenesis, 1865-1914," in *Manliness and Morality: Middle-Class Masculinity in Britain and America, 1800–1940*, J. A. Mangan and James Walvin, eds. (New York: St. Martin's Press, 1987), 163.

42. Joe L. Dubbert, "Progressivism and the Masculinity Crisis," in *The American Man*, Elizabeth H. and Joseph H. Pleck, eds. (Englewood Cliffs, NJ: Prentice Hall, 1980), 307; Welch and Camp, *Yale*, 244; Porter, *Sketches of Yale Life*, 13, 17; Canby, *Alma Mater*, 11; Nicholas L. Syrett, *The Company He Keeps: A History of White College Fraternities* (Chapel Hill, NC: University of North Carolina Press), 123–26.

43. Beers, *The Ways of Yale*, 7–9; Porter, ed., *Sketches of Yale Life*, 91–120.

44. Syrett, *The Company He Keeps*, 134–36; Beers, *The Ways of Yale*, 5.

45. Eating clubs in WCCC, SII, B58, f409; Bagg, *Four Years at Yale*, 51–189.

46. Wolf's Head competed with Bones and Keys after 1885. Camp, "Senior Society Elections," WCCC, SII, B58, f408; Alexandra Robbins, *Secrets of the Tomb: Skull and Bones, the Ivy League, and the Hidden Paths of Power* (New York: Back Bay Books, 2002), 58–70, 84–94.

47. Syrett, *The Company He Keeps*, 80–81.

48. See, e.g., Thomas Donnelley's signoff to Camp: "Sincerely yours in 322," April 21, 1896, WCCC, SI, B9, f250; George Woodruff to Camp, January 24, 1903, WCCC, SI, B27, f768.

49. Skull and Bones in *The Yale Illustrated Horoscope*, May 1890, B272, f8, Amos Alonzo Stagg Papers, University of Chicago Archives and Special Collections (hereafter referred to as Stagg Papers).

50. Camp's cumulative grade point averages for his freshman through senior years were 2.77, 2.61, 2.43, and 2.59. Borkowski, "The Life and Contributions," 46; diary entry, January 16, 1879, WCCC, SV, B66, f2; Powel, *Walter Camp*, 29; Anthony, finding aid to Walter Camp papers, 2, 8.

51. Draft, June 20, 1913, WCCC, SII, B52, f322; Welch and Camp, *Yale*, 578–579.

52. Walter Camp, *The Book of Foot-ball* (New York: Century Co., 1910), xv–xvi.

53. *Walter Camp's Book of College Sports* (New York: Century Co., 1900 [revised ed.]), 1–9; Camp, *The Book of Foot-ball*, xvi, xx.

54. Rader, *American Sports*, 78; Ronald A. Smith, *Sports and Freedom: The Rise of Big-Time College Athletics* (New York: Oxford University Press, 1988), 165–174; Camp, *Book of College Sports*, 5–6; Henry P. Wright to Camp, November 23, 1893, WCCC, SI, B27, f776.

55. Albert G. Keller, *Reminiscences (Mainly Personal) of William Graham Sumner* (New Haven, CT: Yale University Press, 1933), 3–4; Kelley, *Yale: A History*, 250–251; Miller, *Big Scrum*, 88.

56. Diary entry, April 4, 18[80], WCCC, SV, B66, f2; "William Graham Sumner," *Yale Review*, May 1910, 2–3; Donald Pickens, "William Graham Sumner: Moralist as Social Scientist," *Social Science*, October 1968, 202–209; Michael Kimmel, *Manhood in America: A Cultural History* (New York: Oxford University Press, 2006), 63; Kelley, *Yale: A History*, 264–271.

57. Richard Hofstadter, "William Graham Sumner, Social Darwinist," *New England Quarterly*, 14, September 1941, 460–461.

58. J. C. Schwab in *Yale Review* XIX, May 1910, 4; Keller, *Reminiscences*, 29, 61.

59. Borkowski, "The Life and Contributions," 51; Camp, "A Historic Game of Football," *The Youth's Companion*, November 29, 1900, 625–626.

60. Camp, *The Book of Foot-ball*, 85–86; Borkowski, "The Life and Contributions," 36.

61. Caspar Whitney likely exaggerated when he described the graduating Walter Camp as 5' 11 ¾" and 170 pounds. Richard Goldstein wrote that Camp entered Yale at a taller 6', but at a slighter 157 pounds. See Whitney, "Walter Camp," *Harper's Weekly*, March 5, 1892; Goldstein, *Ivy League Autumns*, 11.

62. Camp, "A Historic Game of Football"; Powel, *Walter Camp*, 20; Borkowski, "The Life and Contributions," 41.

63. F. P. Vernon to Camp, January 29, 1915, WCCC, SI, B25, f721; William H. Edwards, *Football Days* (New York: Moffat, Yard and Co., 1916), 71–72; Martin, "Walter Camp and his Gridiron Game."

64. On Roosevelt, WCCC, SII, B54, f346; Powel, *Walter Camp*, 20–21; Miller, *Big Scrum*, 19–25, 54, 94; John Kasson, *Houdini, Tarzan and the Perfect Man: The White Male Body and the Challenge of Modernity in America* (New York: Hill and Wang, 2001), 4–5; Davies, *Rivals!*, 2; White, *The Eastern Establishment and the Western Experience*, 61–62.

65. "Rough and Tumble Play," *New York Times*, November 23, 1879.

66. On Remington, WCCC, SII, B33, f15, 20; Camp, "Some Football Stories," *The Companion*, October 15, 1915, 507; Peggy and Harold Samuels, *A Biography of Frederic Remington* (Austin, TX: University of Texas Press, 1985), 16–27; Benjamin Lamb, "As I Remember Frederic Remington," *Chicago Tribune*, January 9, 1910, SIII.

67. Vernon to Camp, January 29, 1915; Benjamin Lamb to Camp, January 24, 1913, WCCC, SI, B15, f421; Powel, *Walter Camp*, 21, 28.

68. "Yale College News," *New Haven Register*, November 14, 1879; Edwards, *Football Days*, 75–76.

69. Powel, *Walter Camp*, 26–27; Gerald R. Gems, *For Pride, Profit, and Patriarchy: Football and the Incorporation of American Cultural Values* (London: Scarecrow Press, 2000), 14.

70. "Foot-ball Matters at Yale," *Boston Daily Globe*, November 25, 1877; Nelson, *The Anatomy of a Game*, 41.
71. Parke H. Davis, "Walter Camp—The Dean of American Foot Ball," tribute in *Spalding's Foot Ball Guide*, 1925, WCCC, SV, B67, f15.
72. Camp, "The Game and Laws of American Football," *Outing*, October 1886; Powel, *Walter Camp*, 60.
73. Davis, "Walter Camp—The Dean of American Foot Ball"; Nelson, *The Anatomy of a Game*, 50; Martin, "Walter Camp and His Gridiron Game."
74. Camp, *The Book of Foot-ball*, 34.
75. Powel, *Walter Camp*, viii–ix, 32–33; Martin, "Walter Camp and His Gridiron Game."

Chapter 2

1. Whitehead, "Class of '80," 6–9; Welch and Camp, *Yale*, 22–25; Beers, *The Ways of Yale*, 97.
2. Mark C. Carnes, *Secret Ritual and Manhood in America* (New Haven, CT: Yale University Press, 1989); Kimmel, *Manhood in America*, 114–16; Rotundo, *American Manhood*, 62, 90, 143; Dana Nelson, *National Manhood: Capitalist Citizenship and the Imagined Fraternity of White Men* (Durham, NC: Duke University Press, 1998); Syrett, *The Company He Keeps*, 106.
3. Harvey Green, *Fit for America: Health, Fitness, Sport, and American Society* (New York: Pantheon, 1986), 137–140; Gail Bederman, *Manliness and Civilization: A Cultural History of Gender and Race in the United States, 1880–1917* (Chicago: University of Chicago Press, 1995), 14–15, 84–88.
4. Rotundo, *American Manhood*, 174–187, 225, 267; Whitehead, "Class of '80."
5. Kimmel, *History of Men*, 38, 63.
6. Joseph Kett, *Rites of Passage: Adolescence in America 1790 to the Present* (New York: Basic Books, 1977), 173.
7. On the crisis in American masculinity in this period, see Dubbert, "Progressivism and the Masculinity Crisis," 303–320; Kasson, *Houdini, Tarzan and the Perfect Man*.
8. Beers, *The Ways of Yale*, 131–132; Whitehead, "Class of '80."
9. Parke Davis, speech, February 5, 1915, WCCC, SV, B68, f34; National League Baseball Clubs to Camp, November 21, 1883, WCCC, SI, B18, f501; Caspar Whitney, "Walter Camp"; Rader, *American Sport*, 62; Borkowski, *Life and Contributions*, 52.
10. Roberta J. Park, "Sport, Gender and Society in a Transatlantic Victorian Perspective," in *From "Fair Sex" to Feminism: Sport and the Socialization of Women in the Industrial and Post-Industrial Eras*, eds. Roberta Park and J. A. Mangan (London: Frank Cass, 1987), 58–87; Donald J. Mrozek, *Sport and American Mentality, 1880–1910* (Knoxville, TN: University of Tennessee Press, 1983), 69–72, 81; Kasson, *Houdini, Tarzan, and the Perfect Man*, 45–46.

11. Welch and Camp, *Yale*, 265–266; Kelley, *Yale: A History*, 255; Valenzi, *Champion of Sport*, 27.

12. "Foot-ball at Yale," *New York Times*, October 22, 1882; on knee injury, WCCC, SII, B60, f444.

13. Borkowski, "Life and Contributions," 55.

14. "Camp to Visit Harvard: Will Bear Yale's Final Proposition for Harmony," [1890], WCCC, SIII; Alexander Agassiz to Professor Wheeler, February 26, 1882, WCCC, SI, B30, f815; "Yale College News," *New Haven Register*, October 6, 1883; clipping from *The Yale News*, February 12, 1884, 12; WCCC, SII, B52, f328.

15. Henry Chadwick to Camp, March 29, 1884, WCCC, SI, B5, f135; To the Editor, *Outing*, April 1884.

16. John Rickards Betts, "The Technological Revolution and the Rise of Sport, 1850–1900," *Mississippi Valley Historical Review*, 40, September 1953, 238–242; Michael Oriard, *Reading Football: How the Popular Press Created an American Spectacle* (Chapel Hill, NC: University of North Carolina Press, 1993), 57–85.

17. Camp, "College Athletics: Youth the Time for Physical Development," *New Englander and Yale Review*, January 1885.

18. Draft on Tompkins, WCCC, SII, B33, f17; Camp, "The First Yale-Harvard Rugby Game," *Boston Sunday Globe*, November 6, 1892.

19. Harford Powel, "Walter Camp: Chapter II. The Call of the Field," *Youth's Companion*, October 7, 1926, 718; Borkowski, "Life and Contributions," 53.

20. Aphorisms, WCCC, SII, B58, f420.

21. "Varsity Veteran," *Harper's Weekly*, November 12, 1892.

22. Sources differ as to whether the Manhattan Clock Company was also organized by Hiram Camp, and whether Hiram and Walter were related. Ellsworth Grant says both statements are true in *The Miracle of Connecticut* (Hartford, CT: Connecticut Historical Society, 1992), 160; Hiram Camp is described as Camp's grandfather in the May 1917 edition of *The National Jeweler*, but the relation is not confirmed elsewhere. See WCCC, SIII; William G. Daggett, ed., *A History of the Class of Eighty, Yale College, 1875–1910* (New Haven, CT: [n.p.], 1910), 104; "Clocks," [n.d.], WCCC, SII, B58, f405.

23. Kimmel, *Manhood in America*, 71; Rotundo, *American Manhood*, 209.

24. O. G. Jennings to Camp, April 7, 1891, WCCC, SI, B14, f395; Henry W. Taft to Camp, September 21 and 25, 1891, WCCC, SI, B24, f668.

25. Powel, *Walter Camp*, 45, 147–149; Advertisement for the "Dollar Yale" in *Ladies Home Journal*, January 1906, 41.

26. "Do Likewise," *New England Farmer and Horticultural Register*, May 5, 1883, 2; Camp to E. Dana Caulkins, May 19, 1920, WCCC, SI, B18, f503.

27. Robert Kangiel, *The One Best Way: Frederick Winslow Taylor and the Enigma of Efficiency* (Cambridge, MA: MIT Press, 2005); Elliott Gorn and Warren Goldstein, *A Brief History of American Sports* (Urbana, IL: University of Illinois Press, 2004), 159–160; Oriard, *Reading Football*, 23–24.

28. Rader, *American Sport*, 73–81; Mrozek, *Sport and American Mentality*, 103–135.
29. The Social Register got its name in 1887. Francis Gerry Fairfield, *The Clubs of New York* (New York: Henry L. Hinton, 1873), 7–28; White, *Eastern Establishment and the Western Experience*, 11–21, 28–29.
30. Walter Jennings to Camp, January 23, 1902, WCCC, SI, B14, f396.
31. "City Athletics," *Harper's Weekly*, 68, 1892, 297–305; Caspar Whitney, "Evolution of the Country Club," *Harper's New Monthly Magazine*, 90, December 1894, 16–33.
32. Pope, *Patriotic Games*, 19–23.
33. Announcement in *Daily Princetonian*, February 1, 1886.
34. Aphorisms, WCCC, SII, B58, f418; on self-management, February 18, 1884, WCCC, SII, B52, f325.
35. WCCC, SII, B52, f326; Constitution of the Yale Athletic Association, June 15, 1892, WCCC, SI, B29, f799; Camp, "College Athletics," *Century Illustrated Monthly*, 6, 1893.
36. Alan Tonelson, "Heffelfinger was the Greatest Roman of Them All," *Daily Princetonian*, November 16, 1973, A-6, A-7.
37. Camp on Financial Union, January 1, 1900, WCCC, SI, B29, f796; WCCC, SII, B52, f321.
38. Yale Field Corporation, Articles of Association, May 27, 1882; Hartwell, "On Physical Training in the United States," 1885, 33–34.
39. L. W. Robinson to Camp, November 1, 1905, WCCC, SI, B28, f793, 794; Bergin, *Harvard-Yale Football Rivalry*, 22.
40. On faculty control, WCCC, SII, B52, f326; "Answering Dr. McCosh," *New Haven Register*, April 9, 1883.
41. Bergin, *Harvard-Yale Football Rivalry*, 24; Heisman's recollections in Allison Danzig, *Oh, How They Played the Game: The Early Days of Football and the Heroes Who Made it Great* (New York: MacMillan Co., 1971), 69–71.
42. "College Athletic Sports," *New York Times*, November 4, 1882; "Harvard Football," *Boston Daily Globe*, November 24, 1883; "College Foot-ball," *New York Times*, November 24, 1883; Bergin, *Harvard-Yale Football Rivalry*, 24–25.
43. The committee existed until 1893. Parke Davis on Camp in Dartmouth-Harvard Game of 1926 program, WCCC, SV, B69, f40; Nelson, *Anatomy of a Game*, 61–62; Bergin, *Harvard-Yale Football Rivalry*, 29; Goldstein, *Ivy League Autumns*, 13; Powel, *Walter Camp*, 37; F. H. Tackaberry, president of Wesleyan Football Association, to Camp, October 25, 1891, WCCC, SI, B24, f667.
44. Camp, "Football," *Outing*, January 1888; *The Book of Foot-ball*, 61–62.
45. Oriard, *Reading Football*, 28.
46. "Still a Mystery: Was It a Jealous Rival that Shot Condit Smith?" *Lewiston Saturday Journal*, March 7, 1887, 1.
47. "Stole Mr. Camp's Overcoat," *New Haven Register*, November 20, 1886; "Young Camp is Arrested," WCCC, SIII; "Followed A False Clue," *New York Times*, March 6, 1887.

48. "A Lesson for Detectives," *Boston Globe*, March 1887, WCCC, SIII.
49. "Loves Plot Miscarries," 1887, WCCC, SIII; George Condit Smith and Per. R. S. Smith to Camp, March 8, 1887, WCCC, SI, B23, f636.

Chapter 3

1. "Followed a False Clue," *New York Times*, March 6, 1887.
2. Bruce Curtis and Joy Curtis, "The Harder, Nobler Task: Five Victorian Women and the Work Ethic," in *Ideas in America's Cultures: From Republic to Mass Society*, ed. Hamilton Cravens (Ames, IA: Iowa State University Press, 1982), 108–109; Hofstadter, "William Graham Sumner," 457, 474; Bruce Curtis, "Victorians Abed: William Graham Sumner on the Family, Women, and Sex," *American Studies*, 18 (Spring 1977), 103; Alice Sumner to William Graham Sumner, April 16 [1878], William Graham Sumner Papers, Yale Manuscripts and Archives, B22, f622.
3. Alice Sumner to "Brother Will," n.d., Sumner Papers, B22, f626; Curtis and Curtis, "The Harder, Nobler Task," 109; Keller, *Reminiscences*, 51–52.
4. Curtis and Curtis, "The Harder, Nobler Task," 112–115.
5. "New Haven Public Schools Report to Board of Education" (New Haven, CT: Tuttle, Morehouse, and Taylor, 1883), 51–52; "Mrs. Walter Camp Dies in New Haven," *New York Times*, December 19, 1934, 23.
6. Canby, *Alma Mater*, 14–15; Syrett, *The Company He Keeps*, 175–76; Bagg, *Four Years at Yale*, 523; Cox[?] to Camp, September 20, 1886, WCCC, SI, B31, f844.
7. Camp to Professor W. G. Sumner, August 30, 1886, Sumner Papers, B3, f73; Alice Sumner to Graham Sumner, 31 August 1886, Sumner Papers, B22, f623; Jeannie W. Sumner to Camp, September 15, 1886, WCCC, SI, B24, f662; Curtis, "Victorians Abed," 118.
8. Curtis and Curtis, "The Harder, Nobler Task," 111; "Board of Education Meeting," *New Haven Register*, May 12, 1888; Rotundo, *American Manhood*, 118; "Camp-Sumner," *New York Times*, July 1, 1888; "Wedded at Trinity" [1888], personal clippings, WCCC, SIII.
9. Curtis and Curtis, "The Harder, Nobler Task," 111–112; Canby, *Alma Mater*, 13–14; Tim Cohane, *The Yale Football Story* (New York: G. P. Putnam's Sons, 1951), 60; Alice as a local socialite, in personal clippings, n.d., WCCC, SIII.
10. Powel, *Walter Camp*, 41–42; Amos Alonzo Stagg to Charles Willing, December 17, 1941; to Herbert Baumgartner, June 11, 1951, Stagg Papers, B25, f3; "Dedication of the Walter Camp Memorial," *Yale Alumni Weekly*, November 9, 1928, 220; Vance McCormick to Camp, December 5, 1892, WCCC, SI, B16, f451; "Guarded Like A Prison, Patrol System at Yale Field," *New Haven Register*, November 18, 1893; George Chadwick to Camp, November 25, 1902, WCCC, SI, B5, f135; clipping from *Boston Daily Traveler*, October 9, 1893, SIII.

11. Kimmel, *Manhood in America*, 60; Dubbert, "Progressivism and the Masculinity Crisis," 306–307; Henry James, *The Bostonians* (New York: Modern Library, 1965), 343.

12. For Camp's research notes and writings on women as spectators and participants in sports, including football, see WCCC, SII, B50, f290; B55, f368; B60, f439; Park, "Sport, Gender, and Society," 58–87; Mrozek, *Sport and American Mentality*, 136–160; Putney, *Muscular Christianity*, 48, 147.

13. Alice to Graham [Sumner], July 18 [n.y.], Sumner Papers, B22, f624.

14. Camp, "Gridiron Mother," WCCC, SII, B59, f428.

15. Hornstein, "Golden Days with Walter Camp."

16. Kimmel, *Manhood in America*, 107–108; Alice Sumner Camp to Graham Sumner, July 26, 1900, Sumner papers, B22, f625.

17. Alice Sumner Camp to Graham Sumner, July 16 [1901], letter 9; [n.d.], Sumner Papers, B22, f624; Walter Camp to Sumner, July 29, 1903; July 30, 1903, Sumner Papers, B3, f73.

18. "Mrs. Walter Camp Dies in New Haven"; Alice Camp to Arthur J. Sloane, December 28, 1908, WCCC, SV, B66, f7.

19. Correspondence on Alice Camp's work in *Woman's Home Companion*, 1900–1903, WCCC, SI, B27, f764; Elizabeth Wright to Camp, August 25, 1902, WCCC, SI, B27, f775.

20. Susan Cahn, *Coming On Strong: Gender and Sexuality in 20th Century Women's Sport* (Cambridge, MA: Harvard University Press, 1994), 28–29.

21. Camp on women's exercise, WCCC, SII, B56, f378; Dubbert, "Progressivism and the Masculinity Crisis," 314–315; Roosevelt, "The American Boy," 73–77; Aphorisms, WCCC, SII, B59, f424; Josiah Strong, *The Times and Young Men* (New York: Baker and Taylor Co., 1901), 179–180; Roberts, "Strenuous Life," 53; Camp on Walter Jr., WCCC, SII, B53, f338.

22. "Our New Gymnastics" (paper by Luther Gulick before the 28th International Convention of the Young Men's Christian Association), Philadelphia, May 8, 1889, Stagg Papers, B270, f5; Roberts, "Strenuous Life," 73; Rader, *American Sports*, 105–109.

23. Clipping on Yale Athletic Banquet, 1888, Stagg Papers, B253.

24. "Religious Work at Yale," October 3, 1888, Stagg Papers, B253; "Letter on Religious Life at Yale," 1889, Stagg Papers, B270, f7; *The Young Men's Journal*, June 1889, 66, Stagg Papers, B271, f3.

25. "Our New Gymnastics"; "Stagg and Reynolds," *Toronto Empire*, December 10 1888; "Yale's Missionary Work," *New York Times*, January 11, 1889; "A Muscular Christian," *Minneapolis Times*, September 25, 1892; "Yale's Pitcher," *Brooklyn Eagle*, October 29, 1888, Stagg Papers, B253; "Oak Street Urchins," *Palladium*, April 22, 1890, Stagg Papers, B272, f5; Putney, *Muscular Christianity*, 100.

26. Luther Gulick to Stagg, March 8, 1890, Stagg Papers, B273, f3.

27. Camp, "Football," *Outing*, November 1890; Robin D. Lester, *Stagg's University: The Rise, Decline and Fall of Football at the University of Chicago* (Urbana, IL: University of Illinois Press), 32–64.

28. Charles E. Clay to Camp, December 23, 1889, WCCC, SI, B26, f738; Camp's claims in *Collier's* were also in *Spalding's Football Guide*, 1898. See insert dated November 4, 1951, WCCC, SI, B12, f328. Janet Camp took offense at the allegation made by author Tim Cohane that Caspar Whitney, not her father, thought up the All-America team, and she researched to confirm her father's originating role. See WCCC, SV, B72, f61–65. Journalists looked to "old-timers," including Stagg, to weigh in on the controversy. See Cohane, *Yale Football Story*, 68; Stagg to Charles Willing, December 17, 1941, Stagg Papers, B25, f3; WCCC, SII, B38, f84.

29. Valenzi, *Champion of Sport*, 105; Anthony, finding aid, 5.

30. Pope, *Patriotic Games*, 29–31; Oriard, *Reading Football*, 148.

31. Camp was asked to serve on the *Yale Alumni Weekly's* board of directors in 1894. See R. B. Mason to Camp, June 18, 1894, WCCC, SI, B28, f781; Whitney to Camp, October 13, 1892, WCCC, SI, B12, f329; September 11, 1890; October 9, 1890, WCCC, SI, B26, f738; September 16, 1891, WCCC, SI, B12, f328; March 5, 1900; March 28, 1900; Camp to Whitney, April 3, 1900, WCCC, SI, B19, f521.

32. Camp to Whitney, November 11, 1890, WCCC, SI, B12, f328; June 12, 1894, WCCC, SI, B12, f331; January 26, 1900, WCCC, SI, B26, f750; December 19, 1901; Whitney to Camp, December 31, 1901, WCCC, SI, B19, f522.

33. Oriard, *Reading Football*, 147–162; Michael Oriard, *King Football: Sport and Spectacle in the Golden Age of Radio and Newsreels, Movies and Magazines, the Weekly and Daily Press* (Chapel Hill, NC: University of North Carolina Press, 2001), 260–261.

34. Camp, "Team Play in Football," *Harper's Weekly*, October 31, 1891.

35. Camp, *American Football* (New York: Harper and Brothers, 1894 [1891]); Whitney to Camp, September 10, 1891, WCCC, SI, B12, f328.

36. Camp, "The Game and Laws of American Football," *Outing*, October 1886.

37. Camp quoted in Michael Oriard, "The Father of American Football," in *Sport in America: From Colonial Leisure to Celebrity Figures and Globalization*, vol. 2, ed. David K. Wiggins (Champaign, IL: Human Kinetics, 2010), 175–191.

38. Camp, *American Football*, 69–105.

39. Camp, "Football of 1891," *Outing*, November 1891; *American Football*, 89–90, 122–123; Gorn and Goldstein, *Brief History of American Sports*, 159.

40. Whitney to Camp, August 17, 1891; September 10, 1891; September 16, 1891, WCCC, SI, B12, f328; October 28, 1892, WCCC, f329.

41. Samuels and Samuels, *Frederic Remington*, 92.

42. Camp to Gilbreth, May 29, 1917, WCCC, SI, B11, f299; Gems, *Pride, Profit, and Patriarchy*, 97.

Chapter 4

1. Sal Paolantonio, *How Football Explains America* (Chicago: Triumph Books, 2008), 1–13.

2. Camp, "Football," *Outing*, December 1890.

3. Paolantonio, *How Football Explains America*, 37; Gems, *Pride, Profit, and Patriarchy*, 21–22, 152–155; Camp, "College Football," *Outing*, February 1891.

4. Charles Martin, *Benching Jim Crow: The Rise and Fall of the Color Line in Southern College Sports, 1890–1980* (Urbana, IL: University of Illinois Press, 2010), 4, 8, 14–15; "Foot-ball," *Fort Worth Weekly Gazette*, November 8, 1891; Andrew Doyle, "Turning the Tide: College Football and Southern Progressivism," in *Sporting World of the Modern South*, 102, 111.

5. Theron Field to Camp, March 24, 1894, WCCC, SI, B10, f277; C. P. Dunham to Camp, December 14, 1899, WCCC, SI, B10, f258; Whitney, "Amateur Sport," *Harper's Weekly*, December 17, 1892.

6. Whitney to Camp, July 24, 1894, WCCC, SI, B12, f331.

7. Camp, "A Day's Foot-Ball Practice at Yale," *Harper's Weekly*, November 24, 1888; Whitney, "Walter Camp" [1892]; Gorn and Goldstein, *Brief History of American Sports*, 159.

8. Whitney, "Walter Camp."

9. Whitney to Camp, January 14, 1897; March 20, 1899, WCCC, SI, B26, f750; Whitney, "Important to Foot-Ball Men. The Season of 1891," *Harper's Weekly* [1892], WCCC, SI, B12, f329; Whitney to Camp, September 15, 1892, WCCC, SI, B12, f329; G. A. Merriam, U.S. Navy, to Camp, December 30, 1891, WCCC, SI, B17, f473; February 7, 1893, WCCC, SI, B25, f703.

10. "Yale Men As Coaches, Harvard and Princeton about the Only Colleges without Instructors," September 30, 1893, WCCC, SIII; Francis Preston Venable to Camp, September 15, 1893, WCCC, SI, B19, f511; Duncan Lee, Wake Forest, to Camp [1890], WCCC, SI, B15, f426; D. M. Prince, Wake Forest, to Camp, October 3, 1892, WCCC, SI, B26, f725; L. L. Young, University of Virginia, to editor of *Week's Sport*, May 18, 1890, WCCC, SI, B25, f723; Harold Lee Berry to Camp, January 6, 1899, WCCC, SI, B3, f85; Hollis Gray, manager, University of Vermont, to Camp, May 19, 1902, WCCC, SI, B25, f721; George Filius, manager at Western Reserve, to Camp, January 9, 1903, WCCC, SI, B26, f742; R. S. Greeman, manager, Union College, July 30, 1895, WCCC, SI, B25, f694; Cooper Schmitt, University of Tennessee, to Camp, May 22, 1899, WCCC, SI, B24, f671; W. M. Johnston, manager, University of Nebraska, to Camp, December 3, 1892, WCCC, SI, B18, f505; George Spear, University of Minnesota, to Camp, August 27, 1892, WCCC, SI, B17, f478; Jesse Maley, manager, Indiana University, to Camp, March 6, 1893, WCCC, SI, B14, f385; J. G. Blackwell, Rutgers, to Camp, June 7, 1893, WCCC, SI, B21, f600; Alex Shepard, Jr., captain, University of the South, to Camp, August 23, 1892, WCCC, SI, B23, f639.

11. Charles James to Camp, November 5, 1892, WCCC, SI, B5, f147; James Kivlan to Camp, September 20, 1892, WCCC, SI, B19, f511.

12. Joseph Hamblen Sears, "Modern Coaching of Modern Football," *Harper's Weekly*, November 11, 1893; "Yale Men as Coaches."

13. Until World War I, Camp deliberated on rules regarding sideline coaching and substitutes communicating information. See "Revised Rules Bar Side-Line Coaching," *New York Times*, September 2, 1917, 17; Oriard, "The Father of American Football," 177–178; Nelson, *Anatomy of a Game*, 67; Paolantonio, *How Football Explains America*, 120–121.

14. Stan W. Carlson, *Dr. Henry L. Williams: A Football Biography* (Minneapolis, MN: Stan W. Carlson, 1938), 7–13; "Summer School in Football Pedagogy for Coaches, Captains and Quarter-backs conducted by Henry L. Williams," 1915, WCCC, SI, B17, f478.

15. Camp on new innovators in WCCC, SII, B33, f27; John Watterson, "Reputation Reclaimed," *College Football Historical Society*, November 2003, 3; "New Work on Football" (1893); "Football Made Clear," *Philadelphia Times*, November 12, 1893, B253; Camp to Henry Williams, September 23, 1893, Stagg Papers, B25, f3.

16. Carlson, *Dr. Henry Williams*, 69; Charles Gill to Camp, November 12, 1890, WCCC, SI, B11, f299; "Hod" Walker to "Fats," October 6, 1889; October 20, 1889, WCCC, SI, B26, f727.

17. "How Harvard Beat Yale, Secrets of the Famous Game of 1890," *Boston Traveler*, October 9, 1893, 10; W. Cameron Forbes [to Camp], November 14, 1900, WCCC, SI, B11, f286; SII, B33, f27.

18. Camp to John Field, October 26, 1911, WCCC, SI, B10, f277; "The Great Universities' Army of Scouts," *New York Herald*, November 12, 1911, WCCC, SIII.

19. Biography of Michael C. Murphy, online University Archives and Records Center of the University of Pennsylvania; Camp on Murphy in WCCC, SII, B53, f335; B61, f446.

20. "To Coach Western Players," *New York Times*, November 24, 1892, 3; "To Train Western Elevens," *New York Times*, November 28, 1892, 2.

21. "Camp and McClung. Noted Football Coaches Arrive," n.d. [1892], WCCC, SIII; Frank M. Todd to Camp, November 16, 1892, WCCC, SI, B9, f242; "Dinner by the Yale Alumni Association of California to Mr. Walter Camp and Mr. T. L. McClung"; William Thomas to Camp, December 2, 1892, WCCC, SI, B25, f713; SII, B34, f28.

22. "Walter Camp at Palo Alto" [1892]; clipping on Camp speech from December 13, 1892, WCCC, SIII.

23. "Hilarious Yale Students," November 24, 1889; "To Editor of the Palladium," Stagg Papers, Box 270, Folder 4; "Men of Better Business" to Camp, November 26, 1890, WCCC, SI, B31, f845.

24. This quote from "Football and Study," in *Harper's Weekly*, December 3, 1892, is not Camp explicitly, but he likely wrote this anonymous piece for Whitney.

25. The training table was the advent of scientific coaching. Specially prepared meals were served at particular times of day at a team dining table separate from

the eating quarters of other undergraduates. See Mrozek, *Sport and American Mentality*, 94–96.

26. "The Camp in the Hills" [1892]; "Preparations at Stanford. Walter Camp Tells How His Warriors are Fixing for the Fight," *San Francisco Examiner* [1892]; "The Team Has Gone, *Daily Palo Alto*, December 16, 1892, WCCC, SIII.

27. "Rush and Tackle," *San Francisco Chronicle*, December 18, 1892, WCCC, SIII; James Wilson to Camp, June 29, 1893, WCCC, SI, B27, f760; C. D. Bliss to Camp, September 20, 1893, WCCC, SI, B3, f80; W. Walter Heffelfinger to Camp, September 20, 1893, WCCC, SI, B13, f348.

28. O. V. Eaton to Camp, August 26, 1895; Camp to Eaton, August 29, 1895, WCCC, SI, B10, f260.

29. Clipping by Alice Rix, *San Francisco Examiner*, November 3, 1895, front page, WCCC, SIII.

30. "Chicago's Eleven," *San Francisco Morning Call*, December 24, 1894.

31. "Dinner by Yale Alumni Association of California to Mr. Walter Camp and Mr. T. L. McClung at the University Club," December 9, 1892, WCCC, SI, B28, f780.

32. Oriard, *Reading Football*, 90.

33. Pope, *Patriotic Games*, 85–89.

34. Patrick Miller, "The Manly, the Moral, and the Proficient: College Sport in the New South," in *Sporting World of the Modern South*, 31.

35. Camp, "Intercollegiate Foot-ball in America," part 3, *St. Nicholas*, January 1890.

36. Rader, *American Sport*, 123; Paul Thompson, *The Illustrated Sporting News*, to Camp, December 7, 1904, WCCC, SI, B14, f383; Camp to *The Independent* (Hamilton Holt), November 21, 1899, WCCC, SI, B14, f384; Bradford Merrill, *New York American*, to Camp, April 1, 1911, WCCC, SI, B19, f507; W. C. Reick, city editor, to Camp, September 7, 1891, WCCC, SI, B19, f508; Alfred Eyre to Camp, January 16, 1902, WCCC, SI, B10, f271.

37. Oriard, *Reading Football*, 57–85, 138–139.

38. For this shift from nineteenth-century "inner-directedness" to twentieth-century "other directedness," see David Riesman, *The Lonely Crowd* (New Haven, CT: Yale University Press, 1950); Richard Harding Davis, "The Thanksgiving Day Game," *Harper's Weekly*, December 9, 1893, 170–171; Oriard, *Reading Football*, 113–115; 147–148; Rader, *American Sports*, 97.

39. Thorstein Veblen, *Theories of the Leisure Class* (Mineola, NY: Dover, 1994 [1899]); Mark Bernstein, *Football: The Ivy League Origins of an American Obsession*, (Philadelphia: University of Pennsylvania Press, 2001), 44.

40. Bernstein, *Football*, 43–48.

41. "Twas a Physical Cyclone," Stagg Papers, B253.

42. Camp, "Football," *Outing*, January 1891; Oriard, *Reading Football*, 224–226.

Chapter 5

1. Cohane, *Yale Football Story*, 71–72.
2. See tallies of points scored by Yale and opponents game by game, season by season, in Cohane, *Yale Football Story*, 357.
3. "A Dinner to Walter Camp," 1892, WCCC, SV, B67, f32; "The Walter Camp Dinner," *Yale Alumni Weekly*, March 1, 1892, cover, WCCC, SIII; Whitney, "Walter Camp"; "A Big Yale Love Fest," *New York Daily Tribune*, February 27, 1892, WCCC, SIII.
4. "The Walter Camp Dinner."
5. For the American emphasis on *outcome*, see Mrozek, *Sport and American Mentality*, 73–81.
6. Speech notes, 1892, WCCC, SII, B32, f1.
7. B. Arkell to Camp, November 1, 1892, WCCC, SI, B15, f429; Samuels and Samuels, *Frederic Remington*, 27. Richard Harding Davis recalls the Remington story in "A Day with Yale's Team," *Harper's Weekly*, November 18, 1893, 1110; A Yale Player, "The Development of Football," *Outing*, November 1889.
8. Camp, "The American Game of Football," *Harper's Weekly*, November 10, 1888, 858–859; *Book of Foot-ball*, 53–54.
9. Camp, *Book of Foot-ball*, 52. Gerald Gems claims that Woodrow Wilson was the first to introduce "running interference" as a strategy of the Princeton team in 1879. See *Pride, Profit, and Patriarchy*, 16.
10. "Flying Wedge," *Boston Globe*, November 24, 1892; Scott A. McQuilkin, "The Rise and Fall of the Flying Wedge, Football's Most Controversial Play," *Journal of Sport's History*, Spring 1993, 57–64.
11. "Flying Wedge"; WCCC, SII, B33, f22.
12. Camp, "A Plea for the Wedge in Football," *Harper's Weekly*, January 21, 1893; "Football Studies for Captain and Coach," *Outing*, November 1890.
13. On Trinity and cleat rules, WCCC, SII, B32, f14; B33, f24; Camp, "The Football Season of 1886," *Outing*, January 1887; Walter Camp and Lorin Deland, *Football* (Boston: Houghton Mifflin, 1896), 27; "The American Game of Football," 1888.
14. Andrew White, "How to Choose a College," *Youth's Companion*, August 27, 1891, 462; John Sayle Watterson, *College Football* (Baltimore, MD: Johns Hopkins University Press, 2000), 32.
15. J. C., "The Crusade Against Football," *Outing*, January 1894.
16. Camp, "Is Football a Dangerous Sport?" *Boston Sunday Globe*, November 13, 1892.
17. Rotundo, *American Manhood*, 226–227.
18. Elliot Gorn, *The Manly Art: Bare-Knuckle Prizefighting in America* (Ithaca, NY: Cornell University Press, 1986), 138, 140–202; "Boxing at Yale," *New York Times*, March 27, 1892, 3.
19. Camp, "Brawn and Brain," *Harper's Weekly*, February 22, 1892; Oriard, *Reading Football*, 208, 211, 228.

20. Edwards, *Football Days*, 390.
21. "Can a Gentleman Play Football?" *World Magazine*, November 5, 1905, WCCC, SIII; "The Ring," *San Francisco Morning Call*, November 25, 1894; "The Gridiron and the Prize Ring," *Statesville, NC Landmark*, November 29, 1894.
22. Watterson, *College Football*, 30.
23. Eugene Richards, "Intercollegiate Football," *New Englander and Yale Review*, June 1886; "The Football Situation," *Popular Science Monthly*, 45, October 1894, 721–733; "The Football Question, Why the Game is Approved of by the Yale Faculty," *Evening Post*, November 22, 1893, WCCC, SIII.
24. William Conant Church, "Foot-ball in Our Colleges," *Century Illustrated Monthly*, December 1893; B. W. Mitchell, "A Defense of Football," *Journal of Hygiene and Herald of Health*, 45, 1895, 93; Green, *Fit For America*, 233.
25. "President Eliot's Report," February 21, 1894, WCCC, SIII; Smith, *Sports and Freedom*, 92.
26. Roberts, "The Strenuous Life," 105; Oriard, *Reading Football*, 183.
27. Davies, *Rivals*, 11; Watterson, *College Football*, 27–29.
28. H. H. Almond, "Football as a Moral Agent," *Nineteenth Century*, December 1893, 903; White and Wood, "Intercollegiate Football," *North American Review*, January 1894, 100–109; *Medical News*, November 18, 1893; "Football or No Football," *New York Times*, February 18, 1894; S. J. Watt, "A Plea for Association Football," *Outing*, May 1894.
29. Watterson, *College Football*, 30.
30. "The Football Question, Why the Game is approved of by the Yale Faculty"; Powel, *Walter Camp*, 100. Camp's claims about grade point averages were quantified in White and Wood's "Intercollegiate Football," 106; Camp, "The Current Criticism of Football," *Century Illustrated Monthly*, January 1894.
31. Clippings, WCCC, SI, B16, f451; *Harvard Daily Herald* editorial clippings, 1882, 1889, WCCC, SII, B34, f37; Danzig, *Oh, How They Played*, 62.
32. Davis, "A Day with Yale's Team"; Speech notes, 1892, WCCC, SII, B32, f1; Danzig, *Oh, How They Played*, 64–68; Gems, *Pride, Profit, and Patriarchy*, 56.
33. Davis, "Walter Camp—The Dean of American Football"; Laurence Bliss to Camp, March 13, 1895, WCCC, SI, B3, f80; Borkowski, "Life and Contributions," 99; Smith, *Sports and Freedom*, 93.
34. C. K. Adams to Camp, March 13, 1895, WCCC, SI, B1, f2.
35. Nelson, *Anatomy of a Game*, 70–71; Smith, *Sports and Freedom*, 94; Bernstein, *Football*, 55; "To Revise Football Rules," *New York Times*, March 11, 1894, 3; "New Rules for Football," *New York Times*, May 9, 1894, 2.
36. Camp, "College Athletics," June 1893; "Football of 1893: Its Lessons and Results," *Harper's Weekly*, February 3, 1894, 117.
37. "Football and Its Dangers," *New York Times*, January 7, 1894; "Cadets Must Not Play Football," *New York Daily Tribune*, November 25, 1894; Watterson, *College Football*, 32, 36.

38. Oriard, *Reading Football*, 204; Camp, "Open Letters," *Century*, February 1894, 633–634.

39. Ben S. Cable to Camp, November 21, 1894, WCCC, SI, B30, f819; "Yale is the Conqueror," *New York Sun*, November 25, 1894.

40. Watterson, *College Football*, 14–17.

41. Kieran, "Sports of the Times," *New York Times*, November 19, 1937, in Danzig, *Oh, How They Played*, 63.

42. Goldstein, *Ivy League Autumns*, 23; *Waukesha Freeman*, February 28, 1894; "College-bred Brutality," *New York World*, November 28, 1894; W. D. Simmons to Camp, December 11, 1894, WCCC, SI, B22, f630; Nelson, *Anatomy of a Game*, 72.

43. Accounts vary widely as to what happened in the Harvard-Yale game of 1894. William Edwards, for instance, maintains that Hinkey was not even involved in the play against Wrightington. See Edwards, *Football Days*, 428; Camp to "Sam" [n.d.], WCCC, SI, B31, f848; "Hinkey's Play. Opinions on the Injury to Wrightington"; "An Exoneration of Hinkey," *Boston Herald* [1894], WCCC, SIII.

44. Camp, "The Safety of Football," *Outing*, October 1894; Watterson, *College Football*, 33.

45. "Football Investigating Committee Reports and Comments," WCCC, SII, B43, f160.

46. "Introduction: Origin of the Committee, 1893," WCCC, SII, B43, f160; "Wants Football Statistics," *New York Times*, March 9, 1894, 6.

47. W. T. Bradbury to Camp, March 20, 1894, WCCC, SI, B3, f88; D. W. Abercrombie to Camp, March 23, 1895, WCCC, SI, B1, f1; G. H. Thurber to Camp, March 7, 1894, WCCC, SI, B5, f159.

48. Frederic Remington to Camp, April 3, 1894; WCCC, SII, B33, f15; WCCC, B60, f436.

49. "Football Investigating Committee Report and Comments"; Harry Brown to Camp [n.d.], WCCC, SI, B4, f106; Jas. R. Church to Camp, March 18, 1894, WCCC, SI, B5, f151.

50. S. Cheesman to Camp, March 25, 1894, B5, f148; David Boviard Jr. to Camp, March 3, 1894, WCCC, SI, B3, f84; Church to Camp; W. Heffelfinger to Camp, March 5, 1894, WCCC, SI, B13, f348.

51. George Albert Carpenter to Camp, March 12, 1894, WCCC, SI, B4, f124.

52. Church to Camp; Charles Clark Camp to Camp, March 5, 1894, WCCC, SI, B4, f119.

53. WCCC, SII, B44, f185; W. S. Harvey to Camp, April 20, 1894, WCCC, SI, B12, f337.

54. Eugene Baker to Camp, March 12, 1894, WCCC, SI, B2, f59; H. W. Cowan to Camp, January 17, 1894, WCCC, SI, B8, f210; Heffelfinger to Camp, March 5, 1894, WCCC, SI, B13, f348.

55. Carpenter to Camp; George R. Carter to Camp, March 9, 1894, WCCC, SI, B4, f125.

56. Bacon in WCCC, SII, B45, f206.

57. Charles Clark Camp to Camp, March 27, 1894, WCCC, SI, B4, f119.

58. Trafford in "Is Football a Dangerous Sport?" *Boston Sunday Globe*, November 13, 1892; Gems, *Pride, Profit, and Patriarchy*, 81.

59. J. H. Sears to Camp [1894], WCCC, SII, B45, f206; Camp, *Football Facts and Figures* (New York: Harper and Brothers, 1894); "Conclusions of the Committee," WCCC, SII, B43, f160.

60. Davis, "A Day With Yale's Team."

61. George Woodruff to Camp, March 20, 1894, WCCC, SI, B27, f768.

62. "Nursing Their Wounds," *New York Daily Tribune*, November 26, 1894; Smith, *Sports and Freedom*, 92–93; Watterson, *College Football*, 33.

63. WCCC, SII, B45, f206.

64. Ray Tompkins to Camp, March 5, 1894, WCCC, SI, B24, f682; Kimmel, *History of Men*, 61.

Chapter 6

1. "New Rules for Football," *New York Times*, May 9, 1894; Camp, "Football of '95 A forecast of the Season," *Outing*, November 1895; Nelson, *Anatomy of a Game*, 74–75.

2. Theodore Roosevelt to Camp, March 11, 1895, WCCC, SI, B21, f593.

3. Ray Tompkins to Camp, July 3, 1895, WCCC, SI, B24, f682; "Yale Is Mad Clear Through" [1895]; "Harvard Firm," May 18, 1895, WCCC, SIII; Philip B. Stewart to Camp, October 30, 1895, WCCC, SI, B23, f657.

4. Report of the Yale University Football Association, 1893, WCCC, SI, B30, f819.

5. "Can Camp be Had?" *Waterbury American*, March 24, 1897, WCCC, SIII; "Among the Sick" [1895]; "Principal Camp and Wife Ill," [1895]; "Death of Mrs. Camp, [1895], in personal clippings, WCCC, SIII; Camp to Frank B. Smith, July 19, 1900, WCCC, SI, B23, f636.

6. J. H. Sears to Camp, September 19, 1895, WCCC, SI, B12, f331; "Uncle Dudley"; "The Way to Save Football" [1895], WCCC, SIII.

7. "Football Defended. Theodore Roosevelt Thinks Broken Bones Are Nothing to College Glory," *Boston Advertiser*, February 8, 1895, WCCC, SIII.

8. "May be Friends Again. Mssrs. Camp and Deland Trying to Bring Yale and Harvard Together," special to the *World*, February 16, 1896; Deland, "Football at Harvard and Yale" [1910], WCCC, SIII.

9. Contract for *Football*, October 10, 1896, WCCC, SI, B9, f240; Powel, *Walter Camp*, 47; Camp and Deland, *Football* (Boston: Houghton Mifflin, 1896).

10. "Lift Football. Mission of the Book by Camp and Deland" [1896], WCCC, SIII; Deland to Camp, October 14, 1896; November 18, 1896, WCCC, SI, B9, f240.

11. "Yale and Harvard. Walter Camp Will Go to Boston as a Mediator," February 4, 1897; "Mr. Camp Will Try Again," February 12, 1897, WCCC, SIII.

12. "The Yale-Harvard Trouble," *New York Times*, February 14, 1897, 13; "Agreement of Reconciliation between Harvard and Yale Signed by Walter

Camp for Yale and Dr. W. A. Brooks for Harvard," February 13, 1897, WCCC, SI, B29, f799; "Yale and Harvard," February 15, 1897, WCCC, SIII.

13. "Walter Camp is the Hero for Bringing the Blue and Crimson Together Again in Athletics" [1897], WCCC, SIII; Record of annual gate receipts in records of Financial Union, WCCC, SI, B29, f797; Camp in "Amateur Sport," *Harper's Weekly*, January 16, 1897; Ollie Jennings to Camp, February 15, 1897, WCCC, SI, B14, f395.

14. Personal clippings [1897], WCCC, SIII; Alice Sumner Camp to William Graham Sumner, September 5 [1897], B22, f627, Sumner Papers.

15. Roberts, "The Strenuous Life," 188.

16. Kristin Hoganson, *Fighting for American Manhood: How Gender Politics Provoked the Spanish-American and Philippine-American Wars* (New Haven, CT: Yale University Press, 1998), 10; Mrozek, *Sport and American Mentality*, 46.

17. William James wrote of the "moral equivalent of war" for this generation in *Memory and Studies* (New York: Longmans, Green, and Co., 1912); Camp, "Football in 1893: Its Lessons and Results," *Harper's Weekly*, February 3, 1894, 117–118.

18. Hoganson, *Fighting for American Manhood*, 107; Wanda Ellen Wakefield, *Playing to Win: Sports in the American Military, 1898–1945* (Albany, NY: State University of New York Press, 1997), 2.

19. Christian K. Messenger, *Sport and the Spirit of Play in American Fiction* (New York: Columbia University Press, 1981), 141; Hoganson, *Fighting for American Manhood*, 25, 112; Joseph Paul Vasquez III, "America and the Garrison Stadium: How the U.S. Armed Forces Shaped College Football," *Armed Forces and Society*, 38, November 2011, 353, 357; White, *The Eastern Establishment and the Western Experience*, 149–170.

20. Veblen, *Theory of the Leisure Class*, 151; Ben Merchant Vorpahl, *My Dear Wister: The Frederic Remington-Owen Wister Letters* (Palo Alto, CA: American West Publishing Co., 1972), 215–17; White, *The Eastern Establishment and the Western Experience*, 98–9, 102–3, 114–5.

21. Messenger, *Sport and the Spirit of Play*, 143.

22. Kelley, *Yale: A History*, 295–296; Welch and Camp, *Yale*, 164–165.

23. "Walter Camp is Ill," *New Haven Register*, September 8, 1898.

24. Tompkins to Camp, November 28, 1898; Camp to Tompkins, December 7, 1898, WCCC, SI, B24, f682.

25. Danzig, *Oh, How They Played*, 131–133.

26. W. J. Hyland to Camp, September 11, 1899, WCCC, SI, B14, f382; Mrozek, *Sport and American Mentality*, 77.

27. The Doubleday series was abandoned in 1903. William Patten to Camp, December 13, 1901; June 2, 1902, WCCC, SI, B9, f251; Pope, *Patriotic Games*, 32; Camp, *How to Play Foot Ball: A Primer on the Modern College Game, with Tactics Brought Down to Date*, Spalding Athletic Library no. 183 (New York: American Sports Publishing Co., 1903).

28. Walter Camp, ed., *Spalding's Official Foot Ball Guide* (New York: American Sports Publishing Co., 1899, 1902).

29. Julian Curtiss to Camp, January 12, 1899; August 15, 1894; April 25, 1902; Curtiss to Alice Camp, December 13, 1902; Camp to Curtiss, October 26, 1907, WCCC, SI, B23, f640–644; Paul Dashiell to Camp, November 4, 1902, WCCC, SI, B9, f235; Gems, *Pride, Profit, and Patriarchy*, 185.

30. "What Does Mr. Camp Mean?" *New Haven Register*, September 12, 1893; Ronald A. Smith, *Big-Time Football at Harvard, 1905: The Diary of Coach Bill Reid*, (Urbana, IL: University of Illinois Press, 1994), 42–51.

31. Alan Fox to Camp, November 5, 1902; 1906, WCCC, SI, B11, f287.

32. "Walter Camp Burned Out," February 9, 1899, personal clippings, WCCC, SIII; "Walter Camp's Home Burned," *New Haven Register*, February 9, 1899; "No Yale Trophies Lost," *New Haven Register*, February 11, 1899.

33. "Walter Camp's Purchase," *New Haven Register*, June 16, 1897, 5; Arthur Foote to Alice Camp, February 11, 1899, WCCC, SV, B66, f6; Camp to Caspar Whitney, March 27, 1899, WCCC, SI, B12, f332; Alice Sumner Camp to Graham Sumner [n.d.], B22, f624, Sumner Papers; Miller, *Big Scrum*, 90.

34. Bruce Curtis, *William Graham Sumner* (Boston: Twayne Publishers, 1981), 56; Keller, *Reminiscences*, 9.

35. Canby, *Alma Mater*, 250.

36. Pope, *Patriotic Games*, 90–91; WCCC, SII, B36, f68.

37. Richard Thayer Holbrook, *Boys and Men: A Story of Life at Yale* (New York: Charles Scribner's Sons, 1900), 32; Welch and Camp, *Yale*, 221.

38. Canby, *Alma Mater*, 250–251.

39. Keller, *Reminiscences*, 4, 83; Bruce Curtis, "William Graham Sumner, 'On the Concentration of Wealth,'" *Journal of American History*, March 1969, 823–832; Norman Erik Smith, "William Graham Sumner as an Anti-Social Darwinist," *Pacific Sociological Review*, July 1979, 332–347.

40. Sumner in WCCC, SII, B53, f331; Keller, *Reminiscences*, 59, 68.

41. Walter Camp and Lilian Brooks, *Drives and Putts* (Boston: L. C. Page, 1899); Camp and Welch, *Yale, Her Campus, Classrooms, and Athletics*. Correspondence regarding Camp's publications for Page in WCCC, SI, B19, f529, 530.

42. Daggett, ed., *History of the Class of '80*, 104; "A Chair of Athletics at Yale," *Yale News* [1892], WCCC, SIII; William Burnet Wright to Camp, November 2, 1896, WCCC, SI, B28, f777; Hadley to Camp, August 31, 1899, SI, B11, f313; President Hadley to Mr. Berton, June 29, 1900, WCCC, SI, B11, f313; Gems, *Pride, Profit, and Patriarchy*, 88.

43. "Graduates Tackle Regulars," *New Haven Register*, November 3, 1899; "Arrival of Gov. Roosevelt Former Colonel of Rough Riders Here with Lieuts. Goodrich and Greenway," *New Haven Register*, November 20, 1899.

Halftime

1. The Yale players on Camp's first team were Bloomer at tackle, Brown at guard, Olcott at center, Stillman at tackle, Fincke at quarterback, Chadwick at halfback, and Hale at fullback. The second team included Gould at end, Sheldon at guard, and Coy at end. Sharpe was the man on the third team. Report of the Financial Union for 1900–1901 Season, WCCC, SI, B29, f796; Program for Yale University Club Dinner, December 10, 1900, WCCC, SV, B68, f33.

2. "Walter Camp and Gordon Brown Honored Guests at Yale Dinner," 1901, WCCC, SIII.

3. "Walter Camp's Use of Football in Fiction" [1909 or 1910], WCCC, SIII.

4. "Sudden Death of Famous Yale Football Leader," *Daily Princetonian*, May 11, 1911, cover.

5. Syrett, *The Company He Keeps*, 126; Gorn and Goldstein, *Brief History of American Sports*, 167–168; Kelley, *Yale: A History*, 298, 303.

6. Canby, *Alma Mater*, 137; Kelley, *Yale: A History*, 279.

7. Stephen Steinberg, *The Academic Melting Pot* (New York: Carnegie Foundation, 1974), 14.

8. Owen Johnson, *Stover at Yale* (Boston: Little, Brown, 1931 [1912]), 26, 30.

9. Allen Sack, "When Yale Spirit Vanquished Harvard Indifference," *Harvard Magazine*, November 1975, 26–29, 50–51; Kelley, *Yale: A History*, 303–304; Henry Wright to Camp, May 17, 1901, WCCC, SI, B27, f776.

10. Davis, "A Day with Yale's Team."

11. Welch and Camp, *Yale*, 10; Canby, *Alma Mater*, 25–26.

12. "Work for Rockefeller: Yale Football Manager to Enter Standard Oil Trust," *Meriden Morning Record*, September 24, 1900, 5; "Award the Yale Y," *New Haven Register*, January 31, 1900.

13. Welch and Camp, *Yale*, 143–144; Gorn and Goldstein, *Brief History of American Sports*, 164–166; Camp in Sack, "When Yale Spirit Vanquished Harvard Indifference."

14. Canby, *Alma Mater*, 235–236.

15. Kelley, *Yale: A History*, 308–309.

Chapter 7

1. John C. Collins, National Friends of Boys, to Camp, March 19, 1909, WCCC, SI, B18, f501; "Camp Talks on Athletics," *New York Times*, March 14, 1897, 4; Edwin Milton Fairchild to Camp, March 4, 1905, WCCC, SI, B10, f271.

2. Camp, "Daily Dozen Thoughts for Parents," WCCC, SII, B58, f416; Aphorisms, WCCC, f417, 421; Camp, *Keeping Fit All the Way* (New York: Harper and Brothers, 1919), 35; Camp, "Life and Sport," *Colliers*, March 27, 1915, WCCC, SIII.

3. Roberts, "The Strenuous Life," 29–51.

4. Roberts, "The Strenuous Life," 109–110; Bederman, *Manhood and Civilization,* 77–120; Rotundo, *American Manhood,* 262; G. Stanley Hall, *Adolescence: Its Psychology and Its Relation to Physiology, Anthropology, Sociology, Sex, Crime, Religion, and Education,* 2 vols. (New York: D. Appleton, 1904); Kett, *Rites of Passage,* 111–244; Putney, *Muscular Christianity,* 101.

5. Freud's notions about aggressiveness in men found fuller expression later in *Civilization and Its Discontents,* published in 1929. Camp in Valenzi, *Champion of Sport,* 57; Joseph Lee, *Play and Education* (New York: Macmillan, 1915); Henry Curtis, "The Proper Relation of Organized Sports on Public Playgrounds and in Public Spaces," *Playground,* 3 (1909); W. B. Forbush, *The Boy Problem* (Boston: Pilgrim, 1901); Rader, *American Sport,* 110–111; Kett, *Rites of Passage,* 215–226; Putney, *Muscular Christianity,* 6.

6. Camp's views on eugenics in chapter 2 of manuscript in WCCC, SII, B56, f375; "Building Your Baby," 1922, WCCC, f378; chapter draft, WCCC, SI, B19, f528.

7. On tomboys, WCCC, SII, B55, f364; Kimmel, *Manhood in America,* 89.

8. Albert Beveridge, *The Young Man and the World* (New York: D. Appleton, 1905).

9. Gems, *Pride, Profit, and Patriarchy,* 54.

10. Kimmel, *History of Men,* 37–59.

11. Hall actually died in 1894 at the age of thirty-seven, not five years after graduation as Camp claimed. See Whitehead, "Class of '80," 6–9; "Thoroughbred in College the Ideal of Camp," November 27, 1915, WCCC, SII, B56, f376.

12. Camp, *Daily Dozen,* 5–6; Kasson, *Houdini, Tarzan, and the Perfect Man,* 190–207.

13. Roberts, "The Strenuous Life," 107–132; "The Country Life Movement," *Colliers Weekly,* January 1909; Condé Nast to Camp, June 16, 1919, *Vanity Fair* folder, WCCC, SI, B25, f719.

14. Boy Scouts, WCCC, SI, B3, f86; Jeffrey P. Hantover, "The Boy Scouts and the Validation of Masculinity," *American Man,* 285–301; Alexander Wilson to Camp, February 16, 1912, WCCC, SI, B27, f760.

15. S. S. McClure to Camp, August 7, 1891, WCCC, SI, B16, f448; *Boys Magazine* to Camp, August 14, 1911; Scott Redfield to Camp, September 15, 1911, WCCC, SI, B3, f87; Camp, "Athletics," *Boys Magazine,* December 1911, 14–15; Tudor Jenks to Camp, August 26, 1890, WCCC, SII, B21, f601.

16. "The Athlete in Fiction," WCCC, SII, B53, f331; Mark Sufrin, " 'Boys' Sports Books Portrayed An Idealized World of Many Virtues," *Sports Illustrated,* September 1, 1975; Michael Oriard, *Dreaming of Heroes: American Sports Fiction, 1868–1980* (Chicago: Nelson Hall, 1982), 28, 32, 263–330.

17. Harriet Hinsdale, ed., *Frank Merriwell's 'Father': An Autobiography by Gilbert Patten* (Norman, OK: University of Oklahoma Press, 1964), xiii; George Brooke to Camp, September 23, 1907, WCCC, SI, B4, f95.

18. Walter Camp, *The Substitute: A Football Story* (New York: D. Appleton, 1908), 2–5.

19. Arthur Shipman to Camp, September 30, 1911, WCCC, SI, B22, f628; Charles Mayser to Camp, November 28, 1908, WCCC, SI, B17, 471; Edward K. Hall

to Camp, October 25, 1908, WCCC, SI, B12, f318; Rufus S. Woodward to "My Dear Fairfax," October 29, 1908, WCCC, SI, B27, f769; William Ford to Camp, November 9, 1908, WCCC, SI, B11, f287.

20. Walter Camp, *Danny Fists* (New York: D. Appleton, 1913); Montrose Moses, "Various Other Books for Boys," *Bookman*, December 1913, 446; "As Great a Writer as He is a Football Strategist," WCCC, SII, B58, f413; Rotundo, *American Manhood*, 225.

21. "The Favorite Books of Red-Blooded Boys: By Renowned Yale Football Authority, Walter Camp," WCCC, SII, B58, f413; Book reviews, WCCC, f414; Moses, "Various other Books for Boys"; "Buying Christmas Books for Children," *Dial*, December 1, 1911, 457.

22. Heyliger also wrote under the pseudonym Hawley Williams. See Oriard, *Dreaming of Heroes*, 290; William Heyliger to Camp, September 10, 1914; May 24, 1915; July 27, 1915; August 13, 1915, WCCC, SI, B13, f352.

23. Contract with Hurst and Company, February 1, 1910; Camp to Richard Hurst, July 7, 1911; Hurst to Camp, July 13, 1911, WCCC, SI, B14, f381; Everard Thompson to Camp, February 15, 1912, WCCC, SI, B30, f821.

24. Shevlin in WCCC, SII, B34, f29; B38, f86; "An Eastern View of 'Our Tom' Shevlin" [1905]; "Tom Shevlin One of Yale's Most Interesting Figures," *New Haven Evening Register*, November 2, 1915; "Big Hearted Tom Shevlin," *New York Sun* [1904], WCCC, SIII.

25. Camp on Shevlin and Hogan in WCCC, SII, B38, f88; Stokes to Walter Camp, January 11, 1908, WCCC, SI, B30, f828; Oriard, *King Football*, 237.

26. Steinberg, *Academic Melting Pot*, 5; Welch and Camp, *Yale*, 154–158, 446; Syrett, *The Company He Keeps*, 168; Marcia Graham Synnott, *The Half-Opened Door: Discrimination and Admissions at Harvard, Yale, and Princeton, 1900–1970* (Westport, CT: Greenwood Press, 1979).

27. Canby, *Alma Mater*, 128–131.

28. William Wilhelm to "Sir," June 5, 1909, WCCC, SI, B26, f752; Paolantonio, *How Football Explains America*, 59–60.

29. Canby, *Alma Mater*, 49–50.

30. "The Faculty Takes a Stand, A Request that Sanford be Disqualified as a Yale Athlete," February 7, 1893, WCCC, SIII; Watterson, "Reputation Reclaimed," 1.

31. Camp to Anson Phelps Stokes, October 12, 1900, WCCC, SI, B30, f826; Camp to Arthur Hadley, March 19, 1900, WCCC, SI, B11, f313.

32. Statements of R. E. Larendon and H. Miller in letter to newspapers, 1900, WCCC, SI, B15, f409.

33. Watterson, *College Football*, 51–53; Camp to Hadley, March 19, 1900, WCCC, SI, B11, f313.

34. Eligibility oaths [1889], WCCC, SI, B30, f819.

35. "A Dual Football League" [1889], Stagg Papers, B270, f1; Herbert C. Leeds to Camp, October 28, 1889; November 2, 1889, WCCC, SI, B15, f427.

36. Camp to Charles Gould, May 3, 1901, WCCC, SI, B30, f820; George Sawyer to Julian Curtiss, February 11, 1903, WCCC, SI, B23, f642; Rader, *American Sports*, 183–184; Henry B. Needham on Hogan in Rader, *Major Problems in American Sports History*, 119–120.

37. Pope, *Patriotic Games*, 25–27.

38. Alan Fox to Camp, June 20, 1899; Camp to Fox, July 27, 1909, WCCC, SI, B11, f287; Camp to H. S. White, November 14, 1903, WCCC, SI, B26, f747; Camp to B. Winslow, July 19, 1902, WCCC, SI, B27, f761.

39. Camp, "College Training Tables, Their Use and Abuse," *Century*, June 1901, 307–312.

40. For the Lord Greystoke/ape analogy, see Oriard, *King Football*, 346; "College Football," *Outing*, November 1889. Camp also argued that there was good and bad professionalism in "College Athletics" [1885].

41. Heffelfinger in "Is Football a Dangerous Sport?" *Boston Globe*, November 13, 1892, 399.

42. Yale undergraduates later chose to rescind the undergraduate rule. William Burnet Wright to Camp, January 9, 1893, WCCC, SI, B28, f777; WCCC, SI, B4, f109; Camp to Willard B. Luther, March 9, 1906, WCCC, SI, B16, f439; "The Faculty Takes a Hand"; "That Troublesome Rule," *New York Times*, September 28, 1893, 11; Camp, "Undergraduate Limitation in College Sport," *Harper's Weekly*, February 11, 1893.

43. Whitney to Camp, November 2, 1900; November 7, 1900; Camp to Whitney, November 15, 1900, WCCC, SI, B19, f521; Camp to Anson Phelps Stokes, November 6, 1900; November 7, 1900, WCCC, SI, B30, f826; "The Managers Propose a Still Clearer Statement of Yale's Standards," *Yale Alumni Weekly*, February 13, 1901; "Yale's New Rules: Amateur Requirements Made More Strict in Interest of Purity," *Boston Post*, February 17, 1901, WCCC, SIII.

44. Letter from President of the AAU, December 20, 1906, WCCC, SI, B1, f20; Bert J. Jenkins to Camp, November 7, 1900, WCCC, SI, B14, f394; Francis R. Hoffman to Camp, January 28, 1903, WCCC, SI, B13, f362.

45. Arthur Allin to Camp, January 23, 1902, WCCC, SI, B1, f18.

46. Allen Hubbard to Walter Camp, October 27, 1900, WCCC, SI, B14, f376; "Edgar T. Glass, Yale's Giant Guard, the Greatest Football Player in the History of the Game in America," *World*, November 24, 1902, WCCC, SIII.

47. Camp to Arthur Hadley, October 28, 1901; "Statement," November 11, 1901; Camp to Charles Gould, October 11, 1901, WCCC, SI, B11, f313; Samuel J. Elder to Camp, November 9, 1901, WCCC, SI, B10, f264.

48. Julian [Curtiss] to Camp, December 10, 1901, WCCC, SI, B10, f281.

49. Camp to Hollis, November 21 and 22, 1901; Hollis to Camp, November 21, 1901, WCCC, SI, B13, f365; Receipt of Irving R. Fisher, Haverford, PA, July 16, 1899; WCCC, SI, B13, f365; "Walter Camp Won't Talk" [1901], WCCC, SIII.

50. Hollis to Camp, November 14, 1901; Camp to Hollis, November 15, 1901, WCCC, SI, B13, f365; Camp to Theodore Woolsey, January 15, 1902, WCCC, SI, B27, f771; Camp to Hadley, January 17, 1902, WCCC, SI, B11, f313.

51. Hollis to Camp, February 10, 1902; "Memorandum of meeting with Hollis on Harvard's invitation," February 14, 1902, WCCC, SI, B13, f366; "Prof. Hollis, Master of Harvard Athletics" [1901]; Hubert M. Sedgwick, "The New Yale-Harvard Athletic Agreement," *Leslie's Weekly* [1902], WCCC, SIII; Camp to Hollis, April 15, 1902; Hollis to Camp, April 22, 1902, WCCC, SI, B13, f366.

52. Alonzo Stagg to Camp, October 17, 1902, WCCC, SI, B23, f652; Charles King to Camp, November 3, 1902; King to Lewis S. Welch, November 10, 1902, WCCC, SI, B28, f786; Fred H. Winter to Camp, November 1, 1902; November 10, 1902; November 12, 1902, WCCC, SI, B27, f762.

53. Camp to Julian Curtiss, January 26, 1903, WCCC, SI, B23, f642; H. S. White to T. S. Woolsey, February 21, 1906, WCCC, SI, B26, f747; Samuel J. Elder to Camp, January 13, 1906; January 17, 1906, WCCC, SI, B10, f265; H. B. Fine to Camp, January 16, 1906; "Eligibility rules agreed upon with some possible changes in wording by Yale, Harvard, and Princeton," February 1906, WCCC, SI, B10, f278.

54. Watterson, "Reputation Reclaimed," 1–4; Stokes to Camp, July 24, 1905; July 27, 1905; Camp to Stokes, April 9, 1907, WCCC, SI, B30, f827, f828; Anson Phelps Stokes to Charlie Sherrill, July 21, 1906, WCCC, SI, B22, f626; McCormick's letter enclosed in Fred Murphy to Camp, January 23, 1906, WCCC, SI, B18, f497.

55. Anson Phelps Stokes to Sanford, August 11, 1905, WCCC, SI, B30, f827; Lewis Welch to David Twitchell, June 16, 1906, WCCC, SI, B28, f790; Stokes to Professor Morris, March 22, 1907; William G. Thayer to Stokes, March 27, 1907, WCCC, SI, B30, f828.

Chapter 8

1. Charles F. Thwing, "The Ethical Functions of Foot Ball," *North American Review*, November 1901 (reprinted in *Spalding's Official Foot Ball Guide*, 1902, 39).

2. John Heisman to Camp, December 21, 1903; February 27, 1904; n.d. [1904], WCCC, SI, B13, f349.

3. "Suggestions to Remove Its Homicidal Character"; "Fatalities of the Football Season, 1903," *Philadelphia Press*, December 3, 1903, WCCC, SIII.

4. "The Pathology of Football," 1903, WCCC, SIII; Clark W. Hetherington, "Analysis of Problems in College Athletics," paper read at the American Physical Education Association, December 29, 1906; Hetherington to Camp, December 13, 1905; December 18, 1905, WCCC, SI, B13, f352; Gems, *Pride, Profit, and Patriarchy*, 185.

5. William Verbeck to Camp, November 25, 1905, WCCC, SI, B25, f721.

6. Camp to Ray Tompkins, March 11, 1903, WCCC, SI, B24, f683.

7. "Physical Effect of Football," 1903, WCCC, SIII.

8. William Lee Howard, M.D., *Football and Moral Health* (New York: William Wood Co., 1906), WCCC, SII, B56, f386; "Football the Best Life Tonic," *World*, November 29, 1903; E. L. Richards, "Physical Education and Athletic Sports at Yale," 453, WCCC, SII, B43, f160; Scott McQuilkin, "Brutality in Football and the Creation of the NCAA: A Codified Moral Compass in Progressive America," *Sport History Review*, 33, 2002, 2–3, 12; Mrozek, *Sport and American Mentality*, 28.

9. Watterson, *College Football*, 85–88; McQuilkin, "Brutality in Football," 4.

10. Fred Murphy to Camp, December 20, 1905, WCCC, SI, B18, f497; "Boxing Bill Passed; Football Threatened," Special to the *New York Times* [1905]; "Boxing Brutal? No. Pugilistic Parlor Matches in Comparison to Football" [1904], WCCC, SIII.

11. Ray Johnson to Camp, March 7, 1903, WCCC, SI, B14, f399.

12. Dexter, "Accidents from College Football," *Educational Review*, April 1903, 415–428; extract from Dexter's article in *Popular Science Monthly*, March 2006, WCCC, SII, B45, f204; Nelson, *Anatomy of a Game*, 90–91.

13. Camp to Professor E. G. Dexter, February 2, 1903, WCCC, SI, B9, f247; "Injured, 1904," WCCC, SII, B32, f3; Howard Mudie to Camp, February 26, 1900, WCCC, SI, B18, f495.

14. Camp in "Amateur Sport," *Harper's Weekly*, December 26, 1896; "Camp Advises a Radical Change," December 9, 1904; "Experts Divided on Camp's Scheme" [1904]; "Stagg Takes Gloomy View of Football Rules" [1904] WCCC, SIII; John Heisman to Camp, December 5, 1905, WCCC, SI, B13, f349.

15. "Camp Says Game is Not True Test," 1911, WCCC, SIII; "On Camp's Scheme. Coach Stagg Thinks Rule Requiring Ten Yards for First Down Should be Tried," *Pittsburg Press*, December 12, 1904, 10.

16. "Talks Over Rules. Walter Camp, East's Most Famous Football Critic, Here on Visit" [1904]; "Western Football Reform," November 11, 1905, WCCC, SIII.

17. Camp to Julian Curtiss, December 5, 1903, SI, B23, f642; Fielding Yost to Camp, February 20, 1904, WCCC, SI, B31, f838; Gems, *Pride, Profit, and Patriarchy*, 157.

18. Camp on Reid, WCCC, SII, B32, f8; Smith, ed., *Diary of Coach Bill Reid*, xv.

19. Ronald A. Smith, "Harvard and Columbia and a Reconsideration of the 1905–1906 Football Crisis," *Journal of Sport History*, Winter 1981, 11–12.

20. Camp to Julian Curtiss, April 4, 1905, WCCC, SI, B23, f643; Smith, ed., *The Diary of Coach Bill Reid*, 34.

21. Caspar Whitney to Camp, September 18, 1905, WCCC, SI, B19, f522; "Camp Praised for Reform Work; Caspar Whitney Scores the Committee for Not Changing Football Rules," 1905, WCCC, SIII; Whitney, "The View-Point," *Outing*, September 1905, 754; "Review of the Season" [1905], WCCC, SII, B35, f56.

22. "Pigskin Solons to Investigate" [1905]; Roosevelt speech to Harvard men, Cambridge, MA, February 23, 1907, WCCC, SI, B21, f593; "Athletes Are Running This Government," June 24, 1905, WCCC, SIII.

23. "Can a Gentleman Play Football," *World*, November 5, 1905; "Roosevelt Campaign for Football Reform," Special to the *New York Times*, October 10, 1905, 1; Roosevelt to Camp, October 2, 1905, WCCC, SI, B21, f593.

24. Miller, *Big Scrum*, 186–190.

25. Miller, *Big Scrum*, 190.

26. Roosevelt to Camp, October 11, 1905, WCCC, SI, B21, f593; George P. Sawyer to William H. Taft, December 6, 1905, WCCC, SI, B24, f668.

27. Smith, ed., *The Diary of Coach Bill Reid*, 194; Camp to Roosevelt, October 13, 1905; November 28, 1905, WCCC, SI, B21, f593.

28. "Teddy Roosevelt, Jr., is Hurt on Football Field," *Salt Lake City Herald*, October 15, 1905; Miller, *Big Scrum*, 195–196; Davies, *Rivals!* 3; Roosevelt to Camp, November 24, 1905, WCCC, SI, B21, f593.

29. Presidents in WCCC, SII, B45, f205.

30. Smith, "Harvard and Columbia," 7–8; McQuilkin, "Brutality in Football," 9–10; "Blames Camp for the Evils," November 25, 1905; "Eliot Objects to Walter Camp" [n. d.], WCCC, SIII.

31. "Has President Roosevelt Double-Crossed Harvard?" *Evening Mail*, November 22, 1905, WCCC, SIII.

32. Davies, *Rivals!* 3; Jack Owsley to Camp, December 16, 1905, SI, 19, f526; Edwin White to Camp, August 16, 1905, WCCC, SI, B30, f820; Camp to White, August 19, 1905, WCCC, SI, B26, f746; Paul Dashiell to Camp, December 7, 1905; testimony of Shevlin and Quill, WCCC, SI, B9, f235; WCCC, SII, B36, f66.

33. The published numbers on fatalities differ. According to the November 27, 1905 edition of the *San Francisco Call* and other papers, the number of fatalities during the 1905 season was nineteen, eleven occurring in high school games. That others cite more may be attributable to their counting after the end of the season, when injuries that led to later deaths could be accounted for. See McQuilkin, "Brutality in Football," 8; G. W. Ehler to Camp, December 5, 1905, WCCC, SI, B10, f263; "Congressman Landis Sees One Game and Says Football is 'Bum Sport,'" *Salt Lake City Herald*, October 15, 1905, 4.

34. "Yale Men Awaiting Further Harvard Action before Allowing Cambridge Magazine Attack to Cause a Break in University Feeling," *Evening Register*, November 29, 1905; "Good Bye Yale" [1905], WCCC, SIII.

35. Ray Tompkins to Camp, December 2, 1905, WCCC, SI, B24, f683; Julian Curtiss to Camp, December 1, 1905; December 15, 1905, WCCC, SI, B23, f643; "Yale Decides to Await Results," November 27, 1905; "Yale Loyal to Camp"; "Professor Woolsey and Gridiron Experts Talk on Football," *New York Herald*, December 3, 1905, WCCC, SIII; Arthur Hadley to Alice Camp, December 2, 1905, WCCC, SV, B66, f7; Camp to Paul Dashiell, December 12, 1905, WCCC, SI, B9, f235.

36. "Columbia Bars Football," *New York Tribune*, November 29, 1905, 1; "Abolished. University Disregards Student Sentiment and Prohibits Football," December 1905; "Columbia Alumni Protest" [December 1905], WCCC, SIII;

telegram from *New York American* to Walter Camp, December 20, 1905, WCCC, SI, B19, f507; "Football Friends Rally," *New York Tribune*, November 30, 1905, 7.

37. "Move to Oust Camp"; "Game of Football to Be Made Over," 1905, WCCC, SIII; Smith, "Harvard and Columbia," 8–9.

38. Frank Maggio, *Notre Dame and the Game that Changed Football* (New York: Carroll and Graf, 2007), 47; "Fusion in College Football"; "Old Football Committee Will Not Act with New," 1905, WCCC, SIII.

39. Captain N. J. Koehler to Camp, December 15, 1905, WCCC, SI, B15, f419.

40. Mike Murphy to Camp, January 24, 1906, WCCC, SI, B18, f498; Maggio, *Notre Dame*, 48; Smith, "Harvard and Columbia," 14–15.

41. Stagg to Camp, January 11, 1906; December 16, 1906, WCCC, SI, B23, f652; Nelson, *Anatomy of a Game*, 108.

42. "Rational Football Talk from Hadley," *Richmond Times Dispatch*, January 28, 1906, sporting pages 1–2; "Yale for Football," *New York Tribune*, January 20, 1906; "President Hadley Defends Football," *New York Times*, January 20, 1906, 4; "Harvard denounced by Angry Men at Yale," *Pittsburgh Press*, January 18, 1906, 14.

43. Palmer E. Pierce to Hadley, April 17, 1906; Camp to Hadley, December 19, 1906; March 7, 1908, WCCC, SI, B11, f314; McQuilkin, "Brutality in Football," 19–20; "Yale and Harvard Meet on Football," *New York Times*, October 10, 1909, 12.

44. "Football Committees Ready with Reports" [1906], WCCC, SIII; Maggio, *Notre Dame*, 50.

45. *Official Foot Ball Rules, 1906* (New York: American Sports Publishing Co., 1906).

46. "Camp Still 'It' In Football. Yale Authority Practically Controls the College Game," *Record*, May 7, 1906; "Camp to Explain Rules"; "Camp Will Lecture to Coaches Today"; "Coaches Study Football Today. Walter Camp Here to Untangle the Puzzles of the 1906 Code," 1906, WCCC, SIII; *New York Sun* article reprinted in *Toronto Star*, November 28, 1906, WCCC, SII, B37, f81.

47. Arthur Hadley to Camp, January 1, 1905, WCCC, SI, B11, f313; Camp to L. M. Dennis [n.d.], WCCC, SI, B9, f244; "Obituary Record of Graduates of Yale University, deceased during Academic Year Ending June, 1905"; Camp to Stokes, March 20, 1905; April 6, 1905, WCCC, SI, B30, f827; Camp to Pierce N. Welch, April 10, 1905, WCCC, SI, B26, f739; Camp to G. E. Stevens, April 6, 1905, WCCC, SI, B23, f656.

Chapter 9

1. Benjamin Ide Wheeler to Camp, March 24, 1894, WCCC, SI, B26, f745.

2. Camp to Wheeler, January 17, 1905, WCCC, SI, B26, f745.

3. Wheeler to Camp, December 23, 1904; December 19, 1905, WCCC, SI, B26, f745; Statement from Office of the President of University of California, Berkeley, 1911, WCCC, SI, B26, f745; Nelson, *Anatomy of a Game*, 141.

4. Wheeler to Camp, February 15, 1906, WCCC, SI, B26, f745; Statement from Office of the President.

5. Wheeler, "Shall Football Be Ended or Mended?" *American Monthly Review of Reviews*, January 1906, 72–73, WCCC, SIII; Henry Wick Jr. to Camp, April 5, 1907, WCCC, SI, B26, f752.

6. Wheeler, "Shall Football Be Ended or Mended?"

7. Wheeler to Camp, March 10, 1906, WCCC, SI, B26, f745; "Will Confer on Football," *San Francisco Call*, December 5, 1905; Oscar Taylor, "Trying Out Rugby," *Sunset*, November 1906, WCCC, SIII; W. H. Middleton to Camp, February 18, 1909, WCCC, SI, B17, f476; Roberta Park, "From Football to Rugby—and Back, 1906–1919: The University of California-Stanford University Response to the 'Football Crisis of 1905,'" *Journal of Sport History*, Winter 1984, 5–40.

8. John Morgan to Editor of *Collier's Weekly*, January 3, 1908; Walter Camp to A. Ruhl, January 11, 1908, WCCC, SI, B7, f187.

9. "Amazing Growth of Gridiron Sport within Past Five Years" [1908], WCCC, SIII; Morgan to Editor.

10. On British "fair play," see Wakefield, *Playing to Win*, 44; Camp, "The Harvard Stroke," *Outing and the Wheelman*, July 1884, 306; Welch and Camp, *Yale*, 465–466.

11. "What are Athletics For?" [*Outing*, 1913], WCCC, SII, B52, f322.

12. "Jordan Writes on Football," 1909, WCCC, SIII; Jordan to Camp, January 20, 1908, WCCC, SI, B15, f404.

13. Jordan to Charles Van Hise, January 3, 1911; Jordan to Camp, January 1, 1908, WCCC, SI, B15, f404.

14. Berkeley has since earned distinction in rugby, having won twenty-six national championships since 1980 and achieved success internationally. David Huddlestone to Camp, April 26, 1910; August 9, 1910; August 17, 1910; October 17, 1913, WCCC, SI, B14, f377; "Will California Produce Rugby's World Champions," *San Francisco Call*, July 31, 1910.

15. WCCC, SII, B33, f17.

16. "Thayer and Camp Poke Fun at Fair Harvard," 1906, WCCC, SIII.

17. "Yale Ridicule of Harvard," *Advertiser*, 1906, WCCC, SIII; Camp to Allen Hubbard, February 2, 1906, WCCC, SI, B14, f376.

18. "Yale Surplus is Made Public"; "The Great Money Power at Yale," 1905, WCCC, SIII; Pope, *Patriotic Games*, 25.

19. "Deming After Walter Camp," January 1906, WCCC, SIII.

20. "Deming After Walter Camp."

21. Camp to Malcolm McBride, March 15, 1909, WCCC, SI, B16, f445.

22. Camp to Hadley, March 5, 1906, WCCC, SI, B11, f314; Camp to A. M. Stevens, March 19, 1906, WCCC, SI, B23, f656; "Mr. Camp Under Criticism," January 19, 1906; "Who is Deming?" [1906]; "Lake Favors an M.A. for Mr. Camp" [1908], WCCC, SIII; Hubert Sedgwick [n. d.], WCCC, SV, B66, f1; on honorary degree, WCCC, SII, B58, f409.

23. "Dr. Jordan Flays American Football," *New York Times*, December 22, 1907, WCCC, S1; Anson Phelps Stokes to Camp, February 24, 1908; March 13, 1908, WCCC, SI, B30, f828.

24. Report of the Investigatory Committee appointed in November 1905, WCCC, SI, B29, f801; "The Yale Investigation," October 30, 1906; "Woolsey to Head Inquiry Board"; "Yale's Athletic House Cleaning," WCCC, SIII.

25. "Western Football Reform"; "Deals Football Knockout Blow," 1906, WCCC, SIII; B. S. Milliken to Camp, December 18, 1905, WCCC, SI, B17, f478; Watterson, *College Football*, 85–88.

26. "The Great Money Power at Yale."

27. Powel, *Walter Camp*, 114; "Walter Camp of Yale" [1910]; "Abuse in Athletics. W. G. Dole Knocks Methods at Yale and Elsewhere" [1906], WCCC, SIII.

28. Camp to Arthur Hadley, March 12, 1900, WCCC, SI, B11, f313; Joel Pfister, *The Yale Indian: The Education of Henry Roe Cloud* (Durham, NC: Duke University Press, 2009), 37.

29. Pfister, *The Yale Indian*, 36–38.

30. W. G. Anderson to Camp, January 5, 1910, WCCC, SI, B30, f823.

31. Owen Johnson, *Stover at Yale* (New York: Frederick A. Stokes, 1912); Pfister, *The Yale Indian*, 38; Higgs, "Yale and the Heroic Ideal," 169–170.

32. "Sudden Death of Famous Football Leader"; Tom Thorp, "College Preparedness Saves Athletes' Lives" [1917], WCCC, SIII.

33. "Athletes Long-Lived, Says Dr. W. G. Anderson," *New York Times*, January 3, 1907; WCCC, SII, B53, f341. Anderson noted than only four of the fifty-eight deceased Yale athletes suffered heart attacks when Americans collectively suffered around 60,000 fatalities due to heart disease annually. See "Mortality Statistics," United States Census Bureau, Bulletin 104 (Washington, DC: Government Printing Office, 1909), 15.

34. Samuels and Samuels, *Frederic Remington*, 41, 127, 202, 206, 438–439.

35. Guttmann, *The Erotic in Sports*, 63; Dr. Frank J. Born, "A Study in Physique as Represented by the Crew, Football, and Track Teams at Yale," Yale reprints, #4, 1908 (reprinted in *Yale Alumni Weekly*, April 1, 1908).

36. H. M. Clymer to Camp, April 8, 1920, WCCC, SI, B1, f21.

37. "A Game for Fat Boys," *New York Times*, February 10, 1910, 6.

38. Keller, *Reminiscences*, 59, 64.

39. Graham Sumner to Eliot Sumner, December 28, 1909; April 5, 1910, Sumner Papers, B118, f885; Camp to Dr. W. L. Dudley, January 11, 1910, WCCC, SI, B10, f257; Keller, *Reminiscences*, 72, 80–81, 98–100, 109.

40. Keller, *Reminiscences*, 83, 92–93, 98; Sumner to Mrs. Camp [n.d.], WCCC, SV, B66, f10; William Howard Taft to Sumner, August 12, 1909, WCCC, SI, B24, f668.

41. "G.O.P. Drafting Walter Camp to Top of Ticket" [n.d.], personal clippings, WCCC, SIII; Camp, *The Book of Foot-ball* (New York: Century Co., 1910).

42. Camp to Albert Britt, October 16, 1910, WCCC, SI, B19, f523.

43. Various papers list slightly different fatality numbers, though the trends are the same. The *Herald* reported fourteen dead in 1906 and fifteen in 1907. The discrepancies may be due to whether or not collegiate and high school fatalities were combined or whether indirect deaths were factored into the totals. Nothing refutes, however, that 1905 and 1909 saw marked increases in fatalities. "1909 Death Toll 33, 'Well Worth the Cost,' Say College Athletes" [1909]; "Whitman Stops Football," December 1, 1909; "Deaths to Renew Football Fight," *Boston Herald*, November 28, 1909; "Death of Young Christian Casts Deep Gloom Over Hill," November 15, 1909, WCCC, SIII; James D. Wilson to Camp, December 16, 1911, WCCC, SI, B27, f760; Nelson, *Anatomy of a Game*, 141.

44. L. M. Dennis to Camp, November 1, 1909, WCCC, SI, B9, f245; Josh Hartwell to Camp, November 22, 1909, WCCC, SI, B12, f336.

45. Nelson, *Anatomy of a Game*, 142–143; McQuilkin, "Brutality and the NCAA," 22.

46. Camp to Oliver Jennings, December 20, 1909, WCCC, SI, B14, f395; Gems, *Pride, Profit, and Patriarchy*, 29.

47. The *Chicago Tribune* refuted Camp's contention that more high school boys died than did college men "trained by expert coaches." See "Football's Death Toll Twice that of Last Year" [1909]; "Football Perils for the Unfit" [1909]; "Walter Camp Talks Interestingly Upon His Pet Hobby—American Football" [1909], WCCC, SIII; W. A. Lambeth to Camp, November 17, 1909, WCCC, SI, B15, f421.

48. "'Mike' Murphy Suggests Safeguards for Football"; Changing Football Rules Might Injure Sport—Camp"; "Schools Vote to Abolish Football"; "No More Football for New York Boys," 1909, WCCC, SIII.

49. For a more contemporary discussion of the "pain principle," see Don Sabo, "Pigskin, Patriarchy, and Pain," in Michael Kimmel and Michael Messner, eds., *Men's Lives* (New York: Macmillan, 1989), 185.

50. Camp in "Predictions Point to 1910 as a Record-Breaking Year in All Branches of American Sport," *Evening Sun*, January 3, 1910; "Southerners Change Football Methods," 1910, WCCC, SIII.

51. "Women Want Complete Modifications to Make Football Less Brutal," 1909, WCCC, SIII; Grace Hastings Sharp, "Mothers and the Game," *Outlook*, November 12, 1910, 589–591.

52. John Heisman to Camp, November 16, 1909, WCCC, SI, B13, f349; Josh Hartwell to Camp, November 26, 1910, WCCC, SI, B12, f336.

53. "Football is Tamed," 1909, WCCC, SIII; "Forward Pass is Left in Football," *New York Times*, May 14, 1910, 11.

54. "End to Football Heroics" [1911]; "Wail from Yale Over New Football Rules," 1910, WCCC, SIII; Corbin in Danzig, *Oh, How They Played*, 74.

55. "Football Will Be Brilliant and Fast," *New York Times*, February 6, 1912, 8; Camp, "Improvement in Football," *New York Times*, December 29, 1912, 31;

"Football Now to Be Running Game, Says Camp, 1911," WCCC, SIII; Maggio, *Notre Dame*, 61; Oriard, *Reading Football*, 53.

56. "Look to Yale to Show Strength of New Game," *New York Times*, October 2, 1906, 7; "Yale and Forward Pass," Special to *New York Times*, December 3, 1907, 10.

57. "Forward Pass," WCCC, SII, B34, f28; "Walter Camp Poisoned," Special to *New York Times*, January 27, 1907, 1; Gems, *Pride, Profit, and Patriarchy*, 166.

58. Gems, *Pride, Profit and Patriarchy*, 161; Maggio, *Notre Dame*, 52–56, 98–99.

59. C. A. Kiler to *Collier's Weekly* Editor, January 1, 1909, WCCC, SI, B15, f412; J. E. Vetter to Camp, December 18, 1913, WCCC, SI, B25, f721; "Mr. Camp's Lazy Mind," in E. T. Lee to Camp, September 26, 1910, WCCC, SI, B15, f426; R. S. Crowl, "A Justification for the Grudge of the West Against Walter Camp," *Wisconsin Athletic Bulletin*, December 14, 1912, 23–24; Doyle, "Turning the Tide," 115.

60. "Parke H. Davis '93 Analyzes Game in Selection of All-American Team," *Daily Princetonian*, December 6, 1912, 1.

61. "Camp Back From South," *New York Times*, March 24, 1910, 10; Clifton McArthur to Camp, December 3, 1909; November 15, 1910, WCCC, SI, B16, f442; Roscoe Faucett, Sporting Editor of the *Oregonian*, to Camp, December 5, 1911, WCCC, SI, B19, f516.

62. All-America Team history, WCCC, SII, B38, f84; Camp, "How I Pick the All-American Team," *Collier's*, December 10, 1921, 17.

63. "Many Westerners on this Honor List," *New York Times*, December 19, 1910, 10; Gems, *Pride, Profit, and Patriarchy*, 158–162.

64. "Small Colleges Shake Up Prestige of Big Elevens," 1911, WCCC, SIII.

65. Louis A. Sanchez to Camp, January 3, 1923, WCCC, SI, B21, f604.

Chapter 10

1. Rockne in *Collier's Weekly*, October 18, 1930, in Danzig, *Oh, How They Played*, 244–254; Michael Oriard, *King Football*, 7.

2. "Thorpe a Favorite Subject Among Many Newspaper Commentators," *Carlisle Arrow*, December 20, 1912; Lars Anderson, *Carlisle vs. Army: Jim Thorpe, Dwight Eisenhower, Pop Warner, and the Forgotten Story of Football's Greatest Battle* (New York: Random House, 2008), 308.

3. "World's Great Athlete is Greatest Football Player Too, And May Be Big League Baseball Star Next Year," *Pittsburgh Press*, November 8, 1912, 26; "Carlisle Honors Her Olympic Victors on the Return from Stockholm," *Carlisle Arrow*, September 13, 1912.

4. *St. Joseph Gazette* quoted in "The Victory at Stockholm," *Carlisle Arrow*, September 27, 1912.

5. James E. Sullivan to Camp, February 21, 1907, WCCC, SI, B1, f20.

6. Anderson, *Carlisle vs. Army*, 83–103; Bill Crawford, *All American: The Rise and Fall of Jim Thorpe* (Hoboken, NJ: John Wiley and Sons, 2005), 8–22.

7. John Bloom, *To Show What an Indian Can Do* (Minneapolis, MN: University of Minnesota Press, 2000), 10; Tom Benjey, *Wisconsin's Carlisle Indian School Immortals* (Carlisle, PA: Tuxedo Press, 2010), 7–8.

8. Gerald R. Gems, "Negotiating a Native American Identity through Sport: Assimilation, Adaptation, and the Role of the Trickster," in *Native Athletes in Sport and Society*, C. Richard King, ed. (Lincoln, NE: University of Nebraska Press, 2005), 1–21. "Muscular assimilation" is a term borrowed from Patrick Miller in reference to African American athletes in this period, but the term is apt here. See Miller, "To 'Bring the Race along Rapidly': Sport, Student Culture, and Educational Mission at Historically Black Colleges during the Interwar Years," in *Sporting World of the Modern South*, 130.

9. Benjey, *Wisconsin's Carlisle School Immortals*, 11–12; David Wallace Adams, "More than a Game: The Carlisle Indians Take to the Gridiron," *Western Historical Quarterly*, 32, Spring 2001, 25–26, 48; Sally Jenkins, *The Real All Americans* (New York: Broadway Books, 2007), 163–164.

10. C. Richard King, "Identities, Opportunities, Inequities," in *Native Athletes*, xi; Bloom, *To Show What an Indian Can Do*, 13–14.

11. Richard Henry Pratt, *Battlefield and Classroom: Four Decades with the American Indian, 1867–1894*, ed. Robert M. Utley (New Haven, CT: Yale University Press, 1964), 317.

12. M. Friedman, "Purpose of the Carlisle School," *Indian Craftsman*, February 1909, back matter.

13. "Carlisle's Great Football Record," *Indian Craftsman*, December 1909, 9–18; Jenkins, *The Real All Americans*, 124–127.

14. Benjey, *Wisconsin Carlisle School Immortals*, 12; Jenkins, *The Real All Americans*, 143–146; Bloom, *To Show What an Indian Can Do*, 16–17.

15. Adams, "More Than a Game," 31, 40; Benjey, *Wisconsin Carlisle School Immortals*, 12; Caspar Whitney, "Amateur Sport," *Harper's Weekly*, November 14, 1896; Stephen Crane, "Harvard University Against the Carlisle Indians," *New York Journal*, November 1, 1896, WCCC, SIII.

16. Adams, "More than a Game," 33–34; cover caption of *Leslie's Weekly*, November 4, 1897; Camp, "The Football Season," *Harper's Weekly*, October 30, 1897; Langdon Smith, "Carlisle Indians Score Nine Points Against Yale," *New York Journal*, October 24, 1897, WCCC, SIII; Oriard, *Reading Football*, 244; *King Football*, 285–287.

17. Jenkins, *Real All Americans*, 148; Oriard, *Reading Football*, 236.

18. Camp on Carlisle in WCCC, SII, B35, f46, 56.

19. Benjey, *Wisconsin's Carlisle School Immortals*, 15; "Carlisle's Great Football Record"; Jenkins, *Real All Americans*, 168–170.

20. Jenkins, *Real All Americans*, 171.

21. Adams, "More Than a Game," 45; Sally Jenkins, "The Team That Invented Football," *Sports Illustrated*, April 19, 2006, http://sportsillustrated.cnn.com/

2007/more/04/19/carlisleo423/index.html; *Real All Americans*, 171; Bloom, *To Show What an Indian Can Do*, 19.

22. "Carlisle Indians Outplay Penn and Land the Victory by 16 to 6," *Philadelphia Press,* November 15, 1903; "Famous the Country Over Have Been the Carlisle Football Elevens," *Philadelphia Ledger,* November 14, 1909, WCCC, SIII.

23. Mrozek, *Sport and American Mentality*, 78; "Carlisle Football Team One of the Most Remarkable of the Year," *Carlisle Arrow,* December 20, 1912; "Carlisle's Great Football Record"; Jenkins, *Real All Americans*, 173; Tom Benjey, "The Beginnings of Modern Football," LA84 Foundation (www.la84foundation. org/SportsLibrary/CFHSN/CFHSNv18/CFHSNv18n4c.pdf), November 7, 2012, 4; Jenkins, "The Team That Invented Football."

24. Benjey, "Beginnings of Modern Football," 5; *Wisconsin Carlisle School Immortals*, 22.

25. "Carlisle Indians Defeat West Point"; "Indians Crush West Point," *Carlisle Arrow,* November 15, 1912, cover; Adams, "More than a Game," 47; Anderson, *Carlisle vs. Army,* 277–292; Gems, "Negotiating a Native American Identity through Sport," 6.

26. Jenkins, *Real All Americans,* 286; Anderson, *Carlisle vs. Army,* 295–296; Crawford, *All American,* 192.

27. Gems, "Negotiating a Native American Identity through Sport," 4; Camp, "A New Religion," WCCC, SII, B55, f364; on Indians, WCCC, B56, f374; Oriard, *King Football,* 290.

28. Excerpt from the *New York Sun,* April 8, 1906, WCCC, SII, B45, f204; Crawford, *All American,* 150; Gems, "Negotiating Native American Identity through Sport," 5; Smith, ed., *Diary of Coach Bill Reid,* 64–65.

29. "Carlisle Football Methods," 1907, WCCC, SIII; "Athletics at Carlisle Help Academic Work," *Carlisle Arrow,* December 19, 1913; Warner to Camp, December 12, 1907, WCCC, SI, B25, f701; President Hughes to Camp, November 25, 1908, WCCC, SI, B14, f378.

30. Major W. A. Mercer to Camp, December 13, 1906, WCCC, SI, B25, f701.

31. Glenn Warner, "Athletics at Carlisle," *Indian Craftsman,* March 1909, 9–14.

32. Camp tells of incident in WCCC, SII, B35, f48; Benjey, *Wisconsin Carlisle School Immortals,* 17–18; Jenkins, "The Team That Invented Football."

33. Camp to W. H. Edwards, November 6, 1908, WCCC, SI, B10, f262; Review of Seasons, 1903, WCCC, SII, B34, f42.

34. Gems, "Negotiating Native Identity through Sport," 8–9; Edwards, *Football Days,* 258; Oriard, *Reading Football,* 235–247; Bloom, *To Show What an Indian Can Do,* 23–24.

35. Adams, "More than a Game," 37; Glenn Warner to Camp, January 8, 1910, WCCC, SI, B26, f731; Oriard, *King Football,* 289.

36. M. Friedman to Camp, October 24, 1913; November 13, 1913; January 4, 1913, WCCC, SI, B25, f701; "Advisory Committee for the Athletic Association," *Carlisle Arrow,* November 28, 1913, cover; Benjey, *Wisconsin's Carlisle School*

Immortals, 27; Bloom, *To Show What an Indian Can Do*, 28–29; Jenkins, *Real All Americans*, 289–290.

37. "The Amateur," *Outlook*, February 8, 1913, 293–295; Jenkins, *Real All Americans*, 287–289; Crawford, *All American*, 197–210; Pope, *Patriotic Games*, 51–52.

38. Charles Fruehling Springwood, "Playing Football, Playing Indian: A History of the Native Americans Who Were the NFL's Oorang Indians," in *Native Athletes in Sport and Society*, 123–142.

39. The cultural need for "modern gladiators" is analyzed in Kasson, *Houdini, Tarzan, and the Perfect Man*, 68–69; Oriard, "The Father of American Football," 178–179.

40. Clarence J. Smith to Camp, December 1, 1916, WCCC, SI, B23, f635.

41. Camp in *Collier's*, December 30, 1916, in WCCC, SII, B38, f100; Ocania Chalk, *Black College Sport* (New York: Dodd, Mead, and Co., 1976), 176.

42. John M. Carroll, *Fritz Pollard: Pioneer in Racial Advancement* (Urbana, IL: University of Illinois Press, 1992), 9–22.

43. Carroll, *Fritz Pollard*, 37–38.

44. Martin, *Benching Jim Crow*, 9–10; Chalk, *Black College Sport*, 151; Arthur R. Ashe, Jr., *A Hard Road to Glory: A History of the African-American Athlete, 1619–1918* (New York: Amistad Press, 1988), 102; Mark Soderstrom, "Weeds in Linnaeus's Garden: Science and Segregation, Eugenics, and the Rhetoric of Racism at the University of Minnesota and the Big Ten, 1900–45," (Ph.D. diss. Minneapolis, MN: University of Minnesota Press, 2004); Oriard, *Reading Football*, 232.

45. Carroll, *Fritz Pollard*, 43–45.

46. Pope, *Patriotic Games*, 28.

47. Michael Hurd, *Black College Football: One Hundred Years of History, Education, and Pride* (Virginia Beach, VA: Donning Co., 1993), 13, 28–29; Chalk, *Black College Sport*, 197–201, 222; Ashe, *Hard Road to Glory*, 96–98; Martin, *Benching Jim Crow*, 8–9; Miller, "To 'Bring the Race along Rapidly,' " 134, 137.

48. Managing Editor of the *New York World* to Camp, May 21, 1910, WCCC, SI, B19, f509; Carroll, *Fritz Pollard*, 27–28; Randy Roberts, *Papa Jack: Jack Johnson and the Era of White Hopes* (New York: Free Press, 1983), 85–111.

49. Carroll, *Fritz Pollard*, 55–58.

50. Carroll, *Fritz Pollard*, 60.

51. Carroll, *Fritz Pollard*, 61, 70–71; Goldstein, *Ivy League Autumns*, 54–55.

52. Carroll, *Fritz Pollard*, 66.

53. Carroll, *Fritz Pollard*, 72.

54. George A. Adee to Camp, October 25, 1889, WCCC, SI, B1, f3; Carroll, *Fritz Pollard*, 101; Chalk, *Black College Sport*, 171; Cohane, *Yale Football Story*, 333; Sam Rubin, *Yale Football* (Charleston, SC: Acadia Publishing, 2006), 70.

55. Camp donated to the Temperance, Industrial and Collegiate Institute of Claremont, Virginia; the Manassas Industrial School; and the Kowaliga

School for Colored Youth. Oswald Garrison Villard to Camp, August 5, 1909, WCCC, SI, B25, f722; Jane Clark Hill to Camp, December 10, 1909, WCCC, SI, B17, f464; William E. Benson to Camp, February 12, 1910, WCCC, SI, B15, f419.

56. Carroll, *Fritz Pollard*, 58, 92.
57. Martin, *Benching Jim Crow*, 11.
58. Lloyd Brown, *The Young Paul Robeson: 'On My Journey Now'* (Boulder, CO: Westview Press, 1997), 46.
59. Brown, *Young Paul Robeson*, 77.
60. Miller, "To 'Bring the Race along Rapidly,'" 146; Brown, *Young Paul Robeson*, 76–79.
61. Brown, *Young Paul Robeson*, 60–61, 64; Carroll, *Fritz Pollard*, 65–66.
62. Brown, *Young Paul Robeson*, 61.
63. Brown, *Young Paul Robeson*, 68–69, 83, 93; Watterson, "Reputation Reclaimed," 1.
64. Martin, *Benching Jim Crow*, 17–18, 1–26; Gems, *Pride, Profit, and Patriarchy*, 171.
65. Carroll, *Fritz Pollard*, 94; Al Harvin, "Fritz Pollard Dead at 92; Black Head Coach in NFL," *New York Times*, May 31, 1986, 33; Brown, *Young Paul Robeson*, 98.
66. Carol, *Fritz Pollard*, 110, 118; Brown, *Young Paul Robeson*, 111–112.
67. Paolantonio, *How Football Explains America*, 58; Ashe, *A Hard Road to Glory*, 98–99; Carroll, *Fritz Pollard*, 130–185.
68. On professional football, see WCCC, SII, B32, f13; Oriard, *King Football*, 210–212.

Chapter 11

1. Clancy, "Although Yale's Coach Sits on Michigan Bench"; "Football King, On Side Lines, Unique Figure," 1909; advance galley for *American Magazine*, June 6, 1919, WCCC, SIII.
2. Camp on Coy, WCCC, SII, B38, f92; Kelley, *Yale: A History*, 302; "What Yale Pays for Football," *New York Times* [1909], WCCC, SIII.
3. "Harvard's Man of Iron," *World Magazine*, November 30, 1913, WCCC, SIII; on Haughton, WCCC, SII, B32, f10; Edwards, *Football Days*, 268.
4. "Yale's Football Plans," *New York Times*, September 4, 1910, C6; "Walter Camp Called Back to Yale," *New York Times*, October 13, 1910; "Yale Already Feels Better," *Boston Globe*, November 10, 1910; "Yale Shows Poor Form for Mr. Camp," *New York Times*, October 26, 1910, 11; "Yale Crude in New Football," *New York Times*, April 13, 1910, 12; press release, WCCC, SII, B35, f47; Camp to Tompkins, December 10, 1910, WCCC, SI, B24, f683.
5. Shevlin to Camp, October 24, 1912, WCCC, SI, B22, f627.
6. Tompkins to Camp, December 13, 1910, WCCC, SI, B24, f683.

7. Yale hired professional baseball coach Billy Lush in 1904. Camp on the "czar principle" in WCCC, SII, B34, f31; B36, f65; B52, f322; B58, f419; Camp to Tompkins, November 29, 1912, WCCC, SI, B24, f683, 684.

8. Albert Barclay, "Walter Camp is Taken By Death," *Boston Globe*, March 15, 1925, WCCC, SV, B71, f55; Edwin Oviatt to Anson Phelps Stokes, October 25, 1911, WCCC, SI, B28, f790; "Yale Grads for New Coaching System," Special to *New York Times*, December 7, 1912, WCCC, SIII.

9. Powel, *Walter Camp*, 117–119; Camp to McCormick, April 27, 1916, WCCC, SI, B16, f452.

10. "Yale Men Not Surprised," *New York Times*, November 13, 1910, C6.

11. Wallace Winter to Camp, November 26, 1911, WCCC, SI, B27, f762; [Samuel Finley Brown Morse] to Camp, November 26, 1912, WCCC, SI, B18, f491.

12. Anson Phelps Stokes to Camp, October 23, 1912, WCCC, SI, B30, f830; draft of Camp's piece in the *Sheffield Monthly*, WCCC, SII, B35, f48; "Corwin to be Power in Yale Football," *New York Times*, January 17, 1915; minutes of the Yale University Athletic Association, WCCC, SI, B29, f805; minutes dated April 13, 1913, f806; "Yale's Major Sports," *New York Times*, March 23, 1912, 8.

13. "Yale Football Men Discuss Coaching," Special to *New York Times*, January 5, 1913, S1; "The Football Reorganization," *Yale Alumni Weekly*, January 6, 1913, WCCC, SIII.

14. "Wheat" [H. M. Wheaton] to Camp, January 27, 1914, SI, B26, f744.

15. "Yale Alumni Cheer Promise of Victory," *New York Times*, March 14, 1914; minutes of Yale Athletic Association, January 12, 1914, WCCC, SI, B29, f806; Camp to R. A. Douglas, December 29, 1910, WCCC, SI, B14, f380; SII, B32, f5; Dryden Phelps, "Evolution of the Bowl," *Yale Courant* [1914], WCCC, B58, f412.

16. Rubin, *Yale Football*, 43; "Walter Camp," *New York Times*, November 2, 1910, 10; Deland to Camp, November 11, 1910, WCCC, SI, B9, f240; Deland, "Football at Harvard and Yale."

17. Robert McCormick to Walter Camp, March 3, 1914; Camp to Vance McCormick [1916], WCCC, SI, B16, f452.

18. WCCC, SII, B52, f326; L. H. Semper to President of Yale University, June 15, 1914, WCCC, SI, B30, f831.

19. Walter Jennings to Camp, November 26, 1913, WCCC, SI, B14, f396; M. H. Bowman to Anson Phelps Stokes, November 18, 1912, WCCC, SI, B30, f830.

20. Clipping in Robert McCormick to Camp, March 3, 1914, WCCC, SI, B16, f450.

21. "Coach Walter Camp Has Athletic Rival in Family" [n.d.]; "Walter Camp Takes Great Interest in Yale's Season; Son in Squad" [1911], WCCC, SIII.

22. "Yale Wipes Out Old Brown Score," *New York Times*, November 12, 1911; "Yale Hoodoo End Gets Third Victim," *New York Times*, November 4, 1910, 11; "Yale Drills in Mud," *New York Times*, September 30, 1911, 14; "Papa Walter Camp Wears an Expansive and Satisfied Smile These Days," November 2, 1911; "Walter Camp Jr. May Lead Yale" [1911], WCCC, SIII.

23. E. K. Hall to Camp, December 7, 1911, WCCC, SI, B312, f320; WCCC, SV, B66, f11; "Walter Camp Talks Interestingly upon His Pet Hobby"; W. L. Cushing to Mrs. Walter Camp, September 18, 1911, WCCC, SV, B66, f7.

24. "Walter Camp, Jr., Under the Knife" [1912], WCCC, SIII; "Walter Camp Jr. Ill," *New York Times*, August 18, 1912; "Camp Back in Game," *New York Times*, October 10, 1912; "Walter Camp Ill; Quits Yale Team," *New York Times*, November 6, 1912, 17.

25. "Prom Week in Full Swing," *Boston Evening Transcript*, January 15, 1912; Ann Clifford to Janet Troxell, November 28, 1979, WCCC, SV, B72, f59; "Gives Easter Cotillion," *New York Times*, April 13, 1912, 13; "Yale Juniors Now in Fix of 'Stover,'" *New York Times*, May 12, 1912, Special Section, 12; "Yale 'Taps' in Rain Amid Great Tension," *New York Times*, May 17, 1912, 8.

26. Welch and Camp, *Yale*, 99–102; "Yale 'Taps' in Rain."

27. "The Senior Societies," *Yale Literary Magazine*, May 1911, 362; Goldstein, *Ivy League Autumns*, 45.

28. "'Tap Day' May Ring Knell of Yale Senior Societies," *New York Times*, April 27, 1913.

29. "Seniors' Gibes End Tap Day's Gravity," *New York Times*, May 16, 1913, Special Section, 1, WCCC, SIII.

30. "Camp Discusses the Playground Office" [1913], "Taft Appeals for Camp" [1913]; Robert Peabody to Camp, May 26, 1913; "Walter Camp, Jr., Works in Hartford" [1916], WCCC, SIII.

31. "Walter Camp, Jr.'s Fiancée Talented Amateur Actress," Special Dispatch to the *Herald* [1914], WCCC, SIII.

32. *New Haven Register*, Society Page, October 24, 1913; October 31, 1913; October 11, 1914, WCCC, SIII.

33. Camp to Rudolph Lehmann, May 1, 1914, WCCC, SI, B15, f429; letter introducing Walter Camp, from Bradford Merrill, Publisher of *New York American*, May 18, 1914, WCCC, SI, B19, f507; Paul Rousseau, Secretary, Federation Internationale de Boxe Amateur, to Camp [n.d.], WCCC, SI, B10, f275; Washington Wood to Camp, June 23, 1914, WCCC, SI, B27, f767; Note of N. Savage, Secretary of American Universities Club of London [1914], WCCC, SI, B15, f418.

34. "Walter Camp Jr. to Wed," *New York Times*, September 27, 1913, 13; "Walter Camp Jr. Marries," *New York Times*, October 15, 1914, 13.

35. "Walter Camp, Jr., Goes Under Operation Here," January 2, 1915; "Walter Camp, Jr., Operated Upon," January 2, 1915, WCCC, SIII; "Ways of Smart Society," *New York Courier*, January 9, 1915, 17; Ray Tompkins to Camp, February 26, 1915, WCCC, SI, B24, f684; G. A. D. Jr. to Walter Camp Jr., January 5, 1915, WCCC, SV, B66, f12.

36. "Mrs. Walter Camp Dies in New Haven," 23.

37. Elias Johnson to Camp, November 9, 1905, WCCC, SI, B14, f398; Camp to Julian Curtiss, July 5, 1917, WCCC, SI, B23, f647; Frank Gilbreth to Camp, August 19, 1916, WCCC, SI, B11, f299; SI, B25, f719; Camp, "A Photographic

Analysis of Golf," *Vanity Fair*, August 1916, 62–63; Camp, "Under Forty Too Young for Golf" [1924], WCCC, SIII.

38. Powel, *Walter Camp*, 177; Camp to Edwin Knox Mitchell, April 11, 1912, WCCC, SI, B17, f480; Sam Hughes, Newspaper Enterprise Association, to Camp, August 14, 1911, WCCC, SI, B19, f510; General Manager of the Central Press Association to Camp, April 2, 1915, WCCC, SI, B5, f129; Camp to Donald Scott, June 29, 1910; Scott to Camp, June 2, 1910, WCCC, SI, B5, f133; Camp, *Football for the Spectator* (Boston: Gorham Press, 1911); Janet's recollections in WCCC, SV, B72, f60.

39. Camp to W. D. Moffat, June 14, 1916, WCCC, SI, B17, f481; Camp to Robert Appleton, April 13, 1916; April 28, 1916; "Intercollegiate Athletics in America," WCCC, SI, B17, f482.

40. "Camp resigns from Financial Union," *New York Times*, October 15, 1914, 11; Camp to Stokes, October 10, 1914; Stokes to Camp, January 20, 1915, WCCC, SI, B30, f831; "Picket at Clock Shop Arrested This Morning"; "Clock Shop Strikers at Big Meeting" [1915], WCCC, SIII.

41. Alice Sumner Camp to Vance McCormick, 1916, WCCC, SV, B66, f8.

42. "Camp Retires as Eli Board Member," *New London Day*, January 15, 1915, 12; "Professor Corwin Succeeds Walter Camp, *New York Times*, January 12, 1915; "Walter Camp is Missed at Yale," *Herald* [1915], WCCC, SIII; Corwin to Camp, January 18, 1915, WCCC, SI, B29, f802.

43. W. N. Morice to Camp, February 3, 1915, WCCC, SI, B18, f488; speeches at Hotel Biltmore in WCCC, SV, B68, f34.

44. Yale Athletic Association Minutes, November 2, 1914, WCCC, SI, B29, f806; Arthur Robinson, "Camp is Again on Grid Body" [1917], WCCC, SIII.

45. The NCAA had ninety-five members by 1911, 148 by 1926, and 368 by 1951. See McQuilkin, "Brutality in Football," 32. "Camp's Wrist Watch 'Poser' to College Athletes at Meeting" [1915], WCCC, SIII; "Yale Votes to Join Collegiate A. A.," Special to the *New York Times*, January 30, 1915, 7; Camp's Advice to Yale," *New York Times*, January 19, 1915; Camp to Yale Athletic Committee, January 11, 1915, WCCC, SI, B29, f802; Nelson, *Anatomy of a Game*, 169.

46. To Camp [n.d.], WCCC, SI, B19, f525.

47. "Death of Shevlin," *Yale Daily News*, January 4, 1916, WCCC, SIII; "Tom Shevlin Left a Large Fortune," *Wilkes Barre Times*, January 5, 1916; "Cry for Better Football System at Yale Now General"; "LeGore and Four Other Athletes Barred by Yale" [1915], WCCC, SIII.

48. "'Tad' Jones for Yale Football Coach" [1915]; "Naming of Jones Means Return of Camp to Gridiron," February 2, 1916, WCCC, SIII; Camp to McCormick, March 15, 1916, WCCC, SI, B16, f452.

49. "Tad Jones Yale's Football Coach," Special to *New York Times*, February 3, 1916, 10; Camp to Tad Jones, June 29, 1916, WCCC, SI, B15, f403; "Stagg Joins Staff of Coaches at Eli," Special to *New York Times*, September 12, 1916, 8; Cohane, *Yale Football Story*, 200–201.

50. Camp to Vance McCormick, February 15, 1916; October 18, 1916, WCCC, SI, B16, f452; 1916 Team Notes, WCCC, SII, B32, f5; "General Coaching Plan for the Season"; Condition Chart, WCCC, SII, B32, f10; "Memorandum Made Just Previous to Spring Practice," 1916, WCCC, SII, B35, f49.

51. Cohane, *Yale Football Story*, 202; Camp negotiated a three-year contract for Brides for $3,000 the first year, $3,500 the second, and $4,000 the third. Camp to McCormick, February 22 and 24, 1916, WCCC, SI, B16, f452; 1916 Team Notes, WCCC, SII, B32, f5.

52. Cohane, *Yale Story*, 208.

Chapter 12

1. Cohane, *Yale Football Story*, 210; "President Calls for War Declaration, Stronger Navy, New Army of 500,000 Men, Full Co-operation with Germany's Foes," *New York Times*, April 3, 1917, cover.

2. Camp, "Time and War," *Zenith*, December 1916, 61; Valenzi, *Champion of Sport*, 81; Peter Gabriel Filene, "In Time of War," in *The American Man*, 322–323.

3. "They Crucify American Manhood—Enlist," by M. M. Moyle, War Poster Collection, Manuscripts and Archives, Yale University Library, MSSSA.MS, 0671, B21, fYUS 51–65.

4. Wakefield, *Playing to Win*, 3–7, 14.

5. Editorial page of the *New York American*, September 29, 1914; "Walter Camp Agrees," *Puck*, January 9, 1915, 21; draft [1914], on drilling, WCCC, SII, B61, f448; Pope, *Patriotic Games*, 127.

6. In 1920, a report of the U.S. Surgeon General determined that of 2,753,922 men examined for service, 1,320,934 (48 percent) were rejected for physical defects. The Equitable Life Assurance Society reported that of 1,300,000 men who volunteered for the Army and Navy, 448,859 were physically acceptable for service. See Camp, *Keeping Fit All the Way*, 23; Morris J. Hole, Census Bureau, Department of Commerce, to Camp, May 11, 1917; "Men in the United States Subject to Selective Conscription," Department of Commerce Bureau of the Census, May 1917, WCCC, SI, B25, f698; "Life Laughs at All Laws Save One—'The Strong Survive!'" WCCC, SII, B54, f359; Harford Powel, "Walter Camp, Chapter IV: The Last Tournament," *Youth's Companion*, October 28, 1926, 801.

7. William G. Anderson, "Further Studies in the Longevity of Yale Athletes" (reprint from *Medical Times*, March 1916); "Yale's Spirit Has Not Waned but Infects the Colleges" [1916], WCCC, SIII.

8. D. C. Vandercook to Camp, August 8, 1917, WCCC, SI, B25, f718; excerpt, *Outing*, February 1910; *Outing* Advertiser, 1910, 9–10, WCCC, SI, B19, f523.

9. WCCC, SII, B56, f389; B33, f27.

10. Joseph Paul Vasquez III, "America and the Garrison Stadium: How the US Armed Forces Shaped College Football," *Armed Forces and Society*, November

22, 2011, 357–358; Rader, *American Sports*, 133; Filene, "In Time of War," 330–333; Pope, *Patriotic Games*, 145–147.

11. Camp, "Student Army Training Corps Service Sports," WCCC, SII, B53, f336; [1918], WCCC, SII, B35, f50; Valenzi, *Champion of Sport*, 87; Wakefield, *Playing to Win*, 12–13.

12. Lawrence Perry, *Our Navy in the War* (New York: Charles Scribner's Sons, 1919), 246–259; Camp to Secretary of the Navy, "General Report from the Organization of the Commission in 1917 to 1 July 1918," WCCC, SI, B25, f705; "Rules for Boxing Lessons," *New York Times*, February 3, 1918, 24; WCCC, SII, B54, f353; Camp, "Students Army Training Corps Service Sports"; John Dickinson, *The Building of an Army* (New York: Century, 1922).

13. Draft on military schooling [n.d.], WCCC, SI, BI9, f528; Camp, *Daily Dozen*, 27–28; Valenzi, *Champion of Sport*, 84.

14. Camp, *Daily Dozen*, 29.

15. "Report of Physical Director of 5th Naval District, Hampton Roads, VA," WCCC, SI, B25, f705; "Estimated Number of Navy Men Using the Daily Dozen," August 1919, WCCC, SII, B57, f396; "Athletic Trainers for Flying Cadets," Memorandum for the Air Training Records Section, February 12, 1918, WCCC, SI, B27, f774; "Camp Asks Trainers for Aero Squadron," *New York Times*, January 6, 1918, 26.

16. "Yale Students Expert in Field of Artillery," *Daily Princetonian*, May 17, 1917, cover; press release by Anson Phelps Stokes, August 25, 1917, WCCC, SI, B29, f802; Stokes to Camp, August 24, 1917; September 5, 1917, WCCC, SI, B30, f832; Yale athletics during WWI in WCCC, SII, B58, f409.

17. "Instructions Sent to Colleges by the War Department Regarding Athletics" [1917], WCCC, SII, B56, f388; Camp to Fred Allen, August 18, 1917, WCCC, SI, B17, f482; Robert Corwin to Camp, October 1, 1917, WCCC, SI, B29, f802; "Yale Warriors Start Practice. Army Training Corps and Naval Unit Elevens to Open Season," *Hartford Courant*, October 13, 1918, WCCC, SIII.

18. Henry Williams to Camp, September 11, 1918, WCCC, SI, B27, f753; George Daley, "World War Plowed Deeply into Ranks of College Athletes" [1918], WCCC, SIII; Wakefield, *Playing to Win*, 21; Gems, *Pride, Profit, and Patriarchy*, 79; "Where's Yale's Team of 1916," November 25, 1917, WCCC, SI, B29, f802; Camp to Brinck Thorne, October 15, 1917, WCCC, SI, B24, f676; WCCC, SII, B36, f58; John Heisman to Camp, November 21, 1918, WCCC, SI, B13, f349; Camp on Big Three war training, 1917, WCCC, SII, B55, f365.

19. "Likens Football to War. Walter Camp Compares the Gridiron to Battlefield," *New York Times*, November 4, 1917, E6; "Review of Season, 1917," WCCC, SII, B35, f50; drafts [1918], WCCC, B32, f5; B36, f58.

20. McQuilkin, "Brutality in Football," 4; drafts, October 1918, WCCC, SII, B32, f5.

21. George Brown, Director of Athletics, First Navel District, to Camp, November 20 1918, WCCC, SI, B25, f705; Fred Walker to Camp, General

Report, October 6, 1918, WCCC, SI, B25, f705; "Review of Season, 1917," WCCC, SII, B35, f50; Pope, *Patriotic Games*, 149.

22. Although African Americans were only 10 percent of the U.S. population, they made up 13 percent of draftees in World War I. See Wakefield, *Playing to Win*, 15.

23. E. C. Henderson to Camp, November 13, 1918, WCCC, SI, B25, f705; draft, WCCC, SII, B32, f5; "Camp's All American," *New York Times*, December 31, 1918, 12; All-Service selections, WCCC, SII, B38, f101; Camp, "The All-Service Team," *Collier's Weekly*, January 11, 1919; Vasquez, "America and the Garrison Stadium," 358.

24. Camp, "Football Season of 1914," WCCC, SII, B35, f49.

25. Cohane, *The Yale Football Story*, 211; SATC [1918], WCCC, SII, B35, f50; "Students Army Training Corps Service Sports."

26. "Nine Princeton Football Players Have 'Gone West'" [1918], WCCC, SIII; Goldstein, *Ivy League Autumns*, 48; Baston in WCCC, SII, B38, f102; Poe in WCCC, SII, B34, f29.

27. Camp to E. A. G. Wylie, December 17, 1906; Wylie to Camp, August 24, 1917; Camp to Gentlemen of the American Field Service, August 28, 1917, WCCC, SI, B28, f778.

28. Joseph H. O'Dell, "The New Spirit of the New Army," *Outlook*, November 14, 1917, 414–415; W. G. Price to Joseph Raycroft, October 17, 1917; E. F. Sweet to Camp, December 19, 1917; Daniel C. Roper to Camp, December 20, 1917, WCCC, SV, B66, f12; [Walter Camp Jr., n.d.] (copy), WCCC, SII, B61, f449; "Wally" to [recipient unknown], July 16, 1918, WCCC, SV, B67, f15; *The Recruiter's Bulletin*, New York Marine Corps Mobilization Unit, October 1918, 22.

29. Custodian Hospital Fund to Captain Walter Camp [n.d.]; Frederick Exton to Walter Camp, Jr., November 20, 1918; Arthur Foote to Camp, December 30, 1918, WCCC, SV, B67, f15; Camp to Colonel James M. Kennedy, December 12, 1918, WCCC, SI, B15, f409; "Walter Camp Jr. Wounded" [1918], WCCC, SIII.

30. Clipping in WCCC, SII, B57, f403.

31. Julie Des Jardins, *Lillian Gilbreth: Redefining Domesticity* (Boulder, CO: Westview Press, 2012), 88–90; Kasson, *Houdini, Tarzan and the Perfect Man*, 142–143, 221.

32. C. K. Sanborn to Camp, May 2, 1917, WCCC, SI, B22, f615.

33. "Origins of the SSC," WCCC, SII, B57, f401.

34. "To Form Defense Body of Athletes," *New York Times*, March 25, 1917, S1; Van Tassel Sutphen, "Making Middle-Aged Men Fit to Help in War," *New York Times*, June 24, 1917, 60; Camp, "What the Victory or Defeat of Germany Means to Every American," National Security League's Campaign of Patriotism, 1917, State Historical Society of Wisconsin.

35. Camp to Oswald Garrison Villard, April 18, 1917, WCCC, SI, B25, f722; "Reasons for the Establishment of the Senior Service Work," 1917, WCCC, SII, B57, f399.

36. "Reasons for the Establishment of the Senior Service Work"; William Wright to Camp, April 16, 1917; Edward E. Field to Camp, April 18, 1917; George Tooker to Camp, April 25, 1917; George J. Bassett to Camp, April 25, 1917; Huntington Lee to Camp, May 7, 1917, WCCC, SI, B22, f613–620.

37. SSC Corps General Orders #1, May 18, 1917, WCCC, SI, B22, f615; Camp to C. R. H. Jackson, June 12, 1917; Albert Mattoon to Camp, May 25, 1917, WCCC, SI, B17, f470; Henry Farnam to Camp, June 21, 1917, WCCC, SII, B22, f616.

38. Introduction letter to SSC, April 27, 1917, WCCC, SII, B57, f399.

39. Camp to Herbert C. Hoover, May 22, 1917, WCCC, SI, B13, f370.

40. Marcus Holcomb to Camp, March 23, 1917; Silas Hurin to Camp, September 7, 1917, WCCC, SI, B22, f618; WCCC, SII, B57, f403; Camp to Hamilton Holt, July 18, 1917, WCCC, SI, B13, f369; Camp to Arthur Capper [n.d.], WCCC, SI, B4, f122.

41. Camp, "Patriotic Service by Men Over 45," *Rotarian*, June 1917, 577–579; "Senior Service: Patriotism of Men Over Military Age," WCCC, SII, B57, f400; Camp, "The Need of Being Fit," *Hartford Courant* [May 1917], WCCC, SII, B54, f356.

42. Camp to Robert Garrett, May 24, 1917, WCCC, SI, B11, f294; Camp to Don C. Seitz, May 24, 1917, WCCC, SI, B19, f509; WCCC, SII, B54, f354.

43. Camp to Joseph P. Tumulty, Secretary to the President, June 11, 1917, WCCC, SI, B25, f690; "Keeping the President Fit" [1917], WCCC, SII, B55, f366; Franklin Delano Roosevelt to Camp, June 2, 1917, WCCC, SI, B21, f592; Henry Graves, Forester, U.S. Dept. of Agriculture, to Camp [1917], WCCC, SI, B25, f697.

44. "Cabinet Chiefs Learn How to be Young Again," *New York Times*, July 22, 1917, 52.

45. Warburg's write-up, WCCC, SII, B57, f399.

46. The Scamps included Chief Justice Harry Covington, the Federal Trade Commission's Joseph Davies, Solicitor General John W. Davis, Attorney General Thomas Gregory, Associate Justice William Hitz, Assistant Post Master General John Koons, Secretary of the Treasury William McAdoo, the Bureau of Mines' Van H. Manning, Tariff Commission Vice Chairman Daniel Roper, Franklin Delano Roosevelt, Geological Survey Director G. O. Smith, Assistant Secretary of Commerce Edwin Sweet, Assistant Attorney General George Todd, Secretary of the Interior Alexander Vogelsang, the Federal Reserve Board's Paul Warburg, Secretary of Labor William B. Wilson, Comptroller John Skeleton Williams, State Department Counselor Frank Polk, and the National Defense Council's Daniel Willard. See R. R. Smith to Camp, August 22, 1917, WCCC, SI, B23, f638; Camp to William Thatcher, August 10, 1917, WCCC, SI, B22, f617.

47. Edwin Sweet to Camp, September 5 and 6, 1917, SI, B25, f698.

48. Camp to John Skelton Williams, August 10, 1917; Williams to Camp, August 28, 1917; April 2, 1918, WCCC, SI, B27, f756.

49. Scamps poem in WCCC, SII, B57, f390.

50. Van Tassel Sutphen to Camp, April 23, 1917; Camp to Sutphen, April 26, 1917, WCCC, SI, B12, f333; "Senior Service Corps," WCCC, SI, B16, f440.

Chapter 13

1. http://www.pbs.org/greatwar/resources/casdeath_pop.html; on German defeat and European interest in American sport, WCCC, SII, B60, f439, 441.

2. "Review of Sport for 1919," WCCC, SII, B52, f323, 326; Wakefield, *Playing to Win*, 28–29, 43; Camp to Colonel Isaac Jones, June 13, 1919, WCCC, SI, B15, f402.

3. Camp, *Athletes All: Training, Organization, and Play* (New York: Charles Scribner's Sons, 1929), vii–viii.

4. Harvey Woodruff, "All Sport Faces Greatest Boon Following War," *Chicago Tribune*, December 29, 1918, Stagg Papers, Scrapbook, f198.

5. Oriard, *King Football*, 32, 225, 255.

6. WCCC, SII, B54, f354.

7. Camp, *Keeping Fit All the Way*, 33–34, 44.

8. Wakefield, *Playing to Win*, 36–42, 47; Richard Mandell, *Sport: A Cultural History* (New York: Columbia University Press, 1984), 200; Gustavus Kirby, President of Olympic Committee, to Camp, May 4, 1920, WCCC, SI, B15, f414; Pope, *Patriotic Games*, 40–58.

9. Physical Education, WCCC, SII, B54–57, f354, f360, 388, 390; Pope, *Patriotic Games*, 135, 141; Camp to Julian Curtiss, February 26, 1918, WCCC, SI, B23, f647; correspondence with E. Dana Caulkins, Manager of the National Physical Education Service, WCCC, SI, B18, f503; "The Fess-Capper Bill and the Physical Education of Children," *Southern Medical Journal*, January 1921, 60; "Physically Fit, to be Motto in Public Schools," *Chicago Tribune*, November 25, 1918, Stagg Papers, Scrapbook, f198; "News Notes," *American Physical Education Review*, 27, October 1922, 388.

10. Judith Ann Schiff, "The Original Celebrity Trainer," *Yale Alumni Magazine*, July/August 2013, 23; "Annual Address of the President Walter Camp," at the annual meeting of the Civic Federation in the auditorium of Center Church Chapel, May 17, 1912, WCCC, SI, B5, f151; playgrounds and recreation, WCCC, SII, B57, f398; Recreation Committee minutes, February 7, 1921, WCCC, SI, B11, f312.

11. "Industrial Athletics: How the Sports For Soldiers and Sailors Are Developing into Civilian Athletics," *Outlook*, 122(1919); "What Athletics Mean for Industrial Classes," WCCC, SII, B53, f335; "Develop Industrial Sport is the Cry of the Hour," WCCC, SII, B52, f329; "Play for Labor as Well as Capital," WCCC, SII, B60, f440; Camp, "The Broad Folk Highway of American Sport," *American Scandinavian Review*, 9, 1921, 257.

12. Industrial athletics, WCCC, SII, B53, f333; "Review of Season" [1917], WCCC, SII, B35, f50; review of 1923 sports, WCCC, SII, B52, f323; Camp, "Deflating the Country Club" [1921]; "The Craze for Costliness in Golf," *World's Work*, July 1924, WCCC, SIII; *Football without a Coach* (New York: D. Appleton, 1923 [1920]).

13. Telegram, Coleman DuPont and Committee to Camp, January 9, 1919, WCCC, SI, B10, f259; "Orient or Occident?" WCCC, SII, B57, f397; "Sport as a Factor in Americanization," WCCC, SII, B52, f329; B52, f333, B60, f437.

14. Rufus Steele, Division of Films, U.S. Government, to Camp, October 1, 1918, WCCC, SI, B25, f696.

15. On new physical ideal in WCCC, SII, B55, f365; Camp, *Keeping Fit All the Way*, 132, 136.

16. Green, *Fit for America*, 262; Rader, *American Sport*, 119; Kimmel, *Manhood in America*, 86; Martin, "Walter Camp and His Gridiron Game"; Powel, *Walter Camp*, 164.

17. Nelson, *Anatomy of a Game*, 170; Schiff, "The Original Celebrity Trainer," 23.

18. Powel, *Walter Camp*, 159, 168–169; Camp to L. Mitchell, January 2, 1920, WCCC, SI, B17, f480; E. K. Hall to Camp, February 13, 1920, WCCC, SI, B12, f321; Camp to Arthur Page, May 17, 1923, WCCC, SI, B9, f253.

19. Camp, *Daily Dozen*, 3–4.

20. Transcript of *Daily Dozen*, Community Motion Picture Bureau, WCCC, SII, B57, f396; Camp on overcivilization in WCCC, SII, B55, f366.

21. Advertisement for the phonograph record of the Daily Dozen in *The Independent and the Weekly Review*, February 18, 1922, 108; Camp, *Daily Dozen*, XII, 7, 26, 54, 59; Green, *Fit for America*, 294–300; Mrozek, *Sport and American Mentality*, 92–93.

22. Letters to Walter Camp [n.d.], WCCC, SII, B57, f391.

23. William Crawford to Camp, April 23, 1920, WCCC, SI, B8, f213; on obituaries, WCCC, SII, B55, f363.

24. Life expectancy for American men in 1925 was 57.6 years. See http://demog. berkeley.edu/~andrew/1918/figure2.html; "Walter Camp Shocked," Special to *New York Times*, October 28, 1924, 19; "Dr. W. T. Bull Dies, Once Yale Coach," *New York Times*, November 9, 1924, S5; Camp on Roosevelt, WCCC, SII, B56, f373.

25. Camp, *Daily Dozen*, 13.

26. "A New Religion"; WCCC, SII, B54, f353.

27. "Calisthenics in Army and Navy Condemned by Walter Camp in Address to College Graduates," February 8, 1920, WCCC, SIII; Powel, *Walter Camp*, 172–173.

28. "Men of Fifty and Over Can Keep Fit, Says Walter Camp," *New York Herald*, December 26, 1920, WCCC, SII, B57, f393; personal clipping [1924 or 1925], WCCC, SIII.

29. [1920], WCCC, SI, B24, f668.

30. Brinck Thorne to Camp, May 7, 1919, WCCC, SI, B24, f677; McCormick to "Mrs. Walter," December 27, 1919, WCCC, SV, B66, f8; "Yale Men Shocked When Tim Callahan Drops Walter Camp," *Public Ledger* [1919], WCCC, SIII.

31. "Football's 'Big Three' Dies a Natural Death" [1919]; "Yale Behind the Times" [1920], WCCC, SIII; "Yale Players in Lead," *New York Times*, January 8, 1922, 120; "No Big Three Men on Camp's Eleven," *New York Times*, December 30, 1924, 11; Camp to W. H. Morse, December 3, 1919, WCCC, SI, B18, f491.

32. Kelley, *Yale: A History*, 312–313; "Surgeon's Scalpel Heals Love Wound," *Milwaukee Sentinel*, April 24, 1930, 22; "Mrs. Janet C. Buck Wed to Yale Official," *New York Times*, August 27, 1935, 22.

33. Camp to Starling Childs, May 2, 1917, WCCC, SI, B5, f150; "Flamingos Beaten by Orange County," *New York Times*, July 15, 1923, 20; "Kin of Walter Camp Born," *New York Times*, September 15, 1942, 20.

34. "Illinois Game Amazed Camp; Calls It Year's Best Football," *New York Times*, November 10, 1924, 13; "The New Football," *New York Times*, November 21, 1920; "Review of the Season," 1919–24, WCCC, SII, B35, f51–53; B36, f62; Oriard, *King Football*, 3.

35. Bowls and stadiums, WCCC, SII, B60, f442; B33, f25; Charles Ornstein to Camp, November 17, 1922, WCCC, SI, B19, f516; Rader, *American Sports*, 191; Oriard, *King Football*, 65, 86.

36. Martin, *Benching Jim Crow*, 14–20; Gems, *Pride, Profit, and Patriarchy*, 165–168; Miller, "The Manly, the Moral, and the Proficient," 18–21; Doyle, "Turning the Tide," 102, 110.

37. On coaches, WCCC, SII, B32, f10, 11; B33, f18; B34, f28, 31; B52, f324; on seasonal coaches [1918], WCCC, B53, f338; B54, f347; Mrozek, *Sport and American Mentality*, 73–81.

38. Camp to F. W. Lord, April 30, 1920, WCCC, SI, B16, f436; Julian Myrick to Camp, May 16, 1914, WCCC, SI, B18, f499; George Wightman to Camp, May 10, 1924, WCCC, SI, B15, f424.

39. Notes on the baseball scandal, WCCC, SII, B33, f17; Gems, *Pride, Profit, and Patriarchy*, 184; Roderick Nash, *The Nervous Generation: American Thought, 1917–1930* (Chicago: Rand McNally, 1970), 126–136.

40. Martin, *Benching Jim Crow*, 19; Oriard, *King Football*, 6, 8, 79, 102, 105–107.

41. Philip English to Janet Troxell, July 15, 1980, WCCC, SV, B72, f60; J. E. Lyon to Mssrs. Wells, Potter, Fish and Ustick, Inc., May 10, 1923, WCCC, SI, B19, f514; Powel, *Walter Camp*, 150.

42. Alexander McAndrew, Yale Alumni Association of Northern California, to Camp, November 10, 1924, WCCC, SI, B28, f780; "Walter Camp is Found Dead in Bed," *Los Angeles Herald*, March 14, 1925, WCCC, SIII; Fielding Yost to Camp, January 5, 1925, WCCC, SI, B31, f838; Powel, *Walter Camp*, 184–185.

43. Amos Alonzo Stagg, "Rules," *Time*, March 23, 1925, 22.

44. "Heart Attack is Fatal to Famous Leader in Sport," *New Haven Union*, March 13, 1925; "Walter Camp Dies in Hotel of Heart Disease," *New York World*, March 15, 1925, WCCC, SIII; "Walter Camp Dies of Heart Trouble in New York Hotel," *Hartford Courant*, March 15, 1925, 1–2; "Walter Camp Dies; Sportsmen Mourn," *Baltimore Sun*, March 15, 1925, 7; "Sporting World Mourns Death of Walter Camp," *Daily Princetonian*, March 16, 1925, 3.

45. "Comment on Current Events in Sports," *New York Times*, 16 March 1925, 24; Julian Curtiss, "A College Mate's Tribute to Walter Camp," *Evening World* [1925], WCCC, SIII.

46. "Walter Camp's Sport-Casts," February 1925, WCCC, SIII; Powel, *Walter Camp*, 152, 183.

47. "His Own Medicine Fails," *Fort Wayne Gazette*, March 16, 1925; William Hemmingway, "Elderly Athletes," *Philadelphia Saturday Evening Post*, May 9, 1925; "Age and Exercise," *New York City Review*, March 21, 1925; Thomas Rice, "Are Faddists Endangering Longevity of Middleaged?" *Brooklyn Eagle*, March 16, 1925; "How Much Exercise is Too Much?" *New York City Mirror*, March 16, 1925; Macfadden, "The Passing of a Great Athlete," *New York City Graphic*, March 18, 1925, WCCC, SV, B71, f55.

48. Sandow may have died of a burst blood vessel. See Kasson, *Houdini, Tarzan, and the Perfect Man*, 75; Editorial in *Commonweal*, October 21, 1925, 288; "Mathewson, Camp, Ebbett and Many Others Noted in Sporting World Died in 1925," *New York Times*, December 27, 1925, S4.

49. Eventually, both Walter and Alice Camp were buried at the Grove Street Cemetery. "Old Friends Mourn at Camp's Bier," *New York Times*, March 17, 1925, 21; "Walter Camp Left $328,061; Widow Gets Entire Estate," *New York Times*, June 15, 1926, 27; Curtis and Curtis, "Harder, Nobler Task," 112; "Walter Camp's Widow Dies," *Oakland Tribune*, December 18, 1934, B19.

50. "Jones Succeeds Walter Camp on Football Rules Committee," *New York Times*, July 28, 1925, 26; on sports history, WCCC, SII, B60, f440.

51. "The Point of View," *Bookman*, May 1925, 258; Broun, "Best Books and the Very Best," *Forum*, January 1924, 91.

52. "29 Games Tomorrow Honor Walter Camp," *New York Times*, October 29, 1926, 28; Hall in "Dedication of the Walter Camp Memorial," *Yale Alumni Weekly*, November 9, 1928, 220.

53. SII, B52, f326; Oriard, *King Football*, 136–137.

54. Paolantonio, *How Football Explains America*, 24–25; Humphrey D. Howell to Camp, April 5, 1922, WCCC, SI, B24, f685; Nash, *Nervous Generation*, 126–136; Oriard, *Dreaming of Heroes*, 52.

55. Oriard, *King Football*, 7, 11, 29, 50.

56. Palmer Pierce's 1925 address at the annual meeting of the NCAA, WCCC, SI, B18, f500; Rader, *American Sports*, 148–151; Paolantonio, *How Football Explains America*, 62–64; Oriard, *King Football*, 126–128, 180, 234.

57. Grange in Valenzi, *Champion of Sport*, 105.

58. Oriard, "Father of American Football," 186; Smith, *Sports and Freedom*, 172; Aphorisms, WCCC, SII, B58, f417.

Postgame Analysis

1. On sport and early settlers, WCCC, SII, B52, f328; B53, f339; B60, f440.
2. "Wilson is Praised as Football Coach," Special to *New York Times*, November 14, 1926, E5; WCCC, SII, B33, f20.
3. Oriard, *Reading Football*, 188; *King Football*, 328–329.
4. Tim Rohan, "A Football Widow's Traumatic Journey," *New York Times*, April 8, 2013.
5. Tim Layden, "What Ever Happened to Tackling?" *Sports Illustrated*, September 5, 2011 (www.sportsillustrated.cnn.com/vault/article/magazine/MAG1189947/3/index.htm).

SELECTED BIBLIOGRAPHY

Secondary Works

Adams, David Wallace. "More than a Game: The Carlisle Indians Take to the Gridiron." *Western Historical Quarterly* 32 (Spring 2001): 25–53.

Anderson, Lars. *Carlisle vs. Army: Jim Thorpe, Dwight Eisenhower, Pop Warner, and the Forgotten Story of Football's Greatest Battle.* New York: Random House, 2008.

Anderson, William G. "Further Studies in the Longevity of Yale Athletes." *Medical Times* 44 (March 1916): 75.

Ashe, Arthur R., Jr. *A Hard Road to Glory: A History of the African-American Athlete, 1619–1918.* New York: Amistad, 1988.

Bagg, Lyman Hotchkiss. *Four Years at Yale.* New Haven, CT: Charles C. Chatfield, 1871.

Bederman, Gail. *Manliness and Civilization: A Cultural History of Gender and Race in the United States, 1880–1917.* Chicago: University of Chicago Press, 1995.

Beers, Henry A. *The Ways of Yale in the Consulship of Plancus.* New York: Henry Holt, 1895.

Benjey, Tom. *Wisconsin's Carlisle Indian School Immortals.* Carlisle, PA: Tuxedo Press, 2010.

Bergin, Thomas G. *The Game: The Harvard-Yale Football Rivalry, 1875–1983.* New Haven, CT: Yale University Press, 1984.

Bernstein, Mark. *Football: The Ivy League Origins of an American Obsession.* Philadelphia: University of Pennsylvania Press, 2001.

Beveridge, Albert. *The Young Man and the World.* New York: D. Appleton, 1905.

Blaikie, William. *How To Get Strong and How To Stay So*. New York: Harper and Brothers, 1879.

Bloom, John. *To Show What an Indian Can Do*. Minneapolis, MN: University of Minnesota Press, 2000.

Borkowski, Richard P. "The Life and Contributions of Walter Camp to American Football." Ph.D. diss., Temple University, 1979.

Brown, Lloyd. *The Young Paul Robeson: 'On My Journey Now.'* Boulder, CO: Westview Press, 1997.

Cahn, Susan. *Coming On Strong: Gender and Sexuality in 20th Century Women's Sport*. Cambridge, MA: Harvard University Press, 1994.

Canby, Henry Seidel. *Alma Mater: The Gothic Age of the American College*. New York: Arno Press, 1975 [1936].

Carlson, Stan W. *Dr. Henry L. Williams: A Football Biography*. Minneapolis, MN: Stan W. Carlson, 1938.

Carnes, Mark C. *Secret Ritual and Manhood in America*. New Haven, CT: Yale University Press, 1989.

Carroll, John M. *Fritz Pollard: Pioneer in Racial Advancement*. Urbana, IL: University of Illinois Press, 1992.

Chalk, Ocania. *Black College Sport*. New York: Dodd, Mead, 1976.

Cohane, Tim. *The Yale Football Story*. New York: G. P. Putnam's Sons, 1951.

Crawford, Bill. *All American: The Rise and Fall of Jim Thorpe*. Hoboken, NJ: John Wiley, 2005.

Curtis, Bruce. "William Graham Sumner, 'On the Concentration of Wealth.'" *Journal of American History* 55 (March 1969): 823–832.

———. "Victorians Abed: William Graham Sumner on the Family, Women, and Sex." *American Studies* 18 (Spring 1977): 101–122.

Curtis, Bruce, and Joy Curtis. "The Harder, Nobler Task: Five Victorian Women and the Work Ethic," 103–124. In *Ideas in America's Cultures: From Republic to Mass Society*, Hamilton Cravens, editor. Ames, IA: Iowa State University Press, 1982.

Daggett, William G., editor. *A History of the Class of Eighty, Yale College, 1876–1910*. New Haven, CT: published for the class, 1910.

Danzig, Allison. *Oh, How They Played the Game: The Early Days of Football and the Heroes Who Made it Great*. New York: Macmillan, 1971.

Davies, Richard O. *Rivals! The Ten Greatest American Sports Rivalries of the 20th Century*. Malden, MA: Wiley Blackwell, 2010.

Davis, Richard Harding. "The Thanksgiving Day Game." *Harper's Weekly* (December 9, 1893): 1170–1171.

———. "A Day with Yale's Team." *Harper's Weekly* (November 18, 1893): 1110.

Dexter, Edwin. "Accidents from College Football." *Educational Review* 25 (April 1903): 415–428.

Dickinson, John. *The Building of an Army*. New York: Century Co., 1922.

Doyle, Andrew. "Turning the Tide: College Football and Southern Progressivism." In *Sporting World of the Modern South*, Patrick B. Miller, 101–128. Urbana, IL: University of Illinois Press, 2002.

Dubbert, Joe L. "Progressivism and the Masculinity Crisis." In *The American Man*, Elizabeth H. and Joseph H. Pleck, 303–320. Englewood Cliffs, NJ: Prentice Hall, 1980.

Edwards, William H. *Football Days*. New York: Moffat, Yard, 1916.

Fairfield, Francis Gerry. *The Clubs of New York*. New York: Henry L. Hinton, 1873.

Filene, Peter Gabriel. "In Time of War." In *The American Man*, edited by Elizabeth H. and Joseph H. Pleck, 321–335. Englewood Cliffs, NJ: Prentice Hall, 1980.

Forbush, W. B. *The Boy Problem*. Boston: Pilgrim, 1901.

Gems, Gerald R. *For Pride, Profit, and Patriarchy: Football and the Incorporation of American Cultural Values*. Lanham, MD: Scarecrow, 2000.

———. "Negotiating a Native American Identity through Sport: Assimilation, Adaptation, and the Role of the Trickster." In *Native Athletes in Sport and Society*, edited by C. Richard King, 1–21. Lincoln, NE: University of Nebraska Press, 2005.

Goldstein, Richard. *Ivy League Autumns*. New York: St. Martin's, 1996.

Gorn, Elliot. *The Manly Art: Bare-Knuckle Prizefighting in America*. Ithaca, NY: Cornell University Press, 1986.

Gorn, Elliott, and Warren Goldstein. *A Brief History of American Sports*. Urbana, IL: University of Illinois Press, 2004.

Grant, Ellsworth. *The Miracle of Connecticut*. Hartford, CT: Connecticut Historical Society, 1992.

Green, Harvey. *Fit for America: Health, Fitness, Sport, and American Society*. New York: Pantheon, 1986.

Guttmann, Allen. *The Erotic in Sports*. New York: Columbia University Press, 1996.

Hall, G. Stanley. *Adolescence: Its Psychology and Its Relation to Physiology, Anthropology, Sociology, Sex, Crime, Religion, and Education*, 2 volumes. New York: D. Appleton, 1904.

Hartwell, Edward Mussey. "On Physical Training in the United States," In *Public Health Papers and Reports*, volume 10, 27–35. Concord, NH: American Public Health Association, 1885.

Higgs, Robert J. "Yale and the Heroic Ideal, *Götterdämmerung* and Palingenesis, 1865–1914." In *Manliness and Morality: Middle-Class Masculinity in Britain and America, 1800–1940*, edited by J. A. Mangan and James Walvin, 160–175. New York: St. Martin's, 1987.

Hinsdale, Harriet. *Frank Merriwell's 'Father': An Autobiography by Gilbert Patten*. Norman, OK: University of Oklahoma Press, 1964.

Hofstadter, Richard. "William Graham Sumner, Social Darwinist." *New England Quarterly* 14 (September 1941): 457–477.

Hoganson, Kristin. *Fighting for American Manhood: How Gender Politics Provoked the Spanish-American and Philippine-American Wars*. New Haven, CT: Yale University Press, 1998.

Holbrook, Richard Thayer. *Boys and Men: A Story of Life at Yale*. New York: Charles Scribner's Sons, 1900.

Howard, William Lee, MD. "Football and Moral Health." *Medical Record* 69 (April 7, 1906): 546–547.

Hurd, Michael. *Black College Football: One Hundred Years of History, Education, and Pride*. Virginia Beach, VA: Donning Co., 1993.

James, Henry. *The Bostonians*. New York: Modern Library, 1965 [1886].

James, William. "The Moral Equivalent of War." In *Memories and Studies*. New York: Longmans, Green, 1912.

Jenkins, Sally. *The Real All Americans*. New York: Broadway Books, 2007.

Johnson, Owen. *Stover at Yale*. New York: Frederick A. Stokes, 1912.

Kangiel, Robert. *The One Best Way: Frederick Winslow Taylor and the Enigma of Efficiency*. Cambridge, MA: MIT Press, 2005.

Kasson, John. *Houdini, Tarzan and the Perfect Man: The White Male Body and the Challenge of Modernity in America*. New York: Hill and Wang, 2001.

Keller, Albert G. *Reminiscences (Mainly Personal) of William Graham Sumner*. New Haven, CT: Yale University Press, 1933.

Kelley, Brooks Mather. *Yale: A History*. New Haven, CT: Yale University Press, 1974.

Kett, Joseph. *Rites of Passage: Adolescence in America 1790 to the Present*. New York: Basic Books, 1977.

Kimmel, Michael. *Manhood in America: A Cultural History*. New York: Oxford University Press, 2006.

———. *The History of Men*. Albany, NY: State University of New York Press, 2005.

Layden, Tim. "What Ever Happened to Tackling?" *Sports Illustrated* 115 (September 5, 2011): 60.

Lee, Joseph. *Play and Education*. New York: Macmillan, 1915.

Lester, Robin D. *Stagg's University: The Rise, Decline and Fall of Football at the University of Chicago*. Urbana, IL: University of Illinois Press, 1999.

Maggio, Frank. *Notre Dame and the Game that Changed Football*. New York: Carroll and Graf, 2007.

Mandell, Richard. *Sport: A Cultural History*. New York: Columbia University Press, 1984.

Martin, Charles. *Benching Jim Crow: The Rise and Fall of the Color Line in Southern College Sports, 1890–1980*. Urbana, IL: University of Illinois Press, 2010.

Martin, John Stuart. "Walter Camp and His Gridiron Game." *American Heritage* 12 (October 1961): 50–81.

McQuilkin, Scott. "Brutality in Football and the Creation of the NCAA: A Codified Moral Compass in Progressive America." *Sport History Review* 33 (May 2002): 1–34.

———. "The Rise and Fall of the Flying Wedge, Football's Most Controversial Play." *Journal of Sport History* 20 (Spring 1993): 57–64.

Messenger, Christian K. *Sport and the Spirit of Play in American Fiction*. New York: Columbia University Press, 1981.

Miller, John L. *The Big Scrum: How Teddy Roosevelt Saved Football*. New York: HarperCollins, 2011.

Miller, Patrick. *Sporting World of the Modern South*. Urbana, IL: University of Illinois Press, 2002.

Mrozek, Donald J. *Sport and American Mentality, 1880–1910*. Knoxville, TN: University of Tennessee Press, 1983.

Nash, Roderick. *The Nervous Generation: American Thought, 1917–1930*. Chicago: Rand McNally, 1970.

Nelson, Dana. *National Manhood: Capitalist Citizenship and the Imagined Fraternity of White Men*. Durham, NC: Duke University Press, 1998.

Nelson, David M. *The Anatomy of a Game: Football, the Rules, and the Men Who Made the Game*. Newark, DE: University of Delaware Press, 1993.

Oriard, Michael. *Reading Football: How the Popular Press Created an American Spectacle*. Chapel Hill, NC: University of North Carolina Press, 1993.

———. *King Football: Sport and Spectacle in the Golden Age of Radio and Newsreels, Movies and Magazines, the Weekly and Daily Press*. Chapel Hill, NC: University of North Carolina Press, 2001.

———. "The Father of American Football." In *Sport in America: From Colonial Leisure to Celebrity Figures and Globalization*, volume 2, edited by David K. Wiggins, 175–191. Champaign, IL: Human Kinetics, 2010.

———. *Dreaming of Heroes: American Sports Fiction, 1868–1980*. Chicago: Nelson Hall, 1982.

Osborn, Norris Galpin. *Men of Mark in Connecticut*, volume 1. Hartford, CT: W. R. Goodspeed, 1906.

Paolantonio, Sal. *How Football Explains America*. Chicago: Triumph Books, 2008.

Park, Roberta. "From Football to Rugby—and Back, 1906–1919: The University of California-Stanford University Response to the 'Football Crisis of 1905.'" *Journal of Sports History* 11 (Winter 1984): 5–40.

———. "Sport, Gender and Society in a Transatlantic Victorian Perspective." In *From "Fair Sex" to Feminism: Sport and the Socialization of Women in the Industrial and Post-Industrial Eras*, edited by Roberta Park and J. A. Mangan, 58–87. London: Frank Cass, 1987.

Perry, Lawrence. *Our Navy in the War*. New York: Charles Scribner's Sons, 1919.

Pettegrew, John. *Brutes in Suits: Male Sensibility in America, 1890–1920*. Baltimore, MD: Johns Hopkins University Press, 2007.

Pfister, Joel. *The Yale Indian: The Education of Henry Roe Cloud*. Durham, NC: Duke University Press, 2009.

Pickens, Donald. "William Graham Sumner: Moralist as Social Scientist." *Social Science* 43 (October 1968): 202–209.

Pope, S. W. *Patriotic Games: Sporting Traditions in the American Imagination, 1876–1926*. Knoxville, TN: University of Tennessee Press, 1997.

Porter, John Addison, ed. *Sketches of Yale Life*. Washington, DC: Arlington Publishing Co., 1886.

Powel, Harford, Jr. *Walter Camp: The Father of American Football*. Boston: Little, Brown, 1926.

————. "Walter Camp, Chapter IV: The Last Tournament." *Youth's Companion* (October 28, 1926): 801.

Pratt, Richard Henry. *Battlefield and Classroom: Four Decades with the American Indian, 1867–1894*, edited by Robert M. Utley. New Haven, CT: Yale University Press, 1964.

Putney, Clifford. *Muscular Christianity: Manhood and Sports in Protestant America, 1880–1920*. Cambridge, MA: Harvard University Press, 2001.

Rader, Benjamin. *American Sports: From the Age of Folk Games to the Age of Televised Sports*, 5th edition. Upper Saddle River, NJ: Prentice Hall, 2004.

Riess, Steven. "Sport and the Redefinition of American Middle-Class Masculinity." *International Journal of the History of Sport* 8 (May 1991): 5–22.

Riess, Steven, editor. *Major Problems in American Sport History*. Boston: Houghton Mifflin, 1997.

Robbins, Alexandra. *Secrets of the Tomb: Skull and Bones, the Ivy League, and the Hidden Paths of Power*. New York: Back Bay Books, 2002.

Roberts, Gerald. "The Strenuous Life: The Cult of Manliness in the Era of Theodore Roosevelt." Ph.D. diss., Michigan State University, 1970.

Roberts, Randy. *Papa Jack: Jack Johnson and the Era of White Hopes*. New York: Free Press, 1983.

Rohan, Tim. "A Football Widow's Traumatic Journey," *New York Times*, April 8, 2013, http://www.nytimes.com/2013/04/09/sports/football/eleanor-perfettos-journey-coping-with-dementia-and-death-of-former-nfl-player-ralph-wenzel.html?pagewanted=all&_r=0.

Roosevelt, Theodore. "The American Boy," 73–77. In *The Strenuous Life: Essays and Addresses*. Mineola, NY: Dover, 2009 [1900].

Rotundo, E. Anthony. *American Manhood: Transformations in Masculinity from the Revolution to the Modern Era*. New York: Basic Books, 1993.

Rubin, Sam. *Yale Football*. Charleston, SC: Acadia Publishing, 2006.

Sabo, Don. "Pigskin, Patriarchy, and Pain." In *Men's Lives*, edited by Michael Kimmel and Michael Messner, 184–186. New York: Macmillan, 1989.

Samuels, Peggy, and Harold Samuels. *A Biography of Frederic Remington*. Austin, TX: University of Texas Press, 1985.

Schiff, Judith Ann. "The Original Celebrity Trainer." *Yale Alumni Magazine* LXXVI (July/August 2013): 23.

Smith, Norman Erik. "William Graham Sumner as an Anti-Social Darwinist." *Pacific Sociological Review* 22 (July 1979): 332–347.

Smith, Ronald A. *Sports and Freedom: The Rise of Big-Time College Athletics*. New York: Oxford University Press, 1988.

———— editor. *Big-Time Football at Harvard, 1905: The Diary of Coach Bill Reid*. Urbana, IL: University of Illinois Press, 1994.

————. "Harvard and Columbia and a Reconsideration of the 1905–1906 Football Crisis." *Journal of Sport History* 8 (Winter 1981): 5–19.

Soderstrom, Mark. "Weeds in Linnaeus's Garden: Science and Segregation, Eugenics, and the Rhetoric of Racism at the University of Minnesota and the Big Ten, 1900–45." Ph.D. diss., University of Minnesota, 2004.

Springwood, Charles Fruehling. "Playing Football, Playing Indian: A History of the Native Americans Who Were the NFL's Oorang Indians." In *Native Athletes in Sport and Society*, C. Richard King, 123–142. Lincoln, NE: University of Nebraska Press, 2005.

Steinberg, Stephen. *The Academic Melting Pot*. New York: Carnegie Foundation, 1974.

Strong, Josiah. *The Times and Young Men*. New York: Baker and Taylor, 1901.

Sufrin, Mark. "'Boys' Sports Books Portrayed An Idealized World of Many Virtues." *Sports Illustrated* (September 1, 1975), http://www.si.com/vault/1975/09/01/616283/boys-sports-books-portrayed-an-idealized-world-of-many-virtues.

Synnott, Marcia Graham. *The Half-Opened Door: Discrimination and Admissions at Harvard, Yale, and Princeton, 1900–1970*. Westport, CT: Greenwood Press, 1979.

Syrett, Nicholas L. *The Company He Keeps: A History of White College Fraternities*. Chapel Hill, NC: University of North Carolina Press, 2011.

The Lost Century of American Football. Lost Century of Sports Collection, BookSurge, 2011.

Valenzi, Kathleen, ed. *Champion of Sport: The Life of Walter Camp*. Charlottesville, VA: Howell Press, 1990.

Vasquez, Joseph Paul, III. "America and the Garrison Stadium: How the US Armed Forces Shaped College Football." *Armed Forces and Society* 38 (November 22, 2011): 353–358.

Veblen, Thorstein. *Theories of the Leisure Class*. Mineola, NY: Dover, 1994 [1899].

Vorpahl, Ben Merchant. *My Dear Wister: The Frederic Remington-Owen Wister Letters*. Palo Alto, CA: American West Publishing Co., 1972.

Wakefield, Wanda Ellen. *Playing to Win: Sports in the American Military, 1898–1945*. Albany, NY: State University of New York Press, 1997.

Watterson, John Sayle. *College Football*. Baltimore, MD: Johns Hopkins University Press, 2000.

———. "Reputation Reclaimed." *College Football Historical Society* XVII (November 2003): 1–4.

Welch, Lewis Sheldon, and Walter Camp. *Yale, Her Campus, Classrooms, and Athletics*. New York: L. C. Page, 1899.

White, G. Edward. *The Eastern Establishment and the Western Experience*. New Haven, CT: Yale University Press, 1968.

Whitney, Caspar. "Walter Camp." *Harper's Weekly* 36 (March 5, 1892): 226–227.

———. "Evolution of the Country Club." *Harper's New Monthly Magazine* 90 (December 1894): 30.

Winn, William. "Tom Brown's Schooldays and the Development of 'Muscular Christianity.'" *Church History* 21 (March 1960): 64–73.

Selected Works by Walter Camp

Camp, Walter, ed. *Spalding's Official Football Guides*. New York: American Sports Publishing Co., 1883–1924.

Camp, Walter. "The Harvard Stroke." *Outing and the Wheelman* 4 (July 1884): 306.

———. "College Athletics: Youth the Time for Physical Development." *New Englander* 44 (January 1885): 139.

———. "The Game and Laws of American Football." *Outing* 11 (October 1886): 68.

———. "The American Game of Football." *Harper's Weekly* (November 10, 1888): 858–859.

———. "A Day's Foot-Ball Practice at Yale." *Harper's Weekly* (November 24, 1888): 890.

———. "Hints to Football Captains." *Outing* 13 (January 1889): 357.

———. "Intercollegiate Football in America," parts 1–4. *St. Nicholas Magazine* (November and December 1889, January and February 1890).

———. "Football Studies for Captain and Coach." *Outing* 17 (November 1890): 104–107.

———. "Team Play in Football." *Harper's Weekly* XXXV (October 31, 1891): 845–846.

———. "Is Football a Dangerous Sport?" *Boston Sunday Globe*, November 13, 1892.

———. *Walter Camp's Book of College Sports*. New York: Century Co., 1893.

———. "A Plea for the Wedge in Football." *Harper's Weekly* (January 21, 1893): 67.

———. "Undergraduate Limitation in College Sport." *Harper's Weekly* 37 (February 11, 1893), 143.

———. *Football Facts and Figures*. New York: Harper and Brothers, 1894.

———. "The Current Criticism of Football." *Century* 47 (February 1894): 633–634.

———. "The New Football Rules." *Outing* 25 (November 1894): 26–27.

———. and Lorin Deland. *Football*. Boston: Houghton Mifflin, 1896.

———. and Lilian Brooks. *Drives and Putts*. Boston: L. C. Page, 1899.

———. "A Historic Game of Football." *Youth's Companion* (November 29, 1900): 625–626.

———. "College Training Tables, Their Use and Abuse." *Century* (June 1901): 307–312.

———. *How to Play Foot Ball: A Primer on the Modern College Game, with Tactics Brought Down to Date*, Spalding Athletic Library no. 183. New York: American Sports Publishing Co., 1903.

———. *The Substitute: A Football Story*. New York: D. Appleton, 1908.

———. *The Book of Foot-ball*. New York: Century Co., 1910.

———. *Football for the Spectator*. Boston: Gorham Press, 1911.

———. "Athletics." *Boys Magazine* (December 1911): 14–15.

———. *Danny Fists*. New York: D. Appleton, 1913.

———. "A Photographic Analysis of Golf." *Vanity Fair* (August 1916): 62–63.

———. *Keeping Fit All the Way*. New York: Harper and Brothers, 1919.

————. *Athletes All: Training, Organization, and Play.* New York: Charles Scribner's Sons, 1919.

————. "The Broad Folk Highway of American Sport." *American Scandinavian Review* 9 (1921): 257.

————. *Football without a Coach.* New York: D. Appleton, 1920.

————. *The Daily Dozen.* New York: Reynolds Co., 1921.

————. "The Craze for Costliness in Golf." *World's Work* XLVIII (July 1924).

INDEX